D1272422

Growth and Stability

in a Mature Economy

Growth and Stability in a Mature Economy

John Cornwall

Professor of Economics, Southern Illinois University

A HALSTED PRESS BOOK

John Wiley & Sons
NEW YORK

First published in 1972 by
Martin Robertson & Company Ltd.,
17 Quick Street, London N1 8HL.

Published in the U.S.A. by
Halsted Press, a Division of
John Wiley & Sons, Inc., New York

ISBN 0 470 17508 7

Library of Congress Catalog Card No. 72–7742

Reproduced and printed by photolithography and bound in
Great Britain at The Pitman Press, Bath

Contents

for Ellen

Preface

The recent publication of two important survey articles* has now made it possible to see much more clearly the main thrust and emphasis of post-Keynesian macrodynamics. These surveys make clear that the questions modern macrodynamics have been asking are important.

A study of whether or not a long-run equilibrium growth path exists for some model, concerns itself with the properties of that long-run 'steady state', and the factors that determine the long-run growth rate; and it is important because it can help us understand 'why growth rates differ' over time and between countries. Modern growth theory carries the analysis a step further by raising the question of under what conditions it can be said that the equilibrium is stable. For if we can understand under what conditions the equilibrium growth path of a model is stable, we can begin to understand the workings of a real economy, and thus to regulate and control it in the interests of stability.

Most of the works summarized in the two survey articles have been written at a highly technical and abstract level. The tendency has been to concentrate on the nature of the equilibrium growth paths and mathematical stability conditions of models where maximum output or supply is given, and where problems of effective demand are ignored by simply assuming that the economy operates at maximum output.

Since so much is now known about the properties and implication of models where full employment always prevails, and where supply or production functions are well defined and 'well behaved', it seems appropriate to focus attention on an additional set of factors that, most experts would agree, have a bearing on the growth and stability properties of an economy. This is what has been attempted in this study.

This 'reformulation' of the problems of growth and stability is the natural result of a desire to relax the assumption of continuous full employment that prevails throughout the works of the neoclassical and 'Cambridge' economists, to name but two of the more important schools of modern growth or macrodynamic theory. Surely, a strong case can be made for the need to

* Hahn, F. H., and Mathews, R. C. O., 'The Theory of Economic Growth: A Survey', *The Economic Journal*, December 1964, and Harcourt, G. C., 'Some Cambridge Controversies in the Theory of Capital', *Journal of Economic Literature*, June 1969.

study the problems of growth and stability within a context that allows for fluctuations in unemployment rates (and inflation). Furthermore, if, as will be argued in the pages to follow, the demand and supply sides of the market cannot be treated in isolation (as has been the case in most postwar theorizing), to allow for a possible interaction of these two sides of the market might also have a bearing on our thinking about growth and stability.

These two considerations have a further implication of some importance. To take adequate account of the possibility of unemployment and inflation as well as of interaction between demand and supply, it is necessary and essential to cast the analysis in a more concrete, 'down to earth' mold than that to which we have become accustomed. For example, it will be argued that, in order to understand why it is that a capitalist system is usually stable and not subject to breakdowns of the interwar variety, it is necessary to bring together findings from a broad number of specialized fields in economics. The structure of the construction industry, the reaction of the capital goods industry to changes in demand, the portfolio management of liquid assets by households, the portfolio adjustments of financial intermediaries in response to changes in the flows of funds, are all among the influences that must be taken into account in determining whether deviations from some sort of moving equilibrium growth path will be large and prolonged, or more like the post World War II variety. Yet the sheer accumulation of theoretical and empirical work in the various specialized fields of economics, to say nothing of the increased use of very elaborate statistical and mathematical techniques, has meant that economists have been continually forced to narrow their interests.

The significance of these developments for the study of growth and stability are threefold. First, a researcher interested in the problems of growth and stability must invest a great deal of time in trying to master developments in a wide variety of specialities; but at the same time he must be highly selective if the task is to remain manageable. Second, because of the increasing specialization and narrowing of interests forced upon economists, there is an increasing lack of awareness in the profession of what is taking place in other branches of economics. This makes it very unlikely that research in some particular speciality has followed a strategy that suggests the relevance of the findings for other problems. As a result, a substantial recasting of the research results of others by those attempting to analyze more general dynamic questions is often required. Third, since knowledge is cumulative and special areas tend to develop a jargon and a technical apparatus all their own, any attempt to bring together results from diverse fields of study for another purpose had best proceed in a manner as free from jargon and technical peculiarities as possible. Only in this manner can the 'story' be made intelligible to a wide variety of specialists and students.

All of these considerations have influenced the nature of the analysis that follows, as an attempt is made to explain under what conditions mature economies can, and have, grown without serious interruptions of the growth process. Research findings from a large number of specialized areas have been brought together, often recast so that the relevance of the findings for the overall picture are made clearer, and presented as free as possible from the jargon and technical difficulties peculiar to a particular branch in economics. The first two-thirds of the analysis lays out as carefully as possible an economic theory of growth and stability that attempts to explain the way an advanced capitalist system works. The final one-third attempts to substantiate the theoretical apparatus by describing the way in which two mature economies have operated in the 20th century.

The analysis is basically theoretical rather than econometric, in that while an attempt is made to describe the behavior of the endogenous variables in terms of a set of other variables, no attempt is made to derive new estimates of the weights to be assigned to each of the variables. However, various econometric studies that have a bearing on things like the stability of the moving equilibrium are brought into the analysis when appropriate, together with a fair amount of purely descriptive statistical analysis. The reasons for this compromise in the method of analysis are fairly straight forward. We are interested in describing a mechanism that involves a rather complicated interaction between demand and supply. It is extremely doubtful if the nature of this interaction could be picked up statistically. Second, we are also concerned with the description of the long-run equilibrium of a system undergoing changes in the composition of its output. This is difficult to do within the framework of an econometric model. Third, the bad forecasting record of the large global econometric models suggests that there exist some serious misspecifications of the underlying structural relationships. A little more emphasis on theory and a little less on putting the theory to a formal test is in order. Hopefully, some of the ideas developed here will induce others to carry out a more elaborate form of testing. Finally, the task of data collection and refinement followed by parameter estimation of economy wide models has really become a group effort, if one is to advance beyond the degree of refinement and completeness of such studies as the Brookings and FRB–MIT models. At the same time one is reluctant to conclude that descriptive statistics, and 'sight correlations' are of no value in helping to substantiate a point. Hence the inclusion of a few chapters that are hopelessly lowbrow in terms of statistical techniques employed.

The study was supported at different times by the Ford Foundation, the National Science Foundation, the Fulbright Commission, the Boston Federal Reserve Bank, and Research and Projects at Southern Illinois University. Their financial support was greatly appreciated. Parts of the manuscript were completed while I was working at Cambridge University and the Copenhagen

School of Economics. I wish to express my gratitude to both of these universities for the excellent facilities and other aids provided me at the time. Parts of Chapters III and IV have already been published in the *Quarterly Journal of Economics*, February 1970.

The pervasive influence of James Duesenberry throughout the book should be apparent. His *Business Cycles and Economic Growth* provided much of the early stimulus that made me undertake this study. But a host of others who have also kept the Keynesian faith, in writing as well as words, have also strongly influenced my thinking. References to their works are scattered throughout the book.

Finally I would like to thank Douglas Bohi, Ronald Britto, James Duesenberry, Robert Hartman, Jerome Hollenhorst and Edward Kane for their help and constructive criticisms.

John Cornwall
Spring 1972

Chapter I An Introduction to the Problem of Adjustment Mechanisms

A. The Basic Problem

This study grows out of a concern with a question that has not been adequately analyzed or answered: why is it that advanced capitalistic systems have not been subject to periodic breakdowns such as the United States catastrophe of 1929? Why is it that in the past, when recessions have been severe, they have been short; and when prolonged, they have tended to be mild (with the one exception of 1929)?[1] Or, to pose the question in another way: what is the adjusting mechanism bringing a growing demand into line with a growing supply, or maximum output at a tolerable level of unemployment, so that no secular trend in the rate of unemployment results?

The collapse of the 1930's proved that this sort of adjustment is far from automatic in a predominantly *laissez-faire* capitalistic system. And if we take seriously the implications of models of the Harrod–Domar variety, the amazing thing is that periodic breakdowns of the interwar variety have not been the rule, but the exception. After all, why should the rate of growth of non-consumption spending (and, therefore, demand) be just equal to the rate of growth of capital (and, therefore, full capacity output), and both equal to the growth of the labor force?

A great deal of growth theory of the post-war period has of course been directed at controlling this 'knife-edge'-balance problem posited by Harrod and at evolving an adjustment mechanism somehow to bring demand and supply into line. Two of the more popular mechanisms have been fiscal policy and the price mechanism. But clearly, a model whereby demand (and

---

[1] A question posed in Duesenberry, James, *Business Cycles and Economic Growth*, McGraw-Hill, New York, 1958, Chapter 1.

supply) are manipulated through the use of fiscal instruments is not applicable to many countries, including the United States: with the exception of the 1964 tax cut, there has been no major peacetime attempt to regulate the American economy in order to achieve full employment or any other policy goal. For that matter Lundberg has argued that, given the degree of uncertainty and ignorance of the real world by economists both today and in the past, it is incorrect to give target-instrument models too much credit for regulating (among other things) demand and supply.

> My exposition in the later chapters has been principally aimed at showing how and why there are deficiencies in the present knowledge of economic relationships. The conclusion has been that economic policy has to be conducted without much possibility of knowing with quantitative precision what the effects will be. One of my intentions has been, of course, to draw attention to the "false precisions" which often characterize inflationary gap analysis and the preparation of the national budgets as well as the drafting of fiscal and regulative budgets . . . . This book may be interpreted partly as a reaction against excessively optimistic and uncritical views of our present knowledge . . . on which all the more ambitious forms of state intervention must be based . . . of the manner of functioning of the economic machinery.[2]

This passage is not quoted to argue that the country in question (Sweden) could have achieved as creditable a record as it has in the postwar period without active intervention, or that the 1964 U.S. tax cut was a step in the wrong direction. But Lundberg's statement, together with the creditable historical record of Western capitalism, does suggest that an additional mechanism is at work. And this mechanism evidently works in such a way that when demand and full employment output (or full employment stimulants and leakages) are not equal *ex ante*, adjustments occur on both the demand and supply sides of the market (such as changes in income) so that something like the 1930's is a rarity. Among other things this would tend to make fiscal policy look better than it deserves.

B. The Return of the Invisible Hand

One possible adjusting mechanism, one currently in fashion and therefore demanding extended comment, is the price mechanism. For various reasons, including the post World War II record of growth at high levels of employment, modern dynamic models tend to ignore the demand side of the market.

---

[2] Lundberg, Erik, *Business Cycles and Economic Policy*, Harvard University Press, Cambridge, 1957, p. 298. For that matter, one influential British economist has argued that fiscal policy has played a destabilizing role in postwar Britain. See Dow, J. C. R., *The Management of the British Economy, 1945–60*, Cambridge University Press, 1964.

One such approach, which is aptly termed 'neoclassical analysis', has dominated growth theory during the decade of the 1960's. Its practitioners can be divided into two groups. On the one hand there are those who believe that the price mechanism works in some long-run sense. Consider the following statement:

> In the first place, the long-run relative constancy of the rate of return on capital suggests the operation of an important servomechanism. In the absence of technological advance and labor force growth, the accumulation of capital would tend to push down the rate of return. This tendency was apparently off-set by technological advance and growth of labor input, on balance. But in periods when the latter forces were strong enough to raise the rate of return, this apparently induced an increasing volume of saving and investment which eventually drove the return back down.[3]

Thus, unexplained changes in the rate of technological progress generate adjustments in the rate of growth of capital and output, evidently through changes in relative factor prices. In all fairness this position should be broadened to allow for the influence of monetary policy, and therefore interpreted as the belief: either (*a*) that prices move quickly and efficiently enough to adjust demand and supply at reasonable levels of unemployment over, say, a ten-year period; or (*b*) that whatever inertia there may be in the movement of prices can be offset by the monetary authority adjusting the money supply. Therefore, whenever the amount of investment and savings at full employment are not equal (or more generally whenever the *ex ante* stimulants and leakages forthcoming at full employment are not equal), prices, including the rate of interest, adjust, or will be adjusted by the monetary authority, so that deviations from full employment will be short lived.[4]

The second group of neoclassical model builders do not take their assumptions so seriously. These theorists were greatly impressed with some of the works of Harrod on growth and stability. Harrod had showed that in a very simple (and unrealistic) Keynesian model, it was possible for all variables to grow at the same exponential rate; but that this steady state growth path

---

[3] See Kendrick, J. W., and Sato, R., 'Factor Prices, Productivity and Economic Growth', *The American Economic Review*, December 1963. For a similar view see: Nelson, R. R., 'Full Employment Policy and Economic Growth', *The American Economic Review*, December 1966; and Sato, K., 'On the *Adjustment* Time in the Neo-Classical Growth Models', *The Review of Economic Studies*, July 1966, p. 276. Nelson is concerned lest a change in the rate of disembodied technical progress cause a divergence of the natural rate of interest and the money rate, and thereby generate inflation or unemployment. Sato believes that if the speed of convergence to the long-run equilibrium can be shown to be reasonably fast in a neoclassical model, this is a useful first approximation to reality.

[4] However, there is a logical problem involved here, because while adherents to the described position tend to think in some long-run sense, the structure of the typical neoclassical model is such that the system moves from one instantaneous full employment equilibrium to another, whether on the golden age growth path or not. Meade assumes that the monetary authority is able to regulate demand through monetary policy, so that full employment always results. Meade, J. E., *A Neo-Classical Theory of Economic Growth*, George Allen and Unwin, London, 1961.

was most unstable, for the slightest mistake on the part of the economic actors involved would set in motion violent movements away from the path. A great deal of theoretical work in the postwar period has centered around attempts to discover what were the sources of this instability, how they could be eliminated, and how other models could be evolved capable of steady state growth. A wide variety of models was developed, the variations based upon differing assumptions about technology: e.g., the shape of the isoquants of the production function; whether technical progress was 'neutral' or 'biased', and if neutral, whether it was 'Harrod neutral' or 'Hicks neutral'; whether technical progress was 'embodied' or 'disembodied'; whether there was substitution between factors before and after capital goods had been constructed, etc. The essential point is that these studies involved various alternative assumptions about the *supply* side of the market, but no concern with problems of demand, and in this very basic sense were pre-Keynesian or neoclassical. Their approach has an affinity with the 'as if' doctrine espoused by Friedman and others.[5] Thus they would argue that whatever it is that has kept demand and supply in line historically, it is useful to work out the implications of neoclassical models, because many have implications that accord with the 'stylized facts'. For example, given the right assumptions about technology, neoclassical models can generate long-run solutions involving a rising capital–labor ratio (when technological progress is allowed), full employment and reasonable rates of growth of *per capita* and aggregate output. The economy behaves 'as if' the price mechanism works to adjust demand and supply at full employment. Whether this is literally true or not is left open, since interest is focused on other matters.

C. The Role of the Price Mechanism

One difficulty with the 'as if' methodology is that it still leaves us in a poor position to draw inferences about the truth of our premises, we can show only that the implications of neoclassical models accord with the historical record. In Chapter II it is shown that the same stylized facts can be generated by adjusting mechanisms other than the price mechanism, so some method must be evolved whereby we can take a position on this matter of adjusting mechanisms.

It is argued in the following chapters that the price mechanism in fact plays a minor role in steering the economy along a high employment growth path. Monetary factors do play a role, but hardly in such a way as to keep the natural rate of interest equal to the money rate. However, it will be argued

---

[5] Friedman, Milton, *Essays on Positive Economics*, University of Chicago Press, 1953, Part I. For a discussion of the Friedman position, see the section on 'Problems of Methodology' in the *American Economic Review, Papers and Proceedings*, May 1963.

Diagram 1.1

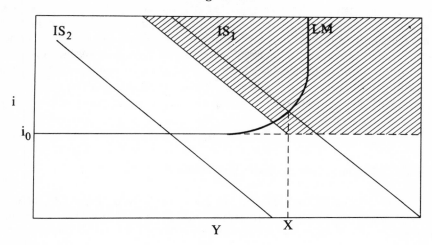

that monetary policy by itself is not enough to keep the system working properly. Consider the standard Hicks *IS–LM* curve diagram, where the intersection of the two curves in Diagram 1.1 depicts the equilibrium level of real income, (Y), and the rate of interest, (i). The position that will be adopted here is that, given the most optimistic assumption about the influence of the rate of interest on spending, what is really of importance and interest is the position of the intercept of the *IS* function. For what matters is whether or not, at any positive rate of interest, spending intentions are such that the *IS* curve intercepts the horizontal axis to the right of full employment output, X. One way of rephrasing the assertion on the role of money is to say that under most circumstances, spending intentions are such that not only does the *IS* curve tend to cut the horizontal axis to the right of X, but that it also tends to cut a line depicting the liquidity trap rate of interest, (i_0), to the right of a vertical line drawn to X. When this mechanism is working properly, monetary policy has a role to play as long as the *IS* curve is not completely interest-inelastic. That role will be to shift the *LM* curve within the shaded area, so that it intersects the *IS* curve at a point as near as possible to full employment and, hopefully, to price stability. But what will also be argued is that when this basic adjusting mechanism breaks down, no amount of movement of the *LM* curve, whether through changes in the money supply or prices, will work.

The original Keynesian argument was that either the liquidity trap (defined as the inability of the interest rate to fall below some positive rate of interest) or wage rigidities could prevent full employment from being realized in the absence of an active fiscal policy. This, however, is a bit misleading, for if the other factors influencing investment (conveniently lumped together in the horizontal intercept of the *IS* curve) are such as to cause the *IS* curve to shift, say, to *IS*$_2$, then it cannot be said that the liquidity trap or wage rigidities prevent full employment. Even in their absence, full employment would be impossible. It is rather the inability of the off-sets at full employment to equal full employment savings or leakages, at a positive rate of interest, and this can and will be traced back to the failure to work properly of an adjusting mechanism that describes an interaction of demand and supply (i.e. full employment output, *X*).[6]

D. The Adjustment Mechanism to be Developed

It will be argued throughout that the price mechanism, defined to include the actions of the monetary authorities, does not by itself work quickly and efficiently enough to equate demand and supply at high levels of employment. Supply or maximum output is also not assumed to be something rigidly defined and uninfluenced by the actual performance of the economy, but to depend very much on demand pressures. However, the rejection of the price mechanism as the means whereby a growing demand and supply are brought into line at high levels of employment necessitates finding some other mechanism as a substitute. Until the advent of neoclassical analysis, the models developed since Keynes to describe the movements of national income aggregates have assumed that when *ex ante* leakages and the offsets forthcoming at full employment are unequal, it is income that adjusts, not prices. Indeed, the spirit of the 'Keynesian revolution' was just this substitution of adjustments in income for adjustments in prices. One need only mention the theoretical models of Hansen, Hicks, Kaldor and Duesenberry, or the econometric models beginning with Tinbergen up to the SSRC–Brookings model, to make the point. But as Keynes showed, there is no *a priori* reason why *ex ante* leakages and offsets *should* be equal in the neighborhood of full employment. This, then, is the main task of this study: to develop a model that can explain why growth in an economy as mature as that of the United States has been accompanied, with one exception, by only relatively minor fluctuations around a high or full employment level of income. It will be argued that the knife-edge problem arises from a too rigid separation of the demand and supply sides of the market. Once such an interaction between demand and supply is allowed, the system becomes much

[6] For convenience, the *IS* curve is assumed to have the same slope before and after any shift. It is always possible to think of such a complete and prolonged collapse of the monetary mechanism that a general and prolonged collapse of the real sector results; but it would be hard to argue that this has ever happened in the United States, with the possible exception of the 1930's. It will be argued later in the text that in the 1930's it was the real sector that was responsible for the most of the trouble.

more stable. In taking account of this interaction, an alternative adjusting mechanism will be developed to account for this amazing record, one that does not depend upon the price mechanism but that is more in keeping with the Keynesian tradition.

The model to be developed borrows many ideas of post-Keynesian model builders, but hopefully combines them with some original elements, so that the final product has some claim to originality. For example, demographic movements either in the form of redistribution of a given population or increase in the size of the demographic base, or both, will play a role. This is not to argue that population growth, or more correctly, growth in the number of family or spending units, is either a necessary or sufficient condition for stability, or rapid growth in aggregate, or *per capita* incomes. Clearly, the Swedish example shows that this is not necessary; while the experience of any number of underdeveloped countries show that demographic growth is also not a sufficient condition. However, arguments can and will be brought forward to show that without demographic movements, or a dynamic fiscal policy, or a situation where there is some given trend in demand (e.g., where exports can be assumed to grow steadily), the system will be much less stable, and much more prone to acute and prolonged recessions that will pull down the growth rate. It will be apparent that this part of the discussion has certain affinities with the stagnation argument of Hansen, but only when the latter is correctly formulated. We now have enough instruments at our disposal to refute the 'vulgar' stagnationist doctrine, whereby a mature capitalistic system is doomed to a secular rise in unemployment, no matter what. What will actually be suggested is that without demographic movements or a sustained export boom, a mature economy may be faced with a slowly rising national debt-to-income ratio.

The Duesenberry emphasis on demand generating its own supply (within limits) also plays a key role, together with a modified version of the ratchet effect developed by Mathews.[7] This 'inertia' effect in the consumption (or any other) function will be seen as a mechanism for introducing the influence of supply on demand. In other words, the model will allow for an interaction between the two sides of the market.

We shall also make a study of several different sectors, considered both separately and as they interact, and for two reasons. On the one hand, it is argued below that the process of growth can only be properly understood as a process of 'transformation'. Only if allowance is made for the rise and subsequent decline of certain goods and industries, can one get to the heart of the matter of growth. For example, as incomes rise, goods that once were luxuries for a few become necessities for mass consumption, as consumers move through a hierarchy of goods. This is mirrored on the supply side by

[7] See Mathews, R. C. O., 'The Savings Function and the Problem of Trend and Cycle', *Review of Economic Studies*, No. 2 pp. 75–95, 1954–55.

consideration of the varying contributions to the overall growth of productivity made by different industries at different points of time. Growth of demand, supply, and productivity is a most unbalanced thing in reality.

Second, it will be argued that the stability of the moving equilibrium of a capitalist system can only be understood in terms of a diffusion process, whereby different sectors are out of phase with some general measure of activity. This by definition requires disaggregation. The possibility of a recession reaching a lower turning point, with net investment still positive, can only be understood in terms of a lack of diffusion of some sectors, which is intimately related to what happened to the various sectors in the previous boom.

E. The Method of Analysis

The following pages deal with an economy of the American type as it has developed during the 20th century, especially since World War I. That is, discussion will center on an urbanized economy with a fairly high rate of population growth (for a developed economy), in which it is assumed that the social overhead capital has been laid, savings is positive at full employment, and consumer capital formation plays an important role in absorbing savings. Thus, it is an affluent society where consumers as investors play an important role in offsetting full employment savings, thereby preventing large-scale unemployment.

An economy of this sort is especially interesting for study. Its success in terms of avoiding recurring depressions of the 1930's variety cannot be explained in terms of stabilization policy, as might be the case for, say, Britain or Sweden. The explanation is more obscure, more difficult and more challenging. It is hoped and intended, however, that some of the analysis will be helpful in understanding the workings of other mature economies. A rather lengthy discussion of the British economy in Chapter XI, together with references to Britain throughout the manuscript, can be viewed as an attempt to indicate the generality of the theoretical model developed in the first parts of the book. For it would be difficult to find two more different mature capitalist economies: Britain, with its heavy dependence upon foreign trade, its much greater commitment to high employment (at the expense of price stability), its relatively small domestic market and its much slower rate of growth of population, provides a perfect contrast to the United States.

Emphasis in the theoretical chapters will be on the moving equilibrium of the system, and its stability. In the moving equilibrium ('steady state' or 'golden age'), all endogenous variables grow at the same (proportional) rate of growth. Stability of this equilibrium implies that if the system is displaced or 'shocked' from its moving equilibrium path, and the variables are assigned some arbitrary set of initial values, the system will move back toward the equilibrium path.[8] In using this frame of reference, the study resembles a currently fashionable branch of growth theory (termed by one economist 'mathematical growth theory'), but here the resemblance mostly ends. The latter studies, with their emphasis on supply and production, can be thought of as a healthy reaction to much early Keynesian (and much current econometric) work, that neglected the supply side of the market. However, the reaction has been allowed to proceed too far. We now have a large body of growth theory that is completely devoid of Keynesian influences: a body of theory that is the logical extension of pre-Keynesian theorizing, distinguished from it chiefly by the use of more elaborate techniques. As suggested above, the present study is in a sense an attempt at synthesis of these two positions, seeing growth as the outcome of an interaction between supply and demand. However, in appearance and in reality it is more Keynesian than anything else.

One final point. There is no single 'problem' of stability in the real world, since one can speak of the stability of employment, prices, the exchange rate, etc. Nevertheless, emphasis here is on the conditions necessary for stability of employment rates. This may seem odd in an age of inflation. However, while it is obviously also important to get at the causes of inflation (i.e., the instability of the price level), much too little is known about conditions necessary for the avoidance of widespread unemployment. And, as will be argued in the Postscript to Chapter VIII, the issue is far from academic. But for fortuitous events, the American economy would very likely have undergone a serious recession in 1969–1970. Furthermore, our discussions of the stability issue even in this limited sense will be helpful in Chapter XI, when it comes to formulating a consistent set of policy instruments for speeding up the growth rate of an economy that shows little likelihood of falling into a serious recession.

F. An Outline of What is to Follow

Chapter II introduces the basic problem of the interaction of the demand and supply side of the market. It sets the stage for the next two chapters, by contrasting two 'pure type' models: one where supply adjusts to demand, and the other where demand adjusts to supply. In the former case demand parameters determine the long-run growth rate, and in the latter only supply parameters have such an influence. In this chapter are also discussed a number of desirable properties that a model of growth should have if it is

---

[8] Beginning in Chapter II, the moving equilibrium will be defined so as to have the additional property of an unchanged rate of unemployment. The notion of stability used here is stability of the steady state path; i.e., part of the problem of equilibrium dynamics as defined by Hahn and Mathews. See Hahn, F. H., and Mathews, R. C. O., 'The Theory of Economic Growth: A Survey', *The Economic Journal*, December 1964, pp. 781–782. However, we allow for the fact that when the system is off the steady state path, markets may not be cleared, in the sense that unemployment may exist.

to be taken seriously—most of which the model offered in subsequent chapters embodies. In Chapters III and IV a simple one-sector model of growth is developed, where the long-run growth rate turns out to be a function of demand as well as of supply parameters. It is argued that only by taking account of an interaction between both sides of the market can one begin to understand how a capitalist system works.

Chapter V puts forward the notion of the family life cycle and a demographic sausage machine, whereby, in a moving equilibrium situation of the type described in Chapters III and IV, families in more advanced stages of the life cycle 'pull' individuals into the initial stages of the life cycle, thus preparing them for later stages. This is of extreme importance in an economy of the type described here, because of the important role played by consumer capital formation in maintaining high and rising levels of employment. And consumer asset formation is clearly related to stages of the life cycle. Chapter V also briefly discusses another type of spending, which is closely related to the distribution and size of the population: spending by governments, especially at the state and local level. This type of spending, and certain types of consumer investment, have played an important stabilizing role, and the manner in which they lend stability to the economy is outlined in Chapters VI and VII. (Chapter V may be skipped over by those concerned with stability issues.)

Chapters VI and VII contain a discussion of the stability of the moving equilibrium of the model outlined in previous chapters. The analysis continues with a moderate amount of disaggregation, since, as already argued, the stability of a capitalistic system very much depends upon a lack of diffusion in different sections in booms as well as recessions. Recessions are mild because recession tendencies are not widely diffused over wide sectors of the economy, and many sectors are out of phase because during the previous boom the growth of some sectors is held back, thereby introducing a lack of diffusion in the boom, and so on. This requires a consideration of the level of the moving equilibrium income relative to full employment income, together with a general consideration of the relative responsiveness of different types of spending to changes in economic conditions.

Chapters VIII–X are descriptive, and can be viewed as an attempt to put to a test the different hypotheses proposed earlier. The behavior of the American economy during the postwar period is discussed in Chapters VIII and IX. In Chapter X additional support is offered for the theory when the interwar period is examined. An attempt is made to explain what went wrong in the 1930's in terms of the earlier analysis. Chapter XI attempts to broaden the analysis with a theoretical and descriptive study of the British economy. It too can be seen as an attempt to test much of the theory contained in the earlier portions of the book. Chapter XII extends the analysis into the future, when an attempt is made to assess the growth and stability properties of the system, given certain projected trends in the composition of output.

Chapter II Two Basic Adjustment Mechanisms

A. The Matter of 'Realism'

In this chapter our attention will be devoted to the question of what is required before it can be said that a growth model qualifies as a 'good first approximation' to reality. This, we shall argue, is basically a matter of developing a realistic adjustment mechanism that brings demand and supply into line; that allows one to speak in a general way about a moving equilibrium, and under what conditions it is stable. But there are also certain other properties that a model should have, and we will begin with a brief discussion of these.

B. The 'Stylized Facts'

Model builders of the postwar era have with few exceptions constructed models where all endogenous variables grow at the same rate. This 'golden age' framework implies that such things as the capital–output ratio, the ratio of profits to wages, and the ratio of outputs of any two sectors of the model (in multisector models), are constant in equilibrium. Unfortunately, the historical evidence suggests a quite different picture of the stylized facts.

Studies of both the American and British economies indicate that neither the capital–output ratio nor the ratio of profits to wage income have remained constant.[1] Both have tended to fall in the 20th century, with the former ratio

[1] See Kuznets, S., *Capital in the American Economy*, National Bureau of Economic Research, New York, 1961, pp. 78–90; and Deane, P., and Cole, W. A., *British Economic Growth, 1688–1959*, Cambridge University Press, 1967, Tables 80 and 81; and Solow, R. M., 'A Skeptical Note on the Constancy of Relative Shares', *American Economic Review*, September 1958. A recent study suggests that there may have been a reversal of the downward trend of the capital–output ratio in the United Kingdom. See Mathews, R. C. O., *Some Aspects of Post-war Growth in the British Economy in Relation to Historical Experience*, Manchester Statistical Society, 1964.

tending to follow an inverted **U**-shaped pattern—if the 19th century is considered as well. Figures for consumption (including durables), and government expenditures as a per cent of aggregate activity, show a notable decline and rise respectively, in both the United States and Britain. Consumer durables expressed as a per cent of either total consumption outlays or of GNP show a strong upward trend in both countries (and others as well).[2] These last two features illustrate particularly clearly the differences in growth rates of different sectors of a capitalist economy as it matures, and numerous others could be cited: for instance, one of the more interesting developments, and one that will receive more extensive comment later, has been the rising importance of consumer investment as a share of GNP. Table 2.1 depicts the changing importance of 'consumer investment' and 'business investment' in the United States for a period spanning most of the 20th century.[3] Similar developments in consumer investment outlays have undoubtedly occurred in other mature economies.

All this evidence supports the view advanced later that growth in a developed capitalist economy is a very unbalanced thing, and should be viewed as a process of 'transformation'. Chapters III and IV, however, are highly aggregative and assume that capital, output, consumption and investment all grow at the same rate. In this sense the model developed in them is at variance with some of the stylized facts. But the assumption is not essential for the main argument and is made only for expositional purposes, while the model does have other features that should strengthen its explanatory power. In later chapters this assumption of equal and steady growth in all sectors is largely discounted.

C. The Stylized Facts—Some Other Considerations

Whether one chooses to work within the framework of golden age equilibria or not, one can insist that the long-run growth rate generated by a model be reasonable. For example, very simple accelerator-multiplier models were first made popular in economics partly because of their ability to generate cycles as part of the interaction of the endogenous variables and nothing else.

[2] Kuznets, S., *op. cit.*, Table R-11; Deane and Cole, *op. cit.*, Table 68; *Historical Statistics on Governmental Finances and Employment*, Bureau of the Census, U.S. Department of Commerce; and various issues of the *Survey of Current Business*, U.S. Department of Commerce, Office of Business Economics and *National Income and Expenditures*, Central Statistical Office.

[3] See Juster, F. T., *Household Capital Formation and Financing, 1897–1962*, National Bureau of Economic Research, New York, 1966. Juster defines consumer investment to include additions to the stock of owner-occupied housing, automobiles, furniture, household appliances and the 'entertainment complex'; i.e., T.V., radios, high fidelity equipment and pianos. Business investment includes, as well as fixed non-residential investment, additions to the rental housing stock.

Table 2.1

	Consumer investment as a share of GNP	Business investment as a share of GNP
	(per cent)	(per cent)
1899–1908	4·4	12·4
1909–1918	5·2	10·6
1919–1928	9·3	9·6
1946–1962	9·8	9·7

Source: F. Thomas Juster, *Household Capital Formation and Financing, 1897–1962*, National Bureau of Economics Research, New York, 1966.

Unfortunately, when these same models are used to generate growth; the long-run growth rate turns out to be prohibitively high.[4] Consider the simple accelerator-multiplier model:

$$Y_t = C_t + I_t \tag{1}$$

$$C_t = \alpha Y_{t-1} \tag{2}$$

and

$$I_t = \beta(Y_{t-1} - Y_{t-2}) \tag{3}$$

where C, I and Y represent consumption, investment and income respectively, all in real terms. If β, the desired capital–output ratio, is set equal to 2 and $\alpha = 0.9$, the long-run growth rate is 77 per cent. A model generating this type of long-run behavior would have to be rejected for this reason alone. We will assume that a model with a long-run growth rate of less than 10 per cent on an annual basis would be a reasonable approximation to reality and, *ceteris paribus* acceptable.

A related point is that of 'structural stability', i.e. 'the ability of the model to withstand changes in its parameters without its performance undergoing a major transformation'.[5] In order to bring out clearly the various forces, interactions etc., that determine the growth and stability propensities of a model, the latter must be kept simple, with a limited number of equations and variables (although simulation work takes some of the edge off this condition). But the fewer the relations and number of independent variables, the more likely are the parameters to be changing over time. But if this has a significant effect on the long-run rate and character of growth, the value of the model, especially for pedagogical purposes, is questioned, since in the

[4] Alexander, Sidney, 'The Accelerator as a Generator of Steady Growth', *The Quarterly Journal of Economics*, May 1949.

[5] Mathews, R. C. O., 'Duesenberry on Growth and Fluctuations', *Economic Journal*, December 1959.

Table 2.2

	Average rate of unemployment in the United States	Average rate of unemployment in the United Kingdom
	(per cent)	(per cent)
1900–1908	4·3	4·5
1909–1918	5·4	2·7
1919–1928	4·5	9·8 (11.7)
1929–1938	17·0	15·9
1946–1959	4·5	1·8
1960–1970	4·8	1·9

Source: S. Lebergott, *Manpower in Economic Growth,* McGraw-Hill, New York, 1964, Table A-3; and *The British Economy—Key Statistics, 1900–70,* The Times Publishing Company, 1971.

real world economies seldom undergo such transformations. For example, in the model just discussed, if α is assigned a value of 0.85, the growth rate falls to 60 per cent. If β is changed from 2 to 1.73, the growth rate becomes 32 per cent. What one would hope for is a model that can withstand a wide range of parameter changes without a dramatic effect on its long-run performance.

A dynamic implication appropriate to the United States experience (and to a lesser extent to the United Kingdom) is a relative constancy of the rate of unemployment; at least in the 20th century. This is seen in Table 2.2. Aside from the 1930's, unemployment has varied within a fairly narrow range.[6] This is nothing more or less than saying that a model should imply that the rate of growth of demand and supply, i.e. full employment output, will be more or less equal. Not only have demand and supply grown approximately at the same rate during this century, but they have done so at tolerable rates of unemployment. Thus, it is not enough for the model to generate a rate of growth of demand and supply of the same order of magnitude. It should do so at unemployment rates of say 3 to 7 per cent on an annual basis, rather than 7 to 10 per cent. Table 2.2 also contains average unemployment rates in the United Kingdom over the same period. The lack of any sort of recovery following World War I is quite apparent—and even more apparent when the unemployment figures for 1919 and 1920 are omitted from the 1919–1928 average. (Thus, the average unemployment rate for the period 1921–1928 is shown in parentheses in the third column of the table.) This inability of demand and supply to grow together at reasonable rates of unemployment

[6] Leaving out the war years and those of the Great Depression, unemployment seldom fell outside a range of 3–7 per cent on an annual basis. The British and U.S. data in Table 2.2 are not strictly comparable.

indicates an even more serious and prolonged breakdown of a capitalist system than the 1930's in America. Britain's difficulties during this period can be attributed to certain long-run technological and economic developments that tended greatly to depress British exports; and to her desire to return to the gold standard at prewar parities.[7]

D. Two Explanations of the Adjustment Process

Any number of models are consistent with the historical record, in the sense that each can generate reasonable values for the variables as part of their dynamic implications. But to treat them on a par with one another because the world behaves 'as if' each model is correct, is poor science. A comparison of two quite different types of models brings out this point: a simple version of Duesenberry's 'Keynesian' model, and a one-commodity Solow–Swan neoclassical model.[8] Duesenberry's model consists of the following four equations:

$$Y_t = C_t + I_t, \tag{1}$$

$$C_t = \alpha_1 Y_{t-1} + \alpha_2 K_{t-1}, \tag{2}$$

$$I_t = \beta_1 Y_{t-1} - \beta_2 K_{t-1}, \tag{3}$$

$$K_t = K_{t-1} + I_t, \tag{4}$$

where Y, C, I and K represent income, consumption, investment and capital, all in real terms. Simple algebraic manipulation allows one to write both the rate of growth of output, r_y, and the rate of growth of capital, r_k, as functions of the capital-output ratio. Thus we have:

$$r_k = \beta_1 Y_{t-1}/K_{t-1} - \beta_2$$

and

$$r_y = (\alpha_1 + \beta_1 - 1) + (\alpha_2 - \beta_2)K_{t-1}/Y_{t-1}.$$

If it can be assumed that the four demand parameters α_1, α_2, β_1 and β_2 are such that the system is capable of sustained growth, then the solid lines in Diagram 2.1 depict the two growth rates as functions of the capital-output ratio.

Both intersection points, A and B, are equilibrium points, in the sense that if the right initial conditions are picked, the system would remain at one or the other in the absence of outside disturbances. However, only point A is a

[7] Arndt, H. W., *The Economic Lessons of the Nineteen-Thirties*, Augustus M. Kelley, New York, 1965, Chapters 1 and 4.

[8] See Duesenberry, *op. cit.*, Solow, R. M., 'A Contribution to the Theory of Economic Growth', *Quarterly Journal of Economics*, February 1956; and Swan, T. W., 'Economic Growth and Capital Accumulation', *Economic Record*, November 1956.

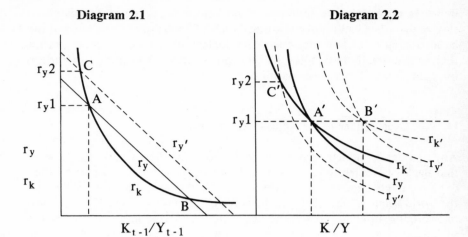

Diagram 2.1   Diagram 2.2

stable equilibrium and our attention will be confined to it. In the long-run, all variables grow at the same rate. If this growth rate is in excess of the rate of growth of the labor force and population, the capital–labor ratio rises over time as does *per capita* income. For plausible parameter values the long-run rate of growth of output (and capital) is reasonable, although the model does lack structural stability.[9]

Now assume time to be continuous and contrast this with the standard neoclassical model. We have

$$Y = Y_0 e^{gt} K^\lambda N^{1-\lambda}, \qquad (5) \qquad\qquad K = I, \qquad (8)$$

$$S = sY, \qquad (6) \qquad\qquad \partial Y/\partial N = w, \qquad (9)$$

$$I = S, \qquad (7) \qquad\qquad N = N_0 e^{(r_n)t}, \qquad (10)$$

where g, N, S, w and r_n represent an exogenous rate of growth of neutral disembodied technical progress, the labor force, savings, the real wage and the rate of growth of the labor force respectively. All other variables have their previous meanings. Equations (5) and (6) can be used to determine the rates of growth of output and capital, once again as functions of the capital–output ratio. Taking logarithms of both sides of equation (5) and then computing the total differential, we may write: $r_y = g + \lambda r_K + (1 - \lambda) r_n$ (5′). Since equation (6) can be written: $S/K = r_K = sY/K$, (6′) the rate of growth of output can also be expressed as a function of the capital–output ratio; i.e., $r_y = g +$

---

[9] An analytical solution of Duesenberry's model gives two roots:

$$x_1, x_2 = \frac{(1 - \beta_2 + \alpha_1 + \beta_1)}{2} \pm \frac{\sqrt{(1 - \beta_2 + \alpha_1 + \beta_1)^2 - 4[\alpha_1(1 - \beta_2) + \beta_1(1 - \alpha_2)]}}{2}$$

The stable equilibrium growth rate depicted by point A in Diagram 2.1 is equal to the larger (real) root minus one.

$\lambda s Y/K + (1 - \lambda)r_n$ (5″). This is shown graphically in Diagram 2.2. Intersection point A' is a stable equilibrium. Starting from any set of initial conditions, the system moves steadily towards growth rate, r_{y1}, which is also equal to the rate of growth of capital. Both here and in the Duesenberry model, the long-run capital–output ratio is constant. The long-run growth rate, $r_y = g/(1 - \lambda) + r_n$, is a reasonable one and if λ is assumed equal to profits as a share of output, the model displays structural stability for reasonable parameter values. The capital–labor ratio rises at rate $g/(1 - \lambda)$ as does *per capita* income and the rate of growth of real wages relative to the return on capital. As is well known, with a Cobb–Douglas production function, and competitive pricing, the constancy of the factor shares is assured. In this sense, the standard neoclassical model is capable of explaining more than is, say, Duesenberry's. However, a little comparative dynamics brings out some additional points of greater interest.

E. The Effect of Demand Parameter Changes on the Growth Rate

Duesenberry's model of growth generates a rate of growth of demand and supply of the same order of magnitude, and at a reasonable level of unemployment, by assuming that supply adjusts to demand. The rate of growth of productivity and of the labor force are made functions of the actual performance of the economy. This assumption has been the basis of many of the less formal models developed in recent years, especially by European economists.[10] Assume an increase in one of the demand parameters, α_1. This causes a shift outward to the right of the curve depicting the rate of growth of output in Diagram 2.1 to that shown by the dashed line, $r_{y'}$. The intersection point, C, indicates a new equilibrium rate of growth of output, r_{y2} as supply adjusts to the greater demand pressures. In this very basic sense, demand parameters influence supply or maximum output, and the long-run growth rate of the latter through their effect on productivity and growth of the labor force.

Consider now the neoclassical model and assume an increase in s, the average and marginal propensity to save: a parameter change comparable to the change in α_1 in the Duesenberry model. The net effect in this case is to cause a shift to the right of the curves representing the rates of growth of output and capital, to those shown by $r_{y'}$ and $r_{k'}$ in Diagram 2.2, as can be seen by inspecting equations (5″) and (6′). At the new intersection point, B', the capital–output ratio is greater, but the long-run growth rate is unchanged. In this type of model spending or demand parameters cannot affect the long-run growth rate.

[10] Lamfalussy, A., *Investment and Growth in Mature Economies*, Macmillan, New York, 1961 and *The United Kingdom and the Six*, Irwin, Homewood, 1963; and Maddison, Angus, *Economic Growth in the West*, Twentieth Century Fund, New York, 1964.

The basic differences between these two 'pure type' models and their different explanations of the adjustment process can be seen in another way. In the Duesenberry model an increase in the long-run rate of growth of demand induced a higher rate of growth of productivity (or 'technical progress').[11] Consider now the neoclassical model and allow an increase in the supply parameter g, the rate of growth of technical progress, which falls like manna from heaven. This shifts the r_y line in Diagram 2.2 to $r_{y''}$ in a manner similar to the shift in the same curve in Diagram 2.1 caused by increased demand pressures. The new intersection point, C', like point C, indicates a higher growth rate; i.e., r_{y2}. In both cases the long-run growth rate is higher, but the kinds of adjustment, as well as the side of the market doing the adjusting, are quite different. If there is to be any adjusting in this model, demand must adjust to supply, while in the Duesenberry model supply must adjust to demand. In the Duesenberry scheme of things, the means whereby supply adjusts to demand consists of such things as higher growth of the labor force, and induced effects on productivity or technical progress through better utilization of existing resources, together with shifts in the distribution of resources. The price mechanism plays no role whatsoever. In the neoclassical model, a change in technical progress is the cause rather than the effect of certain adjustments that are required, if the two sides of the market are to grow at the same rate. The unexplained increase in the supply parameter, g, necessitates that the price mechanism work in such a way that changes in relative factor prices clear markets, and bring demand into line with changed supply conditions; i.e. Say's Law.

F. A More Eclectic Approach

Here then are two alternative explanations of the manner in which the demand and supply sides of the market adjust. The implications of both allow one to argue that the economy behaves 'as if' Say's Law applies (supply creates its own demand), and also applies in reverse (demand creates its own supply). If we are forced to choose between the two explanations, our choice comes down to whether we think adjustments of maximum output or price bring one side of the market into line with the other.

---

[11] The terms 'technical progress' and 'growth of productivity' actually measure our ignorance. They denote the unexplained part of growth, or the 'residual', and are used more or less interchangeably in the text. For example, if we measure labor and capital conventionally—i.e. without regard to things like differences in quality or 'vintage'—and combine them with weights depending upon factor shares, we have a geometric index of total factor productivity, A. If λ represents the share of output going to capital and $1 - \lambda$ the share going to labor we have $A = Y/K^\lambda N^{1-\lambda}$ or $\Delta A/A = \Delta Y/Y - \lambda \Delta K/K - (1 - \lambda)\Delta N/N$. However, if λ and $1 - \lambda$ are fixed, the expressions denote a Cobb–Douglas production function when solved for Y or $\Delta Y/Y$, where $\Delta A/A$ is the rate of growth of neutral technical progress.

In the model to be developed in Chapters III and IV, elements of both models are used in such a way that both demand and supply parameters can be said to determine the long-run growth of the system. This joint interaction should add to the stability of the model, and give some insight into the question of why there has been no secular trend in the unemployment rate. Unlike the Duesenberry model, we will limit the extent to which demand can affect maximum output and the long-run rate of growth of supply. Unlike the neoclassical model, small reliance is placed on the price mechanism as a means of adjusting demand and supply; instead a different mechanism is introduced. Monetary policy will have a role to play, and will add to the stability of the moving equilibrium; but the manner in which it and the price mechanism work is quite different from that envisaged in neoclassical analysis. For the most part the final product will be more Keynesian than pre-Keynesian. This fact, together with the increased interest in neoclassical models, necessitates some additional comments on the latter before building anew from a Keynesian base.

G. The Neoclassical Approach

Before one can determine to what extent neoclassical analysis contributes towards our understanding of the process of growth, it is necessary to take account of the fact that the basic model outlined above has been altered in many different ways in the interest of realism. It is important first to distinguish between two aspects of neoclassical analysis:—the supply or production side, and the demand side or market-clearing mechanism—for most of the important modifications have been on the supply side. For example, the assumptions of *ex ante* and *ex post* substitution in production have been questioned; and dissatisfaction with the notion of technical change unrelated to the performance of the economy has given rise to concepts such as embodied technical progress, learning by doing, biased technical progress, etc. But the assumptions about markets, about the environment within which economic units operate, have been little changed, and these assumptions are critical in neoclassical models for explaining phenomena such as the distribution of income, growth of demand (at full employment) and the stability of the models. Basically this type of analysis relies on an equilibrium analysis that assumes instantaneous adjustments at the margin, static expectations, pure competition and perfect foresight.

The assumption of perfect foresight, for example, implies that businessmen work in a situation where they have blueprints for all techniques for combining capital and labor for each period (and in the future), and that they have all relevant information about costs. On the demand side, perfect foresight and pure competition mean that there is never any uncertainty about demand conditions. Marginal revenue curves are known with absolute certainty, and are therefore relevant for price policy. The assumption that product prices are flexible, and always adjust to clear markets, is also in keeping with a world without monopoly, uncertainty and constraints on behavior.

Neoclassical analysis also assumes smooth, perfect and instantaneous workings in factor markets. The demand for labor is treated as a function of the real wage, with the supply of labor treated either as given, or as an increasing function of the same variable: in any short period, a situation of excess demand or supply is only momentary, as the real wage adjusts to clear markets. Furthermore, the return on capital, or natural rate of interest, in neoclassical models is usually thought of like the rental rate on a machine: over a period, the stock of machines grows if savings are positive; the owners of the machines lease them to other businessmen, and, within a very short time, the rental rate is so adjusted that all machines are employed in a manner analogous to the alleged workings of the labor market.

When evaluating the demand side of neoclassical analysis and its explanatory value, the issue comes down to whether in the real world of lags, rigidities, ·uncertainty and monopoly, changes in relative factor prices are rapid enough to eliminate, within the multiplier period, any *ex ante* discrepancy between full employment leakages, and non-consumption expenditure at full employment. For example, assume for convenience of one period an expenditure lag for consumption (and induced investment) behind income. Then, starting from a position of full employment, allow for a decline in investment such that, at the beginning of the next period, *ex ante* investment is less than full employment savings. If relative prices do not adjust within the period, income will fall by the amount of the autonomous decline in investment. By the end of the next period the price adjustment must be sufficient to offset the original decline in investment, plus the induced decline in consumption and investment—and so on.

Given what we know about product and factor markets, it seems extremely unlikely that price adjustments are ever rapid or strong enough to generate full employment in the above example, even in the long run. From inflation theory and studies of the structure of industry, we know that firms in most product markets do not behave according to the neoclassical precepts. Demand pressures may influence price eventually, but not in any neat short-run market clearing sense. Nor can we find much about factor markets that resembles the above description. For example, most evidence indicates that there is no correlation between movements of real wages and unemployment, one reason being that there may be no way for employees to affect the real wage. It can and will be argued that, given the kinds of pricing policy most likely to be pursued by business, there is little or no way for adjustments in the real wage to take place in such a way that labor markets are always cleared.[12] The same lack of appropriateness is found in the neoclassical description of the manner in which markets for capital goods work. In a frictionless world of perfect foresight and pure competition, such a theory of market adjustment or clearing might be useful; but it is inappropriate to describe the workings of the market for capital goods in the real world. Typically, say, when demand falls below production in the capital goods industry, order books shorten; rentals or prices don't adjust.

The question arises as to what is gained by assuming away all the institutional and behavioral rigidities and lags of the real world, and ignoring what makes for excess demand and supply situations, and the subsequent dynamic adjustments, in the real world. We wish to understand how it is that an economic system may be stable, that the demand and supply (or maximum output) side of the market adjust, and have adjusted historically, to one another in the long run. At the same time, we need a theoretical framework that can dispense with perfect markets and permit short-run disequilibria. It is thus necessary to develop a framework that can accommodate sticky prices and uncertainty about demand and cost conditions; one where rules of thumb may be the best strategy (and good sensible utility or profit maximizing behavior) in the face of uncertainty. And such a model need be in no way less 'theoretical' because it lacks tidiness.

Thus, it has become fairly common in economics to criticize model builders for 'ad hoc theorizing'; i.e. for constructing behavioral relationships between variables that cannot be said to 'flow from a basic profit or utility function'. To the extent that the complaint against 'ad hockery' is a complaint against measurement without theory, it is a point well taken. There is little to be said in support of relating variables in a way that suggests causation when on a priori grounds there is good evidence that no such relationship exists. But what critics usually have in mind when the charge of ad hoc theorizing is leveled, and what they would like to substitute, is more often than not of more dubious value. Those most intent on escaping from the charge of ad hoc theorizing can usually offer no more than some smooth simple profit or utility function (usually twice differentiable) that is to be maximized. From this flows 'good theory'; from the lack of an explicit function, 'bad theory'. The position adopted here is that the real world is much too complicated to be summarized in such a convenient manner: some account must be taken of the constraints, uncertainties and frictions of the real world. The resulting theories may be somewhat 'messy', but the behavioral relations employed can at least be said to flow from underlying maximization principles, and to have the added value of enhancing our understanding of the real world.

---

[12] Kuh, Edwin, 'Unemployment, Production Functions and Effective Demand', *Journal of Political Economy*, June 1966.

H. The Neoclassical Contribution

It was suggested earlier that neoclassical analysis should be seen partly as a matter of adjusting mechanism, partly as an aspect of production theory. As will become clear in Chapter IV, various notions developed in the neoclassical analysis of production and capital will be employed in our analysis. The question of measuring the contribution of the different inputs, the question of the 'embodiment' of technology in investment, and the notion of 'switching-techniques', are among the many ideas springing from neoclassical developments that are incorporated in the analysis.

However, these very useful notions will be incorporated into an analysis that employs two fundamental departures from the usual neoclassical tenets. First, it will be necessary to drop the assumption so prevalent in modern production and neoclassical theory that there is a simple, well-defined relationship between maximum output and the different inputs. Various rather complex interactions between the inputs and 'technological progress' will be allowed for. Second, and related to the first point, maximum output and its growth rate will not be treated as something independent of the present and past behavior of the system. In particular, demand pressures, their intensity and duration, will be seen as factors influencing supply or maximum output.

One final point of comparison. The notion of a long-run equilibrium and its stability, so central to neoclassical analysis, also plays a very important role in the analysis that is to follow. An advanced capitalist system will be viewed as an economy with a 'steady rate' growth path with the relevant endogenous variables growing at the same exponential rate. It will also be viewed as a system subject to periodic shocks which set in motion cyclical movements. Chapters VI and VII, and to a lesser extent Chapters III and IV, will discuss the question of under what conditions this economy tends to move back towards its equilibrium path. Unlike neoclassical analysis, stability will not turn out to be a matter of the relative capital intensity of production in the different sectors, or of whether a production function is 'well behaved' in the usual sense. The relevant factors are much more commonplace but no less important for all that.

I. Growing Needs and Growing Demands

There is one final point to be made in this discussion. Demographic movements will play a role in the model as a stabilizer, even though these movements need not be anything but a redistribution of a population of fixed size. However, a positive rate of growth of population, whether through natural increase, migration or both, strengthens the stabilizing tendencies. This reliance on demographic movements as a stabilizer suggests that in the model developed here, at least, an additional stylized fact requires explanation.

Somehow growing needs associated with a growing population get translated into growing demands and *per capita* output. Just how this is accomplished deserves an explanation.

There are several sorts of problems here, the Malthusian one of growing population leading to falling rather than rising *per capita* incomes, being the most obvious. The actual historical rise of *per capita* incomes in the face of increasing numbers of people, shows the deficiency of the simple Malthusian argument. However, consider the following position: assume for the sake of argument that the capital–labor and capital–output ratios are constant. Then, the higher is the rate of growth of the labor force, the higher must be the rate of growth of capital, and the higher the share of output devoted to investment, if capital per worker is to remain constant ($I/Y = (K/Y) \cdot (I/K)$). If it is assumed that output per worker varies with capital per worker, then after a point the more rapid is the rate of growth of the labor force, the slower is the income per worker likely to rise (since there is a limit to the size of I/Y).

> When viewed in aggregate terms, the effects of demographic variables on the economy form a paradox of sorts: the growth arising from high fertility increases aggregate demand but reduces the full employment capability of the economy to increase its output per head.[13]

This raises two more problems. Is labor productivity simply a matter of capital per worker? Second, the statement just quoted assumed full employment. If full employment is dependent upon the rate of growth of the population, then the argument must also be modified.

With regard to the first problem, it has been argued that output per worker rises with an expanding population, because it induces entrepreneurs to add the more efficient newer vintage capital at the margin. Thus, average productivity per unit of capital will be pulled up, in a world of population and labor force growth, faster than in a world where the new vintage is incorporated only as part of the replacement process. Furthermore, demographic growth may permit entrepreneurs to reap economies of scale.[14]

With regard to the second point, a growing labor force requires that the demand for additional labor must always precede the ability of that labor to purchase its output, if rising unemployment is to be avoided, and this must come about in the face of rising productivity. The fact that savings is positive at full employment output merely adds force to the argument. One of the cornerstones of the secular stagnation argument was the importance of demographic growth in generating enough demand, so that full or high employment savings were offset, and new entrants to the labor force continuously absorbed. The effect of demographic movements on the nature of the moving equilibrium and its stability is a matter that should be met head on in a study of growth. This will be taken up in Chapter V.

[13] Coale, Ansley, *Introduction to Demographic and Economic Change in Developed Countries*, Princeton University Press, Princeton, 1960, pp. 13–14.
[14] Harrod, Roy, *The British Economy*, McGraw-Hill, New York, 1963, pp. 69–75.

Chapter III The Influence of Supply on Demand: How the Natural Rate of Growth Affects the Actual

A. The Harrod–Domar Problem

The basic problem of growth theory is to find an adequate explanation of the long-run stability of the unemployment rate. As we saw in Chapter II, demand and supply in the United States and Britain have grown at approximately the same rate, with tolerable rates of unemployment, except during the inter-war period. For a country like the United States especially, where active discretionary fiscal policy is still unheard of, an explanation of the lack of any trend in unemployment rates is certainly in order. In the last chapter the price mechanism was discussed, and considered insufficient in itself to bring a growing demand into line with a growing supply or maximum output. This poses no difficulty provided an alternative mechanism can be found to take its place. Otherwise we may be left with a vague sense of uneasiness that only 'God's grace' has kept us from experiencing repeated recessions of the inter-war variety. Furthermore, a whole body of literature has developed since the end of World War II which, if taken literally, strongly suggests that we should be uneasy about this problem of stability. One of the main implications of what has come to be known as the Harrod–Domar model is that a capitalist system is perpetually tottering on the brink of disaster. Fortunately, this conclusion follows only because this type of model has been stripped down until there is no mechanism left that could bring demand and supply into line.

Write $Y = \sigma K$ for the Harrod–Domar supply equation and $Y = uI$ for the demand relationship where u is the multiplier, and K is capital in existence. Ignore the government and foreign sectors. Since, in the first instance, maximum output is proportionate to the stock of capital and demand is proportionate to the level of investment, demand and supply grow at the same rate if investment and capital grow at the same rate. If demand or investment is growing more rapidly than the stock of capital, full employment of capital is soon achieved and it is usually assumed that inflation will set in. Secular stagnation results when the inequality is reversed. This happens in the former case because it is assumed that investors will try to step up the rate of growth of investment in response to the strong demand pressures; and in the latter because excess capacity develops causing investment to be cut back. Since it is most unlikely that capital and investment will always grow at the same rate, the conclusion follows directly that a capitalistic system is inherently unstable. And further, even if capital and investment grow at the same rate there is still a problem if this growth rate is not equal to the rate of growth of the labor force (or the rate of growth of the labor force plus the rate of growth of productivity).[1] Thus, if the rate of growth of investment, capital and demand is not the same as the rate of growth of labor (given the usual assumption of fixed coefficients) then either inflation or mass unemployment results for reasons just described.

The sources of instability in these types of models are not hard to find. They arise from a failure of Harrod–Domar models to contain any sort of mechanism that would, first, bring the rate of growth of investment and demand into line with the rate of growth of capital; and, second, bring all of these things into line with the rate of growth of the labor force plus some allowance for productivity increase.

The neoclassical model discussed earlier had its origin in an attempt to overcome the 'knife edge' problem. By allowing for substitution in production and a market-clearing mechanism, the two sides of the market were brought into line with each other. Neoclassical analysis—like much of post-Keynesian growth theory, including the present study—can be viewed as an attempt to eliminate some of the instability of the Harrod–Domar models. The procedure adopted here is to approach the problem in two stages. In this chapter supply or maximum output is treated as exogenous, uninfluenced by the actual performance of the economy. This enables us to isolate and study the influence of supply on demand. In the next chapter maximum output is treated as something endogenous depending on demand or the actual performance of the system. This allows the development of a model where demand and supply interact.

[1] The knife edge problem is usually posed in terms of the requirement that all variables grow at rate, σ/u. This ensures full utilization of capital. However, this problem can be formulated for any degree of capital utilization, as in the text, which facilitates comparison with a model to be developed subsequently.

B. Eliminating One Source of Instability

The first step in eliminating one source of instability is to develop a very simple capital stock-adjustment model which incorporates a mechanism bringing the rate of growth of investment and capital into line. Write:

$$C_t = aY_t, \tag{1}$$

$$I_t = bY_{t-1} - cK_{t-1}, \tag{2}$$

$$Y_t = C_t + I_t + Z_t, \tag{3}$$

$$K_t = K_{t-1} + I_t, \tag{4}$$

and

$$Z_t = Z_0 (1 + r)^t, \tag{5}$$

where K is the stock of capital in existence, Z is some unexplained 'autonomous' variable (introduced primarily for expository purposes) to be contrasted with what we will term for the time being 'induced investment' represented by I. All other symbols have their previous meanings. This familiar textbook model contains a generalized accelerator–multiplier mechanism—equations (1)–(4)—and an exogenous trend—equation (5). Equations (1)–(4) make up the endogenous mechanism which is capable of generating different types of behavior over time. For our purposes the different types of behavior can be divided into two classes; stable or unstable. Reverting to an earlier definition, the endogenous mechanism can be said to generate stable movements if a 'shock' is followed by a movement back to the equilibrium path. This movement may be one of smooth asymptotic convergence, or it may be one where the system oscillates around the equilibrium path, but in cycles of ever decreasing amplitude.

Various kinds of evidence can and have been cited to show that a capital stock-adjustment or generalized accelerator–multiplier interaction is most likely to generate damped cycles.[2] Much of the discussion in Chapters VI and VII lends further support to this position, and it will be adopted here. However, a clearer understanding of the important issues is enhanced by using an analytical solution of the model: i.e. $Y_t = A_1(x_1)^t + A_2(x_2)^t + Y_t^E$. For our purposes it is enough to note that the A_1 and A_2 are constants, x_1 and x_2 are the 'roots' of an equation obtained from the endogenous part of the model: i.e. equations (1)–(4), and Y_t^E is the equilibrium growth path where $Y_t^E = vZ_t$.[3]

---

[2] This is born out, for example, by a simulation study using an econometric model which is for all practical purposes a simple capital stock-adjustment model. See Cornwall, J., 'Economic Implications of the Klein–Goldberger Model', *The Review of Economics and Statistics*, May 1959.

[3] There are any number of mathematical economics textbooks describing in detail the methods for solving difference equations. One of the very first was Baumol, W. J., *Economic Dynamics*, 2nd ed., The Macmillan Company, New York, 1959.

Alternatively, we may say that $Y_t^E = vZ_t$ is the particular solution which introduces the root, $1 + r$. The assumption that the capital stock adjustment mechanism generates a damped cycle is equivalent to the assumption that $|x_1| < 1$ and $|x_2| < 1$. Therefore, as t takes larger and larger values, Y_t^E increasingly dominates the behavior of Y_t (and all other variables). Ignoring a possible physical constraint on output, we obtain: $\lim_{t \to \infty} Y_t = Y_t^E = vZ_t$, where v is the super multiplier.[4] While this is a very simple model, it does have some dynamic properties worth discussing.

First, assume that the age composition of the population is constant and that the latter and the labor force grow at rate r. Then Z_t can be interpreted as some type of expenditure dependent upon population growth. And in the absence of any change in labor productivity, the rate of growth of employment will be equal to the rate of growth of the labor force, since demand, output, Z, and the labor force all grow at the same rate. By the same token, if the rate of growth of labor productivity is positive, this would result in an ever increasing rate of growth of unemployment. Second, in simple models of this sort all endogenous variables grow at a rate determined by the rate of growth of Z_t.[5] If the latter grows at the same rate as the labor force, then the capital–labor—as well as the capital–output—ratios will approach a constant. This is certainly not consistent with the stylized facts. However, the fact that new workers 'bring along' their own capital takes a good deal of sting out of the knife edge problem, provided, of course, it really is a problem. In any case, the rate of growth of capital and investment are now equal.

Third, write, $Y_t^E/N_t^e = l$ where l is the average and marginal productivity of employed labor and N^e is the amount of labor employed. Since $Y_t^E = vZ_0$ $(1 + r)^t$ and $N_t = N_0(1 + r)^t$, $Y_t^E/N_t = vZ_0/N_0$ and $N_t^e/N_t = v(Z_0/N_0)/l$. In other words, in the long run the employment rate is positively related to the super multiplier, and to the initial level of Z per member of the labor force; and negatively related to the productivity of labor. Finally, still assuming that the rate of growth of Z depends on growth in the demographic variables, changes in the latter have a one-to-one effect on the rate of growth of demand and supply. Among other things this means that the model has structural stability. It also brings out the dual role of demographic movements on the demand and supply side. However, *per capita* income is always constant whatever the rate of growth of the demographic variables.

---

[4] By solving the system for the particular solution it is found that

$$v = [u(c + r)(1 + r)] \div [(1 + r)^2 - (bu + 1 - c)(1 + r) + bu],$$

where $u = 1/[1 - a]$. In the special case where $c = 1$, this becomes $v = u/(1 - h)$, where $h = [ubr] \div [(1 + r)^2]$. For any reasonable set of parameter values, $1 > h > 0$ and, therefore $v > u$; hence the expression 'super multiplier'. By the same token, if $r = 0$, $h = 0$ and, therefore, $u = v$.

[5] See Goldberger, Arthur, *Impact Multipliers and Dynamic Properties of the Klein–Goldberger Model*, North-Holland, Amsterdam, 1959, pp. 133–134, for similar results.

C. Consumption, Demand and Growth: the Smithies Model

The model outlined in the previous section implies a constant level of *per capita* income, and a secular rise in unemployment if there is any growth in labor productivity. It is unsatisfactory for these reasons alone. What is required is a model that permits a positive rate of growth of labor productivity, and rising *per capita* demand and output. A useful starting point in altering the model is Smithies' model of growth and fluctuations.[6] Smithies argues that growth and cycles can be generated from an endogenous mechanism similar to the one used here, but with one important difference: a ratchet effect is introduced in the consumption function. ·Write

$$C_t = dY_t + e\bar{Y}_t, \text{ where } \bar{Y}_t \tag{1'}$$

is the highest aggregate income to date. No account is taken of any sort of exogenous trend in spending in his model. Yet, if the capital stock mechanism generates a strong enough boom, and if the ratchet effect is strong enough, i.e., consumers strongly resist a cut back in consumption standards, Smithies shows that cycles around a trend in income will be generated.[7]

These conditions are most likely to be satisfied if there is a strong trend component in demand other than that generated by the ratchet effect. With this added trend in demand, booms will be more prolonged compared with recessions, and the latter will be relatively milder and shorter. Such conditions are necessary if a ratchet effect is to be realistic, since the ability to maintain living standards is primarily a function of the duration and amplitude of the recession. This is true whether consumption is defined to include consumer durables, as in the Smithies model, or to exclude them. Similarly this trend in demand will promote strong booms (and perhaps an investment ratchet), since the mildness of the past recessions will be projected into the future, leading to stronger and quicker reactions of consumers and investors to increases in incomes. This should be especially true when the trend is related to demographic variables, since less risk would certainly be attached to that part of investment which is to satisfy the demands of an expanding market based on an expanding number of similar consuming units. For example, a public utility would show much less hesitation and react more quickly in building ahead of demand, if it felt that any excess capacity in the short run would eventually be eliminated by new consumers and/or rising per family incomes, rather than just the latter. Similarly, a state or local government would be less likely to hold back on capital expenditures if its tax base was increasing for these two reasons instead of for just one of them.

---

[6] Smithies, Arthur, 'Economic Fluctuations and Growth', *Econometrica*, January 1957.
[7] Interestingly enough, when the parameters of the Smithies model were estimated, they implied damped oscillations. See Choudhry, N. K., and Mohabbat, K. O., 'Economic Fluctuations and Growth: Notes on Testing the Smithies Model', *Oxford Economic Papers*, March 1965.

In developing the implications of the Smithies model, it is convenient to drop equation (5) entirely from the model. If we then substitute equation (1') for (1), retain equations (2)–(4), and assume that Smithies' conditions are met, cycles around a rising trend in income will result. This can be seen in the following way. In the Smithies model there are two equilibria found from two different particular solutions of the model, one solution corresponding to periods when $Y_t = \bar{Y}_t$ and the other when $Y_t < \bar{Y}_t$. However, the solution of the 'recession model' is the only one relevant. Equations (1') and (2)–(4) can, after substitution, be combined and expressed as:

$$Y_t = \left(\frac{b}{1-d} + 1 - c\right)Y_{t-1} - \left(\frac{b}{1-d}\right)Y_{t-2} + \left(\frac{ec}{1-d}\right)\bar{Y}_t$$

This has as its solution:

$$Y_t = Y_t^E + B_1(x_1)^t + B_2(x_2)^t.$$

The last two expressions contain the cyclical components and describe the behavior of the endogenous mechanism. The first expression is a particular (equilibrium) solution where

$$Y_t^E = u'Y_t = \left(\frac{e}{1-d}\right)\bar{Y}_{t'}.^8$$

Assume again that the endogenous mechanism generates cyclical movements. Given our assumptions, $\bar{Y}_t$ increases from one cycle to the next, which process will introduce a 'floor' in the model that will be shifting upward over time. This result is depicted in Diagram 3.1. Assume that in period t actual income is Y_1 and the highest income to date is $\bar{Y}_0 > Y_1$. Ignoring the damped cyclical components, $Y_{t0}^E = u'\bar{Y}_{t0}$ describes the initial recession equilibrium level of income. Assume further that from period t until $t + 3$ a boom ensues. The previous peak is reached in $t + 1$ and the new peak, $\bar{Y}_1$, in $t + 3$. Following $t + 3$, the economy now moves towards the new recession equilibrium, $Y_{t1}^E = u'\bar{Y}_{t1}$. Following the upturn, the second boom carries income above $\bar{Y}_1$ to $\bar{Y}_2$. In the next recession the economy moves towards still another recession equilibrium, $Y_{t2}^E = u'\bar{Y}_{t2}$, etc. In the long run, the actual trend in income is depicted by the thick solid line.[9]

Whether or not this rising trend in income and expenditure is equal to the

---

[8] Note that we have written the highest income to date as a function of time. This calls attention to the increases in $\bar{Y}$ over time.

[9] The Smithies model in effect incorporates shocks; i.e., arbitrary departures of the economy from the time path implied by the equations. If the model is incapable of steady growth, then when it turns down, a shock is introduced when the consumption relation changes from $C_t = (d + e)Y_t$, to $C_t = dY_t + e\bar{Y}_t$. Of more relevance is the fact that when the economy turns up again and surpasses its previous peak, the consumption relation changes to $C_t = (d + e)Y_t$; i.e. another shock. This makes the amplitude of each boom independent of the amplitude of the previous boom, and only dependent on the initial conditions prevailing when the model switched over to the new equilibrium path.

Diagram 3.1

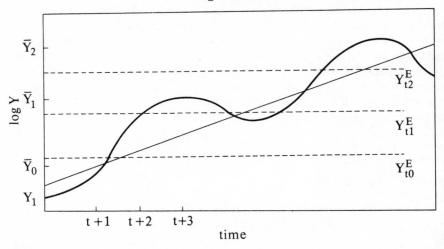

rate of growth of supply cannot be determined. In the special case where each successive peak income is also a full employment income, there will be a close relation. And if they are approximately equal, secular stagnation (and exhilaration) can be avoided. What the ratchet term does is to adjust spending levels upward in such a way as possibly to prevent the rate of unemployment from increasing.

D. A Modified Ratchet Model

Presently it will be argued that supply and labor productivity are not parameters but very much a function of the performance of the economy. This will increase the likelihood that demand and supply grow at the same rate. However, even assuming that the natural rate of growth in general, and the rate of growth of productivity in particular, are rigidly fixed, it is possible to show that the equality of the rate of growth of demand and supply are the likely outcome of the growth process, at least in the moving equilibrium. This will be helpful for another reason, for if the elimination of secular stagnation (and constant *per capita* incomes) hinged on one particular type of consumption function, the results would certainly have very precarious foundations. However, it is possible to work with other consumption functions and achieve similar results, and one such function has the additional benefit of explicitly generating rates of growth per demand and supply that are equal when the rate of growth of labor productivity, ρ, is positive.

Mathews has argued that if one uses an aggregate version of the Duesenberry–Modigliani function, there is no unique time path for consumption for any given time path for aggregate income, aggregate consumption depending also upon the way unemployment is distributed.[10] For example, if unemployment is unequally distributed, in the sense that it falls entirely on one group of workers, then, for a given recession income, consumption will be higher than if that same level of unemployment (measured in man hours) is distributed equally over the entire labor force—provided one condition is met: that those who experience no unemployment during a recession also experience rising incomes. This is so because those experiencing rising incomes will be moving along their long-run consumption function with a high marginal propensity to consume (MPC), while those experiencing some unemployment will be moving down their short-run, low MPC function. On the other hand, if unemployment is equally distributed, all will be moving along the short-run function. Thus, for the same given recession aggregate income, consumption will be higher in the former case because the MPC of those experiencing an increase in income is higher than the MPC of those experiencing a decline.

This can be seen if we write the Duesenberry–Modigliani, (D–M), function in a manner more in keeping with Modigliani's formulation. Thus write; $c_t = \cdot5y_t + \cdot4\bar{y}_t$, where the lower case letters c_t, y_t and $\bar{y}_t$ represent family consumption, current income, and peak income attained, which may be the current income. Then the aggregate version of the (D–M) function becomes $C_t = \cdot5Y_t + \cdot4\bar{Y}_t$, where each higher case letter represents the aggregate version of the family measures. The coefficients chosen are of no consequence, as the argument is independent of their values.

Now assume that there are only three families whose incomes are represented by y_1, y_2 and y_3. Table 3.1 brings out the essential issues. Given the numbers in the three columns for family income, and assuming each family behaves according to the (D–M) theory, consumption for each family can be computed according to: $c_t = \cdot5y_t + \cdot4\bar{y}_t$. Adding the three consumption figures so computed, we obtain the figure for aggregate consumption, C, given in the adjoining column. By simple aggregation Y is obtained, and if, for convenience, it is assumed that $\bar{y} = 40$ in the first period for all three families, $\bar{Y}$ is known. Assigned values for maximum output X are given in the final column.

Reading down the Y column, it is apparent that a trendless cycle of constant amplitude is taking place. Compare now the figures for family incomes beginning in period 3. The figures without parentheses depict a situation where from period 3 to 4 income rises for the first and second family but falls to zero for the third. Here unemployment has fallen solely on one family (head). By period 5, the second family experiences a decline in income, until by period 7 only one family receives any income.

---

[10] Mathews, R. C. O., *op. cit.* A similar type consumption is found in Mincer, J., 'Employment and Consumption', *Review of Economics and Statistics*, February 1960. Also see Duesenberry, J., *Income, Savings and the Theory of Consumer Behavior*, Harvard University Press, Cambridge, Mass., 1949. Duesenberry defined consumption to include consumer durables. Consumption as defined here does not.

Table 3.1

Period	y_1	y_2	y_3	C	Y	$\bar{Y}$	X
1	40	40	40	108	120	120	120
2	50	50	50	135	150	150	150
3	60(40)	60(40)	0(40)	128(120)	120	150	180
4	75(50)	75(50)	0(50)	155(135)	150	150	225
5	90(40)	30(40)	0(40)	146(120)	120	150	270
6	105(50)	45(50)	0(50)	167(135)	150	150	315
7	120(40)	0(40)	0(40)	158(120)	150	150	360

In contrast, the family income figures in parentheses depict a situation where each family receives the same income, thereby sharing equally the hardship of (partial) unemployment during each recession. Beginning in period 3, aggregate consumption, C, is always higher when unemployment is unequally distributed, as can be seen by comparing the figures not in parentheses with those so enclosed in the C column.

More to the point are the growth implications of Mathews' theory. Assume unemployment is unequally distributed. Then, over time, because of productivity increases and growth of the labor force, i.e., because maximum output, X, is growing, aggregate consumption will rise for any given level of aggregate income. This follows because unemployment will be higher over time for any level of aggregate income, and therefore a larger number of people will be moving along their short-run schedule. In terms of the average propensity to consume (APC), from one cycle to the next the number of people with the higher short-run APC increases. The figures without parentheses in the C column bring this out quite clearly. Note that these figures would not be predicted by the equation $C_t = \cdot 5Y_t + \cdot 4\bar{Y}_t$.

Thus the figures in the C column also reveal that an aggregate version of the (D–M) function will underestimate aggregate consumption, unless unemployment is equally distributed. Only in this one case will the aggregate consumption figures predicted by the aggregate (D–M) consumption function coincide with the consumption figures obtained by summing up the family consumption levels predicted by $c_t = \cdot 5y_t + \cdot 4\bar{y}_t$; i.e., the figures in parentheses. As it is unlikely that unemployment will be equally distributed in reality, the problem remains of how to retain the essential spirit of the (D–M) theory for the individual family, and yet correctly explain and predict aggregate consumption. Clearly some account must be taken of the amount of unemployment associated with any level of income. This, in turn, depends upon the size of the labor force and the average productivity of labor or, what comes to the same thing, the level of maximum output, X_t. For example, in periods 3, 5 and 7 actual output is constant at 120, while maximum output moves from 180 to 360. As a result unemployment rises from one-third to two-thirds of the labor force (each family or spending unit containing one worker). Thus, if maximum output had been growing more rapidly than assumed in Table 3.1, so that by the 5th period $X = 360$ and the first family head produced the entire output of 120, family consumption levels would be: $c_1 = \cdot 9 \times 120 = 108$, $c_2 = \cdot 4 \times 75 = 30$ and $c_3 = \cdot 4 \times 50 = 20$ for a total consumption of 158, instead of 146 as in the table.

While Mathews suggests that productivity and the size of the labor force be substituted for the ratchet term as independent variables, maximum output, or the level of unemployment, will do just as well. Write:

$$C_t = mY_t + nX_t, \tag{1''}$$

where X represents maximum output. Equation $(1'')$ indicates that for any given income Y_t, the greater is maximum output, the greater is consumption. This follows, since unemployment increases with X_t (for a given Y_t) and so does the number of consumers with income below their previous peaks. Next assume

$$X_t = X_0(1 + r_x)^t, \tag{6}$$

where r_x is the rate of growth of X which can be divided up bween the rate of growth of the labor force, r_n, and the rate of growth of labor productivity, ρ; i.e., $r_x = r_n + \rho$. Equations $(1'')$ and (6) can be combined with equations (2)–(4). Thus, the model can again be solved down to a 'final equation' for income:

$$Y_t = \left(\frac{b}{1-m} + 1 - c\right) Y_{t-1} - \left(\frac{b}{1-m}\right) Y_{t-2} + \left(\frac{n}{1-m}\right) \cdot \left(\frac{c+r_x}{1+r_x}\right) X_t.$$

The complete solution of this difference equation is

$$Y_t = Y_t^E + C_1 (x_1)^t + C_2 (x_2)^t.$$

As before, the last two terms are obtained from solving the endogenous part of the system, and contain the cyclical components. The first term is the particular solution where this time $Y_t^E = v'X_t$ (instead of $Y_t^E + u'\bar{Y}_t$).[11] The complete solution has three roots. The capital stock adjustment mechanism introduces two, x_1 and x_2, while the particular solution introduces a real root greater than one, $(1 + r_x)$. If it is again assumed that the endogenous mechanism is damped, the long run behavior of the model is dominated by the rate of growth of supply or maximum output. In other words, $\lim_{t \to \infty} Y_t$ $= v'X_t$.

---

[11] The constant v' is equal to:

$$Y_t^E/X_t = \left[\frac{n}{1-m}(c+r_x)\right](1+r_x) \div \left\{(1+r_x)^2 - \left[\frac{b}{1-m}+1-c\right](1+r_x) + \frac{b}{1-m}\right\}.$$

The fact that m is significantly smaller than the long run average and marginal propensities to consume, and that $1 > c > 0$, lend support to the view that the endogenous mechanism will be damped.

E. Implications of the Model

This long-run equilibrium has all the desirable properties of the original model, plus several others. First of all, not only do capital and investment grow at the same rate, but the long-run rate of growth of demand and supply are now also equal. The expression $Y_t^E = v'X_0 (1 + r_x)^t$ determines the growth rate of all variables including actual output, Y_t, or demand, so that it too grows at rate r_x, the rate of growth of maximum output. This is the Mathews' notion of similar forces at work on both the demand and supply side, and is easily generalized to allow supply factors to affect investment demand as well.[12] This means that the problem of secular trends in the unemployment rate is eliminated and, in addition, a means is introduced whereby growing needs become growing demands. For in the moving equilibrium, assuming that the age distribution of the population is constant, demand grows at a rate equal to the combined growth of the labor force and productivity. Employment will then grow at the same rate as the labor force, since $r_n^e = r_y$ $- \rho = r_x - \rho$ and $r_x = r_n + \rho$ where r_n^e and r_y are the rate of growth of the labor force and output respectively. Furthermore, given an unchanged pattern of marital behavior, the rate of family formation will also be equal to the rate of growth of the labor force and employment. Thus, in the moving equilibrium, the assumption that family formation proceeds at the same rate as the growth of the labor force is justified.

Second, the model is structurally stable. Any change in the parameters of the endogenous mechanism (within some relevant range) will have a minimum effect on the behavior of income, while any change in the rate of growth of productivity or of the labor force will have a one-to-one effect on the long-term growth rate. Third, if only the dominant term in the solution is considered, we can write: $Y_t^E = v'X_t$ or $Y_t^E/N_t = v'X_t/N_t$. Next, to facilitate comparison with the earlier model, assume that $X_t/N_t = Y_t^E/N_t^e = l$; i.e. the average productivity of labor at full employment is the same as the average productivity of labor on the equilibrium path. Then, $N_t^e/N_t = v'$; i.e. the employment rate is independent of the level of productivity, as v' does not contain the term l. The explanation of this is fairly straightforward. Any change in the level of productivity affects both demand and supply proportionately, so that it is no longer true, as it was with the first model, that the higher the level of productivity the harder it is to maintain full employment.

---

[12] Mathews, R. C. O., *The Business Cycle, op. cit.*, Chapter 13. A Friedman type consumption function was also tried where $C_t = \sigma_1 Y_t + \sigma_2 C_{t-1}$ was combined with the other relevant equations that form a complete model. When reasonable values are assigned to the parameters, this model is capable of generating growth in excess of the likely growth rate of the number of families. Such a model has two shortcomings, however. First, there is no explicit tie-in between the rates of growth of family income and productivity; and second, the model is subject to a certain amount of structural instability. For the rationale behind the Friedman function see Friedman, M., *A Theory of the Consumption Function*, Princeton, 1957.

In summary, the two chief sources of instability contained in the Harrod–Domar model have now been eliminated. All endogenous variables behave in the same way in the moving equilibrium. Capital and investment grow at the same rate, so there is no conflict between what corresponds to Harrod's actual and the 'warranted' rates of growth. Since the natural rate of growth, r_x, i.e. the rate of growth of the labor force plus the rate of growth of productivity, determines the behavior of all the variables, it too is in line with the actual and warranted growth rates. The long-run capital–output ratio approaches the constant:

$$K_t^E/Y_t^E = \frac{b}{c + r_n + \rho},$$

while the capital–labor ratio grows exponentially.

None of these conclusions are peculiar to the model used. Any amount of disaggregation and any number of complications in the form of distributed lags could be introduced without altering the results. These changes only increase the order of the system. Thus, we could distinguish between a large number of capital (and consumer) goods, and allow investment in each to be determined by a capital stock-adjustment mechanism or some variant. Assume that this gives rise to an nth order system. This will have as its complete solution:

$$Y_t = Y_t^E + \sum_{i=1}^{n} A_i(x_i)^t,$$

where Y_t^E is, once again, the particular solutions and the term

$$\sum_{i=1}^{n} A_i(x_i)^t$$

depicts the n roots obtained from the homogeneous solution of the system, i.e. the roots implied by the more complicated endogenous mechanism. As long as the largest of the roots is less than one in absolute value, i.e. as long as the endogenous mechanism is stable, the same results follow.

F. Some Disequilibrium Economics

As mentioned earlier, the fact that workers bring along their own capital takes some of the sting out of the knife edge problem. In this case they bring along successively larger amounts of capital as additions to output are reproduced by increasingly more capital intensive methods of production. But the important point is that something is adjusting the rate of growth of capital, investment, and demand and supply, so that the Harrod–Domar difficulties seem to have been resolved. This is just as true when the system is displaced from its equilibrium path as when it is in equilibrium. For, unlike the Harrod–Domar models, it is in the very nature of a model which includes a capital stock adjustment mechanism, that possible shortages or excesses of capacity can be eliminated by their feedback effect on investment (when the system is capable of sustained growth). The result is that if, initially, capital, output and investment are all growing at the same (natural) rate of growth, and a disturbance causes a displacement, the inequality between the growth rates of capital and investment caused by the shock can be corrected.

Thus, if a shock pushes down the capital–output ratio, then, when the capital stock adjustment mechanism again determines investment, capacity will be strained, and large (monopoly) profits are to be made if the capital stock is increased relative to output, and, of course, labor. The rates of growth of investment, demand and capital will then rise above their long-run rates. For a time the multiplier effect of investment may exceed the capacity effect, causing the capital–output ratio to fall further. But since the cyclical component is assumed to be damped, capital will eventually grow more rapidly than investment and output. This rising capital–output ratio will then lead to an overaccumulation of capital, causing all the variables to decline. The model may overshoot on the other side, but eventually it will move toward the equilibrium growth path where investment, demand and capital grow at the same rate governed by the growth of the labor force and productivity. In this manner, the capital stock adjustment mechanism works to keep investment, capital and output growing at the same rate, while the influence of supply factors on demand causes these variables to grow at the same rate as supply; i.e. the rate of growth of labor plus enough more to offset productivity increases. Analogous results would be generated by a shock that caused a rise in the capital–output ratio.

Thus, even without the aid of a deliberate stabilization policy, a capitalistic system need not always be tottering on the brink of disaster. There are forces at work tending to cause demand and supply to grow at the same rate. The fact that there has been only one prolonged deep depression should have made us suspicious of the explanatory value of the Harrod–Domar model.[13] It stacked the cards in favor of instability, by completely divorcing the demand and supply sides of the market, while incorporating the notion of the dual role of investment and greatly limiting substitution in production. What is essential to the model developed here is that it allows some short-run variability in the rate of growth of the capital intensity of production, whenever

---

[13] The important conclusion to be drawn from the Harrod–Domar analysis was that spelled out by Domar. Investment has a capacity effect as well as an income effect, and in a world where savings are positive at full employment, investment must grow if unemployment is to be avoided. Unfortunately, the models of Harrod and Domar were grouped together by economists so that Domar's important point became blurred with Harrod's unrealistic assumptions.

output deviates from the long-run growth path. If the capital stock is measured in terms of the deflated value of machines and buildings, then the model requires some *ex post* substitution. This is not implausible, because of the possibility of multiple shifts, overtime for labor and the adaptability of business plant to various amounts of labor. The fact that the assumption of unlimited substitution between capital and labor *ex post* is unrealistic, does not mean that an assumption of a total lack of any such substitution is any more realistic.

G. Prices as 'Signals'

In the discussion of the convergence of the system back to its long-run growth path following a disturbance, no mention was made of the behavior of relative factor prices, either as a market clearing mechanism, or as a system of 'signals' steering the economy back to this path. The task of clearing markets has already been assigned another mechanism. However, it is quite possible to graft onto what would otherwise be a 'fix-price' model, a mechanism whereby relative factor prices could function as signals inducing directed changes in the capital intensity of production. Without too much simplification, indeed less than that involved in neoclassical analysis, it is possible to show, for example, that when the cyclical components cause the system to move above its long-run growth path, the return on capital is likely to be high relative to the real wage and to its long-run equilibrium rate.

For example, with the capital stock-adjustment model of investment generating damped cycles, the early stages of a boom will be a period when the rate of capital growth is less than the rate of growth of output and investment, though all are growing more rapidly than their equilibrium growth rates. Not only will the capital–output ratio be falling, but the capital–labor ratio will be rising less rapidly than on the equilibrium growth path. This can be shown to result in changes in relative factor prices, that generate an increase in investment and capital sufficient to bring the growth of the capital-labor ratio, capital and output back to their equilibrium growth rates. We will proceed indirectly by discussing first pricing policies in product markets. This entails a down-grading of the importance of short-run marginal revenue and marginal cost curves in output price decisions, followed by an emphasis on stock adjustments to any disequilibrium situation. Once this is done we can return to the main task and discuss directly the role of relative factor prices.

First, it is necessary to dispose of the assumption that firms know their present and future cost and demand conditions with certainty. Certainly in a growth situation where demand constantly changes, products are constantly

Diagram 3.2

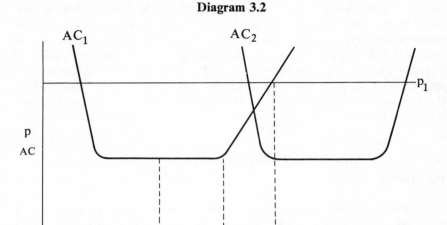

being varied and new competitive and complementary products introduced to the market, while trends towards monopoly increase the impact of one firm's policy on another, it is doubtful if firms have any knowledge of demand conditions except at those prices and outputs at which they have been operating in the immediate past. In this case, marginal revenue is at best a very vague concept. And once the existence in the mind of the entrepreneur of a marginal revenue curve is challenged, the assumption that he thinks in terms of short-run marginal cost curves is also called into question, for without marginal revenue curves there is nothing to which to equate marginal cost.

If the assumption that firms know exactly the nature of their costs, including the effect of changes of plant size on costs, is dropped, a very reasonable conclusion to draw is that in the short run firms assume that marginal cost equals average cost over some range of output. However, firms would certainly be aware that average costs eventually rise, as is depicted in Diagram 3.2. Here short-run average cost curve AC_1 represents the cost situation for a typical firm in the present (short-run) period. It corresponds to a given stock of capital that was thought to be appropriate when forecasts of demand conditions for the present period were made. Alternately we can think of it as the capital stock that resulted from the adjustment through investment to last period's discrepancy between actual and desired stocks of capital. Let output q_1 be what was thought to be the most likely level of sales and production and plant for the period were drawn up with this output in mind.

The next question is how firms in a world of monopoly, oligopoly and uncertainty about demand and cost conditions, will go about setting price. A very plausible assumption is that pricing is on a mark-up basis, whereby firms seek to achieve some targeted rate of return on their capital. For example, let price p_1 result in the realization of the targeted rate of return on the firm's capital (that amount of capital giving rise to curve AC_1), if sales actually turn out to be q_1. If sale and actual output turn out to be greater than q_1 (but less than q_3), the realized return will be greater, etc. Let this firm experience an unforeseen increase in demand. Let the price of the product remain at p_1 and let output expand beyond q_1 to something like q_2. If it also happens that the response is not such as to increase output beyond q_3, then the targeted rate of return will be exceeded and the capital–output and capital–labor ratios will turn out to be too low *ex post*, labor inputs having been expanded to increase from q_1 to q_2.[14] If we relax the assumption that prices remain fixed (but hold money wages constant), and allow the firm to increase its price, then the likely result is an even higher rate of return.

In either case, the ratio of the return on capital, absolutely and relative to the real wage, has exceeded expectations. These 'signals' will act as inducements for adjusting the capital–labor ratio through greater investment in the next 'period' (or, more correctly, over the next several periods). Next period's capital stock will be increased through investment by a larger amount than if sales had turned out to be q_1. Let the adjustment give rise to something like average cost curve AC_2. If price p_1 still permits the targeted return to be realized, it may be felt unnecessary to alter price. If additions to the capital stock affect productivity in such a way that a different price is consistent with the desired return on capital, or if the firm wishes to take advantage of a seller's market, price may be changed. In other words, it can be argued that the immediate response to short-run disequilibrium is to adjust labor inputs and capacity utilization rates. Prices may or may not be adjusted, but in either case the higher return on capital will set in motion a chain of events that reflect an attempt to adjust the capital–labor ratio in the long run, through induced changes in capacity.[15]

At the aggregate level, factor prices can be seen to influence the behavior of the aggregate capital–output and capital–labor ratio, when the system is not in long-run equilibrium in a similar way. The unforeseen increase in

[14] By making the assumption that firms never expand output beyond the intersection of the AC_1 curve and the price line, we ensure that any unexpected increase in sales relative to capacity also gives rise to an increase in profits relative to capacity over what had been expected. At the aggregate level this correlation between Y/K and P/K allows us to say something about the behavior of P/K in terms of the behavior of Y/K as the system converges towards its long-run equilibrium.

[15] 'A further implication of the findings for the theory of the firm is the relationship found between price and investment decisions. The information on this aspect is limited, nevertheless the setting of and attempt to follow specific target returns on investment are manifest at two separate levels of operations: short-run pricing and investment decisions. The investment decision presupposes a price (and usually a market-share) assumption, which, in turn, determines short-run price decisions thereafter. Thus, investment decisions in effect are themselves a form of pricing decisions, and over time become an inherent part of price policy.' Lanzillotti, R. F., 'Pricing Objectives in Large Companies', *American Economic Review*, 1958, p. 940.

demand for firms on the average, means that sales in the aggregate are larger than expected. Now the aggregate return on capital will be greater than the target rate, and higher than expected relative to the real wage, while money wages are unchanged. In addition, since the unanticipated expansion could only be achieved through hiring more labor (plant size being fixed within the period and some *ex post* substitution allowed), the capital–labor ratio will be lower, and the output–capital ratio higher, than expected. The abnormally high return on capital will lead to an increased rate of expansion of capacity either by existing firms or new ones, or both.

During a boom, this process will continue until the capacity effect of investment outstrips the multiplier effect. This sets the stage for a downturn. During this phase, firms individually and in the aggregate over-estimate actual sales in the next period and therefore over-expand capital relative to actual sales and labor utilized. Adjustments will take place in the opposite direction. The actual return on capital will be less than the targeted return, which will act as a signal to cut back the rate of growth of capital. Again, this can be the result of a decrease in the number of firms in the industry, or a cutback in the output of the existing firms, or both. The convergence towards equilibrium is simply a process whereby the rate of growth of capital relative to output and labor is continuously adjusted, so that the actual return is pushed up or down relative to the targeted rate. Because of lags, the convergence need not be asymptotic, but the assumption that cycles are damped ensures, in the absence of further shocks, that equilibrium is eventually attained.

It must be stressed in conclusion that none of this analysis is meant to imply that firms do not maximize profits. Given a world of uncertainty with regards to costs and demand conditions, the assumption that firms price in an effort to achieve some rate of return may be consistent with profit maximization. Nor does the fact that prices may or may not be relatively fixed in the short run, imply that productivity considerations do not eventually affect prices. They, along with the money wage rate and the general price level, determine what price must be set to achieve the targeted rate of return.[16] The main lesson here is that, in thinking about adjustments to imbalances between demand and supply, product price adjustments play a somewhat minor role, given money wages. Capacity adjustments are the critical responses that bring the system back to long-run equilibrium. It is also to be emphasized that there is nothing in what has been said here to justify the assumption that the behavior of factor prices from one period to the next is sufficient to clear markets and maintain some constant rate of employment of labor and capital in the long run.

---

[16] Assume that the long run target of the ith firm (a mirror image of business in general) is to achieve a fixed rate of return on its capital; i.e., $P_i/K_i = \gamma$, where P_i represents money profits deflated by the GNP price deflator, p, and K_i is the capital stock valued in constant prices. If intermediate products are ignored, money profits P'_i are given by $P'_i = p_i q_i - \hat{w} N_i$ where $\hat{w}$ is the money wage rate, p_i, q_i and N_i are respectively the price and quantity sold of the ith product and labor employed. A little substitution gives $P_i = \gamma p K_i/q_i + \hat{w} N_i/q_i$, where K_i/q_i and N_i/q_i measure average capital and labor productivity.

H. A Postscript—The Long and Short Run Elasticity of Supply of Labor

Whether off the equilibrium path or not, changes in the real wage come about through actions of entrepreneurs, given the state of technology. Any change in money wages will cause firms to price output so that in some aggregate sense a certain return on capital is earned. This suggests that it might be better to treat the supply curve of labor within the short period as perfectly elastic at the going real wage. This is shown in Diagram 3.3 with the real wage, w, measured on the vertical axis and labor, N, on the horizontal. Assume that there is a mechanism such as that described above that maintains a constant rate of employment, and for convenience let this be full employment. Then, S_t depicts the short-run supply curve of labor in period t. Employment is equal to N_t, the available labor force during period t. In period $t + 1$ the supply of labor increases to N_{t+1}, etc. By connecting up the kinks in the different curves a long-run supply curve for labor can be constructed. Its elasticity depends upon the rate of growth of the labor force, and the speed at which the short-run curves are moving upward. This in turn is given in the first instance by the identity $w = K/N[Y/K - P/K]$. Since the output–capital ratio and the return on capital, P/K, are fixed in the long-run equilibrium, the rate of growth of the real wage depends upon the rate of growth of the capital–labor ratio, K/N. As already shown, in equilibrium the rate of growth of the capital stock is the same as the rate of growth of output; i.e. $r_n + \rho$. Therefore, the rate of growth of the real wage is simply the difference between this and rate of growth of the labor force or ρ, the rate of growth of labor productivity. The latter is unexplained at this point and will be treated as something endogenous in the next chapter. But both in the long and short run, movements of the real wage are the outcome of technological change and actions and desires of entrepreneurs. The elasticity of the long-run 'supply' curve of labor will reflect these influences, and not such factors as the trade-off between work and leisure.

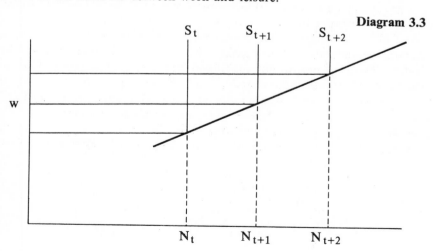

Diagram 3.3

Chapter IV The Interaction
of Demand
and Supply

A. A Comparison with Hicks' Model

The final model developed in Chapter III is repeated here:

$$C_t = mY_t + nX_t, \tag{1''}$$

$$I_t = bY_{t-1} - cK_{t-1}, \tag{2}$$

$$Y_t = C_t + I_t, \tag{3}$$

$$K_t = K_{t-1} + I_t, \tag{4}$$

$$X_t = X_0(1 + r_x)^t. \tag{6}$$

The model utilized the notion of a well-defined level of maximum output, X_t, which plays a critical role, since its growth determines the long-run growth rate of the system. In some respects it is similar to a related group of cycle and growth models, where explosive movements of the endogenous mechanism are constrained by a growing limit to output. The most notable is the model of Hicks, whose efforts were directed toward generating a cycle of constant amplitude by constraining an explosive accelerator–multiplier model.[1] The economy would supposedly move toward a ceiling level of income, i.e. X_t, hit the ceiling, and bounce off into a recession. However, as has been shown in the case where the endogenous mechanism is capable of generating steady growth, the economy may simply move along the ceiling after an encounter and never turn down.[2]

Assume that the endogenous mechanism of the Hicks model is capable of

---

[1] Hicks, J. R., *The Trade Cycle*, Oxford University Press, 1950.
[2] Alexander, S. S., 'The Accelerator as Generator of Steady Growth', *The Quarterly Journal of Economics*, May 1949. A necessary condition for crawling along the ceiling is that the growth rate of the ceiling be bracketed by the growth rates implied by the two real roots of the (second order) difference equation.

generating steady growth, and that the model does not bounce off the ceiling. Then this endogenous mechanism, if unconstrained, has a definite long-run growth rate for all the endogenous variables where capital, output and investment all grow at the same time. Alternatively, we can say that in this case there is a feedback mechanism that brings the growth rates of capital, output and investment into line. However, there is nothing yet to bring these things into line with the rate of growth of supply, or with the ceiling, as in the final model developed in Chapter III. Now assume that the growth rate generated by the endogenous mechanism in Hicks' model is greater than the ceiling rate of growth, $(r_n + \rho)$, so that the economy sooner or later encounters the ceiling. In this case, the economy will eventually adjust to the ceiling so that all variables grow at rate $(r_n + \rho)$ as with the model developed here.

However, there are important differences between the two models. First, the equilibrium level of income relative to full employment income, Y_t^E/X_t, is not necessarily one in our model as it is in the constrained Hicks model. This greatly increases the possibility of secular inflation in the latter model, especially when the growth rate of demand generated by the accelerator–multiplier model greatly exceeds the rate of growth of the ceiling. Second, in Hicks' model, there is a distinction between the rate of growth generated by the interaction of the endogenous variables, and the rate of growth of the ceiling or supply, whereas no distinction is necessary in the model developed here. This gives rise to another difference. Assume that the rate of growth of the labor force is given. Then, in models of the Hicks type there will be a certain rate of growth of the capital–labor ratio as the economy moves towards the ceiling, followed by another slower rate of growth of this ratio as the economy moves along the ceiling. But unless productivity grows more rapidly before the ceiling is encountered than after, there is nothing to offset the more rapid rate of growth of the capital–labor ratio during the movement towards the ceiling. If productivity does not behave this way, we would expect the return on capital to be declining as the economy moved toward the ceiling, and this is clearly inconsistent with steady growth during the unconstrained phase.

In our model there is no distinction between a rate of growth generated by demand forces, and one determined by supply factors. And since the rate of growth of capital equals the rate of growth of actual and maximum output, i.e., $r_x = r_n + \rho$, the capital–labor ratio always grows at rate ρ. Assume that the rate of return on capital is given in the moving equilibrium. Then if we wish to describe this in more neoclassical terms, we can think of this growth path as one where a given rate of growth of Harrod neutral technical progress is just offsetting the higher rate of growth of capital relative to labor. This prevents the return on capital from falling as the real wage grows. Thus, the long-run properties of our model are quite consistent with the conventional views on productivity, even though assumptions of perfect and frictionless markets have been discarded.

B. A Model of Joint Interaction

But in spite of these improvements, a model that allows the supply side of the market to affect demand, but assumes that the rate of growth of supply is independent of the actual performance of the economy, is still quite unsatisfactory. While it need not be argued that economic events always induce a one-for-one change on the supply side, it is essential for the argument of those who stress the role of demand in growth that, whatever causes maximum output to grow at a rate greater than the growth of the labor force, it should be something related to demand. This is the core of the stability question in demand-determined growth models. Supply adjusts to demand through changes in productivity and factor supplies, so that inflationary pressures are dampened. Thus, instead of equation (6) a very simple additional relation between demand and supply could be introduced such as (6')

$$X_t = F(Y_t, t),$$

where t represents a time trend. On the one hand, the expression resulting from equations (1")–(4) describes the influence of supply on demand, while (6') gives the cause and effect relation in the opposite direction. Together, equations (1")–(4) and (6') determine the actual and maximum output from one period to the next.

However, to bring out this interaction in more detail, a different procedure will be followed. We retain equation (6) and add an additional equation:

$$r_x = f(r_y) \tag{7}$$

so that the complete model consists of the following six equations:

$$C_t = mY_t + nX_t, \tag{1"}$$

$$I_t = bY_{t-1} - cK_{t-1}, \tag{2}$$

$$Y_t = C_t + I_t, \tag{3}$$

$$K_t = K_{t-1} + I_t, \tag{4}$$

$$X_t = X_0(1 + r_x)^t, \tag{6}$$

$$r_x = f(r_y). \tag{7}$$

Next the first five equations (1")–(4) and (6) can be combined and solved to form a final equation, i.e.,

$$Y_t = \left(\frac{b}{1-m} + 1 - c\right) Y_{t-1} - \frac{b}{1-m} Y_{t-2} + \left(\frac{n}{1-m}\right)\left(\frac{c+r_x}{1+r}\right) X_t.$$

The solution of this is:

$$Y_t = Y_t^E + C_1(x_1)^t + C_2(x_2)^t.$$

However, with the endogenous part of the model damped, the cyclical component of this part of the model can be ignored, as the long-run behavior

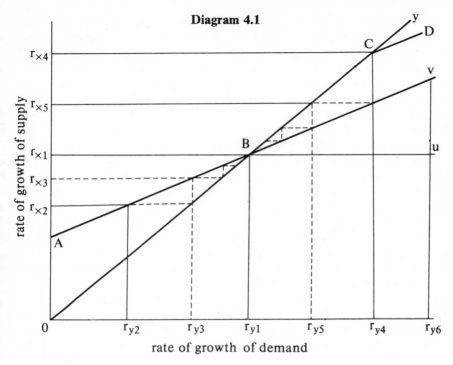

Diagram 4.1

of output is determined by the behavior of X_t; i.e. $\lim_{t \to \infty} Y_t = Y_t^E = v'X_0(1 + r_x)^t$.

This last expression, together with $r_x = f(r_y)$ (7) gives the two basic relations which again describe the joint interaction, but in a more concise form.

Take the former expression first. This tells us that as X_t grows at some rate, say, r_{x1}, Y_t will eventually grow at this rate. If it grows at a higher rate, $r_{x2} > r_{x1}$, Y_t will also grow at this higher rate. And so for any permanently maintained value of r_x, there will be a long-run rate of growth of Y_t of the same magnitude, and we can write $(I)r_y = r_x$ to represent equations (1")–(4) and (6). This is shown graphically in Diagram 4.1 by the 45° line labeled y.[3] This line indicates the long-run growth rate of demand, output and capital (and all other endogenous variables) that will result if some rate of growth of supply, r_x, is maintained indefinitely. In other words, it indicates how the natural rate of growth influences the warranted and actual rates of growth. As r_x increases, the X_t term in the consumption equation (1") ensures that in the new long-run equilibrium, the rate of growth of consumption and all other endogenous variables, including capital, will increase by the same amount. Thus, whatever the rate of growth of supply, the capital–output ratio will approach a constant in the long run. The actual long-run rate of growth of supply has yet to be determined.

[3] As r_x is increased, the dominant root of the set of equations (1")—(4) and (6) increases by the same amount, causing the long-run rate of growth of Y to change by the same amount. This is nothing but a family of particular solutions describing the first relation between demand and supply with the causation running from the latter to the former.

It is possible to depict graphically the second relation between the rates of growth of demand and supply. Diagram 4.1 illustrates the effect of the rate of growth of demand upon the rate of growth of supply, under different assumptions as to the responsiveness of supply to demand pressures. The assumption that r_x is independent of demand is shown in the diagram by the horizontal line u. However, in the amended model of this section a mutual interaction between the two sides of the market is desired. This requires developing a second relation between demand and supply, showing what would be the long-run rate of growth of supply if the growth of demand were maintained at a certain rate.

One possibility is to allow supply to respond to demand in rather a simple way. Thus, line v assumes that as r_y increases, so does r_x, but the slope is less than one. For the moment this can be taken to indicate that an increase in r_y induces a higher rate of growth of capital, labor and/or productivity, but never in such a way that the resulting increase in r_x is as great as the changes in r_y. The positive intercept can indicate that supply grows even in a stagnant economy, because of growth in the labor force and/or productivity.

In this case it is easy enough to show that point B, where demand, supply, output and capital all grow at the same rate, is a stable equilibrium point. Assume initially a situation where $r_y = r_{y1}$ and $r_x = r_{x1}$, and allow for a displacement to the left so that $r_y = r_{y2}$. This causes a decline in r_x but not as much as the decline in r_y. However, $r_y = r_{y2}$ cannot be maintained, since $r_{x2} > r_{y2}$ will mean that X_t/Y_t is rising (as the unemployment rate increases), causing an increase in the rate of growth of consumption relative to demand and output. This rising ratio of consumption to output will also cause an increase in the rate of growth of demand and output to something greater than r_{y2}; say, r_{y3}. The whole process will continue as long as X_t/Y_t is rising, so that eventually the influence of supply, X_t, on demand, Y_t, will cause the rate of growth of all endogenous variables to converge on a growth rate given by r_{x1}.

Thus, we could think of the process of convergence back to $r_{y1} = r_{x1}$ as an initial displacement of demand to r_{y2}, which is associated with a rate of growth of supply $r_{x2} > r_{y2}$. This growth of supply causes the rate of growth of demand to increase to r_{y3}, causing a further increase in the rate of growth of supply from r_{x2} to r_{x3}, etc., until equilibrium is restored. This example (like those to follow) ignores the likely cyclical nature of the convergence process, but this is of no consequence.

Alternatively, we could assume that starting from $r_{y1} = r_{x1}$, something causes the rate of growth of supply to fall to r_{x2}. This generates a decline in the rate of growth of demand to r_{y3}, but this situation cannot be maintained. This lower rate of growth of demand is associated with a lower rate of growth of supply than the original equilibrium, but nonetheless higher than r_{x2} as shown by line v. As in our first example, $r_{y3} > r_{x2}$ must cause the rate of growth of supply to increase, etc., until once again $r_{y1} = r_{x1}$.

On the other hand, assume a displacement such that initially $r_y = r_{y4} > r_{x5}$.

If there are unemployed resources it is possible that demand can temporarily grow more rapidly than supply, but once these resources are exhausted, the rate of growth of output in real terms is given by line v. Since consumption in real terms is related to the rate of growth of real output, i.e., r_{x5}, this unbalance will eventually pull down r_y to something like $r_{y5} > r_{x5}$, which leads to further movements until equilibrium is restored.[4] Finally, a displacement initiated by a change in the rate of growth of supply to, say, r_{x4} can also be seen to be only temporary. The increase in r_x to r_{x4} will induce an increase of r_y to r_{y4} initially. But this higher rate of growth of demand, while associated with a higher rate of growth of supply than r_{x1}, will soon cause r_x to fall back to something like r_{x5}, etc. Thus, while the 45° line represents the effect of the rate of growth of supply on demand, and the v line represents the effect of the rate of growth of demand on supply if each is maintained in some long-run sense, no other r_x or r_y can be maintained except those corresponding to point B.

The equation for line v can be written

$$r_x = \gamma_0 + \gamma_1 r_y. \tag{II}$$

Once again, this shows the rate of growth of maximum output for any rate of growth of demand. The causal relation emanating from the supply side as shown as the y or 45° line in the diagram has been written as:

$$r_y = r_x. \tag{I}$$

Equations (I) and (II) in the unknowns r_x and r_y can be solved to determine the long-run equilibrium: $r_y = r_x = \gamma_0/(1 - \gamma_1)$. Even without specifying what γ_0 and γ_1 represent, the long-run growth rate appears to be independent of demand parameters. Something more is evidently necessary before it can be said that demand (in this sense) is one of the determinants of the long-run growth rate. This is true not just for the particular form of equation (II) assumed here, but for a whole class of supply responses provided each satisfies the conditions: $f' > 0$, $f(0) > 0$ and $f'' \leq 0$.

The relation between demand and supply illustrated by line v can be compared with Kaldor's technical progress function. Kaldor denies the possibility of separating the influences on labor productivity of changes in capital per worker from that of technical progress. Instead he posits a relation between the rate of growth of capital per worker and output per worker, which, using a linear approximation, can be written:

$$r_x - r_n = \alpha + \beta(r_k - r_n)$$

[4] Some care must be taken in interpreting the diagram when discussing a displacement to the right of the equilibrium point; then it is necessary to make a distinction between the rate of growth of demand and the rate of growth of output. If there is full employment to begin with, an increase in the rate of growth of demand from, say, r_{y1} to r_{y4} does not result in an increase in real output of the same magnitude. The rate of growth of real output can only increase by an amount indicated by line v. No such distinction between demand and output is necessary when discussing displacements to the left of point B.

or:

$$r_x = \alpha + (1 - \beta)r_n + \beta r_k.^5$$

This looks suspiciously like line v, and also a Cobb–Douglas production function, if β is interpreted as the elasticity of output with respect to capital and α as the rate of disembodied technical progress. The main difference is that we can use the rate of growth of demand instead of capital.[6] Thus, if the rate of growth of capital is measured on the horizontal axis of Diagram 4.1., line v is a linear version of Kaldor's technical progress function, and, given certain assumptions, can be integrated to give a Cobb–Douglas function. Furthermore, the long run equilibrium in the Kaldor model can be written: $r_x = (\alpha)/(1 - \beta) + r_n$. This is identical with our results if $\gamma_0 = \alpha + (1 - \beta)r_n$ and $\beta = \gamma_1$ and the standard neoclassical results, given the above-mentioned interpretations of β and α. In all three cases demand parameters have no long-run effect and it is difficult to distinguish one model from the other in the 'golden age'. While Kaldor's adjustment mechanism is certainly not neo-classical, his assumptions about supply clearly fit into the neoclassical supply determined framework.

The decision to work throughout this paper in such general terms as the effect of demand on supply, rather than specifying a technical progress or a Cobb–Douglas production function, has been deliberate. In view of the arguments advanced in the next section, to explain how supply in general and productivity in particular depend on the actual performance of the economy, this seems most appropriate. The use of simple aggregate production and technical progress functions lends a feeling of exactness that is unwarranted, given how little we know about the supply side. In addition, the more formal functions overlook many sources of growth. By working in general terms we don't pretend to any such exactness and hopefully pick up some of these other sources.

C. Growth as a Transformation

What must now be shown is that if it is to be argued that demand determines or helps to determine the long-run growth rate, a different sort of response of supply to demand must be assumed from those just discussed. As will soon

[5] One of Kaldor's earliest formulations is found in Kaldor, Nicholas, 'A Model of Economic Growth', *Economic Journal*, December 1957.

[6] It should be noted that while Diagram 4.1 measures the rate of growth of demand on the horizontal axis, any rate of growth of supply or maximum output associated with some rate of growth of demand, is itself associated with some given rate of growth of capital, investment and consumption. For example, as r_y is increased, say, from r_{y1}, this would, if maintained, induce an increase in the rate of growth of capital, r_k, equal to the increase in r_x. In the immediate vicinity of the equilibrium point, B, all these growth rates are approximately equal.

become clear, this is essentially a matter of higher rates of growth of demand inducing equal increases in the rates of growth of supply. However, unlike the purely demand-determined growth models, we will limit the possibility of this sort of response to a certain range of growth rates. Much of the literary exposition that is to follow runs in terms of a multi-sector economy. Even so it will often be convenient to refer to the simple one-sector model depicted in Diagram 4.1.

We can begin by recognizing that the process of growth is anything but balanced. Growth rates of individual sectors vary considerably, both over time, and relative to one another at a point in time. One can go further and characterize growth as a movement through a hierarchy of goods. In terms of final output, we can think of an initial period when certain goods are considered luxuries by most spending units, given the level and distribution of income of the period, but eventually these goods will become necessities in a later period, say, $t + \alpha$, when incomes have risen sufficiently. Then in period $t + \alpha$ goods that were unknown in period t classify as luxuries, only to be reclassified as necessities in period $t + 2\alpha$, when incomes have risen even further. Over time, as goods pass from the luxury to necessity classification, the rate of growth of demand first increases and then levels off as the market becomes more and more saturated. The same pattern will be true for the output of industries supplying intermediate products.

This type of development can be seen more clearly with the help of Diagram 4.2. On the vertical axis is measured household or family consumption with income on the horizontal axis. Following the usual definitions of luxury goods and necessities as goods with an income elasticity of demand greater than or less than one respectively, Diagram 4.2. describes different goods that at low incomes are luxuries and at high incomes necessities. For example, the consumption pattern for Good 1 is such that from zero income to income y_1 the marginal propensity to consume is greater than the average, i.e., the good is a luxury, while for incomes greater than y_1 it falls in the necessity category. Similarly Good 2 is a luxury item until income y_2 is achieved (indeed is not even purchased until family income reaches some minimum), at which point it becomes a necessity. In the meantime, the consumption of Good 1 has reached a saturation point.

For the economy as a whole, as incomes grow from a very low level, the rate of growth of demand for Good 1 will first rise (Good 2 not even being purchased) then decline and eventually become zero. Before that happens, though, Good 2 will start to be consumed as demand for it first grows slowly, then speeds up and eventually falls to zero as with Good 1. The rate of growth of market demand for each good will be a function of the distribution of income as well as the shape of any curve.[7] But for any given distribution of total in-

[7] Aitchinson, J., and Brown, J. A. C., 'A Synthesis of Engel Curve Theory', *The Review of Economic Studies*, No. I, 1954. Out of this early study a fairly sizeable body of literature has developed with special emphasis on consumer durable expenditures.

Diagram 4.2

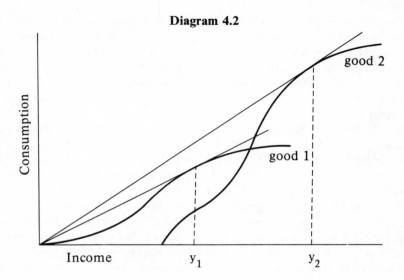

come, it is apparent that as average family income grows consumer purchases will eventually shift from Good 1 to Good 2, and eventually on to other goods further along in the hierarchy.

D. Demand and Productivity

With different income elasticities of demand for different goods at any point in time, and with the income elasticities of demand for any one good changing as income rises in the manner just described, the higher the rate of growth of demand, the more rapidly will the distribution of demand change. How rapidly this changing composition of demand results in a changing composition of output depends upon the levels and rates of growth of productivity in different sectors (since the latter is the basis of rising *per capita* incomes) and the rate of transfer of resources. It can also be argued that the behavior of productivity, as well as the rate of transfer of resources, itself depends on the rate of growth of demand. Take the case of the influence of demand on productivity first. Assume that any firm trying to work out its production plan is faced with the problem of having only a limited number of ways of combining capital and labor. For convenience we can think of there being two basic techniques available: one highly capital intensive, the other highly labor intensive. However, for both techniques we allow a limited amount of substitution of capital and labor *ex post*, as machines can be worked more or less intensely, workers can be given more or less space to work in, etc. Assume further that the possibility of achieving economies of scale and productivity increases through mass production, and the extent of the problem of indivisibilities are both positively related to the capital intensity of the technique chosen. Then reaping the benefits of mass production becomes a function of the rate of growth of demand and sales (rather than just the level of sales). For the more acute is the problem of indivisibilities, the more rapidly must demand grow, if the fear of excess capacity is not to deter business from adopting the more capital-intensive methods and realizing economies of scale.

In a market where demand is growing relatively slowly, the likelihood is that firms will be content to use methods of production that are 'sub-optimal' and of low capital intensity, rather than face the possibility of excess capacity. The alternative is to opt for the 'optimal' production possibility and engage in fierce competition, in an effort to increase one's market share and eliminate the excess capacity in fairly short order. On the other hand, in a market where demand is growing rapidly, existing firms can introduce mass production techniques without having to live with excess capacity for any extended length of time, thereby reducing the need to try to increase their share of the market.

This tendency to switch to highly capital-intensive techniques when demand has been growing rapidly, is reinforced by two other factors: the tendency of technological progress to be 'localized', and the past and projected trend in factor prices.

Thus, one assumption of a large number of currently popular production functions is that technological progress is such that it leads to 'spill-over' effects; that is, technological progress acts to increase the labor productivity of all available techniques of production. For example, write: $Y = Y_0 e^{gt} K^\lambda N^{1-\lambda}$ or $Y/N = Y_0 e^{gt} (K/N)^\lambda$ where g is the rate of growth of technical progress. The fact that this function rules out increasing returns to scale and indivisibilities is unimportant. What is important is it assumes irrespective of the technique of production employed in the past (i.e. the chosen capital intensity of production), that it is possible to switch today to an entirely different capital–labor ratio and still reap the benefits of past technical progress, because by its very nature such progress applies or spills over to all techniques. But what if technical progress does not fall like manna from heaven to be spread evenly over all techniques, but results either from experience in production (i.e., from a kind of learning process), or from research activity induced by and embodied in investment?[8] Then it is most likely that technological progress will be localized; i.e., it will act to improve only those techniques of production that have been put into use or those that will be put

---

[8] Assume that technical progress is embodied in investment in the usual way and write $Y = Y_0 J^a N^{1-a}$ or $Y/N = Y_0 (J/N)^a$, where J is capital measured in efficiency units. Then it still remains true, even if a totally different technique is adapted today, that newer capital goods realize a higher efficiency than any and all earlier vintages.

into use when research activities prove them to be feasible techniques of production.[9] In such a case it not only pays to switch to the more capital-intensive techniques, in spite of the short-run excess capacity (in order to be prepared to service the expanded markets of the future), it may be absolutely essential; for a firm that first adopts an improved method of production may gain a permanent cost advantage over one that lags. This possibility forces all firms in a fast growing industry not only eventually to switch to the new technique, but to do so as soon as possible after a competitor has taken the step. On the other hand if technical progress is not localized, the laggards would not be penalized to the same degree, since they eventually obtain the same benefits of technical progress as those that switched early. This is true whether progress is simply a function of time, or embodied in investment, provided the spill-over effects are present.

Another factor speeding the tendency to switch to high capital-intensity techniques is the projection of past behavior of factor prices into the future. If the wage rate is expected to continue its upward historical trend, then the projected trend in factor prices becomes much more important if technical progress is localized than if it is not. For the growth of labor productivity and the reduction of labor costs are a function of the time expended working with the new technique (and related research activity). As before, a firm cannot wait and still expect to obtain the cost-reducing effects of technical progress that would accrue if the latter spilled over to all techniques.

Thus, the projected trend in factor prices and the localization of technical progress work to offset any negative factors associated with building ahead of demand. This results in a substantial reduction in risk for firms with rapid growth prospects, if they choose to switch to more modern mass production techniques, even if current demand does not justify the expansion of capacity involved.

The fact that the possibilities of exploiting economies of scale may be limited, does not diminish the force of the argument. It is at this point that the notion of a hierarchy of goods is useful. All that really needs to be argued to support the economies of scale position is that growth of productivity in some firm or industry is more responsive to demand conditions when the rate of growth of demand is high and rising. When the market for the good becomes relatively saturated and demand shifts to other industries, a slowing down in the rate of growth of productivity and the exhaustion of scale economies can be expected. Furthermore, it comes at a time when it is less consequential for the overall growth of productivity. What an increase in the overall rate of growth of demand may accomplish is a speed-up in the time of adoption of mass production techniques in those sectors about to produce 'necessities', and thereby a shortening of the time needed to move through the hierarchy.

---

[9] See Atkinson, A. B., and Stiglitz, J. E., 'A New View of Technical Change', *The Economic Journal*, September 1969.

E. Demand and the Transfer of Resources

Demand also affects the rate of transfer of resources. For example, the mobility of labor from one sector to another depends upon the vacancy rates and opportunities for advancement in the expanding sectors, and these depend upon the actual and expected rates of expansion in those sectors. Similar arguments could be put forward to show that the rate of transfer of capital and the rate of growth of demand are positively related. The rate at which resources will be transferred from one sector to another is also very much dependent not only on the desire of entrepreneurs to introduce the most advanced or best practice techniques, but also on the willingness of (organized) labor to permit changes in plant layout and in the type of capital installed. Other things being equal, the higher the rate of growth of demand, the lower will be the rate of growth of unemployment. High employment will, in turn, decrease the reluctance of organized labor to accept innovations and organizational changes, and speed up the movement through the hierarchy. However, a rapid shift in the distribution of resources and output caused by an increase in the rate of growth of demand will be helpful, and lead to an increase in the overall rate of growth of productivity and aggregate output, only if the shift is towards sectors with higher than average productivity. In this case, it will feed back and provide the basis for a higher rate of growth of demand, which in turn will stimulate productivity, and so on.

Historically, this seems to have been the case in the United States as well as in other developed capitalistic economies, and for several reasons. First, as has just been argued, higher rates of growth of demand induce higher rates of growth of productivity within a sector. Even if a relatively new but growing sector had a rather low average productivity early in its development, the increase in demand for the good as it moves into the 'necessity' category may soon raise average productivity in that sector above that in the older sectors.

But second, even if higher rates of growth of demand did not induce higher rates of growth of productivity, i.e. if the rate of growth within any sector is somehow given but not necessarily zero, we would expect demand to tend to shift towards sectors with higher than average rates of growth of productivity, which would generate the same result. This can be seen in the following way. The rate of growth of demand for some good depends both upon its income and price elasticity of demand. At any point in time there will be a group of goods whose prices are rising relative to others, because rates of growth of productivity are below average. This will tend to retard the rate of growth of demand for these goods. Therefore, the distribution of demand will have a tendency to shift towards those sectors which produce under conditions of rapid growth in productivity, and which have attained, or are likely soon to attain, high average productivity status.

Third, new industries can 'borrow' the technology of other industries through their use of the same capital goods industry. We frequently stress the importance for underdeveloped economies of borrowing technology from the industrial leaders. This supposedly allows them to collapse the period required to move from one level of per capita income (read average labor productivity) to another. But if anything, this possibility is even more likely within a country. This enables any new industry to start from or quickly attain a relatively high level of average productivity.[10]

As a final point, the influence of demand on the growth of the labor force might be mentioned. This can be divided into two parts: the effect on participation of the existing labor force; and the effect on migration of labor into the country. The former process can best be thought of as a factor adjusting the level of demand to that of supply. But though the effect of induced migration on the rate of growth of aggregate income and maximum output is also fairly straightforward in an advanced economy, its effect on *per capita* output and productivity is anything but obvious. It has been argued by some that higher rates of growth of the labor force and population can lead to higher rates of growth of output both in the aggregate and *per capita*. Demands of immigrant workers for consumer and social overhead capital are often weak for some time after the date of immigration, due to a variety of cultural factors, or simply to the fact that the migrant either leaves his family behind him or delays forming a family. Whatever the reason, this would allow for a larger share of output to be devoted to business investment, which should have a beneficial effect on productivity. The long-run effects, taking this position, are less certain unless the theory is coupled with some sort of economy of scale argument.

Alternatively, it can be argued that the higher the rate of growth of the population and the labor force, the more likely are all firms and industries to be retaining, if not expanding, employment. This reduces the amount of frictional unemployment for any level amount of total unemployment. This, in turn, would have the effect of reducing the amount of inflationary pressure

[10] The idea that, even if overall growth can be thought of in terms of some sort of 'steady state', the underlying process is one of the successive rise and fall of different sectors is well expressed by Svennilson, I., *Growth and Stagnation in the European Economy*, E. C. E., Geneva, 1954. The notion of borrowing technology previously developed by the capital goods industry for sectors that had industrialized earlier is found in Rosenberg, N.,'Technical Change in the Machine Tool Industry", *Journal of Economic History*, December 1963. The Rosenberg study finds support in two empirical studies, Massell, B., 'A Disaggregated View of Technical Change', *Journal of Political Economy*, December 1961, and Slater, W. E. G., *Productivity and Technical Change*, Ch. XI, London, Cambridge University Press, 1960. Massell uses a geometric index of total factor productivity to show the importance of shifts in resources, especially capital, for the overall growth rate of the index in the United States, while Slater uses a simple labor index of productivity to show the same thing for the United Kingdom.

The fact that the composition of output may be shifting towards services need not lead to pessimism. The historical record suggests that the response to this might well be something like computerized medicine, to take but one example. If not, the price elasticity effect may reverse this tendency. In the appendix these ideas are spelled out in a different manner.

for any given rate of unemployment, allowing more sustained and higher demand pressures, and the induced effect this has on productivity.

F. Say's Law in Reverse

However, and this is the crux of the matter, the degree to which these influences operate depends upon whether or not the rate of unemployment is rising. As the rate of growth of demand rises above zero, we may expect some increases in the rate of growth of maximum output, but not by much, relatively speaking, as long as $r_x > r_y$, for several reasons. First, an increase in the rate of growth of demand tends to reduce the risks of building ahead of demand, *other things being equal*. But the unemployment rate is surely one of the other things, and it is unlikely that firms on the average will undertake investment projects involving indivisibilities and excess capacity, as long as the unemployment rate is rising. Second, the rate of transfer of both capital and labor will be low when unemployment rates are rising, so that any growth of productivity due to interindustry shifts can be expected to be relatively small until unemployment rates stabilize. Third, labor will be most unreceptive to innovations when unemployment is rising. And finally, immigration will tend to be low.

The assumption that demand creates its own supply can now be reinterpreted. An increase in the rate of growth of demand may induce in the rate of growth of supply an increase which is of the same order of magnitude over a certain range. This possibility is shown by the line segments $ABCD$, in Diagram 4.1. The response of supply to demand to the left of r_{y1} is small, for reasons just discussed. However, at that point where the rate of growth of demand is as great as r_{y1}, there is a sharp break in the relationship. Once the economy passes beyond those growth rates of demand which, if they were maintained, would generate secular stagnation, the line segment BC indicates demand which creates its own supply. However, there is a limit to the rate of migration into a country, to the rate of exploiting economies of scales, and to the rate of transfer of resources. Beyond point C, the induced effect is again smaller. Equation (II) must be rewritten:

$$r_x = \gamma_0 + \gamma_1 r_y \text{ for } r_y \leq r_{y1};$$ (II')

$$r_x = \gamma_0' + \gamma_1 r_y \text{ for } r_y \geq r_{y4} \text{ with } \gamma_0' > \gamma_0 \text{ and};$$

$$r_x = r_y \text{ for } r_{y1} \leq r_y \leq r_{y4}.$$

We have already discussed the behavior of the model for growth rates less than r_{y1}. It is also apparent that with the line segments $ABCD$ describing the response of supply to demand, a growth rate of demand (or supply) greater than r_{y4} is not sustainable. However, the BC segment requires further discussion. Starting from a possible equilibrium where $r_{y1} = r_{x1}$, allow a onceover increase of the rate of growth of demand to r_{y4} due to an increase in the propensity to invest. At the micro level, we can think this the result of entrepreneurs expecting sales to grow at a rate greater than r_{y1}, say r_{y4}, and so stepping up investment, and therefore demand, in order to meet this expected higher level of sales. In this case, the increase in the rate of growth of demand induces an equal increase in the rate of growth of maximum output, so that the original increase in the rate of growth of demand can be sustained.[11]

The capital-output ratio is again constant in the new equilibrium since whatever the point actually chosen on the BC segment, all endogenous variables grow at the same rate; but demand, supply, capital and the capital-labor ratio grow more rapidly than before. In neoclassical terms, the increase in the long-run rate of growth of the capital–labor ratio, *per capita* income and other endogenous variables corresponding to this movement along the BC segment, would be attributed to an assumed higher rate of growth of technical progress, unrelated to the actual behavior of the economy. Because of this, a more rapid rate of growth of capital is possible for a given rate of growth of the labor force, without causing a secular decline in the rate of profit. The interpretation here is quite different. It assumes that the entrepreneur is something more than a mere co-ordinator, and it rejects the notion that technical progress falls like manna from heaven. Technical progress and productivity gains are very much embodied in investment, but not in any simple, rigid way. Expecting higher profits and trying to protect his market position, our entrepreneur searches for new ways to expand capacity through newer and better machines and superior plant layouts, and for new products with favorable profit prospects; and, in the process, he increases the rate of growth of productivity. The rate of investment becomes very important indeed in these circumstances. And even the less dynamic, less innovating entrepreneur benefits. The more rapid rate of growth of demand and capital, and the induced higher rate of growth of productivity, result in a more rapid increase in *per capita* income. If the income elasticity of demand is positive, even the laggards may find that their profits relative to their capital stock have increased, because of the higher rate of growth of the capital stock overall and its effects on productivity and income.

However, the neoclassical result can be treated without any difficulty. Assume the economy had been growing for some time at $r_{y1} = r_{x1}$ and that for some unexplained reason there is a onceover increase in the rate of technical progress, causing the rate of growth of supply to increase to r_{x4}. This results eventually in a higher rate of growth of demand, capital and the capital–labor ratio, as the ratchet influence in the consumption function

---

[11] The line segments are drawn as straight lines. This is done for convenience, since line segment BC could take any shape as long as it is above the 45° line between points B and C. Nor is it necessary that segments AB and CD be straight lines.

causes all types of spending to grow more rapidly. (Stress here is on the causation running from demand to supply.)

G. Capital Formation and the 'Residual'

Viewed in macro terms, the BC segment implies that the rate of growth of productivity, however measured, is positively related to the rate of growth of demand, output and capital. So much so that the elasticity of output with respect to capital is one. If a geometric index of total factor of productivity is chosen, with weights for each factor depending upon factor shares, and if each factor is measured in 'natural' units, then over the BC segment there is a positive correlation between the rate of growth of demand, output and capital, and this more conventional type of 'residual'. If we choose to embody technical progress in capital at some fixed rate, a similar interpretation is appropriate. As suggested in the appendix, it is possible for technology at the individual firm level to be of a very conventional type, say Cobb–Douglas, and still have aggregate productivity positively correlated with the rate of growth of capital.

What is being argued here can perhaps be seen more clearly if the analysis proceeds more formally with the help of Frankel's 'modifier'.[12] Write for the aggregate production function: $Y = \sigma H \, K^{\beta} N^{\alpha}$ where σ is a constant and the other variables have their previous meanings. Assume that H, the modifier, is a function of the level of development of the economy which can be approximated by the capital–labor ratio. Specifically write $H = (K/N)^{\lambda}$, which upon substitution in the production function yields: $Y = \sigma(K/N)^{\lambda} \, K^{\beta} N^{\alpha}$, or, in terms of growth rates: $r_y = (\beta + \lambda)r_K + (\alpha - \lambda)r_n$.

As is clear, the modifier modifies or increases the contribution that capital makes as an economy develops; i.e., as the capital–labor ratio rises. In the special case where $\alpha = \lambda = 1 - \beta$, the function reduces to: $Y = \sigma K$, which is the Harrod–Domar production function, which assumes that the elasticity of output with respect to capital is one. In this case a higher rate of growth of demand resulting in a higher rate of growth of capital will cause an equal increase in the growth of maximum output.[13]

While the final result is the same as ours, the conclusions are arrived at somewhat differently. We would allow for the contribution of a given amount of capital and labor to rise over time as K/N rises, just as we have already argued that a higher rate of growth of capital and the capital–labor ratio can result permanently in a higher rate of growth of supply. However,

[12] See Frankel, M., 'The Production Function: Allocation and Growth', *American Economic Review*, December 1962.
[13] Viewed in these more conventional terms, we would also argue that the elasticity of output with respect to capital varies depending upon the rate of growth of demand.

we have argued that all this is the result of induced increases in productivity growth and resource movements. Among other things we do not preclude the possibility of more unconventional technology at the firm level, which allows for indivisibilities, localized technical progress, a limited number of techniques and variable returns to scale.

What has been said can be properly understood and justified only within the context of an economy that is undergoing a 'transformation', i.e. change in the composition of output. When this is the case, it is not enough to speak merely of the quantity of capital somehow measured. The structure of the capital stock must also be considered. Traditional marginal productivity doctrine tends to view the capital stock as a collection of homogeneous units, in the sense that additional units by definition must be competitive with one another. Once the changing composition of demand and output due to rising *per capita* income is stressed, it is much more sensible to view the capital stock as a collection of qualitatively different units: so different that new units of capital may be complementary with existing units as well as with units yet to be produced.[14] If, then, we take account of the fact that a higher rate of growth of demand, capital and output represents a more rapid change in the composition of output and the structure of capital, the possibility that the rate of growth of productivity may be positively correlated with these variables does not seem unreasonable.[15] The movement from point B to C in Diagram 4.1 does imply a more rapid rate of growth of both capital and total factor productivity. But it also should be interpreted as a more rapid movement through a hierarchy of goods, and a more rapid change in the structure and composition of the capital stock.

The length of the BC segment is another matter and will depend upon many things. Obviously, such things as the quality of entrepreneurship, the organization of the labor and capital markets, and the adaptability of the capital goods industry are important; as is the ability to borrow technology abroad. The rate at which a managerial class will move capital and provide the inducements to get labor to move are critical, and so is labor's willingness to move. How quickly consumers will adapt themselves to new goods will have an important bearing on how rapidly increases in productivity and *per capita* income get translated into new demands. Finally, various fiscal and monetary policies undertaken in the interests of altering the growth rate must be taken into consideration. These influences can be largely ignored in a discussion of the United States economy. But as we shall see in Chapter XI, the possibility

---

[14] This notion of complementary was first developed by Lachman, L. M., in 'Complementary and Substitution in the Theory of Capital', *Economica*, May 1947, and 'Investment Repercussions', *Quarterly Journal of Economics*, November 1948.

[15] This can be seen in another way. The relative performances of different West European economies in the postwar period provide the basis for a cross section analysis. In actual fact, the higher rate of growth of capital and output of the German economy relative to the British was also accompanied by a higher rate of growth of total factor productivity and a more rapid rate of growth of the capital–labor ratio.

that the length of the BC segment can be influenced by policy cannot be ignored when dealing with the British economy.

The actual point chosen on the BC segment is indeterminate without expanding the model. This involves several considerations. For instance, no regard has been taken of the effect of changes in demand pressures on the behavior of prices. It is most likely that as the rate of growth of demand is increased from r_{y1} towards r_{y4}, inflationary problems will intensify. A point may then be reached when this rate of inflation is politically and economically intolerable. This will set limits to the rate of growth of output, as the authorities through policy measures may try to limit growth rates for the economy to a subsegment of the BC segment.

Another possibility is that stepping up the rate of growth of demand gives rise to balance of payments difficulties after a certain point. This is related to the inflationary 'constraint' just mentioned, although payments difficulties could arise for other reasons as well. But even allowing for these constraints, it still remains true that demand as well as supply parameters determine the long-run growth rate, and that the rate of investment may be very important indeed.

H. Some Contrasts with Current Theories

Much of what has just been said can be put in its proper perspective if a further comparison is made with some of the developments in current growth and capital theory. First, a contrast between some of the views of Kaldor and those expressed here are in order. As one of the few 'Keynesian' growth theorists writing in the 1960's, his views deserve additional comment. Running through Kaldor's writings on growth is a strong distaste for the type of model building that assumes perfect competition, perfect foresight, rigid, over-simple technological relations and instantaneous adjustments at the margin.[16] However, there are important differences between Kaldor's approach and that stressed here. Earlier in the chapter, Kaldor's model of growth was described as a model of supply determined growth. The model developed here allows for a joint interaction between demand and supply. In addition, there is a basic difference in the mechanism used to bring demand and supply into line. In Kaldor's models any short-run discrepancy between the rate of growth of demand and maximum output is supposed to lead to a change in the price–money wage relation, which alters the distribution of income. This, in turn, is supposed to stabilize demand at the full employment

---

[16] See Kaldor's rebuttal to Modigliani and Samuelson in: Kaldor, N., 'Marginal Productivity and Macro-economic Theories of Distribution', *Review of Economic Studies*, October 1966.

level (although it is not clear whether this mechanism is a sufficient condition for full employment or not).

There is good reason to reject the Kaldor adjustment mechanism, as it has serious shortcomings. Not only must the distribution of income change so as to bring savings into equality with investment, but this (previously determined) level of investment is assumed to be a full employment level of investment. This latter assumption is purely arbitrary. In addition, Kaldor neglects the possibly destabilizing influence on investment of a shift in the distribution of income. For example, an increase in investment demand may lead to an increase in profits and savings because of higher profit margins, but this may stimulate investment even more.[17]

Next consider the earlier discussion of the effects of a higher rate of growth of demand on the choice of techniques. It was argued that a choice between a high or low capital-intensive technique would be dictated largely by the current and anticipated future growth of demand for the output of the firm. This followed from the assumption that the problem of indivisibilities increased with the capital intensity of the technique chosen. The discussion in this earlier section suggested certain affinities with some of the problems that have emerged in modern capital theory. For example, switching from a technique of production involving a low capital intensity to one with a high capital intensity, clearly involves a high rate of investment and an entirely new type of capital structure. Therefore, the more rapid increase in productivity or technical progress that this would generate would have to be embodied in the investment outlay. This notion of embodied technical progress plays an important role in neoclassical analysis; though in neoclassical models the rate of embodied technical progress is independent of the type and size of investment outlay, an assumption that has a lot to do with the 'unimportance of investment'. A dollar's worth of equipment investment, other things being equal, is assumed to add the same amount to productive capacity, whether a high capital-intensive mass production technique is used, or a small scale, low capital-intensive technique. This does not appear to be a tenable position. For example, any shift of an investment program from one that is 'defensive' in nature (i.e. primarily concerned with reducing costs and protecting a share of a stagnate market), to one aimed at expanding capacity in a growing market (an 'enterprise' investment program), would surely, dollar for dollar, have a differential effect on productivity.[18]

It was also suggested that technological progress was most likely to be localized. While new investment projects were necessary for taking advantage of potential increases in factor productivities, these possibilities would be limited to certain techniques of production. For example, in a textile firm

---

[17] See Kaldor, N., 'A Model . . .', *op. cit.* For a thorough analysis of the possibility of instability in the Kaldor models see Britto, R., 'A Study in Equilibrium Dynamics', *The Economic Journal*, September 1968.

[18] The distinction between defensive and enterprise investment was first developed by Lamfalussy, *op. cit.*

organized along cottage industry lines, an investment project aimed at increasing productivity might, together with the learning (and research) experience that accompanied it, have a substantial effect on labor productivity. But if the firm eventually switched to more modern mass production techniques, it could hardly be expected that the technical progress embodied in the older techniques could be automatically transferred to the new technique.

The notion of limited possibilities of factor substitution *ex ante* (as well as *ex post*), has also been stressed. This can be contrasted with much of neoclassical analysis, which works with smooth production functions that assume unlimited ways of combining capital and labor *ex ante* or *ex post*. Subsequent developments in capital and neoclassical growth theory illustrate a serious attempt to get away from the assumption of perfectly malleable capital, that can supposedly be molded to form any desired capital-intensive technique of production even after the capital goods have been built. Instead, models have been developed that allow for no substitution *ex post*.[19] There are *ex ante* substitution possibilities, but once an investment project has been completed factor substitution is no longer possible. These additions to the capital stock must be combined with labor in fixed proportions, and each new capital good just becomes another one of a collection of heterogeneous capital goods of a certain age.

However, the factors inducing a change in technique in these amended neoclassical models are quite different from what is being implied here. For example, in the neoclassical world of perfect competition, changes from less to more capital-intensive techniques are responses to a decline in the rate of profit relative to the wage rate, whether *ex post* substitution is ruled out or not. In some models the switching may not occur for small changes in relative factor prices, because the number of techniques of production may be limited, as in our model; i.e. *ex ante* substitution is limited. However, a higher (lower) capital-intensive technique is always associated with a lower (higher) rate of profit.[20] The 'factor price frontier' which traces out the rate of profit and real wage that perfect competition would generate for some given capital-intensive technique (when the number of techniques is unlimited), requires this association. This is not necessarily the case in the model developed here. The switching to a more capital-intensive technique described earlier in the chapter was induced by an increase in the rate of growth of demand for output. This enabled the firm to overcome more easily any problems associated with indivisibilities. It is true that profit considerations are undoubtedly behind such a switching process, but in the real world of uncertainty and limited competition it can just as easily be argued that the switch would be associated with the earning of a higher rate of profit on the new technique. For even if

[19] This extreme position was also rejected earlier. See p. 62. An example of a 'putty-clay' model is found in Johansen, Leif, 'Substitution vs. Fixed Production Coefficients in the Theory of Economic Growth', *Econometrica*, May 1959.

[20] This conclusion has been challenged on other grounds than those stressed in the text. For a summary of the debate see Harcourt, J., 'Some Cambridge Controversies in the Theory of Capital', *The Journal of Economic Literature*, June 1969, pp. 386–395.

long-run competition did cause firms to scale down their targeted return on capital, a higher risk associated with such a venture would require a higher realized return. In addition, this switch, should it lead to scrapping of the old capital, need not imply that the old capital was incapable of earning profits or quasi rents.

I. Some Comparative Dynamics

In Chapter III it was argued that the relative factor prices could play a role in bringing the system back to its equilibrium growth path. The model developed there had a unique long-run growth path, where demand and supply grew at a rate dictated by supply. In this chapter it was argued that there may be no unique long-run golden equilibrium growth path. This indeterminacy allows some concluding remarks about the long-run inter-action between relative factor prices and the capital intensity of production. It was argued in Chapter III that pricing is most likely undertaken with a view towards obtaining some targeted rate of return. What factors deter-mined this rate of return were not discussed. In the real world of frictions, uncertainty and other imperfections, these factors would certainly include the stage of development of the capital markets, technology, the degree of com-petition and ease of entry into any industry, governmental regulations and attitudes, and the actual performance of the economy.[21] Any serious attempt actually to explain the determinants of the targeted return would have to consider these factors. But by merely assuming that there is some given target rate of return, we were able to show in the last chapter that the capital stock-adjustment theory of investment was quite consistent with, and actu-ally part of, a system whereby relative factor prices acted as signals. However, the problem to be dealt with here lies more in the area of comparative dynamics, than in an analysis of the path back to one long-run equilibrium. We allow for the fact that for any given, sustained long-run rate of growth of demand along the BC segment, there will be a long-run equilibrium path for the system, and any deviations from that path will be self-correcting—partially because relative factor prices will help to induce a movement back to that equilibrium path. But the question we ask here is, what is the relationship between relative factor prices and the capital intensity of production at different points on the BC segment (i.e. in long-run equilibria), and this can best be seen by comparing two different points on the BC segment.

Thus, at any point along the BC segment in Diagram 4.1 the capital–output ratio is constant, as is P/K by assumption and, therefore, P/Y (al-though the value of K/Y and P/Y will differ according to the position on the BC segment). This means that the rate of growth of the real wage depends upon the rate of growth of the capital–labor ratio; as does the rate of growth

---

[21] If one subscribes to a branch of the Cambridge (England) School of Growth, it would be necessary to add that this rate of return or profit must depend on the growth rate of the economy and the saving propensity of capitalists.

of wages relative to the return on capital, since $w = K/N[Y/K - P/K]$. Assume that the rate of growth of the labor force is given. Then, starting from a growth rate corresponding to point B, an increase in the rate of growth of demand that is permanently maintained results in an equal increase in the rate of growth of capital. This, in turn, means that, as we move from a growth rate corresponding to B to, say, one corresponding to C, the rate of growth of wages relative to the return on capital increases. Viewed in these terms, the long-run behavior of real wage relative to the return on capital turns out to be a by-product of the process of growth, and is intimately connected with demand as well as supply. If real wages grow more rapidly in one golden age than in another, absolutely and in relation to the return on capital, this need not be attributed to differential treatment by Divine Providence. Techno-logical change, as we have argued, depends upon economic considerations which are most immediately felt and embodied in investment, but not in any simple way. Instead of describing growth rate r_{y4}, compared with growth rate r_{y1} in Diagram 4.1., as a situation where the higher rate of growth of disembodied technical progress permits (and a more rapid increase in the real wage relative to the return on capital induces) a higher rate of growth of capital relative to labor, we can reverse the direction of causation. The high rate of growth of productivity (and the real wage) is the result of a high rate of growth of capital relative to labor. And this 'switching' to a more rapid rate of increase of the capital–labor ratio in one long-run equilibrium compared to another, is ultimately related to Schumpeter's entrepreneur, heroic or other-wise. Furthermore, the rate at which the real wage grows should be a matter of complete indifference to business as long as it gets its targeted return on capital.[22]

What is important is that there be a joint interaction between the two sides of the market. When *ex ante* stimulants are not equal to *ex ante* high employ-ment leakages, adjustments are set in motion to correct the disequilibrium. The corrections are not necessarily instantaneous, but will involve a certain amount of time. Historically they seem to have worked rapidly and effectively enough to generate a credible record.

Chapter V discusses the equilibrium growth path in a less formal sense, by bringing in one very important type of expenditure whose growth tends to dominate growth of aggregate activity. Following Chapter V, we return in Chapters VI and VII to the important issue of the stability of the moving equilibrium growth path. The reader interested in the stability issue can proceed directly to Chapter VI without fear of losing the main thread of the argument.

[22] Nothing said in this section should be construed as contradicting what was said in Chapter III. For some given or permanently maintained rate of growth of demand along the BC segment, it is still true that movements of relative factor prices help to correct any temporary deviation from that long-run growth path. What we are saying here applies to the comparative dynamics of the matter. Comparing one permanently maintained growth rate with another along the BC segment, it is more correct to say that the chosen capital intensity determines the long-run behavior of relative factor prices than vice-versa.

Appendix

Define γ as the overall rate of growth of a geometric index of productivity; i.e., $\gamma = r_y - \lambda r_k - (1 - \lambda)r_n$ when r_y, r_k, and r_n are the rates of growth of output, capital and labor, and λ and $(1 - \lambda)$ the weights used to measure the contributions of the inputs. Following Massell and working with a two sector model, it is possible to divide the rate of growth of productivity into two parts, as in the text: that due to shifts of resources between the sectors, and that due to growth of total factor productivity within each sector. Write:

$$\gamma = (Y_1/Y)\gamma_1 + (Y_2/Y)\,\gamma_2 + Y_1/Y\,[\lambda_1(r_{k1} - r_k) + (1 - \lambda_1)]\,(r_{n1} - r_n)$$
$$+ Y_2/Y\,[\lambda_2(r_{k2} - r_k) + (1 - \lambda_2)]\,(r_{n2} - r_n)$$

where the subscripts denote one or the other of the two sectors. For example, Y_1/Y measures the importance of the first sector in total output, λ_1 represents the elasticity of output with respect to capital in the first sector, r_{k_1} represents the rate of growth of capital in the first sector (which may be negative), etc.

The first two terms measure the contribution of the rate of growth of productivity within a sector to the growth of overall productivity, while the last two measure the contribution of shifts in resources. However, it is possible to rewrite the expression to bring out the points discussed in the text. Thus:

$$\gamma = (Y_1/Y)\,\gamma_1 + (Y_2/Y_2)\gamma_2 + (N_1/Y)\,[1 - \lambda_1]\,(Y_1/N_2)$$
$$- (1 - \lambda_2)\,(Y_2/N_2)\,(r_{n1} - r_n) + (K_1/Y)\,[\lambda_1\,(Y_1/K_1) - \lambda_2\,(Y_2/K_2)]\,(r_{k1} - r_k),$$

where K_1 and N_1 represent capital and labor inputs in the first sector, and Y_1/N_1, Y_2/N_2, Y_1/K_1, and Y_2/K_2 represent average productivities of the inputs in their sectors.

Assume $\gamma_1 = \gamma_2 = 0$; i.e. the rate of growth of productivity within any sector is unresponsive to demand and zero. Further, assume that the expressions in the brackets are positive. Then it is still possible that $\gamma > 0$ provided that $r_{n1} - r_n > 0$ and/or $r_{k1} - r_k > 0$. Even in this case a higher rate of growth of demand can lead to an increase in the rate of growth of productivity, if it speeds up r_{n1} and r_{k1} relative to r_n and r_k. This is the effect of the rate of growth of demand on the rate of transfer of resources and, eventually, the overall rate of growth of productivity, γ, just discussed.

But there is an additional influence, whereby a higher rate of growth of demand speeds up the rate of growth of productivity within a sector (i.e., increases γ_1 or γ_2). Similar reasons why higher rates of growth of demand induce higher rates of growth of productivity within a sector are found in Lamfalussy, *op. cit.*, and T. Scitovsky, 'Economies of Scale and European Integration,' *American Economic Review*, March 1956. For the general methodology, see Massell, *op. cit.*

Chapter V Growing Needs and Family-Related Expenditures

A. Growing Needs and Growing Effective Demand; the General Problem

It will be recalled that in Chapter III an unexplained type of spending category, Z, was rather casually related to demographic growth, and then dropped. It was easily excluded from the analysis of Chapter IV since the long-run equilibrium of the system was dominated by factors growing in excess of the rate of growth of demographic variables. Some mention was made of the importance of demographic growth as support for the use of a ratchet term such as $\bar{Y}$ or X in the consumption function: a growing demographic base was singled out as a factor tending to generate strong booms and mild recessions because of its favorable effect on entrepreneurial expectations. However, it would be difficult to argue that a positive rate of growth of the population introduces an expansion bias, if there is not some mechanism whereby the growing needs associated with population growth are translated into growing demands and rising output. It will be recalled that a failure to make this mechanism explicit was a source of endless confusion and debate in the secular stagnation argument.

Chapter V serves an important function. It attempts to spell out in a more concrete and detailed manner the nature of the moving equilibrium discussed in the two previous chapters, emphasizing the manner in which growing needs become growing demands. This is facilitated by concentrating on those types of expenditure that are closely related to certain demographic characteristics of a population, including its growth rate. These 'family-related expenditures' comprise a large share of nonconsumption expenditures, and are important for this reason alone. In Chapter VII the discussion will take up the question of how expenditures that are closely related to demographic movements are affected by recessions. What will be argued is that family-related expenditures are, of the different spending categories, among the least sensitive to declines in the overall activity. Thus, population growth has an additional stabilizing role. It introduces an expansion bias into the system and, together with several other factors to be discussed, it is helpful in reversing downswings. Furthermore, in Chapter VI it is argued that the behavior of this type of spending plays a stabilizing role during boom periods.

After a few preliminary remarks on definitions, follows a short and rather general discussion of the influence on spending of the distribution of population by age and stages of the life cycle.[1] This notion of a family life cycle together with that of a demographic 'sausage machine' can then be brought in to show that in the moving equilibrium families in a more advanced stage of their life cycle 'pull' other economic groups into and through the earlier stages, thus preparing the latter for future movements. In this way, needs become demands, and the moving equilibrium of an economy can be discussed and described, so as to emphasize the influence of the composition of the population on the demand and supply sides of the market. The analysis is quite general in the sense that it applies to economies experiencing high, low or zero population growth.

B. Family-related Expenditures

The first problem is to give some meaning to the expression family-related expenditure, since ultimately all types of expenditures, whether by government, consumers or business, are somehow related to the demographic base. As the expression suggests, this type of spending is related to family formation. This would be true whether changes in the number of families arise from a change in the composition of a given population, or an increase in population. As a first step, we can sharpen the analysis by assuming that changes in the composition of a given population do not affect aggregate consumption; i.e. consumer expenditure on non-durables and services.[2] (Note that this does not

[1] Much of what is being said in the text applies to an economy experiencing a geographical redistribution of a fixed number of families. As we shall see in Chapters VI and VII, growth in reality is an unbalanced thing, with the spatial distribution of employment opportunities seldom if ever corresponding to the spatial distribution of families or the labor force. This has the effect of generating both internal and external migration of labor, leading to lags in the satisfying of family-related needs and demands. This, in turn, introduces a stabilizing influence on the economy. A positive rate of growth in the number of families merely strengthens these stabilizing effects.

[2] In many respects the term 'spending-unit related expenditures' might convey better the intent than 'family-related', but we will neglect such distinctions and use the less awkward expression. Unless otherwise stated, the terms 'households', 'families', and 'spending units' are used interchangeably. For a discussion of the distinctions between these concepts when they are precisely used, see Glick, Paul, *American Families*, John Wiley and Sons, Inc., New York, 1957, Appendix A.

mean that a change in the composition of a given population cannot affect total spending.) It will be argued that consumer investment outlays and spending by other sectors, both on current and capital account, will be very much influenced by changes in the composition of a population (whether growing or stationary).

Family-related expenditures will be defined as those nonconsumption expenditures which will provide services that are connected with and related to a particular locality occupied by families as a place of residence. Three different types of such spending can be distinguished, depending upon whether they are undertaken by consumers, business or government. First, there are those investment expenditures undertaken by consumer units themselves, that are related to setting up and maintaining a household. Typically, the services of those items of consumer capital formation are not shared between families (or spending units) but are shared within a family (although rising family incomes can and have led to multiple ownership of durables). Secondly, there are certain business investment outlays that are undertaken in order to provide services for a particular residential area, e.g. rental housing, some public utility investment and the construction of new suburban shopping centers. Finally, there are those expenditures by government bodies that provide services specific to some place of residence, e.g. school construction, teachers' salaries and outlays for public safety.[3] In contrast to consumer outlays, these government expenditures include outlays on current as well as capital account. What is included in this bundle of family-related expenditures will vary over time depending upon such things as income, tastes, access to credit, stage in life cycle, etc. For example, the amount of consumer investment undertaken by families today is much larger than that of fifty or one hundred years ago. In part, this reflects higher incomes but it also reflects a switch in preference toward (or availability of) private rather than public services. The discussion in this chapter will center around consumer capital formation and government outlays.

The consumer capital component of family-related expenditure is quantitatively the most important. Its increasing importance has already been noted

---

[3] Excluded from this category would for instance be defense spending, and investment as well as consumption by an auto company. As will presently be seen, any type of spending that can be explained without specifying some demographic trait of the population as an independent variable, is excluded. While rather vague, the text definition is a workable one. In any case: 'In science, we take care that the statements we make should never *depend* upon the meaning of our terms. Even where the terms are defined, we never try to derive any information from the definition, or to base any arguments upon it. This is why our terms make so little trouble. We do not overburden them. We try to attach to them as little weight as possible. We do not take their "meaning" too seriously. We are always conscious that our terms are a little vague (since we have learned to use them only in practical applications) and we reach precision not by reducing their penumbra of vagueness, but rather by keeping well within it, by carefully phrasing our sentences in such a way that the possible shades of meaning of our terms do not matter. This is how we avoid quarreling about words.' Popper, K., *The Open Society and Its Enemies*, Princeton University Press, 1950, p. 216.

in Chapter II.[4] However, 'consumer investment' outlays ignore rental housing and other important types of family-related expenditures. One method of getting a better measure of family-related investment is to introduce the notion of 'house-induced' investment, which arises from the concept that certain types of investment (in this case housing) induce other types of investment. The construction of a dwelling unit is likely to induce other types of private and public construction which can be broken down into two types: 'house-connected' investment, e.g. public utility outlays; and 'house-oriented' investment, e.g. stores, restaurants and garages, and investment in educational facilities.[5] As the examples suggest, these induced types of investment are undertaken both by the business and government sectors. However, these expenditures, at least in some long-run equilibrium sense, are really best thought of as different kinds of family-related expenditures, since, in a situation where vacancies, withdrawals from the housing stock and conversions add up to zero, the number of dwelling units started and new households formed are by definition equal. These outlays, as well as some of those items of consumer capital just discussed, rental housing and certain other government expenditures, must be considered in order to arrive at the full impact of family formation on family-related expenditures, and the effect of the former on the nature of the moving equilibrium.

When it is a matter of measuring the quantitative importance of this spending category, it seems best not to include all consumer capital formation and all house-induced investment under the heading 'family-related expenditures'. Not all public utility investment is undertaken to service a place of residence. Public utility sales (net of those provided by transportation firms) to residental users amount to less than 50 per cent of total sales in the United States, and not all investment in stores, restaurants, etc. can be attributed to the need to provide services connected with family formation and residential housing. On the other hand, much is excluded when, say, only the construction expenditures of state and local governments are included, since this ignores the large current expenditures component that is family-related. There seems to be no clear cut attitude to take here, so that what is excluded and what is included must be somewhat arbitrary. Under the general heading of family-related expenditures we will include: consumer investment in 'household furnishings and equipment', 'residential buildings' (nonfarm), 'commercial investment in stores, restaurants and garages', 'other nonresidential buildings' (private) and, for the public sector, construction of 'residential buildings', 'education, and hospitals and institutional nonresidential build-

---

[4] See Table 2.1, p. 25.

[5] Mattila, J., and Thompson, W., 'Residential-Service Construction: A Study of Induced Investments', *The Review of Economics and Statistics*, November 1965. In this study the authors argue that house-connected investment occurs simultaneously with housing construction, while house-oriented construction tends to lag behind it. A lag of one year for schools, private hospitals, churches and social and recreational facilities is suggested, together with a longer lag of two years for municipal highways and public hospitals.

Diagram 5.1

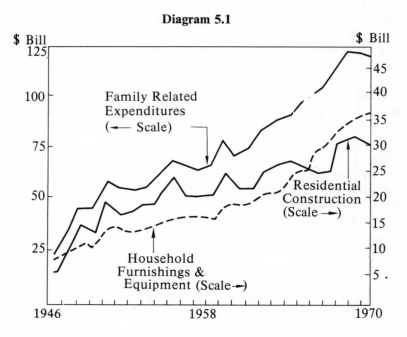

Sources: *U. S. Dept. of Commerce, Construction Reports—Value of New Construction Put in Place*, various issues. U.S. Dept. of Commerce, *Survey of Current Business*, various issues.

ings', 'sewer and water systems', and all current outlays. From time to time, public utility and some forms of business investment can be included as a reminder that other outlays very much related to family formation have been excluded from the category.[6]

The post World War II behavior of total family-related investment, so defined, is shown in Diagram 5.1 with two of its more important sub-categories: residential buildings and one of the consumer investment components. As is clear, a strong trend is introduced into the American system by the behavior of these types of spending. During the postwar period, family-related expenditures were over one-tenth of GNP. Since total spending other than consumption is approximately 45 per cent of GNP this means that about one-fourth of the offsets to the 'leakages' fall within the meaning of the term 'family-related expenditures'.

[6] Most of the categories are taken from the breakdown of construction found in issues of *Construction Review*, U.S. Department of Commerce. Equipment investment by business and government related to family formation must unfortunately be left out. Estimates of consumer investment in household furnishings and equipment are those of the Department of Commerce published in the *Survey of Current Business*. It will be noted that consumer purchases of autos has been excluded. This is somewhat arbitrary, since part of annual auto sales are certainly related to family formation. However, such a high percentage of auto purchases is unrelated to family formation *per se* and since auto purchases play such a small stabilizing role they have been excluded from our measure.

C. Demographic Traits and Their Influence on the Economy

Formally, the influence of demographic movements on spending in Chapter III was written as $Z_t = Z_0(1+r)^t$ where r represented the rate of growth of the population, labor force and number of families, given certain assumptions about sociological patterns and the age composition of the population. This simple method of handling demographic growth was used only for convenience, since the long-run behavior of the system was dominated by other forces, and a more general and realistic 'explanation' of the influence of demographic movements would only have confused things. Now matters are quite different. Write: $Z_0 = er/(1+r)F_0$ and $F_t = F_0(1+r)^t$, F representing the number of families giving: $Z_t = er/(1+r)F_t = e\Delta F_t$. Thus, the very casual connection between Z_t and demographic growth posited in Chapter III implicitly assumed that the ratios of family-related expenditures to both the number and changes in the number of families are constants in equilibrium. Alternatively, Z_t/Y_t must fall secularly, since Y_t grows at rate: $r_y = \rho + r_n$. More importantly, the use of the expression: $Z_t = Z_0(1+r)^t$ assumes that there is always a perfect adjustment between family formation, and expenditures which are induced by family formation. This could arise only when the system is on its long-run equilibrium growth path, but even then the expression has no explanatory power.

An alternative expression suggests itself for explaining family-related investment outlays, which has the benefit of being simple and appropriate both in equilibrium and when off the long-run path. The basic model is simply a variant of the capital stock adjustment mechanism. Total family-related investment is broken into two parts; net investment $I^{c'}$, and depreciation ($=$replacement), $I^{c''}$. Net investment is a function of the difference between the desired stock of capital (variously defined), $\hat{K}^c$, and the actual stock, K^c. Current consumption can be expressed as $I^{c''} = \gamma K^c$ where γ is the rate of depreciation. For convenience the equation can be written as before in its simplest form as $I^c = \pi(\hat{K}^c - K^c) + \gamma K^c$, where π is a reaction coefficient.[7]

[7] See Stone, R., and Rowe, D. A., 'Market Demand for Durable Goods', *Econometrica*, July 1957, and 'The Durability of Consumers' Durable Goods', *Econometrica*, April 1960. In Arnold Harberger (Ed.), *The Demand for Durable Goods*, University of Chicago Press, Chicago, 1960, the same type of model is employed using *per capita* permanent income and expenditure variables together with various measures of cost. Other models employ a logarithmic form of the capital stock adjustment model. Alternatively a very similar type of function can be derived from a permanent income theory applied to consumer durables. Assume that the stock of consumer durables is proportioned to a moving average of past levels of income (i.e., permanent income), such that:

$$K^c = \sigma' \sum_{i=0}^{\infty} \lambda^i Y_{t-i-1}$$

with $0 < \lambda < 1$. Using the Koyck transformation we obtain:

$$I_t^{c'} = \sigma' Y_{t-1} - (1-\lambda)K_{t-1}^c$$

or

$$I_t^c = \sigma' Y_{t-1} - (1-\lambda-\gamma)K_{t-1}^c$$

with $(1-\lambda)$ equivalent to π in the text formulation.

It should be noted that these types of models are only applicable to market demand when consumer investment outlays are considered, since indivisibilities prevent marginal adjustments by individual consumer units when desired stocks diverge from actual.[8]

If the desired capital stock is made a function solely of income, the capital stock adjustment equation is no different from that used earlier for business, and this seems incorrect.[9] We are dealing with investment that will provide services for families, and would expect the desired capital stock to be a function of certain demographic traits of population as well. Furthermore, previous studies suggest the importance in this type of analysis of price, attitudinal and liquid asset variables, various measures of credit conditions and, as we shall see presently, 'outside grants'. However, the concern here is with the influence of demographic variables on demand and, therefore, most factors other than income and demographic variables can be neglected. Thus, introduce time explicitly and write: $\hat{K}_t^c = f(Y_{t-1}, V_t)$ where V_t is as yet some unspecified set of demographic influences, giving: $I_t^c = \pi[f(Y_{t-1}. V_t) - K_{t-1}^c] + \gamma K_{t-1}^c$.[10] The question is to determine the relevant set of demographic influences represented by the expression, V_t.

Many times series studies, including the large econometric models, utilize a single variable such as the size of the population, to pick up the influence of demographic movements on various types of family-related expenditures, without regard to the distribution of this demographic base by, say, age, family composition, housing tenure, color, etc. However, to take the most obvious example even if outlays per family or household did not vary by age group, changes in the age composition of the population could have an appreciable effect on family-related spending. The matter is seen clearly with the help of the data in Table 5.1. Define the headship rate of the ith class as

[8] There have been several attempts to circumvent this problem using cross section data. Two of the more recent are: De-min Wu, 'An Empirical Analysis of Household Durable Goods Expenditure', *Econometrica*, October 1965, and Huang, David, 'Discrete Stock Adjustment: The Case of Demand for Automobiles', *International Economic Review*, January 1964.

[9] The Brookings Quarterly Econometric Model uses no demographic variable to explain purchases of cars or 'other durables.' An income variable, the relevant stock variable lagged, and an attitudinal variable in the former case and a liquid asset variable in the latter, make up the independent variables. On the other hand, the models for the housing market and government capital outlays are much more complicated. The former employs the change in the number of new households as one of the explanatory variables (which is itself a dependent variable), but neglects to include a stock variable. See Duesenberry, J., *et al.* (Eds.), *The Brookings Quarterly Econometric Model of the United States*, Rand McNally & Co., Chicago, 1965, Chapters 6 and 7. The Wharton Model gives no consideration to demographic variables in any of the equations for 'family-related expenditures.' See Evans, M. K. and Klein, L., *The Wharton Econometric Forecasting Model*, Wharton School of Finance & Commerce, University of Pennsylvania, 1967.

[10] The income variable used in the text was chosen purely for purposes of illustration. Other studies have used variations of Friedman's permanent income variable, feeling that temporary changes in actual income in the current or previous period are less relevant than some moving average. See Harberger, *op. cit.*

Table 5.1

Age of household head	Headship rate	
	1950	*1967*
	(per cent)	(per cent)
Under 25	3·2	3·9
25–34	36·3	46·1
35–44	44·6	49·9
45–54	49·0	52·6
55 or over	52·2	58·7

Source: *Historical Statistics of the United States,* pp. 8, 14.

the ratio of household heads to total number of people in the ith class. Then Table 5.1 indicates how headship rates vary by age of household head for two postwar years. Taking the headship rates for 1967 for example, if a population of 500 is distributed equally between the five age categories, this will result in 211 households, If, instead, the population is predominantly in the lower age groups, such that 160 people fall into each of the two youngest categories and the remaining 180 are distributed equally among the older classes, the projected number of households falls to 177.

More formally, the use of the headship rate concept in estimating present and future needs for, say, housing is seen as follows. Given some assumed headship rates and various projected age distributions of the population, changes in the number of households are easily forecast. If α_i represents the headship rate of the ith class (where $i = 1; 2 \ldots n$), and P_{it} represents the number of people in the ith class in period t, then $\sum_{i=1}^{n} \alpha_i P_{it}$ represents 'housing needs' in period t and $\sum_{i=1}^{n} \alpha_i P_{it+1} - \sum_{i=1}^{n} \alpha_i P_{it}$ represents the additional needs in $t + 1$ assuming headship rates unchanged. As a predictor of the actual number of new households formed, changes in effective demand, new housing units started, and as a possible (partial) explanation of family-related investment outlays, its success will depend upon the accuracy of the headship rates assumed, and economic conditions, some of which affect headship rates.[11] But even so, these exercises suggest at the very least taking into account the number of households in trying to define the desired stock of family-related capital.

[11] This method of explaining or forecasting housing demand is based on Campbell, B. O., 'Long Swings in Residential Construction: The Postwar Experience', *American Economic Review*, Papers and Proceedings, May 1963.

D. Consumer Investment Outlays and the Family Life Cycle

Differences in headship rates for age groups point up the importance of the age composition as a determinant of demand for housing, as well as other items of family-related capital formation. But this approach is always limited. Even if it could be assumed that headship rates do not vary over time, such an approach only predicts needs for (and physical quantity demanded of) dwelling units.[12] As a forecasting tool, it does not attempt to predict the amount spent on housing even in the special case where there is no speculative building, no large number of vacancies and no downswing in the economy. Even this would involve additional information on how expenditures vary between families with different demographic and other characteristics. Various studies employing cross-section data have attempted to pick up the importance of demographic traits on expenditures. Age, place of residence, race and stage of the life cycle have been singled out as significant causes of differences in spending patterns between households or families. This is suggested in a general way by Diagram 5.2, where households are classified by age of head.[13] On the vertical axis is measured the age of the husband of a married couple while the horizontal axis measures the per cent of any group so defined displaying certain characteristics. The data is taken from the 1960's. For example, the lines 'families with own home' and 'families who rent' show the per cent of families by age group that own or rent. The difference between 100 per cent and the sum of these two percentages represents households without a home of their own. This tends to fall rapidly from the first to second age class, indicating a sizeable increase in the disposition of married couples either to rent or buy a house of their own. The relative higher percentage of young families without a home of their own suggests that not all family formations need generate much in the way of family-related expenditures. The marked increase in home ownership with age, until old age is reached, also is to be expected. The diagram indicates clearly that tenure arrangements vary consistently with age. More to the point, housing expenditures will then also vary with age of household head, since the average cost of an apartment is roughly one half that of an owner-occupied dwelling. The remaining line tells something about the changing composition of families as a function of age. The number of families with children under

[12] This is merely to say that other variables such as income, stock of housing, etc., are also needed to explain current investment. On the other hand some of the determinants of expenditures such as the distribution of dwelling units between apartment and single family units are related to age and would be partially picked up by taking account of the age distribution of the population.

[13] The family concept used to measure with or without household is 'married couples', that for measuring percentage with children of a certain age, 'husband-wife families'; and that for the per cent owning their own home, 'husband-wife primary families'. See Glick, *op. cit.*, Appendix A for the meanings of these related terms. As the expression 'family without own home' suggests, a household can contain more than one family.

Diagram 5.2

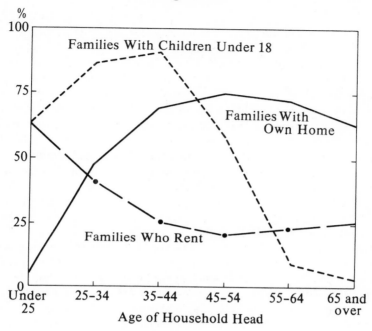

Source: George Katona *et al.*, *1966 Survey of Consumer Finances*, Institution for Social Research, The University of Michigan.

18 rises during the childbearing years and falls drastically after age 44, at which point we see the first step in the dissolution of the family. Changes in the composition of a family which are a function of age can be expected to have an important influence on all types of consumer investment outlays.

The matter can be approached in a slightly different manner. It can be argued that, to use the age composition of the population in some manner as an independent variable influencing spending, is to use a proxy for the 'true' explanatory variable: namely, the stage of the life cycle.

From one point of view the use of the life cycle as an explanatory variable in an investigation of economic behavior may be regarded as an alternative to the use of age, age being expressed in calendar years. The stage at which an individual finds himself in the life cycle is, of course, related to his age. Hence any variable strongly related to the one is certainly to be related to the other.

Which to use in a particular investigation must depend on the problem at hand. In an investigation of such a topic as housing, the direct causal relationship is probably between the life cycle stage and type of housing. That is, one may become interested in buying a house for the first time at the age of 29. But it is not the fact that one is 29 which makes an apartment seem inadequate; it is the fact that one has a wife and two children. True, more men aged 29 than aged 21 have a wife and two children, and in this sense a man may be said to be interested in buying a house because he is 29. The causal sequence runs from calendar age to stage in the life cycle to the desire to buy a house.[14]

This notion of a life cycle, and the association of certain consumer investment outlays, is not to be confused with what has come to be known as the life cycle hypothesis of consumer behavior. The latter is an attempt to explain expenditures on nondurables and services (plus depreciation of durables), while the studies summarized here are concerned with consumer investment outlays, which include housing as well as consumer durables.[15] The life cycle begins with the setting up of a separate household accompanied or followed by marriage, and continues throughout the lifetime of the husband and wife with appropriate subdivisions for the birth of children and the eventual departure, change in home ownership status, change in place of residence, etc.[16] Each of the subdivisions marks a rather drastic change in the life of the family unit. With each change it could be expected that pronounced alterations in spending, ownership and even work patterns would take place.

A common method of life cycle stage classification is to subdivide families or spending units according to whether the head is over or under 45, married or single, and if married, whether or not he has children, and of what age. Each of these stages can then be related to certain economic traits. In Diagram 5.3 cross section data have been used to depict the relationship between stage of the life cycle, and the proportion of the families in that stage in the sample who possess a certain characteristic. For example, the tenure status of families changes more slowly from rental to home ownership as a family moves through the stages than does car ownership, where the probability of ownership reaches its maximum by the second stage. The likelihood of being faced with instalment debt follows a somewhat different pattern (although the likelihood of having 'large' amounts of indebtedness, i.e., above some absolute level, shows a profile more similar to that of home ownership).

[14] See Lansing, J., and Morgan, J., 'Consumer Finances over the Life Cycle', *Consumer Behavior*, Vol. II, New York University Press, 1955, p. 38. The Survey Research Center of the Institute for Social Research at The University of Michigan conducts annual surveys that employ extensively the life cycle concept.

[15] See Ando, A., and Modigliani, F., 'The "Life Cycle" Hypothesis of Saving: Aggregate Implications and Tests', *American Economic Review*, March 1963. One consumption function derived in their study very much resembles the one developed in Chapter III, with the size of the labor force instead of maximum output used as an independent variable.

[16] In one study only 4 per cent of those in the sample failed to fit into a neat orderly progression, because of such things as failure to marry, early death of one spouse, etc. See Lansing, John, and Kish, Leslie, 'Family Life Cycle as an Independent Variable', *American Sociological Review*, October 1957, p. 513. The authors argue that while age and stage of the life cycle are correlated, the latter is the 'more powerful' independent variable. This is certainly borne out by their comparison of the influence of age versus life cycle stage on the likelihood of home ownership by elderly people, and the likelihood of the wife of a couple working.

Diagram 5.3

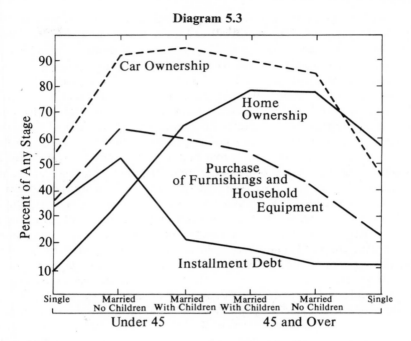

Source: G. Katona, *et al.*, *1966 Survey of Consumer Finances*, Institute for Social Research, The University of Michigan, 1967, Tables 2-3, 3-2, 4-17, 5-2.

Taken together the findings build up a general picture of young married people buying homes, cars and all sorts of household appliances. Coming at a time when the spending unit income is still rising and 'below normal', these outlays exert heavy pressure on the family's liquid assets which tends to be relieved by the use of credit, not only for house purchases, but for the car and durables as well.[17]

The influence of life cycle stage is also revealed in terms of the proportion of any group in some stage making purchases. Diagram 5.3 indicates that the first two stages mark a critical transition in the purchase of home furnishings and large household appliances or equipment, in the sense that a large increase in the probability of purchase between the single and married with no children stage takes place. There is additional evidence that not only moving from one stage depicted in Diagram 5.3 to the next is critical in this sense, but that even within a stage certain events may induce additional outlays. Thus, in one study, holding income (but not current stocks held, tenure or age) constant, the probability of purchase of a refrigerator, stove and TV set has been found to rise in a pronounced fashion as family size increases from one to two. On the other hand, the probability of purchase

[17] Lansing and Morgan, *op. cit.*, p. 47.

of a washing machine, dryer and deep freezer shows a large increase when family size increases from two to three for the first item, and from three to four for the last two. This suggests a substitution of home services for commercial services within a stage when family composition changes. It also suggests a certain ordering in the purchase of durables, as has indeed been borne out by other studies. What is being suggested here is that the nature of the ordering is very much related to certain basic characteristics of the family and its circumstances.[18] There is no reason to believe that these results would be any different if age or life cycle stage had been held constant. Indeed, there is every indication that holding these constant while allowing family size to vary would bring out more clearly the importance of changes in household circumstances. For the difficulty with using the number of persons in a household as an explanation of differences in spending patterns, without holding age or life cycle stage constant, is that it tends to introduce a mixed bag. For example, a two-person household can be a young married or a retired couple. Taking account of family size merely introduces a more detailed amount of subclassification than that depicted in Diagram 5.3.

Unfortunately, the studies that attempt to measure the importance of demographic traits on investment outlays do not for the most part take account of current stocks held.[19] Without holding stocks constant, a given sample might show no significant change in the probability of purchase between one stage and the next, when in actual fact the probability would be very much affected if stocks were taken into account. To some extent the influence of stocks held can be captured by holding age of household head or stage of life cycle constant, since first purchases will be correlated with age or life cycle stage. But to get any sort of true measure of the importance of certain demographic characteristics of a population, some account has to be taken of current stocks.

Finally it should be noted that, as incomes rise relative to the cost of consumer capital items, and as built-in economic obsolescence becomes an important feature for these items, replacement expenditures will become a larger proportion of total outlays.[20] This will tend to make changes in the

[18] See David, Martin, *Family Composition and Consumption*, North-Holland Publishing Company, Amsterdam, 1962, Chapter 4. A pattern of ordering similar to David's was found by Paroush, J., 'The Order of Acquisition of Consumer Durables', *Econometrica*, January 1965. A different sequence was found by Pyatt. The difference is perhaps accounted for by differences in cultural patterns between countries. See Pyatt, F. G., *Priority Patterns and the Demand for Household Durable Goods*, Cambridge University Press, Cambridge, 1964.

[19] An exception is Schipper, L., *Consumer Discretionary Behavior*, North Holland Publishing Co., Amsterdam, 1964. Time series studies are more likely to include some measure of stocks held, although the distribution of stocks held by, say, life cycle stage is more to the point.

[20] In one study replacement expenditures for house furnishings and equipment amounted to 70 per cent of total expenditure in a period covering the years 1929–1956. See Lippitt, Vernon, *Determinants of Consumer Demand for House Furnishings and Equipment*, Harvard University Press, 1959, p. 109.

distribution of households by life cycle stages less important in explaining differences in aggregate outlays. But given the present levels of affluence, and the items of consumer capital we have chosen to include under family-related expenditures, the importance of first purchases associated with moving from one 'critical stage' to another must still loom very large as a per cent of total purchases. This has important implications for stability, since the motives behind and the ability and willingness to postpone first purchases can be assumed to be different from those associated with replacement outlays. There would certainly be less tendency to postpone expenditures during recessions if they are first purchases, than if they are replacements.

Ideally, then, our set of demographic traits summed up on V_t should at least include the number of families or households, and the distribution of those families either by age or stage of their life cycle. While changes in the distribution by either of these traits may or may not affect consumption, they will certainly affect consumer investment outlays. The analysis could be further refined by subdividing the married with children categories according to the number of people in the family. How properly to weight the different subgroups in order to come up with some sort of distributional demographic variable is another matter. Clearly the under-45 married groups will stimulate more family-related expenditures than either the over-45 group or the young bachelors. Any bulge or decline in the high investment household groups is bound to cause important changes in demand pressures. Fortunately, in order to describe the manner in which growing needs become growing demands in the moving equilibrium, it is possible to ignore entirely this problem of weighting different family types because of their different spending patterns.[21]

E. Growing Needs, Demands and the Demographic Sausage Machine

The manner in which the growing needs of a growing population are satisfied can be seen more clearly if only the consumer investment component of family-related expenditures is considered. Later in the chapter the government sector will be treated in a similar manner.[22] For this purpose, assume

[21] Lippitt is one of the very few investigators to try to quantify the importance of changes in the demographic composition of the population. He utilizes analysis of variance techniques on cross-section data to try to estimate the importance of changes in the distribution of population by such traits as occupation, place of residence, income and family type. The latter is a fairly elaborate life cycle classification. This he converts to a 'combined distributional effect' variable. See Lippitt, *op. cit.*, Chapters III and IV.

[22] Introducing the other family-related expenditure components in the formal model would only increase the order of the system and add little to our understanding. The effect of demographic movements on different types of business investment, while important, is almost entirely ignored.

initially that the age composition of the population is constant. In such a situation it is only the number of families that need be included in the analysis in order to pick up the demographic influences on spending. Let I' represent all non-consumption spending other than I^c, and r_f the rate growth of the number of families (equal to the rate of growth of the population). Then we can write as a modified version of the model developed in Chapter III:

$$C_t = mY_t + nX_t, \qquad (1)$$

$$I'_t = bY_{t-1} - cK'_{t-1}, \qquad (2)$$

$$I^c_t = uY_{t-1} - vK^c_{t-1} + wV_t, \qquad (3)$$

$$Y_t = C_t + I'_t + I^{c_1}_t, \qquad (4)$$

$$K'_t = I'_t + K'_{t-1} \qquad (5)$$

$$K^c_t = I^{c_1}_t + K^c_{t-1}, \qquad (6)$$

$$I^c_t - I^{c_1}_t = \gamma K^c_t, \qquad (7)$$

$$X_t = X_0(1 + r_x)^t, \qquad (8)$$

$$V_t = V_0(1 + r_f)^t. \qquad (9)$$

Alternatively the more complicated response of supply to demand developed in Chapter IV could be substituted for equation (8). The former model has as its solution:

$$Y_t = Y^E_{1t} + Y^E_{2t} + D_1(x_1)^t + D_2(x_2)^t + D_3(x_3)^t,$$

where x_1, x_2, and x_3 are the roots obtained from the endogenous part of the model; i.e. equations (1″) through (7) with X_t and V_t surpressed. Y^E_{1t} and Y^E_{2t} are particular solutions where: $Y^E_{1t} = EX_t$ and $Y^E_{2t} = FV_t$, E and F being constants. Y^E_{1t} dominates the long-run behavior of the model, since $X_t = X_0(1 + r_x)^t = X_0(1 + \rho + r_n)^t > V_t = V_0(1 + r_f)^t$. As the rate of growth of r_x is by definition equal to the sum of the rate of growth of the labor force, r_n, and labor productivity, ρ, we can write: $r_n = r_x - \rho$. And since the rate of growth of employment, r_{ne}, must be equal to the rate of growth of demand minus the rate of growth of labor productivity, we have: $r_{ne} = r_y - \rho$. But $r_y = r_x$, and therefore $r_{ne} = r_n$. In other words, demand in the moving equilibrium grows at a rate sufficient to ensure that employment grows at the same rate as the labor force, the number of families, population and, therefore, needs.

Consider now a division of this growing population into different stages of the life cycle, all groups growing at the same rate. In other words, we can think of a stage in the life cycle of a typical (future) family head just prior to the family formation stage where he enters the labor force, finds employment, develops skills, possibly accumulates assets and prepares for marriage. This can be followed by another stage in which families are formed and separate housekeeping units set up. This could be followed by yet another stage when children are born and raised and additional family-related expenditures undertaken, finally followed by the dissolution of the family, first by children leaving home and eventually by death.

If we make the useful pedagogical assumption that the unemployed are always new entrants to the labor force, then the constancy of the unemployment rate along the long-run growth path, together with the absence of certain constraints to be discussed in Chapters VI and VII, allows for this orderly progression of each family through the life cycle stages. Adverse economic circumstances do not intervene to cause families on the average to postpone movements from one stage to the next. The number of people in each of the stages of the life cycle will also be growing at the same rate in equilibrium, whatever the age of movements from one stage to the next.

This allows the moving equilibrium to be depicted in terms of a demographic 'sausage machine' whereby a growing number of families at certain stages in the life cycle induce a growing level of expenditure, which helps to generate rising per family (or capita) demands of the same magnitude as the growth of *per capita* income and productivity. This helps to ensure that the rate of growth of aggregate demand is sufficient to absorb new entrants into the labor force (the lag between entrance to the labor force and gainful employment being a function of the unemployment rate), thus preparing them for movements through the next stage of their life cycle. It is true that there is a lag between the time that a person enters the labor force and the time that his future family needs induce some family-related expenditures. But even though the additions to the labor force (or supply) are different from the families that are generating growth in demand related to stages in the life cycle, the growing needs of the new entrants to the labor force result in growing effective demand, partly because more established spending units are providing them with employment through the initial and secondary multiplier effects of their spending.

F. Population Growth and the Composition of Output

A little comparative dynamics is helpful in drawing some concluding remarks on the nature of the equilibrium path. Take two mature economies that differ only in that in one population growth proceeds at a higher rate than in the other, say, twice as rapidly. Again assume that the age composition is fixed in both economies. Then, if the rate of growth of labor productivity, ρ, is independent of the rate of growth of the population, and the same in both economies, *per capita* income will grow at the same rate in both, while aggregate income will be higher in the economy experiencing the more rapid demographic growth. The difference, of course, is the difference in the rate of growth of the latter. If, now, a more or less fixed long-run relationship can be assumed between the stock of family related capital, K^c, and income (or total capital and income for that matter), i.e., $K^c/Y = \beta$, then there will be some long-run accelerator relationship such that: $I^c = \beta \Delta Y$ or $I^c/Y = \beta \Delta Y/Y = \beta(\rho + r_n)$. In other words, the composition of output will be more heavily weighted toward non-consumption output and expenditures in the economy experiencing high population growth. Because of this, the economy with the more rapid population growth will have a lower rate of unemployment over the cycle, other things being equal. In Chapters VI and VII this added tightness in the labor and capital markets will contribute to stability in an additional way.

While *per capita* incomes will grow at the same rate, the level of *per capita* consumption will be lower in the high population growth economy if *per capita* incomes are initially the same. But now assume that labor productivity and population growth are positively related. In terms of Diagram 4.1 in Chapter IV, entrepreneurs may be more prone to move the economy close to point C if risks are reduced because of more rapid population growth. Then, while it is doubly true that I^c/Y will be higher in the economy with the more rapid population growth, *per capita* consumption might well be higher whatever the initial levels of income and consumption.[23]

Whether labor productivity is positively related to demographic growth or not, a higher rate of growth of the population—especially when this implies higher rates of growth of all age groups—will have the effect of increasing the long-run equilibrium rate of growth of demand and supply by the same amount. A more rapid growth of needs will be accompanied by a more rapid growth in effective demand and output, as the demographic 'sausage machine' works whatever the rate of growth of the demographic variables. This is in marked contrast to the rigid separation of demand and supply sides of the market in the Harrod–Domar models, and adds an element of stability to the system as suggested earlier.[24] For example, a higher rate of growth of the population and labor force does not merely increase the rate of growth of the full employment ceiling but also the rate of growth of demand.

G. Family-related Government Outlays

A large part of government expenditure, especially at the state and local level, plays a similar role to these consumer investment outlays. In addition to having a strong influence on consumer investment outlays, demographic growth and changes in the distribution of the population by age and life cycle stage have an important influence on government outlays on capital and also current account. These expenditures (or a large part of them) respond to the needs of the economy in the same way as consumer investment outlays, and should be treated as endogenous. This suggests that we might

[23] See the arguments summarized earlier in Chapter II, p. 35.
[24] See pp. 37 and 46.

proceed on similar lines to those followed in previous sections, in explaining capital outlays of government at least. There are some important differences however.

In America a financial arrangement between the different levels of government has arisen, and has come to be known as 'fiscal federalism'. Because of the nature of the type of taxes collected historically by different levels of government, and because of the desire of states and local governments to remain 'competitive', state and local receipts had a tendency to rise more slowly than the needs traditionally satisfied by these governments. As a result, grants-in-aid, first by state governments to locals, then from the federal government to the states, and finally from the federal level to the local governments, have become increasingly important sources of revenue for state and local governments. And it is the latter who typically disburse funds for programs related to demographic characteristics of the population.[25]

This increasing dependence of a lower level of government on a higher one means, for our purposes, that an important determinant of family-related government outlays will be the amount of such grants-in-aid. The exact effect on state and local government spending of outside financing is still a matter of controversy, but there is little in the way of a counterpart for the consumer sector.[26] In addition other demographic characteristics of the population have been considered important in explaining government outlays; e.g. the degree of urbanization, population density, the size of the school age population, etc.[27] Finally some sort of income restraint has been suggested, since legal restrictions require the financing of current expenditures out of current tax receipts, while legal limits to indebtedness may constrain capital outlays.

But changes in the demographic characteristics of a population will still have a pronounced effect on government family-related outlays, as they will for those by private outlays for consumers. Earlier, the 25–45-year-old age group was singled out as the group likely to generate large amounts of family-related types of consumer investment expenditures. An important influence on state and local expenditures would be the number or per cent of the population less than, say, 18 years of age. Or the division could be more detailed. With *per capita* expenditure requirements higher for high school pupils than elementary school, the ratio of high school to elementary school pupils will show up as a significant factor explaining differences in *per capita* expenditures

---

[25] Funds for education, welfare services, hospitals, health, police and fire protection and sanitation are examples of this kind.

[26] See Osman, J. W., 'The Dual Impact of Federal Aid on State and Local Government Expenditures', *National Tax Journal*, December 1966; Smith, D. L., 'The Response of State and Local Governments to Federal Grants', *National Tax Journal*, September 1968, and Pogue, T. F., and Sgontz, L. G., 'The Effect of Grants-in-aid on State-Local Spending', *National Tax Journal*, June 1968.

[27] The pioneering work is that by Fabricant, S., *Trends of Government Activity in the United States Since 1900*, National Bureau of Economic Research, New York, 1952.

between localities.[28] Over time we would expect any bulge in the numbers in the lower age groups to generate a corresponding increase in educational outlays. This is likely to be especially true for capital outlays. Public assistance payments to the needy aged point up the importance of shifts in the composition of the population towards the opposite end of the age distribution.

The analogy with consumer investment outlays can be pushed further. It has just been suggested that there might be an ordering in the purchase of those consumer investment outlays that is closely related to the stage of the life cycle and other social and demographic circumstances. It is fairly easy to envisage an ordering process for government goods and services connected with these same circumstances. A family is formed and a place of residence acquired. This will generate the need for certain municipal services; e.g., streets and roads, public utility facilities, police and fire protection, etc. With the advent of children, educational services are soon required. From the cradle to the grave depending upon custom, technology, income levels and the extent of development of the welfare state, the need for certain public services will be evident and these needs must be satisfied.

Thus, in constructing a model that explains current additions to capacity, we can think of capital outlays by state and local governments (either *per capita*, per family or in the aggregate) as being a function of the discrepancy between desired and actual stocks of government capital, where the former is partly a function of some of the influences already mentioned (e.g., certain demographic traits of the population, V_t, and grants-in-aid). This can be expanded to allow the desired capital stock to be a function of the price of the durable good to be bought, an income or 'ability to pay' variable such as tax receipts, an assessed or market value of the community's property, or a measure that attempts to take into account income and wealth such as the yield of a representative tax system.[29]

Because of the important role played by the property tax in local government financing, either the assessed or economic value of property could also be considered as a possible independent variable. There is also the possibility of capital outlays being postponed or dropped, because of legal limitations on the amount of indebtedness permitted a local government. However, this financial constraint has been weakened somewhat by the increased propensity of state and local governments to (a) bypass legal debt limits by shifting financial responsibility for projects to other less restricted units, or even

[28] Hirsch, W., 'Determinants of Public Education Expenditures', *National Tax Journal*, March, 1960.
[29] In one study the *per capita* desired stock of capital was made a distributed lag function of income, relative prices, an interest rate and certain demographic variables. In the regression runs the distribution of the population was taken into account in explaining *per capita* state and local capital outlays and 'other purchases and employee compensation', while transfer payments were made a function of an unemployment variable. See Gramlich, E. M., 'State and Local Governments and Their Budget Constraint', *International Economic Review*, June 1969.

newly created 'quasi-governments'; and (*b*) to issue non-guaranteed debt.[30] There are obviously other factors influencing state and local expenditures, especially in the short run, but as with consumer investment outlays they may be ignored at this point.

Having then defined the desired stock of government capital, investment outlays can then be viewed as a process to correct any discrepancy between desired and actual stocks. A capital stock adjustment model for state and local government capital expenditures, together with an equation describing current outlays, can be incorporated into a formal model in much the same way as for consumer investment outlays.

H. Government Outlays and Receipts on the Moving Equilibrium Path

For the sake of illustration, let the desired stock of public capital be a linear function of certain demographic traits, the price of capital goods, grants-in-aid, income and the ratio of existing debt to assessed property values; and let tax receipts be some fixed proportion of income. Assume that the demographic composition of the population is fixed, so that changes in the latter are not allowed to generate fluctuations in different sorts of family-related expenditures in the absence of shocks. If the price of capital goods purchased remains constant, and income, wealth and grants-in-aid grow at more or less the same rate in the moving equilibrium, then government outlays on current and capital account, tax receipts and government debt will also grow at the same rate.[31] Like the growing demand for the services provided by consumer capital, there will be a growing demand for public services corresponding to the growing needs generated by a growing population. Since the financing of these demands and needs is forthcoming in the moving equilibrium, these needs will be satisfied.

All of this leads to a kind of balanced growth situation, while in the United States the record clearly indicated a more rapid growth of state and local government expenditures than GNP. To a large extent this imbalance has been made possible by a much more rapid growth of grants-in-aid to these government units. So as not to overstate magnitudes, assume that all

---

[30] See Mitchell, W. E., 'The Effectiveness of Debt Limits on State and Local Government Borrowings', *The Bulletin, No. 45*, October 1967, Institute of Finance, New York University.

[31] A more detailed and formal model that takes into account budgetary constraints is found in Gramlich, *op. cit.* Netzer, among others, makes certain simplifying assumptions about the likely behavior over time of certain key variables, and then derives the implications. For example, given certain assumed values for the responsiveness of taxes to economic conditions, and given certain assumptions about grants-in-aid, by stipulating a certain growth rate for the economy and assuming prices are constant, it is possible to derive the required amount of bond financing for various levels of *per capita* expenditures on public goods and services. See Netzer, D., *Economics of the Property Tax*, The Brookings Institution, 1966.

federal grants-in-aid to states merely 'pass through' the latter as states turn over these funds to local governments. By this measure alone grants-in-aid have risen from approximately $3.5 billion in 1948 to $20.2 billion in 1967, or from 1.4 per cent to 2.6 per cent of GNP. But even after allowance is made for grants-in-aid, growth of state and local tax receipts has been more rapid than overall activity. This rapid rise in expenditures and financing relative to overall growth of the economy must be viewed as partly a catching up of deferred demands, partly the result of a desire to increase 'standards' (e.g., to increase constant dollar expenditures per person for services such as education), and partly a desire to expand into new areas (e.g., pollution control). Only the latter two factors can be expected to exert any future influence. But whether balanced or not, whether standards of public service are maintained, improved or allowed to deteriorate, growing needs are again satisfied in the moving equilibrium, with desired current and capital outlays and the required financial resources simultaneously determined.

I. Conclusion

The importance and relevance of the moving equilibrium concept and the demographic sausage machine, depends very much on the stability of the system. For unless fluctuations in unemployment rates are mild and the convergence back to some 'normal' rate of unemployment fairly rapid, both concepts lose much of their value. With recessions of the 1930 variety occurring periodically, the 'transient path' of the system takes on as much or more value than a moving equilibrium where unemployment rates are constant. Similarly the crises that took place in the interwar period clearly indicated that a progression through stages was not a smooth matter, nor was the sausage machine analogy a very useful way of describing the events of that period. In Chapters VI and VII various factors tending to dampen fluctuations in unemployment are discussed. What it all comes down to is that stability is not a question of one or two conditions being met. The answer to the problem is far less clearcut, because there are a number of conditions to be satisfied, allowing various factors to exert a small but important influence on the system by themselves, and through their interaction with each other. The behavior of family-related expenditure is just one of the causes of mild fluctuations along a growth path: by continuing to grow in the face of a decline in activity, such outlays help dampen recessions, and allow growing needs to become growing demands over the cycle, with only moderate interruptions in the life cycle progression.

Chapter VI **The Stability of the Moving Equilibrium**

Part I **The Ceiling in the Capital Goods Industry**

A. Introduction

The question of the stability of the moving equilibrium has only been touched upon lightly. In Chapters III and IV it was argued that by including a ratchet effect in one or more of the spending equations, the growth of demand would be brought into line with the growth of maximum output or supply. In addition, demand was allowed to influence supply, but the range over which a permanently maintained increase in the rate of growth of demand could cause an equal increase in the rate of growth of supply was assumed to be limited. This limitation, together with the other assumptions of the model, generated a stable moving equilibrium. Any deviation of the rate of growth of demand (or supply) from this limited range of growth rates could not be sustained, and the system would eventually move back to a rate of growth of demand and supply corresponding to some point on the BC segment of Diagram 4.1.

There can be little argument that the response of supply to demand is limited in this way. However, the *influence* of supply *on* demand needs further comment and substantiation. The difficulty with including maximum output, X_t, in the consumption function is the same as using the original ratchet variable, $\bar{Y}_t$; you cannot expect the influence of the past or previous peak to remain undiminished regardless of the length and severity of a depression. As a recession lingers on and intensifies, and the duration of unemployment lengthens for the unemployed, the exhaustion of past savings, unemployment compensation and the like will surely cause the influence of previous peak income to diminish. While there undoubtedly is a ratchet influence at work, it should not be given the sole responsibility for bringing the system back to its long-run growth path. We can strengthen our case therefore, if we can find other forces also at work dampening fluctuations. This is in no sense meant to deny that the stability of the moving equilibrium of a capitalistic system is not the outgrowth of the sort of interaction between actual and maximum output already described. But it must also be seen as affected by additional factors which reinforce and are reinforced by the strong pressure of consumers to maintain living standards. The problem is to determine what are the additional circumstances that are sufficient to keep cyclical movements mild—mild enough for it to be appropriate to assume that maximum output affects demand and actual output throughout a recession. These additional conditions will be seen to be very much tied up with the behavior of the system during the boom. When some of these conditions are not met, we can still speak of a moving equilibrium of a capitalist system, but it is an unstable one. Shocks or disturbances that bring the cyclical components into play may in this case lead to such rapid and prolonged declines in output, that the assumed stabilizing influence of consumption will become a much less potent factor for stability; which further intensifies the difficulties.

Disturbances pushing the economy above the trend line are also a problem, but, as will become clear, to explain the upper turning point and the 'mildness' of booms is easier than to explain their recession counterparts. The conditions or circumstances required for stability will be described first within the framework of a system uncomplicated by a cold war, or the presence or aftermath of a hot one. This does not preclude the existence of a growing public sector. It does omit from consideration the possible stabilizing or destabilizing effects of large and rapid changes in federal government expenditures and taxes, as well as odd initial conditions reflecting backlogs built up during actual earlier hostilities. These complications are introduced later, following a rather extended, theoretical study of the stability question, when the analysis will be brought to bear on an actual economy during a half century of its development. In Chapters VIII–X two historical periods in the development of the American economy are studied, the interwar period and the period following World War II. In each case, the American economy is treated as one having a long-term growth path along which it could move in the absence of shocks. Because of the latter, cyclical movements are brought into play causing it to deviate from some trend line. It is argued that the interwar era illustrates a period of history when the conditions required for mild fluctuations or minor deviations from relatively steady growth were not met. Once the decline of 1929 had set in, conditions were such that the recession would be so severe that the ratchet effect became inoperative and, hence, the joint interaction mechanism between demand and supply broke down. The current period is treated as a period when conditions for stability were met. In Chapter XI we discuss briefly the breakdown of this mechanism in the United Kingdom. The causes of the collapse were quite different, however, from the American case.

B. The Relationship between the Boom and the Subsequent Recession

Consider this problem in terms of the model developed earlier. In Chapter IV a long-run equilibrium growth path for the system was defined simply as a situation where the unemployment rate was constant. The stability of this moving equilibrium was discussed in a very general way, in terms of the reaction of the model to displacements from the equilibrium path. For example, with the model originally growing at rate r_{y1}, a shock (i.e., an arbitrary departure of the model from the path determined by the equations), was introduced that resulted in the growth rate being pushed down to r_{y2}. As we argued, this growth rate could not be substained and the model would eventually grow at r_{y1}. However, this glossed over some problems, since the introduction of shocks will always bring the cyclical components of the model into play and the amplitude of the fluctuations will be related to the size of the shock. The question that now arises is what determines whether shocks and their induced effects are sizable enough to call into question the whole notion of a consumption ratchet.[1]

It can be argued that certain models (and economies) are more shock resistant at one time than another, in the sense that there exist institutional and technological constraints that dampen the response of the system to shocks, whatever their magnitude. The interaction of the endogenous variables by itself may generate a cycle of large amplitude when shocked, but if constrained any unfortunate initial conditions generated by the shock may not have such a pronounced impact. For example, we can think of the system moving along its long-term growth path when it is disturbed in an upward direction. The capital-stock adjustment mechanism would initially cause income to grow more rapidly than capital (while both grow more rapidly than their long-term rate). Even in the absence of some physical constraint on the growth of output, these relative growth rates will be reversed (if the capital-stock adjustment part is assumed to be incapable of generating steady growth by itself) with capital eventually growing more rapidly than output. This sets the stage for the downturn, which could be fairly severe. However, the existence of some kind of constraint may have the effect of prolonging the boom while dampening its amplitude. This would be likely to be the case if the growth of capital were slowed down by more than the rate of growth of output (though it would naturally still exceed the latter during the mid and

---

[1] This is analogous to explaining under what circumstances shocks can cause such a large increase in the capital–output ratio in Diagram 2.1 in Chapter II, that the system plunges into a severe recession.

latest ages of the boom). With a less pronounced over-accumulation of capital, the system would turn down more slowly, and the ratchet influence might remain operative because of the constrained nature of the previous boom. By the same token, the decline would be moderate and slow enough for any interruption of the procession of different age groups through the life cycle stages to be minimal. The trend influences then take effect and a recovery could soon follow.

This is still all very general, but the notion of a constrained cycle does give a clue as to what might be important; spending plans should be somehow stretched out or postponed during a boom. This generates a less dynamic boom as well as a less rapid decline in output during the recession. In other words, the behavior of an economy in one phase of the cycle might be closely related to its behavior in an earlier phase. In order better to distinguish between models and economies that are shock resistant and those that are not, a certain amount of disaggregation is necessary, together with some discussion of certain structural characteristics of an economy. It is also necessary to proceed in a less formal, more literary fashion.[2]

C. The Amplitude of the Cycle and its Diffusion

Most non-consumption types of spending are positively related to some overall measure of economic activity, say GNP, and negatively related to a cumulative measure of past investment. The capital-stock adjustment principle applies in one form or another to such divergent types of spending as inventory investment, and capital outlays of state and local governments. What differs from one such spending category to the next is the speed of response to discrepancies between desired and actual stocks. For a change in any of the determinants of the desired stock, say output, there will be various possible lagged responses, with spending stretched over several periods into the future. The form of the lagged response will depend upon such things as the durability of the investment good, the speed of response of the capital goods industry (which in turn depends upon both current and

---

[2] A more formal approach would not be helpful. Even if it is assumed that demand does not affect supply as in Chapter III, it does not help matters. As described earlier, disaggregation has the effect of increasing the order of the system so that the analytical solution of the model is still composed of the solution of the homogeneous part plus a particular solution. As before, the solution can be written:

$$Y_t = Y_t + \sum_{i=1}^{n} A_i (x_i)^t.$$

If it is again assumed that the endogenous part is stable, i.e., $|x_i| < 1$ for all i, then $\lim_{t \to \infty}$ $Y_t = Y_t^E$. But using a more formal disaggregative approach in no way helps determine under what conditions the model would be more or less shock resistant.

past levels of activity as well as the type of capital good), access to funds for financing and a host of institutional considerations. Because of the positive correlation between these different components of GNP and GNP, it would be expected that a boom (or a recession) would by its very nature be a situation where more and more spending categories get pulled into phase with the general state of the economy. Thus, in addition to the influence of the amplitude of the fluctuations in, say, the more volatile sectors, the relative strength or mildness of a boom or recession is also very much a matter of how widely it is diffused: i.e., of what proportion of the different types of final expenditures grow during each phase of the cycle. The more widely diffused is the boom, the greater will be its likely amplitude and the longer its duration, and the same can be said for any recession. For example, whether we work with industrial production or with investment, a strong correlation holds between the percentage of production and investment sectors expanding, and the growth of production and investment, respectively.[3] Indeed, at the aggregate level, a damped cyclical mechanism may be seen as the analogue both to a mildness in the fluctuations of individual sectors, and to a lack of diffusion of different spending components of final output over the cycle. What must be shown is that the mildness of the fluctuations of individual sectors, especially those with inherently strong destabilizing tendencies, together with the lack of diffusion of the several sectors in any phase of the cycle, can be traced to certain constraints or supply inelasticities. When these are operative, the response to shocks will also be mild at the aggregate level, and the moving equilibrium stable, because the system is in our terminology shock resistant.

Next, consider the following argument. It has been suggested that 'recessions are mild because not widely diffused'.[4] Industries producing goods with high income elasticities continue to expand capacity and production in the face of a general decline in business. New rapid growth industries, it is argued, can be expected to be undertaking large investment programs involving relatively long gestation periods, which are unlikely to be interrupted unless a serious decline in activity takes place. This provides a floor for the economy in much the same way as the ratchet effect. However, while both of these boot strap operations have some force, it can just as well be argued that recessions are not widely diffused because they are mild. While some sectors need not be too sensitive to current economic activities, they are surely influenced by large declines in output. For example, if declines in aggregate output are very large because the declining sectors are greatly contracting, all sectors, including the growth industries, may get into phase.

Fortunately, there is a way out of this circular, somewhat tautological

[3] See Hickman, B., 'Diffusion, Acceleration and Business Cycles', *The American Economic Review*, September 1959.

[4] Hickman, B., 'Postwar Cyclical Experience and Economic Stability', *The American Economic Review*, Papers and Proceedings, May 1958.

argument. If a decline in overall activity is to come to a halt, some sectors must be expanding in spite of the overall decline, to offset the depressing influence of those sectors which either touched off the recession, or reacted early in such a way as to aggravate it. At the same time we have argued that other things being equal, all spending is positively related to the current behavior of aggregate economic activity. This means that for a recession to come to an end (before net investment becomes negative) it is necessary that two conditions be met. First, other things must not be equal for some sectors, so that the decline in overall activity is not too widespread, and some sectors actually increase their outlays. Second, the spending of those sectors responsible for initiating and aggravating the decline must not be falling too rapidly. If these conditions are met, the first influence will soon offset the second, bringing the decline in output to a halt, and eventually reversing its direction. This sets the stage for the next boom, since it will eventually eliminate the causes of the downward movement of spending of those sectors that generated the recession. Both these conditions can be seen to depend to a large extent on the presence or absence of certain supply constraints operating in the previous boom.

These constraints are of two types. First, there are certain characteristics of the markets for labor and real capital goods, that lead to fairly persistent situations of disequilibria, and therefore to delays in the response to excess demand situations. Second, there are those institutional characteristics of the money and financial markets that act systematically to thwart spending plans, and to prevent certain groups from commanding real resources during the boom because of their inability to command financial resources. By common agreement the chief source of fluctuations in final sales is fluctuations in business investment, especially fluctuations in manufacturing investment. The importance of the ceiling in the capital goods industry stems from the stabilizing effect it has on these types of expenditures which are chiefly responsible for instability. In addition, this ceiling will cause a postponement of expenditures by other groups, most of whom are the least sensitive to declines in overall activity. The importance of the 'monetary ceiling' is somewhat similar. It lies in its tendency not only to make fluctuations in certain types of spending more mild than would otherwise be the case, but also to put these fluctuations out of phase with movements of overall activity.

In discussing how these constraints work, we will usually find it more useful to use final sales, i.e. GNP less inventory investment, as the measure of overall economic activity. What is really important for stability is that the rate of decline of final sales be slow, soon halted and eventually reversed, since this will correct any inventory disinvestment. The latter can simply be treated as some sort of moving average of recent changes in GNP or final sales. When discussing monetary policy later, however, it will often be more convenient to speak in terms of the more commonly used measure of overall activity, GNP.

D. The 'Ceiling' in the Capital Goods Industry

The overaccumulation of capital during a boom by the business sector, and especially the manufacturing components, is probably something that must be lived with. Fortunately, there are forces at work dampening these movements. Supply constraints are encountered in the capital goods industry (defined to include construction firms as well as equipment producers) in the course of the boom, and as a result spending plans by even the most aggressive and volatile sectors have to be stretched out or postponed until the subsequent recession. Firms in the capital goods industry, especially those producing producers' durable equipment, are subject to wide fluctuations in demand. If costs of hiring and firing are high because of training costs, the possibility of strained labor relations, etc., there will be a strong desire to stabilize production. During the boom, when new orders for capital goods pick up, the short-run response by firms in the industry can either be to increase prices, sell out of inventory, lengthen the delivery dates for new orders, or to combine two or three of those responses. For purposes at hand, the first possibility can be disregarded.[5] The second possibility permits employment and production to be stabilized and, if forecasts are accurate, allows demand for new capital goods, i.e. new orders, to be satisfied more or less upon receipt. However, 'production to stock' is unlikely for most firms in the capital goods industry to the extent that their output is geared to business investment demands. For the most part production must be geared to unpredictable specific demands by different business customers. Any production in anticipation of demand runs the risk of large losses if the specifications are wrong. The result is that such firms are willing to incur the lesser cost of requiring an increase in the waiting period between receipt of a new order and the supplying of a new capital good to the buyer. Production will be to order rather than to stock. This is true for firms producing equipment as well as for construction firms undertaking non-residential construction projects. One very likely result of all this is described in Diagram 6.1, which depicts in a somewhat idealized fashion the behavior of the demand for the output of the capital goods industry by the business sector, and the supply response by capital goods producers. Again, P and T represent a peak and trough in overall economic activity, CO is contracts and new orders for capital goods, S is the 'supply' of new capital goods and U is unfilled orders. It will be understood that both CO and S include contracts awarded and expenditures respectively, for commercial and industrial plant, as well as new orders and expenditures for producers' durables.[6]

[5] In actual fact it has been shown that both prices and unfilled orders respond to excess demand pressures. See Zarnowitz, V., 'Unfilled Orders, Price Changes and Business Fluctuations', *The Review of Economics and Statistics*, November 1962.

[6] The contracts and orders being discussed correspond most closely to the 'Contract and Orders, Plant and Equipment' series published by the U.S. Department of Commerce in *Business Cycle Developments*, recently renamed *Business Conditions Digest*.

Diagram 6.1

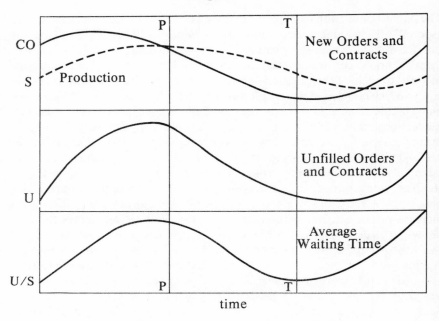

As suggested by Diagram 6.1, the boom is characterized by such a rapid increase in the demand for new capital goods by business, relative to what is supplied to them, that new orders soon exceed production. Once this happens, unfilled orders must rise, and continue to do so until, as shown in the middle panel, demand falls below supply. Eventually demand turns down and falls below supply, the latter often continuing to rise for a period even though exceeding demand. Throughout the recession the unfilled orders are worked off (as long as supply exceeds demand) until the recovery in economic activity causes new orders to rise again and the cycle repeats itself.

The top panel is meant to suggest that there is a partial but still incomplete response by the capital goods industry to excess demand, in the form of increased capacity. Second and third line producers may enter the industry, technical improvement may take place within the industry itself, etc. In addition certain construction firms that are able to undertake both residential and business construction will shift to the latter type of work during the boom. However, these responses would most likely become less and less important as the boom continued. The bottom panel is more illuminating. The ratio of unfilled orders to the supply of new capital goods approximates the average waiting time between an order and the delivery of the capital good. This tends to rise relatively early in the boom and to continue to rise as long as new orders do. Once the latter level off, U/S soon declines. The behavior of U/S illustrates quite well the kind of a constraint or supply inelasticity encountered during a boom that is appropriate for studying the stabilizing effects of constraints. The lengthening of the waiting period reflects the interaction of all the forces brought to bear on the capital goods industry during the boom. Because of this, and the related accumulations of unfilled orders during the boom, as long as orders are not cancelled once the recession sets in, the rate of decline in the production, delivery and expenditure on new capital goods will be much smaller than if demands could be met out of inventory or upon receipt. Since these types of expenditures are among the more volatile and sensitive to current economic conditions, and since they are largely responsible for fluctuations in final sales, the dampening influence of this supply constraint cannot be underestimated when discussing the conditions necessary for stability. How much the fluctuations are damped, and how rapidly investment expenditures decline once new orders have begun to decline, will depend upon several factors, many of which are summarized in the behavior of unfilled orders to shipments during the boom. The further these have risen before new orders decline, the slower will investment expenditures fall. This in turn is partly a matter of how long the boom has lasted, partly a matter of cancellations. But the overall effect must be to slow down the decline in activity once the latter sets in.

E. The Ceiling and the Non-business Sectors

The scheme being discussed here will not eliminate fluctuations in business investment entirely, nor need it make the boom less widely diffused. And unfortunately, like any built-in stabilizer, these constraints cannot lead to a reversal of the decline in business investment and the economy, unless they can lead to a rise in the desired stock of capital relative to the actual stock however measured. This requires largely that the effect on income from the cutback in investment be more than offset by the effect on capacity. This possibility is most unlikely; a mild recession will be one where capacity continues to grow in spite of an actual decline in gross and net investment. If the decline in final sales was initiated by an overaccumulation of business capital, say in the manufacturing sector, and if capacity continues to grow during the early stages of the boom, then other types of spending must increase during the early stages of the downswing, to turn the economy around.

Fortunately, the same kind of supply inelasticity operates naturally for other less aggressive purchasers of capital goods, those that typically undertake what we have termed family-related expenditures. Residential construction, capital outlays by state and local governments, and investment by nonprofit institutions, are less influenced by the fact that activity is increasing *per se* than business activities are, but to the extent that they are, their higher demands will add to the backlogs created during the boom. More important, the greater persistence, ingenuity and resources of the business sector will permit it to increase its share of the output of the capital goods industry when the supply of the latter becomes less elastic at the expense of these groups. This means that the relative lack of aggressiveness by the various non-business groups reduces the likelihood that their desired stock of capital will fall below the actual stock during the boom (provided that the boom is characterized by strong investment demands of the business sector). It also means that so many potential spenders will be squeezed out in their bid for part of the output of the capital goods industry, that the resultant backlogs could lead to increased spending in the subsequent recession. Here the diffusion of the boom may be affected, and the behavior of the economy during the boom would have an important influence on the subsequent recession.

But there is more to it than this, at least for residential construction. Construction workers on industrial projects are paid higher wages than those on residential projects. With the total supply of construction workers very inelastic in the short run, workers will move into the industrial building projects whenever demand picks up, and leave residential home builders with a shortage of workers.

There is also another factor at work over the cycle. The price of housing is the result of the demand for and supply of total housing, newly constructed and old. Since the additions to the housing stock in any year will be a very small percentage of the total stock, the demand for new housing will be very elastic in relation to the price of new houses and ultimately construction costs. If construction costs and prices of new dwelling units rise during a boom, construction will fall off, and so will demand.

In contrast, rising construction costs can be passed on more readily on non-residential construction projects. This is especially true for industrial and commercial building. Both these considerations work to cause residential construction to move countercyclically.[7] We spoke earlier of the ability of the business sector to increase its share of the output of the capital goods industry during the boom: this can now be seen more precisely as an ability of business to increase its share of output of the construction industry.

All this has important implications for stability. It means that at the cyclical peak, certain sectors may find that their actual capital stocks will fall below the desired amount. It is true that the subsequent decline in aggregate output will narrow this gap. On the other hand, it can be argued that those sectors that supply family-related services are not as sensitive to declines in economic conditions as is the business sector. This is partly a matter of a longer time horizon, less concern with profits, and a higher construction content in their investment outlays. The question of sensitivity will be taken up in Chapter VII.

[7] See Evans, M. K., *Macroeconomic Activity*, Harper and Row, New York, 1969, pp. 194–196.

F. Frictions in the Labor Market and Stability

Unfilled orders for capital goods tend to rise before maximum output is reached in the capital goods industry. In an analogous way job vacancy rates rise early in the boom before unemployment rates reach a minimum. However, neither of these responses can be thought of as taking place without some sort of lag. In a frictionless labor market there would be no appreciable rise in the vacancy rate as unemployment fell until the economy reached some minimum level of unemployment; i.e., before an absolute ceiling had been reached. Fortunately, for our purposes, the real world is not frictionless. And this lack of perfect elasticity in the short-run supply of labor before 'full employment' is reached has the effect of slowing down the rate of growth of income and demand in a manner similar to the short-run inelasticity of supply in the market for capital goods.

However, the inelasticity of supply of capital goods is more basic and for two reasons. First, job openings or offers can be cancelled when profit prospects decline. Backlogs of unfilled orders for capital goods, in contrast, tend not to be cancelled on a broad scale once the recession sets in.[8] Second, the increase in demand for labor during the boom is to a large extent the result of the increase in demand for new capital goods. Hence the stretching out or actual postponement of investment demands and expenditures will, through the multiplier effect, be a factor stretching out the growth of demand for labor and therefore employment and income. In both cases output and incomes are kept from rising as rapidly as desired expenditures.

G. Some Concluding Remarks

We have argued that the end of a boom is characterized by an overaccumulation of capital by business. At the same time backlogs of demand for capital goods are built up during the boom, and even during the recession unfilled orders remain positive. The latter condition results from the type of response of firms in the capital goods industry to excess demand situations. The former condition (overaccumulation of business capital) is possible if, in spite of supply inelasticities in the capital goods industries, the rate of growth of business capital during the mid and late stages of the boom still exceeds the rate of growth of business output. This, in turn, can happen if the capital goods industry has a capacity sufficient to allow business capital to grow more rapidly than output, but insufficient to satisfy the demand for business capital

---

[8] One study estimates that the cancellations of machine tool orders is very small. See Zarnowitz, V., 'The Timing of Manufacturers' Orders During Business Cycles', Chart 14.4, p. 454, in *Business Cycle Indicators*, Volume I, New York National Bureau of Economic Research, Princeton University Press, Princeton, 1961.

goods during the boom.[9] Thus supply inelasticities and backlogs of demand for capital goods by business and others can paradoxically be as natural a characteristic of the booms as overaccumulation of capital. However, the essential point is that because of the backlogs the offsetting movements (i.e., the tendency of some sectors to increase outlays in spite of a general decline in overall activity), need be less widespread. This is further strengthened by the realization that certain types of spenders may be forced to postpone investment outlays during the boom.

It was pointed out earlier that the 'billiard ball' theory of the cycle is incorrect in certain cases, as the system may react by moving along the ceiling, provided the rate of capital accumulation slows down also. Further doubt has been cast on the ceiling explanation of the downturn on empirical grounds; there is little evidence that economies do reach 'the' ceiling in the boom. However, none of these arguments need deter one from accepting the notion that the stability of an economic system can be partly explained in terms of certain supply restraints or inelasticities, that operate in different degrees at different stages of each boom, and in such a way as to act as to encourage stability. What is essential is that, soon after the boom gets underway, the lag between the decision to spend, and the acquisition of the good under consideration, be lengthened for some groups. Whether the lengthening of the lag is long enough to postpone completely any expenditures by some group during the boom, or merely to stretch it out over a longer period, will depend upon such considerations as the aggressiveness of the potential spenders, access to funds, etc. The main point here is that, in trying to understand how certain supply inelasticities might operate to dampen cycles and increase stability, it does not help to think in terms of an absolute barrier to growth. While such a barrier might eventually come into play, it is more helpful to think in relative terms, in terms of a collection of constraints that stretch out or cause temporary postponement of certain types of spending.[10] We turn now to another of these constraints.

---

[9] Alternatively, we can say that while this kind of constraint slows down the rate of growth of all types of capital during the boom, non-business capital formation is retarded more than business. There is ample evidence that this is the case.

[10] This argument has certain affinities with that developed by Matthews, R. C. O., *The Business Cycle*, Chapter 9, *op cit.*; and Hickman, B., 'Diffusion . . .', *op. cit.*

Part II The Monetary Ceiling

A. Introduction

The rigid quantity theory of money argued that, since the income velocity of money was constant, a given money stock generated only one level of aggregate expenditures, and could finance only one level of (full employment) income. The supply of loanable funds consistent with any supply of money might vary, because savings was a function of the terms of borrowing, but changes in savings were always matched by changes in consumption of the same magnitude but in the opposite direction; i.e., total spending was constant. The Keynesian position challenged both these implications of the rigid quantity theory. Many different levels of spending and incomes, whether at full employment or not, were consistent with a given money stock, and the supply of loanable funds could vary without an offsetting change in consumption, because changes in interest rates could induce people to alter the manner in which they held their wealth. Thus, rather than argue that there was a rigid fixed monetary ceiling that was defined in terms of the existing money supply, the revisionists argued that total spending, velocity and the supply of loanable funds were variable, but that as the demand for these funds increased the supply became increasingly inelastic.[11] This increasing inelasticity in the supply of loanable funds, and the increasing difficulty in financing higher levels of expenditure and output, suggests something analogous to the increasing inelasticities of the supply of real capital and labor already discussed.

The $IS\text{-}LM$ curve is repeated in Diagram 6.2 for convenience, with the interest rate, i, and real income, Y, measured on the vertical and horizontal axis respectively, the price level and money supply being given. The change in the slope of the LM curve as income changes can be used to indicate the changing inelasticity of the supply of funds. From zero income to one corresponding to Y_1 we have something analogous to the free cycle case for the real sector, as nothing 'constrains' spending over this range of income. As the IS curve shifts from IS_1 to IS_2, only income is affected; because an increase in the income velocity of money, V, and total spending, MV, is forthcoming without any rise in the rate of interest. In effect, the supply of loanable funds is infinitely elastic at interest rate i_0. At the other extreme, beyond income Y_2, an absolute monetary ceiling exists that is analogous to some absolute maximum for output. Here nontransactions balances have been drawn down to a minimum, and the income velocity of money is at a maximum. No further

---

[11] Inelasticity in the supply of loanable funds is usually defined with respect to 'the' rate of interest, but it can also be defined with respect to other terms of credit, such as the maturity of the loan, etc.

Diagram 6.2

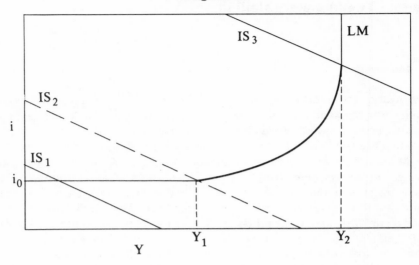

'action' can be obtained from the given money supply, as a shift in the *IS* curve to the right of IS_3 merely drives up interest rates. At incomes between Y_1 and Y_2, however, there exists a situation that is comparable to an inelastic supply of labor and capital: it is not completely inelastic, becomes more so as income and spending increase. Short-run increases in labor participation rates and in capacity are possible as vacancy rates and unfilled orders increase, but this becomes more unlikely the higher are the employment and capacity utilization rates of the capital goods industry. By analogy, a given money supply can generate a large supply of loanable funds and support higher levels of income, as interest rates rise (and the payments system adjusts) to induce dishoarding of idle balances. However, the increasing slope of the segment between Y_1 and Y_2 indicates that the supply of funds available to finance higher levels of income and expenditures becomes increasingly inelastic. A given shift upward to the right on the *IS* curve generates increasingly smaller increases in output, and increasingly larger increases in interest rates. Viewed in these terms, discretionary monetary policy can be seen as a deliberate manipulation of the *LM* curve relative to the shifting *IS* curve over the cycle. The aim of the monetary authorities is to impose a monetary ceiling or remove it by various degrees, in an effort to control aggregate demand.

This is the familiar textbook world of commercial banks and a capital market, with the nonbank public given the option of holding their financial wealth in the form of bonds or money. The nonbank public are induced to alter the form in which they hold this wealth by changing bond prices. However, this comparative statics methodology tends to make the monetary authorities' job look easier than it is. Basically the difficulties associated with monetary policy stem from the fact that the authorities operate within a framework of uncertainty and lags (which permits groups ample opportunity partially or totally to offset the authorities' activities, because of the existence of large blocks of near monies). As a result, during the boom there is a strong desire to make a monetary ceiling operative, but at the same time there is a concern lest policy measures are pushed too far, either causing a financial panic or intensifying an impending recession. The latter introduces a bias towards 'gradualism' in the application of policy.

Be that as it may, what is required is for the monetary authorities to be able in the boom to cause certain types of expenditures to be postponed or cut back, thereby dampening the boom and preventing a more rapid overaccumulation of capital (and a more rapid rate of inflation). If they can do this, then, they will have succeeded in constraining the potentially destabilizing influence of the capital-stock adjustment mechanism brought into play by outside shocks. This sets the stage for a milder recession, increasing the chances of a quick recovery, because the postponed spending will to a very large extent be made up in the recession. This view of discretionary monetary policy as a constraint operating to stabilize the economy will be developed further in the next four sections.

B. The Priority Scheme in the Use of Bank Funds

Consider first a situation where financial intermediaries are unimportant, where there is a market for bonds but not equities, and commercial banks (hereafter referred to as 'banks') keep only noninterest bearing demand deposits. This idealization is useful as a first step not just because this is the traditional way to analyze the channels through which policy works, but also because the impact of monetary policy is felt most immediately by this segment of the money and capital markets and because 'banks are different'. Banks are allowed to hold the full menu of income earning assets and have a general priority scheme in the use of funds on deposit. That is, after taking account of primary and secondary reserve requirements, banks wish to satisfy their 'customer loan demand' to the full extent possible. For the moment all loans, whether mortgage, business or consumer, can be treated as a homogeneous group to be contrasted with 'securities'. The priority scheme argues that only after satisfying loan demand will bank funds be invested for income in securities—always assuming, of course, that we are talking of acceptable loan customers.[12] Next allow a boom to develop that results in a general tightening of credit, and assume that the authorities slow down the growth of unborrowed reserves and the money supply relative to some

[12] See, for example, Robinson, Roland, *The Management of Bank Funds*, New York, McGraw-Hill, 1951.

average growth over the cycle. At first this may result merely in a drawing down of excess reserves. But allow the boom to be strong and prolonged enough for increased borrowing, given the central bank's persistence, to be matched increasingly by open market sales, so that at some point deposit growth more or less reaches the limit targeted by the authorities, and higher rates of growth of loan demand result in more rapid liquidation of securities.

As the boom continues and loan demand continues to increase, the sale from the bond portfolio serves to mop up idle (nontransactions) balances, or to cause an economizing in the use of transactions balances as interest rates rise and induce purchases of securities by the public. If loan expansion by banks accompanies the liquidation, the supply of loanable funds will grow more rapidly than the money supply, as velocity will continue to increase. Assume at this point that those seeking funds are little affected by the kind of changes in the terms of borrowing that arise during an ordinary boom. Then the strength of monetary policy in this kind of world can be measured by the extent to which banks find it necessary to cut back on individual loan demands (assuming that bond purchasers do not cut back their expenditures on goods and services). The possibility of an unsatisfied loan demand, in turn, will to a large extent be a function of the liquidity of the banking system at the beginning of the boom, relative to the strength of the boom (itself partly influenced by policy). These two factors, the initial liquidity of the banking system and the strength of the boom, will largely influence tne willingness and speed with which banks switch from investments to loans—i.e. the amount of credit rationing per unit of time—since together they greatly determine both the extent and duration of tight money policy, and (given the elasticity of demand for money) the extent to which interest rates must rise and capital losses be incurred. If the banking system is particularly liquid at the beginning of the boom and if there is a limit to the speed at which the authorities can proceed, monetary policy might indeed be very ineffective in cutting back spending in the aggregate (or in particular sectors). There would be no reason to believe that new issues in the capital market would have any more difficulty in finding buyers than securities dumped by the banking system. The boom in this case would come to an end eventually, but for other reasons. In the meantime, the side effects considered undesirable by the authorities (i.e. inflation and a very rapid over-accumulation of capital) would have had their undesirable consequences.

C. The Introduction of Fixed-price Near-moneys

There are many ways to improve on the realism of this picture of the response of the flow of funds to a general credit tightening. One is to introduce fixed-price near-moneys and other types of financial intermediaries; another is to drop the fiction that banks treat all types of private loans, commercial, mortgage, personal, etc. as interchangeable; and a third means is to allow for the possibility that the demand for funds might be influenced by the terms of borrowing. All three modifications give added scope for monetary policy.

Consider first the possibility where banks are allowed to pay interest on certain deposits which, while not circulating as a medium of exchange, are highly liquid, both because of a low transaction cost in converting them into money and because of their fixed price. Additional sources of fixed-price near-moneys can also be introduced at this point, by including 'thrift' institutions in the analysis; i.e. savings and loan institutions and mutual savings banks.[13] The increasing importance of these latter two financial intermediaries has been the cause of a certain amount of doubt about the effectiveness of monetary policy. Their ability to create near-moneys (savings deposits, saving and loan shares etc.) by issuing claims and the possible subsequent expansion of the supply of loanable funds, at one time generated the opinion that commercial banks were not unique. Both types of institution were considered capable of generating multiple expansion of credit under their respective fraction reserve arrangements, though banks were subject to legal reserve requirements while the thrift institutions were not. Thus, it was argued, any shift in the flow of funds into the latter and away from the former could give rise to an appreciable increase in the supply of loanable funds, the size depending on the amount of customary reserves held against liabilities.

This view can and has been attacked on two grounds. First, thrift institutions are subject to more substantial leakages than commercial banks in the process of credit expansion. As has been pointed out more than once, the uniqueness of banks lies in the speed with which reserves are restored to the banking system whenever any bank issues claims against itself (issues demand deposits in the process of acquiring assets).[14] But even if commercial banks are not unique (or are unique only because of a legal reserve requirement), the mere fact that a shift of idle bank deposits to other financial intermediaries can affect the supply of loanable funds, and in this sense diminish the effectiveness of monetary policy, does not mean that such shifts will occur. During the course of the boom, as monetary conditions tighten and interest rates rise, all intermediaries may raise the rates they pay on their deposits (and this includes time deposits at commercial banks) in order to attract funds. If the claims they issue are more attractive to some holders of idle balances than primary securities, this will tend to make the flow of funds greater than it would be in the absence of intermediaries.

However, rates paid on deposits at thrift institutions, like the rates paid on time deposits at commercial banks, apply to all deposits of the same type.

---

[13] These are the American counterpart to 'building societies'.
[14] See Smith, Warren, 'Financial Intermediaries and Monetary Controls'. *Quarterly Journal of Economics*, November 1959.

Additional earnings due to higher rates on loans (and other assets) apply only to new loans (and other assets) acquired, which can only be a fraction of deposits; and the longer the average maturity of assets now held, the smaller will be this fraction. This will have the effect of slowing down the pace of increase in rates paid on claims issued by intermediaries. Therefore, unless rates earned on newly acquired assets can be increased much more rapidly than market rates in general (a most unlikely possibility), the differential between rates in the latter and rates on interest earned on fixed-price near-moneys must widen. This will lead to disintermediation—the withdrawal of interest-bearing deposits from financial intermediaries and their direct placement in the securities market. Thus, the most likely development during a period of tight money is not a shift in deposits from banks to thrift institutions, but a shift of deposits out of financial intermediaries in general to the capital markets. Numerous examples of this process of disintermediation will be cited in Chapters IX–XI.

The effects of the process of disintermediation (and intermediation during easy money periods) are quite profound. This is because some financial intermediaries, especially the thrift institutions, match certain assets and liabilities; i.e. deposits. To take but one example, the overwhelming proportion of the assets held by savings and loan associations are mortgages, especially on one to four family housing. In addition, thrift institutions are an important source of construction loans to tract builders. If the flow of funds into thes thrift institutions is cut back, as it would be in a process of disintermediation, mortgage lending and housing must be affected, unless other lenders make up for the cut back in mortgage lending by thrift institutions. This, we will argue, is extremely unlikely.

This effect on mortgage lending and housing would take place even if there were no change in the terms of a mortgage loan. On this reading, one of the main impacts of monetary policy, and the channel through which it works, can be seen to be a somewhat complicated version of an availability of funds argument. As the authorities slow down the growth of reserves, the overall supply of loanable funds will not slow down as much, since the payments system adjusts and interest rates rise to induce a more rapid turnover of the money supply. But the supply of loanable funds available to certain types of borrowers may be very much affected. If intermediaries or banks are legally restricted in the rates they may pay on their deposits, the process of disintermediation may be further heightened and the effect on housing attenuated.

D. Household Portfolio Adjustments and their Effect on Residential Construction

The adverse effect of disintermediation on mortgage lending and housing is basically the outgrowth of portfolio adjustments by the household sector in the face of rising interest rates. Nonfinancial, domestic holders of liquid assets can be divided into three groups—households, business, and state and local governments. The latter two groups customarily hold only commercial bank interest-bearing deposits when they choose to hold fixed-price near-moneys at all, while households choose between these and deposits in the thrift institutions; i.e. savings and loan associations and mutual savings banks. Now if there were a strong relationship between liabilities and mortgage assets at financial institutions other than thrift institutions (and here we can concentrate on banks and insurance companies), then movements of funds into these latter two institutions would be as important for mortgage lending and housing, as flows into thrift institutions are. But all the evidence points to a loose tie between interest-bearing time deposits and mortgages on the one hand, and insurance premiums and mortgages on the other, especially during tight money periods. One implication of this for mortgage lending is that changes in the total amount of fixed-price near-moneys outstanding may be of less importance than changes in its distribution at financial institutions. A shift of a fixed flow of interest-bearing deposits from thrift institutions to banks may have a more adverse affect on residential mortage lending, than would an actual decline in the total, accompanied by a shift in the opposite direction. This suggests that study of the channels through which policy affects housing should be concentrated on changes in the flow of funds into the thrift institutions, such as savings and loan associations and mutual savings banks. Furthermore much of our concern with portfolio management and adjustments can be further narrowed down to the household sector, since it is the latter that hold deposits in these two thrift institutions.

The process of disintermediation whereby the supply of funds available for housing is almost automatically cut back in the boom, causing certain types of expenditure to be postponed, can now be described differently. During the boom, as the demand for loanable funds begins to outstrip the supply, interest rates, especially those on primary securities, begin to rise absolutely and relative to rates paid on fixed-price near-moneys. This induces the non-financial domestic holders of funds to lend to bypass financial intermediaries, and to place them directly in the capital markets. For those institutions which very closely match mortage lending with deposits, such as savings and loan associations, the adverse effect of household portfolio adjustments on mortgage lending (and especially on mortages for one to four family housing) is straightforward. For mutual savings banks holding a wider variety of assets, and showing a greater willingness to substitute different types of assets when yield differentials are large enough, the final effect is almost as straightforward: the same factors causing potential depositors to bypass savings banks are working to make yields on securities relatively attractive, compared to mortgages. Yield spreads will move against mortgages at the same time as flows into savings banks decline. Thus, we have a somewhat ironic situation where behavior of the household sector during tighter money periods acts to curtail residential construction, thereby intensifying any existing housing shortage.[15]

But, as we have just implied, disintermediation is not the only means whereby the supply of credit flowing into the housing market declines during tight money periods. For example, insurance companies, a financial intermediary neglected up to now, operate in the mortgage markets, but are not subject to same instability of 'deposits' as are thrift institutions.[16] But because of the relative sluggishness of mortgage rates relative to rates on different kinds of bonds, there will be a tendency during tight money periods for these institutions to adjust their portfolios in such a way as to take advantage of the more favorable relative yields, say, on corporate bonds. Insurance companies will become increasingly reluctant to make long-term commitments and will back away from the mortgage market. This information will soon become known to those providing short term lending, who will in turn cut back on their interim financing. As we shall see presently, commercial bank mortgage lending is curtailed during tight money periods also, and for the same reason: the tie between deposits and mortgages is comparatively loose.

E. Monetary Policy and the Demand for Loanable Funds

The main concern up to this point has been with the supply of funds and how it comes to be rationed to home owners (and builders) primarily through a redistribution of the flow of loanable funds. Under the set of institutional arrangements just sketched, it is possible to show that a monetary constraint exists that would affect the spending plans of certain types of potential borrowers, even if no actual changes occurred in the terms on borrowing. Even if mortgage rates or monthly payments were not altered in a way unfavorable to the borrower at a thrift institution, financial flows would change in such a way that funds are increasingly unavailable to finance housing. This occurs because certain financial intermediaries tend to match deposit flows and mortgages very closely. Even if terms of borrowing were unchanged, a shift in the distribution of loanable funds away from these thrift institutions during the boom would lead to a decline in the availability of funds for

[15] One study suggests that the countercyclical flow of funds into mortgages has been going on for one hundred years, and for reasons similar to those discussed in the text. See Stevenson, R. F., Ness, J. F., and Winkelman, R. D., 'Mortgage Borrowing as a Frontier Developed', *The Journal of Economic History*, June 1966.

[16] However, a study indicates that something very similar to the kind of disintermediation discussed in the text has been occurring at insurance companies in recent times. See Schoot, F. H., 'Disintermediation Through Policy Loans at Life Insurance Companies', *The Journal of Finance*, June 1971.

mortgages and residential construction. But the argument is incomplete, since it neglects the demand for loanable funds and changes in the terms of borrowing. In particular, the argument has neglected the response to shifts in the supply of funds of potential mortgage borrowers relative to other borrowers. Since the discussion of the last few sections has also neglected the role of banks, and since what applies to banks applies equally well to other financial institutions, the remaining gaps can best be filled by dealing with these.

As suggested earlier, a distribution is made by banks between 'customer loan demand' and other loans, chiefly those to consumers secured by the purchases of real assets. This distinction is made for at least two reasons. First, a large part of customer loan demand is made up of loans that are the outgrowth of a line of credit granted the business borrower by the bank. These continuous borrowing privileges arise from, and are granted in return for, a stable or growing deposit relationship at the bank. Not to grant such loan demands when requested can both increase risk and decrease long-run profits.[17] As a result, customer loan demand receives the highest priority in the allocation of bank funds, after satisfying primary and secondary reserve requirements. If the pinch comes, these types of loan demand should suffer the least given risks. In comparison loan demands by others stand to be refused during periods of tight money or greatly trimmed.

In addition, consumer loans, especially mortgage loans, secured by a real asset financed mainly from the proceeds of the loan, are treated differently because of what has been termed the 'unequal distribution of assets'. Consider the case of a loan to an individual to finance the purchase of a home. The borrower, in contrast to the typical business customer, will be likely to lack saleable assets other than the capital good under consideration. This means increased risk for the lender in the event of default on the loan. Lenders will thus place a high premium on a rapid increase in the amount of equity the borrower has in the asset. The speed of this increase and the initial down payment become a variable subject to manipulation by lenders, depending upon credit conditions.[18] Mortgage rates, for example, are sluggish compared with other market rates; but the response of banks to a general tightening of credit conditions may be to adjust the other terms of the loan in a way unfavorable to the borrower, and to adopt a take it or leave it attitude. Indeed, in terms of long-term good will this may be the most sensible way to act, given the need to be in a position to satisfy higher priority loan demands.

A similar effect is obtained when ceiling rates of interest are placed on certain types of 'guaranteed' mortgages, limiting what the lender may charge. If these same mortgages also contain other terms more favorable to the borrower than 'conventional' mortgages, a refusal of lenders to extend

---

[17] Kane, Edward, and Malkiel, Burton, 'Bank Portfolio Allocation, Deposit Variability, and the Availability Doctrine,' *The Quarterly Journal of Economics*, February 1965.
[18] See Juster, F. Thomas, *Household Capital Formation and Financing, 1899–1962*, New York, National Bureau of Economic Research, 1966.

mortgage loans with a ceiling rate (because rates on other types of mortgages are now more favorable) will mean that borrowers are faced with tougher mortgage terms.

The resulting tightening up on the terms of credit is most likely to apply to the longer term mortgage loans, and especially to those offered by banks with their greater portfolio diversity and their priority scheme. And while banks need not be the most important lenders in the mortgage field, they are an important factor. But there should be some effect even at thrift institutions. By allowing the downpayment and the monthly payment to vary through changes in the amortization periods, banks and other lenders can sizeably affect the amount of funds demanded to finance this and related types of consumer investment. As with the change in the distribution of the supply of loanable funds caused by disintermediation, this increases the likelihood that consumer investment will be systematically cut back whenever the supply of funds is restricted relative to demand. Furthermore, even if the terms for financing consumer purchases of household furnishings and equipment do not vary, the fact that such investment may be complimentary to housing investment will lead to a cutback in the former, during tight money periods.

Of course, this tightening up on the terms of credit will be the outcome of a shift in a supply of funds curve relative to the shift in the demand for funds schedule. Most writers assume that the latter is relatively stable over the cycle for mortgage borrowers, its position being more a function of demographic factors.[19] For business, demand curves will be shifting with the cycle phase. What this all comes down to, then, is that during a tight money period the overall supply of loanable funds is curtailed, as well as the relative flow of funds into thrift institutions. This has the effect of shifting supply curves of available funds at any financial institution, upward to the left. These supply curves will have a positive slope whether it is the rate of interest, the downpayment or the ratio of the value of the residential property to the mortgage loan that is measured on the vertical axis (although for some loans only the interest rate is the relevant term of the loan). The new intersection point of the relevant demand for funds curve for whichever supply curve is chosen, will depict a borrowing term less favorable to the borrower (unless the demand for funds is completely elastic) and fewer funds borrowed and lent (unless the demand for funds is completely inelastic).[20]

This is true for any type of borrower, but mortgage borrowers are easily seen as the most sensitive to changes in the terms of borrowing induced by shifts in the supply of funds schedule. The shortening of the amortization period on a residential mortgage, and the resulting increase in monthly payments, has no counterpart for business. As to the other terms of lending,

[19] See, for example Alberts, W. W., 'Business Cycles, Construction Cycles, and the Mortgage Market', *Journal of Political Economy*, June 1962.

[20] See Guttentag, J., 'Credit Availability, Interest Rates, and Monetary Policy", *Southern Economic Review*, January 1960.

such as the interest rate, only business borrowers are in a position to pass on higher interest costs to their customers.

Thus, the position adopted here is that, in spite of findings of several economy-wide econometric models, there is much less certainty about the effects of the monetary ceiling on the supply of loanable funds to other types of borrowers, and about their reaction to less favorable terms of borrowing. In a general sort of way, it is undoubtedly true that 'marginal' bank customers will find that the supply of funds available to them is cut back or eliminated entirely by commercial banks and other lenders. Even regular loan customers may have their loan demands trimmed. We do know that more emphasis is put on 'compensating balances', the minimum deposits that bankers require loan customers to keep during tight money periods. An increase in these for a given 'line of credit' serves as a credit-rationing device for these types of borrowers. Some lenders in the capital market may also back away from the new issues markets. By the same token, tight money conditions may lead to some cutback in inventory investment, and a postponement of some bond flotations by state and local government, public utilities and non-profit institutions as they await more favorable borrowing conditions. This will even be true to some extent if market rates of interest are below some legal maximum for certain borrowers, since a self-imposed ceiling may be important, and serve to bring about a postponement of bond flotations and subsequent expenditures. All these influences may be helpful, but the position taken here is that the main direct influence of monetary policy must come through its effect on housing. And this is not said in order to imply that monetary policy does not have an important stabilizing role to play.

F. Some Concluding Remarks

There remain only a couple of loose ends in this discussion of constraints and their stabilizing effect. First, the two ceilings, one limiting the supply of capital goods and the other limiting the funds available to command resources, reinforce each other in stabilizing the economy. Without a monetary ceiling, demands on the capital goods industry, especially the construction industry, could be far greater relative to supply.[21] This would strengthen inflationary tendencies during the boom. On the other hand, without the backlogging of new orders and contracts, both by the business and non-business sectors, and the actual postponement of construction projects by home builders, less investment is transferred to the subsequent recession. The monetary ceiling might limit the boom in such a case, but the easy money

---

[21] The expression 'could' is used rather than 'would' since without a strong business investment boom you need not generate a monetary ceiling or inflation. Instead, a housing boom is likely to result.

policy in the subsequent recessions would have a much greater job to do. Both ceilings operate to slow down the rate of growth of output and capital, as well as to allow the share of business fixed investment in total investment to increase. The impact of both constraints is to help ensure an eventual over-accumulation of business capital during the boom.

Second, a great deal was made in Chapter IV of the lack of balance in the growth of demand and supply in a capitalist system. But the process of growth or transformation is unbalanced in another important, although related, sense. As an economy grows and the composition of output changes, it is likely that the spatial distribution of employment opportunities and the labor force will continuously diverge. Historically the most dramatic instance has been the movement of labor out of agriculture into industry. But movements between urban areas and within urban areas are also of importance. Because of this imbalance between the areas of demand for labor and the distribution of the labor force at any point in time, economic growth will always involve a certain amount of migration, external, internal or both. Family-related expenditures by definition are investment outlays that are peculiar to some geographical area. Even a redistribution of a fixed population will require new kinds of construction, and because of the slow depreciation of many of these items of family-related expenditure in depopulated areas, such a process can generate positive net investment. In contrast, many types of business investment are independent of this redistribution.

A boom is merely a deviation from the growth path, and temporarily increases this imbalance even further. If it induces migration because of more plentiful job opportunities in new areas, the first reaction will be a relatively pronounced movement of the male labor force which will involve a short run setback in the movements through the life cycle. And because of this, we can expect the migrants moving into a new area to delay their normal demands for loanable funds and resources, thus permitting those investment demands responsible for the boom to be more readily satisfied. In short, the geographical redistribution of jobs, followed by the redistribution of the labor force, usually will not result in the short run in the migrants demanding and receiving as much in the way of output as they themselves add to output. This surplus of production allows other demands to be satisfied, while certain other family-related types are deliberately deferred. This has the same effect as the different types of ceilings under discussion, in that both build up backlogs and set the stage for offsetting movements when the sectors generating the boom turn down.[22] In this case, though, these demands can be thought

[22] These types of offsetting movements have been used by one economist to generate Kuznets cycles. The initial stimulus to the boom is provided by some kind of investment spurt that induces migration to the areas of new job openings. The eventual increase in family formation induces various kinds of family-related expenditures, which generate continued growth in output for a period longer than the ordinary business cycle. The existence of Kuznets cycles is open to some doubt, but the argument developed in the text is independent of them. See Easterlin, Richard, 'Economic–Demographic Interactions and Long Swings in Economic Growth', *American Economic Review*, December 1966.

more as being deliberately postponed; i.e., they would not be forthcoming even if funds and resources are there and credit terms were favorable.

Finally, let us conclude by raising the following kind of problem. Assume that the direct effects of restrictive monetary policy, and the capital goods ceiling on spending other than housing, are marginal. Does it follow from this that the ceilings are not an important force for dampening the amplitude of fluctuations? Earlier it was argued that a boom would be characterized by an over-accumulation of capital by the business sector. This was partially due to the business sector's persistence in stepping up the rate of growth of business capital. However, the rate of growth of business capital can only be too high relative to the rate of growth of demand for output of business. While the direct effects of the ceilings might be limited, our earlier arguments in Chapter V indicate that there might be some indirect induced effects on other types of family-related investment. Together the direct and indirect effects might cause a sizeable slowdown in the rate of growth of demand and total output during a boom. Even if business were not able to increase its share of the output of the capital goods industry during the boom, both constraints could work towards generating an over-accumulation of capital by business, through their effect on the rate of growth of aggregate demand and output. The increased share of the output of the capital goods industry cornered by business merely speeds up the process of over-accumulation.

Thus, we come back to the original position, that under certain conditions the cyclical movements of a capitalist system might be so damped by certain constraints that recessions would be so moderate and short, that it is reasonable to assume that the ratchet effect remains operative throughout the downswing, and that a fairly orderly movement through the life cycle stages continues even during the recession. To this end our attention has been devoted to understanding why a boom might be fairly mild, preventing a too pronounced over-accumulation of capital, especially by business. Certain constraints were found to be at work (and it cannot be stressed enough that the boom in business investment must be strong) that had two important effects. On the one hand, they worked to stretch out and backlog business investment demands and thus expenditures; and on the other hand they operated to cause an actual postponement of other types of investment by non-business sectors. The former result certainly has the effect of permitting a more gradual decline in activity, once the downswing sets in. In this sense the recession phase and its severity is very much tied in with how certain sectors responded in the previous boom. But the effect of squeezing non-business sectors during the previous boom is as much, if not more, important for the behavior of the economy in the subsequent recession phase. What we must now show is that these sectors, because of their lack of sensitivity to the recession (which in turn is partly due to what happened in the previous boom), will play an important role in pulling the economy out of the recession.

Chapter VII **The Stability of the Moving Equilibrium (Continued)**

A. Lags in the Adjustment Process

In our concern with the question of stability, including the role that monetary policy might play, the analysis has dealt almost exclusively with the boom and the upper turning point. It it necessary now to analyze the response of the economy and certain key sectors to a recession. Following a discussion of the relative sensitivity of different groups to current economic activity, which involves a discussion of lags, we turn to a brief discussion of the role of monetary policy. The concluding portion sketches an outline of a cycle, and discusses what causes one to differ from another, within the context of an economy free of rapid and sustained changes in the government budget.

We argued earlier that, other things being equal, all types of spending are positively related to the general level of economic activity. On the other hand, it was argued that a necessary condition for mild recessions was that enough sectors should not in fact respond to changes in aggregate demand (at least in the short run), so that a lack of diffusion characterized the downswing, putting a floor under the economy and eventually leading to a reversal. In general, what is required is that the insensitive sectors persist in their spending plans, more or less until capacity utilization rates of the destabilizing sectors turn up again. These two views call for some sort of reconciliation, and the obvious way to approach this is to consider what other things may not be equal for certain groups, to cause them actually to step up their expenditures during a decline of general economic activity.

Insensitivity to current economic conditions suggests several things: a good deal of inertia in the adjustment process; isolation of the spending unit from general business conditions; and related to this, a lack of concern with moderate changes in economic conditions because of an unwillingness to associate a general change in overall activity with one's own economic situation. Take the question of a lag in the adjustment of expenditures behind the determinants of expenditures. This lag could be something as simple as a lapse between a change in one of the determinants of expenditures, and a particular date in the future when spending is affected: this is a discrete lag. On the other hand, the effect of a change in a determinant of spending might be distributed over several periods into the future; i.e. a distributed lag. To put the matter somewhat differently, while expenditures today are influenced by what is happening today, past events also have an influence.

The fact that events today may be partially or even largely the result of events in the past can be explained in a number of ways. The example of an unwillingness or inability to adjust one's living standards immediately to changes in income can be described in terms of a distributed lag function. For example, write:

$$C_t = \sum_{i=0}^{\infty} u_i \, Y_{t-i}$$

as a general form for a distributed lag function, C and Y being consumption and income as before and u_i a set of unspecified weights or lag coefficients. A common assumption in econometric work is to assume that the weights decline geometrically; i.e.,

$$u_i = a\lambda^i$$

or

$$C_t = a \sum_{i=0}^{\infty} \lambda^i Y_{t-i}$$

with the usual restrictions that $0 < \lambda < 1$ and $(a + \lambda) \lessdot 1$.

Take two different possibilities; one where $a = \cdot4$ and $\lambda = \cdot5$ and the other where $a = \cdot6$ and $\lambda = \cdot25$. Then, the implications of this kind of distributed lag can be seen in Diagram 7.1 by concentrating on the two curves that slope downward to the horizontal axis. These curves (as well as the two bell-shaped ones) can be read in the following way. Start from a situation where income has remained constant for some time and allow a once-over change in income that is permanently maintained. Moving from left to right, the vertical distance from the horizontal axis to a point on any curve measures what weight to assign to the change in income in successive periods, in determining the period by period change in consumption. In other words, the lag weights trace out a time profile of the adjustment or response to changes in income. In this case, with only one explanatory or independent variable, income (and its lagged values), whichever profile or set of weights is chosen, simply depicts how the effect of a once-over change in the explanatory variable is spread over time. If additional explanatory variables are used, their impact over time will also

Diagram 7.1

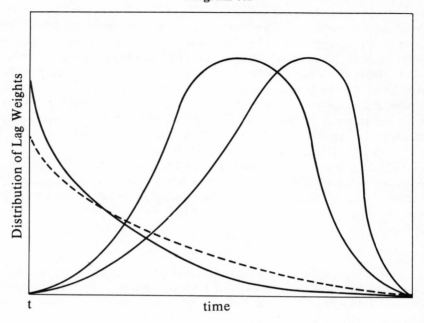

depend upon the distributed lag weights chosen for each one. In the case where $a = \cdot 4$, (representable by the dashed line), the immediate response to an increase in income is less than where $a = \cdot 6$, while the influence in later quarters is greater when $a = \cdot 4$—this in spite of the fact that the ultimate change in consumption, $\Delta C = [a/(1 - \lambda)] \Delta Y$, is the same in both cases. In other words, the larger is a (for a fixed $a + \lambda$), the more sensitive is spending to current economic conditions, as we would expect when $0 < \lambda < 1$. This can be seen in another way by using the familiar Koyck transformation, which allows one to write

$$C_t = a \sum_{i=0}^{\infty} \lambda^i Y_{t-i}$$

as

$$C_t = aY_t + \lambda C_{t-1}.$$

The C_{t-1} term introduces an inertia factor that bears a certain resemblance to the consumption ratchet effect.

Given this type of lagged response, expenditures are only partially dependent upon current conditions. However, such an assumed response cannot lead to expenditures actually moving in the opposite direction to changes in income. This is the result of assuming that the weights decline from the very beginning. Some have argued that the form of the lagged response is in many cases such that the influence of a change in one of the determinants of expenditures, such as overall activity, may be small at first, but then increase for a while before dying out.[1] This is also shown by the bell-shaped curves in Diagram 7.1. Assume again that expenditures depend only upon one determinant, income. Then, the more the curve is stretched out and the more skewed it is to the left, the longer will it take, say, for an unfavorable change in current activity to have a marked depressive effect on expenditures. And if the determinants of expenditures have been changing in a favorable direction prior to the present period, expenditures can continue to rise for some time, even if income continues to decline in the future.

B. Distributed lags and the investment process

At this point it is convenient to switch to different kinds of investment, and to break down the time interval, between a change in one of the determinants of expenditures and actual outlays, into three parts. First, there is the lag between a change in one of the ultimate determinants of investment and the decision to invest; e.g., the appropriation of funds. Second, there follows the lag between the decision to invest and the actual commitment of funds in the form of a contract signed, or an order placed. And, finally, there is the lag between the commitment to invest and the actual outlays. The latter is the kind of construction lag discussed in the last chapter. Various econometric studies have attempted to estimate one or more of these lags, especially for manufacturing investment, sometimes using only one simple profile to encompass all three. The construction lag has been estimated to vary from a lag distributed over 12 months for residential construction, to 20 months for state and local government construction.[2] In general the lagged weights followed an inverted **U**-shaped pattern skewed somewhat to the right. This type of distributed lag seems less applicable to equipment investment, where investment outlays are usually not made until completion of the project.[3] When more than one explanatory variable is used, it is often assumed that each variable influences the dependent variable with the same distributed lag.[4] There is no *a priori* reason

---

[1] See Solow, Robert, 'On a Family of Lag Distributions', *Econometrica*, April 1960.

[2] See Mayer, Thomas, 'The Inflexibility of Monetary Policy', *The Review of Economics and Statistics*, November 1958.

[3] One study that assumes that the lagged response resembles the bell-shaped curves of Diagram 7.1 is that by Almon, Shirley, 'The Distributed Lag Between Capital Appropriations and Expenditures', *Econometrica*, January 1965. The distributive lag weights used in this study, while perhaps satisfactory on statistical grounds, do not seem on theoretical grounds to be correct. Equipment investment is a large proportion of manufacturing investment (the type of investment covered in the study), and investment outlays or payments to the producer are usually made upon completion of the equipment.

[4] The investment equations in the Wharton model and to a lesser extent the Federal Reserve–MIT model retains this assumption for several of the independent variables. A summary of the FRB–MIT model is given by De Leeuw, Frank, and Gramlich, Edward, 'The Federal Reserve–MIT Econometric Model', *Federal Reserve Bulletin*, January 1968.

to expect this to be the case. Indeed we would often expect this assumption to be quite wrong. In most studies the weights are assumed fixed, although variable weights have been used in describing the lag between new orders for capital goods and actual expenditures.[5]

It has been suggested that the deciding factor in determining the degree of sensitivity to current economic conditions is whether economic units within any sector are profit-oriented or not.[6] This distinction does not seem warranted when discussing the distributed lag between commitments and outlays. New orders or contracts are seldom cancelled because of financial penalties and other factors. Economic conditions may deteriorate after a commitment had been made, giving rise to a desire to cut back on future investment outlays, but these desires are seldom fulfilled in reality.[7] Here is a case where other things are not equal, and a decline in activity can, with an inverted **U**-shape pattern of lagged response, be accompanied for a time by an actual increase in expenditures. The longer is the construction period and the more the profile depicting lagged response to income changes is skewed to the left, the longer this can go on.

However, the distinction between groups motivated primarily by profits, and those that are not, is useful in discussing the nature of the lagged response between changes in the determinants of investment and the decision to invest, and between the latter and the actual commitments. This arises partly because of (a) the difference between groups as to the average length of time elapsing between a change in one of the determinants and the decision to invest and (b) the finality of the decision to invest. We might, for example, think of the distributed lag between changes in some measure of capacity utilization rates and the decision to invest, to be one of geometrically declining weights. At the same time there is a lag between the decision to invest and the actual commitment of funds, reflecting the time involved in such things as taking and accepting bids, shopping around for the best price-quality combination, arranging financing, etc., the exact influence depending upon the type of investor involved. As a first approximation we can distinguish between the business sector and other groups, in terms of the average length of the lag between decision to invest and a change in a determinant to invest. This lag is likely to be shorter for business investment than for other types, other things being equal. For example, the 'need' to expand capacity will normally be apparent sooner to corporate officials than to a school committee, if for no other reason than that the corporate business has the more professional organization. In addition, the same distinction between groups will apply to the

[5] See Popkin, Joel, 'The Relationship between New Orders and Shipments: An Analysis of the Machinery and Equipment Industries', *Survey of Current Business*, March 1965.

[6] Hastay, Millard, 'The Cyclical Behavior of Investment', *Regularization of Business Investment*, National Bureau of Economic Research, 1954.

[7] As already mentioned, Zarnowitz's study found little in the way of cancellation of machine tool orders once the latter had been placed. See Zarnowitz, V., *The Timing of . . .*, *op. cit.*

weight to be attached to economic conditions during the interval between the decision and the commitment; in other words, the finality of the 'decision' to invest. In general we would expect the business sector to attach a much higher weight to economic conditions during this period (which will, on the average, be highly correlated with their own sales), than do other groups. For business, even within a period of a year, large discrepancies can occur between a decision to invest a certain amount and the commitment of the funds. The discrepancy can be largely accounted for by the difference between anticipated and actual sales. In contrast we would not, for example, expect a state or local government, once it has decided to build a new school and has obtained whatever approval was necessary, to decide not to go ahead and contract for the construction. Indeed, it may be legally impossible for them to do so. And aside from this, it is difficult to imagine a local government reacting to (or even being aware of) a decline in the economic circumstances of its constituents in the same way as a business would react to a decline in its sales. As we shall soon see, an analogous reaction applies to the majority of household spending units. What has often been termed the 'primary' labor force tends to be isolated in the short run from recessions. As a result, spending decisions made before the downturn tend not to be reversed once the recession sets in, and this is especially true for consumer units making their 'first purchase' of some consumer investment good.[8]

What this all adds up to is that the response of business to changes in the determinants of investment decisions, and the nature of the commitment, will on the average be qualitatively different from that of non-business groups. A different profile of distributed lag weights appears appropriate.[9] It is possible to go further, and argue that the response within business will vary, depending upon things like the share of plant in total investment outlay, the need for external financing, and whether the output or service produced by the capital good is a luxury or a necessity. In any case, in combining these types of lagged responses with that arising because of a construction lag, a very complicated lag structure is appropriate for describing the influence of a change in one of the determinants of investment on actual investment.[10]

---

[8] Thus outlays for household furniture and equipment show little, if any, decline during postwar recessions while auto sales tend to fall off sharply.

[9] In one study an attempt is made to take account of a reconsideration of decisions. The resulting time profile of the lagged response between the determinants of investment and outlays resembles an inverted 'W'. This reconsideration, however, is assumed to precede the actual investment outlays by only one quarter. This would imply that cancellations of contracts and orders are large and frequent, since one would expect the construction lag to be much longer than one quarter, and this is incorrect. In our view, the inverted 'W' lagged response is better thought of as applying to the interval between the determinants of investment and commitments on new orders and contracts. See Evans, M. K. 'A Study of Industry Investment Decisions', *The Review of Economics and Statistics*, May 1967.

[10] Unfortunately, most econometric studies gloss over the separate links in the chain between the determinants and actual outlays of investment, and attempt to encompass two and sometimes all three of the steps in one simple distribution of lag weights.

C. The Need for Variable Lag Weights

But the discussion of the possibility of reconsidering investment decisions suggests that even if several lagged responses are taken into account, this would still involve a vast oversimplification of the true lag structure. Most studies attempting to measure the distributed lag pattern assume that this pattern is fixed, and independent of the size and the rate of change of any determinant of expenditures (or commitment). This is an untenable assumption. The case of an individual and his investment plans brings this point out. We would expect that the head of a spending unit, when be reaches some critical stage in his life cycle such as marriage or the raising of a family, as long as his current and immediate past income has not changed too much, would embark on an investment outlay amounting to some moving average of his income over the past several years. Assume that current stocks held are zero and that the consumer investment outlay equation can be written as: $I_t^c = \cdot 1 Y_t + \cdot 8 I_{t-1}^c$. In other words, with zero stocks, income is the only determinant of expenditures, and the influence of past values of income declines geometrically.[11] If, then, current income has declined (or increased) slightly, we would not expect a large weight to be attached to current income. On the other hand, assume that the potential investor becomes unemployed in the current period, with his income falling from $10,000 per year to $3,000. In this case we would not expect his outlay to fall by only $700 over what he had originally planned; i.e., $\cdot 1 \times \$7,000$. A heavier weight would be given to the current period, the larger is the change in income, (and this weight will also probably differ according to in which way income changed). His outlay is more likely to fall to zero, as he postpones the investment entirely until he is re-employed. Distributed lag weights that do not vary with the size of the change in the determinants of investment, can never pick up this effect. Something like this is surely applicable to other groups. For example, a drastic decline in sales by business would lead to a much larger weight being attached to current sales than if sales fell off moderately.

On the average, then, until the time that funds are committed, in the interval between a change in a determinant of investment and the commitment of funds, current conditions will have a variable effect on actual outlays, the weight depending upon the size (and sign) of the change in a determinant of investment as well as on the type of investor involved. By definition, the less plans or decisions are changed for any given divergence from the anticipated of actual conditions today, the less sensitive is the group or sector to current economic activity. Assuming that the distributed lag of decisions behind the determinants is likely to be longer for nonbusiness groups, and that the decision is less likely to be changed for a given percentage deviation of anticipated conditions from actual, the business or profit-orientated sector will be more sensitive to economic conditions than will be

---

[11] Recall that the variable, I_{t-1}^c, represents a moving average of past values of income.

other sectors. And again among the different business groups, those like public utilities with their large plant outlays and lower risks will be less responsive than, say, manufacturing groups producing luxury items.

D. The Stabilizing Role of the Household Sector

After this rather lengthy discussion we can return to the original formulation of the problem. All economic units, other things being equal, are influenced by current economic conditions. At the same time, if recessions are to be mild, outlays by some sectors must grow during the recession. We now see that this is partly a matter of lags, partly other influences. Backlogs of unfilled orders accumulated by business during the boom, some involving long construction periods, will tend to lead to a slow decline in business investment and therefore final sales once business has overaccumulated. Backlogs will not reverse the downswing, however. The overaccumulation of business capital indicated by a peak and then decline in capacity utilization rates, will result in a decline in new orders and contracts. This must eventually lead to a downturn in outlays whatever the nature of the gestation period, even if outlays increase for a short time at first because of the lagged expenditure effects. What is important if income is to turn around is not just that investment orders be backed up waiting to be filled. Rather 'new orders' and 'contracts' for capital goods by some groups must actually increase during this period or soon afterwards. Since decisions once made can be reversed fairly easily any time before the commitment of funds, one must look elsewhere than the business sector for the upturn. This naturally means the consumer and government sectors. It also means a reliance on family-related expenditures to lead the economy out of a recession.

However, the importance of a slow decline in activity can now be seen more clearly. The slow decline in activity tends in the short run to isolate certain groups or sectors from the rest of the economy, as well as to keep expectations from becoming perverse. As a result these consumer units need not cut back their investments. More than likely they will actually increase expenditures and if the number of households is growing during this period so much the better.

In Chapter III emphasis was laid on the influence of maximum output, X_t, in bringing the rate of growth of demand and supply into line in the long run. However, the short run implications of this consumption function (as well as one that employs the usual ratchet effect or lagged consumption expenditures) are also important. By making consumption a function of maximum output, an element of inertia is introduced into the system that works in the case of recessions to slow down the rate of decline of consumption and therefore of income. This inertia effect, together with those introduced by the backlogs of unfilled orders and other built-in stabilizers, gives a much clearer picture of what to expect once an economy has turned down, than do the formal textbook accelerator-multiplier models.

The relatively slow decline in activity, with its short-run discrepancies between the rate of growth of demand and supply, permits responses by business and members of the labor force that tend to keep employment in general, and employment of the 'primary' labor force in particular, from declining as much and as rapidly as output. Hence the unwillingness of business to discharge workers in proportion to the decline in sales during the sort of recession experienced in the postwar period. There is a cost to hiring and firing labor that is only offset in the event of large declines in sales. This unwillingness to discharge workers has the effect during a recession of shifting the distribution of income from profits to wages. If the marginal propensity to consume out of wage income is higher than the propensity to consume out of profits, a plausible assumption, we have a Kaldor-like mechanism at work that tends to bring down the savings ratio at the same time as the investment ratio has fallen. While usually considered as one of the built-in stabilizers (but not necessarily as a guarantee of long-run full employment), this mechanism is best singled out here as one of the factors stabilizing employment, and permitting the life cycle progression to continue for many households in spite of deviations of output below the long-run path. Naturally, this orderly progression implies a continuation of consumer investment (and total) outlays during the recession, and very likely an increase in the case where population is growing.

But in addition there are forces at work that tend to stabilize the employment rate of the primary labor force; i.e., males between the ages of 25 and 64. The evidence indicates that the participation rate of this primary labor force is little responsive to cyclical movements of the economy. On the other hand, females of various ages, and males less than 25 or more than 64 years of age, tend to move in and out of the labor force in response to economic conditions. The net influence of labor market conditions on participation rates is the outcome of 'the discouraged worker' and 'additional worker' effects, the discouraged worker responding positively to the employment rate, and the additional worker responding positively to the unemployment rate. For example, the semi-retired businessman or potential school dropout are typical of the discouraged worker type, while non-white females represent additional workers. Over all the discouraged worker effect tends to dominate, at least under conditions similar to those of the post World War II period. The estimates of orders of magnitude vary a great deal: one of the more conservative finds that for every change in employment demand of 100 workers, there will be a change of 18–19 workers in the labor force in the same direction.[12]

[12] See Mincer, Jacob, 'Labor-Force Participation and Unemployment: A Review of Recent Evidence', in *Prosperity and Unemployment*, Gorden, R. A., and Gorden, Margaret, (Eds.), John Wiley and Sons, New York, 1966.

It is an easy matter to incorporate this cyclical responsiveness into the analysis and illustrate its stabilizing effect during a recession. As job vacancies fall and unemployment rises, there is a withdrawal of members of the secondary labor force from the labor force. This has the effect of eliminating some of the original imbalance between the demand for and supply of labor, as primary labor force as well as those previously employed can move into jobs made available by the departure of the marginal workers. There are other forces at work also. Seniority regulations, whether formalized or not, would tend to stabilize unemployment rates of the primary labor force, including those in the 25–44-year-old bracket. The net effect is that the average increase from peak to trough in GNP in the male unemployment rate in the five postwar recessions in the United States for the 20–24, 25–34, and 35–44-year-old groups was 4.4., 2.4 and 2.0 per cent, respectively.[13]

The point is that this group of workers with a loose attachment to the labor force tends partially to correct imbalances between the demand and supply of labor. Naturally, if discouraged workers are counted as part of the unemployed (as has been suggested by some economists), fluctuations in employment will be larger by definition. From a welfare point of view their inclusion in the ranks of the unemployed may be justified. But to do so here would obscure the stabilizing role that the secondary labor force plays. For the behavior of discouraged workers works partially to immunize the primary labor force from fluctuations in demand, and it is this group which makes up the heads of families undertaking consumer investment outlays in accordance with some life cycle program.

This picture is given added force when it is recalled that these same groups were most likely to be deterred from carrying out their expenditure plans during the previous boom. And those who were forced to postpone expenditures during the boom and are still employed, are not likely to wait for the next boom before attempting to satisfy their demands. The decision to invest was made some time ago, and the commitment of funds is likely to be made as soon as funds are available, provided the household head is not unemployed in the meantime. Fortunately, unemployment in general and long-term unemployment in particular is more liable to fall on those who would contribute the least to the recovery.

The earlier distinction between first purchases and replacement expenditures is also relevant here. Adverse expectations generated by a decline in general activity will naturally cause a cutback or postponement of some consumer investment outlays, even if the potential spender is still employed. But this is much more likely for those undertaking replacement investment rather than first purchases. And if the pace of the general decline is slow, and if demands for consumer capital goods have been backlogged in the previous boom—

---

[13] Unemployment rates for males, whatever the phase of the cycle, tend to decrease as age increases, until males are in their fifties.

conditions that are most likely, as we argued in Chapter VI—we can expect a kind of bootstrap operation to be at work during a recession. In the last chapter we saw how the household sector helped (inadvertently) to lessen the amplitude of the boom.[14] This same sector now pays a stabilizing role during the downswing. By maintaining or even increasing the outlays in the early stages of a recession, the household sector will help to establish a 'floor' to the economy, and eventually facilitate a recovery. A growing demographic base will only strengthen this operation.

E. The Stabilizing Role of the Non-profit Sector

All of this applies equally if not better for non-profit groups, including state and local governments. It is most unlikely that these groups will increase their actual stocks of capital relative to the desired stocks during the previous boom, however one chooses to define overaccumulation in these sectors. Furthermore, given the nature of the decision process, it is unlikely that decisions made will be cancelled in the light of a gradual decline in income, nor is it likely that new appropiations will be cut back. These outlays will continue to grow during the recession.

This pattern may seem at odds with the persistent belief that the behavior of state and local governments during recessions is such as to aggravate the downswing.[15] However, most of this feeling can be traced to the reaction of state and local governments to the Great Depression, and only then when attention is focused on what happened when the economy was well into the slump. In other words, when discussing the reaction of state and local governments to declines in activity, it is necessary to distinguish between mild and severe recessions, and when discussing the latter to distinguish between the early and late stages of the recession. As we shall have occasion to discuss later in Chapter X, when treating the interwar period in detail, it was not until well into the Great Depression that expenditures by state and local governments got into phase with the rest of the economy.

In contrast, during the period following World War II, outlays by state and local governments have exerted a stabilizing role during recessions, helping to bring about an early recovery after only relatively minor declines in GNP and final sales.[16] The overriding characteristic of state and local government behavior in the postwar period was that of growth, both of expenditures and receipts. To put the matter somewhat differently, total state and local receipts

[14] See pp. 117-118.

[15] The perversity doctrine is usually attributed to Hansen, Alvin, and Perloff, H. S., *State and Local Finance in the National Economy*, Norton, New York, 1944.

[16] As Chapter XI will indicate, this is even more true for economies where discretionary fiscal policy is employed.

were stabilizing in every expansion, and destabilizing or perverse in every contraction. Expenditures were stabilizing in every contraction, but destabilizing in every boom. More important is the net impact when receipts and expenditures are considered together. In a study covering the postwar period up to the early 1960's, the net impact was one of significantly moderating recessions and promoting recovery. During booms, the net impact was expansionary, but this perversity tended to taper off in later stages of the boom.[17] Concentrating on the expenditure side, it is apparent that state and local expenditures have performed much the same sort of bootstrap operation as consumer investment outlays, such as housing and household equipment. Increased outlays by these non-profit groups in the face of a decline in activity in order to satisfy certain needs, have helped to lead to quick reversals of the economy, thereby justifying the optimistic expectations of these same groups.

The question arises as to why this should be so, in the light of the legal strictures on state and local governments against running a deficit on current account over the fiscal year.[18] If the budget on current account was drawn up anticipating a certain level of tax revenue (plus other sources of income), and if these revenues show any sensitivity to the level of economic activity, then one might expect a cutback in outlays if receipts fell below the anticipated levels: either that, or an attempt to bring receipts back up to their projected level through tax rate increases. To a large extent both of these things happened during the 1930's, but it must also be stressed that large numbers of state and local governments simply chose to ignore the budget constraint on current outlays. The net effect was that while attempts were made to increase receipts by raising tax rates, outlays on current account did not show any appreciable decline until 1933 (and on capital account until 1932).[19] But very little of this happened in the postwar United States, and this is what needs explaining.

In an effort to expand their tax base, state and local governments have had to look for new sources of tax revenues. The net effect has been to increase the direct taxes as a share of total tax receipts. This tendency, other things being equal, makes receipts more sensitive to economic activities, and increases the likelihood that expenditures will be cyclically perverse.[20]

---

[17] See Rafuse, R. W., 'Cyclical Behavior of State-Local Finances', *Essays in Fiscal Federalism*, Musgrave, R. A. (Ed.), The Brookings Institution, Washington, 1965.

[18] Deficits within a fiscal year have been permitted because of the lack of synchronization of tax receipts and expenditures. These are financed through the issuance of tax anticipation notes.

[19] See Maxwell, James A., *Federal Grants and the Business Cycle*, National Bureau of Economic Research, New York, 1952, p. 21.

[20] Note that this increased sensitivity of tax receipts is usually cited as an example of decreased fiscal perversity by state and local governments. This is true only if one side of the ledger is considered. It is true that tax receipts will fall off more per dollar decline in GNP the more direct taxes are substituted for indirect taxes. But if outlays must always fall by as much as receipts, there is no gain in stability. There may well be a net loss.

Offsetting this is the increasing importance of grants-in-aid already discussed. These have tended to move countercyclically in postwar recessions, a reflecttion largely of secular growth in the programs.[21]

The explanation of the rise of state and local current expenditures in the face of declines in activity is best explained along the following lines. First of all, state and local governments are in the habit of establishing reserves against appropriations, in case actual receipts fall short of forecasts. To this should be added the tendency for these governments to be extremely conservative in their projected revenue estimates. This means that there is a certan amount of leeway in their spending operations. Should economic activity decline, even if tax receipts move with the general state of the economy there exists a 'surplus' that must first be eaten into before the budget constraint becomes operative. Naturally, if the recession is pronounced enough, this constraint will become operative. But if the decline in activity is slow, even a moderate rise in non-business expenditures during the early stages of the decline can soon offset the decline in the destabilizing types of expenditure. And once a 'floor' is reached, tax receipts will stop declining and the budget constraint need not cause these government units to behave in a fiscal perverse manner.

Most of this applies to state and local expenditures on current account. Expenditures on capital account are influenced to some extent by the behavior of tax receipts, but the fact that a similar kind of budget constraint is not operative here (about one-half of these expenditures are financed through bond flotations) would seem to offer state and local government some additional flexibility. This is borne out in those recession periods for which we have data.[22] A possible explanation of the stabilizing behavior of state and local capital outlays is an alleged sensitivity of these outlays to changes in interest rates and credit conditions. However, during a period of the most extreme tightness on record, high interest rates were found to have led to a cutback of no more than 1 per cent in capital outlays.[23] What monetary policy appears to affect is the timing of long term borrowing. In particular, it has been found that the lag between the authorization by a legislature or referendum to borrow funds, and the actual offering of the bonds for sale, lengthens when interest rates are rising and shortens when rates fall. In addition the amount of issues offered tends to be much higher during slumps than during booms.[24] This behavior is very much related to 'anticipatory borrowing'; i.e. offering issues in advance of financing needs, followed by short term

[21] See Rafuse, *op. cit.*, pp. 70–72.

[22] From fiscal 1957 to 1959 capital outlays by state and local governments rose steadily from $12.6 to $15.4 billion. From 1960 to 1961 they increased from $15.1 to $16.1 billion.

[23] Peterson, John E., and McGouldrick, Paul F., 'Monetary Restraint, Borrowing, and Capital Spending by Small Local Governments and States Colleges, in 1966', *Federal Reserve Bulletin*, December 1968; and 'Monetary Restraint and Capital Spending by Large State and Local Governments in 1966', *Federal Reserve Bulletin*, July 1968.

[24] See Shrapshire, William, 'Interest Rates and Local Government Spending: The North Carolina Experience, 1955–1958', *Southern Economic Journal*, April 1966. Much of this confirmed by Petersen and McGouldrick, *op. cit.*

investment of the funds in Treasury bills or time deposits. It is but one reason why capital outlays seem to be little affected by credit conditions. In addition short term borrowing and the liquidation of short term assets allow state and local governments to escape much of the high cost of borrowing during tight money periods.[25]

Thus, while the fiscal perversity of state and local fiscal behavior may taper off in the later stages of the boom, not too much of this should be attributed to the high interest rates during this phase of the cycle. Nor should increased outlays be attributed to the decline in rates during recessions. A more likely explanation of the lack of any noticeable sensitivity to declines in GNP must be found elsewhere. As already suggested in Chapter VI, the operation of certain constraints during booms acts to cause a deferment of spending plans, whose realization is then carried over to the subsequent recession. Furthermore, because of their non-profit orientation together with lags in the adjustment process, it is not to be expected that state and local governments should react sharply and quickly to declines in activity. Together these influences tend to cause state and local outlays to grow more or less steadily, whatever the phase of the cycle. The only time when this will not be so is when certain conditions are present that permit the destabilizing sectors to cut back sharply in their spending; that this was the case in the interwar period in the United States is argued in Chapter X.

What this and the previous section point up is the importance of relatively insensitive sectors being the least aggressive or in the least favorable position to command resources during the boom. If there were not this matching up of characteristics—if, on the contrary, the least aggressive groups were the most sensitive to declines in output—recessions would certainly be more severe. Fortunately, as long as the boom is strong, it can be expected that some of those sectors least sensitive to declines in general economic conditions will be forced to cut back their proposed spending plans during the boom. Others will continue to increase their expenditures whatever the phase of the cycle. Together with some of the other considerations just discussed, this should lead to highly damped oscillations. We have assumed away a possible destabilizing role for fiscal policy (or any important stabilizing role in the United States for that matter). There still remains the possibility that monetary policy may spoil the story.

F. The Role of Monetary Policy

It was argued in Chapter VI that discretionary monetary policy operated as a kind of ceiling or constraint such as to cause a decline in consumer investment, largely because of a decline in mortgage loans. Marginal business

---

[25] See Petersen and McGouldrick, *op. cit.*

borrowers would also feel the pinch, along with some trimming down of loans even to good loan customers. In addition, the demand for funds by certain nonbusiness groups was considered to be sensitive to the terms of credit, so that shifting supply curves would cause a decline in the amount of funds demanded during the boom. This tended to create backlogs of demands by these groups that could only be satisfied in some later period. At the same time as this postponement of expenditures tended to cut back the rate of growth of demand and output for these groups, it permitted business demands for funds and additions to productive capacity to be satisfied, relatively speaking. This, in turn, would eventually lead to an over-accumulation of capital by business and a downturn. In other words, business over-accumulated capital during the boom, while consumers and other non-business groups tended if anything to develop a shortage of capital. Provided the decline in overall activity was not too great or rapid (and the inelasticity of supply of the capital goods industry would help here), these non-business groups would help reverse the downward movement of the economy. Without such a constraint we have argued that fluctuations in money income and most likely real income would be larger, generating greater instability to the system. On the one hand, booms would be more inflationary, with a greater tendency for all groups to over-accumulate capital, and recessions would be more severe since there would be less of a tendency for backlogging demands during the boom.

Thus, the natural course of events in a recovery is for investment by consumers, and state and local government expenditures, to lead the economy out of the recession and to dominate the early stages of the boom. The business sector will lag here because capacity utilization rates will be low during the recession and early stages of the recovery, thus discouraging this type of investment. However, investment tied in with consumer investment such as stores, restaurants and garages, capital outlays by the public sector and other forms of house-induced investment will soon follow the recovery in consumer investment. Eventually capacity utilization rates for business in general, and manufacturing in particular, will rise inducing an increase in business investment. It is at especially this point that the monetary authorities must decide whether or not a full fledged boom is underway, and if inflationary pressures are soon to develop. Their decision here must be guided by several considerations. Naturally their forecast of government spending is relevant, particularly federal government outlays, since state and local expenditures have a relatively predictable trend. Capacity utilization rates for manufacturing at the trough and during the early stages of the boom are also relevant since they will influence the strength of the boom in investment.[26]

[26] Under certain plausible assumptions, the rate of capacity utilization for manufacturing will be positively correlated with the per cent of firms experiencing shortages of capacity. See Enzler, Jared, 'Manufacturing Capacity: A Comparison of Two Sources of Information', *Federal Reserve Bulletin*, November 1968.

And finally the strength of other kinds of business investment that are perhaps less sensitive to capacity utilization rates than manufacturing, but more related to the past behavior of the economy, must be ascertained. Commercial and public utility investment immediately suggest themselves. All these things must be related to the level and movements of the unemployment rate. If at the point in the boom when all sectors are getting into phase unemployment is high, one kind of decision is called for while a different one is required when labor markets are already tight.[27]

Assume that the authorities feel that a strong boom is under way and that if they merely followed some rule—e.g., a 4 per cent annual growth of the money supply regardless of the state of the economy—inflation would soon get out of hand. In an effort to take some of the steam out of the boom before this happens, they allow credit conditions to tighten, again compared with some rule. Now it should be clear that cyclical fluctuations in the demand for loanable funds will cause market interest rates to fluctuate with the economy even if a rule is followed, resulting in a certain amount of disintermediation. But discretionary policy, although gradual, speeds this up. Various studies of the lags in monetary policy correctly measure the lag in policy, as the interval between the time that the authorities change policy and the time it takes the real sector to react to the policy change. In computing the lag in monetary policy, it is sensible to compare the time it takes discretionary policy to have this added effect on residential construction, the spending of marginal or rationed borrowers, and any other group. This lag, when applied to residential construction, will be seen in Chapter VIII to be relatively short.

Under a discretionary policy, the authorities will allow market rates to rise. Rates will also rise relative to rates on fixed-price near-moneys and mortgage rates; flows into thrift institutions will be slower; and mortgage commitments by all lenders will be less than under a rule. This can take place any time after a boom is underway. It will slow down the rate of growth of demand for the resources of the construction industry, and the rate of growth of residential construction, again compared to a policy of following a rule. In addition it will slow down the rate of growth of demand for 'house-induced' investment, and certain types of consumer durables, so that both a direct and indirect effect are at work. Eventually, this slowing down in the rate of growth of output will help bring about an over-accumulation of capital by the business sector, a recession and less pressure on prices.

This is not meant to imply that the authorities deliberately aim at creating a recession. But in the absence of perfect forecasts, they cannot be expected to reverse a tight money policy in time to avert any decline in output. Generally speaking, the more committed are the authorities to high unemployment at the expense of price stability, the quicker will they shift to a policy of ease

---

[27] All of this assumes that there is only one ultimate target being sought, which is closely related to aggregate demand. When there are multiple targets, either more instruments must be devised or some trade-off between objectives must be accepted.

when there develop signs of a general weakening of a boom. Once the shift to ease has been made, market rates of interest will fall absolutely, and, relative to rates paid on fixed-price near-moneys and mortgages, intermediation will take place and mortgage lending increase. Again, this would be expected even if a rule were being followed. Discretionary monetary policy intensifies and speeds this up in the recession as well as the boom. The task of discretionary policy in a world of uncertainty has traditionally been the modest one of attempting to dampen fluctuations in output and limiting inflation, at least in the United States.

The authorities can, of course, err in either direction. By overestimating the strength of the boom they can cause a slowdown in the growth of demand that causes a mild boom in consumer investment and house-induced investment. This can be mild enough for capacity utilization rates to remain low when business and manufacturing investment begins to pick up, and these utilization rates will continue low because of the failure of housing and investment linked to housing to grow in any sustained fashion. A business investment boom will never get off the ground in this case. On the other hand, they can err by underestimating the strength of the boom. Eventually, an over-accumulation of business capital will be achieved, but undesired inflation will have resulted. It must also be pointed out that in some cases it may be impossible for monetary policy to prevent a serious inflation. The authorities cannot be expected to be able to predict during the early stages of a recovery, that a boom is going to be so strong that if they were to wait to act until unemployment was 'moderate' they would be unable to stop inflation. If authorities can, or are willing to, act only when the boom has already made some progress, there may be times when various types of non-consumption expenditures especially by business are all in phase and are surging. This can lead to a situation where large and increasing backlogs of orders for new capital goods accumulate and prices rise for some time in spite of tight money. This buoyancy will be reinforced by the inflation trends, as investors projecting rising prices into the future attempt to beat the game by investing now. Besides, the real rate of interest may be unaffected during the boom.

But in spite of all the difficulties in formulating policy, the authorities do have some things working in their favor. Working in their favor (and in favor of our ability to interpret their actions) are two factors: (*a*) any boom (or recession) has a certain amount of momentum of its own; and (*b*) a discretionary policy of gradually leaning against the wind can at best have only a marginal direct influence on spending. That this, paradoxical as it may seem, is an advantage, can be seen more clearly by assuming the opposite. For if it is assumed that small changes in the degree of tightness (or ease) in credit markets brought about by policy could have large effects on spending (though with a slight lag), then to be on target from one period to the next would involve fairly sharp and quick reversals in the movements of the instrument variables. Given the commitment to gradualism, i.e., the need to proceed slowly because of constraints and information lags, policy might be quite hopeless. A gradual implementation would most likely be destabilizing, in which case discretionary policy would soon be abandoned.

This result would be intensified if movements in income in the absence of discretionary policy were very erratic. It is very likely that there would be an inclination to fall back on some sort of rule in this case also.

On the other hand, assume that policy can only have a marginal direct effect on spending, and that there is a great deal of inertia in an economic system, so that once a boom gets going it will persist for some time regardless of the kind of policy undertaken. Then, as unemployment rates start to decline and the authorities try to adjust their instrument variables, after taking account in the best way possible all the interactions involved in correctly setting discretionary policy, we can expect the authorities slowly to tighten up credit conditions. Thus, we would expect borrowings and interest rates to rise, and free reserves to fall and eventually become negative—slowly perhaps, but steadily, as the system allows excess liquidity to be mopped up and higher velocity to do an increasingly large share of the work in financing growing levels of expenditures. Credit conditions and the level of monetary aggregates, to be sure, are influenced in the real world by the state of the economy. But the point of the matter is that (given enough time) the authorities as supplier of funds of the last resort, are in a position to compensate for these forces, so that in some long-run sense credit markets can largely reflect their intentions. Where they might go wrong is when the length of any cycle phase in the absence of discretionary policy (i.e., when a rule is followed) is short, compared with the lag between a deliberate change in policy and its effect. And even if this were not a problem, they also might err at cyclical turning points because of information lags.[28] Finally, they will be greatly handicapped in their efforts to stabilize demand if they must also take into account additional targets of policy. This difficulty is discussed in Chapter IX.

G. The Cycle in Outline—a Summary

In summarizing the manner in which damped cycles are generated around a trend, it is helpful to think of the trend as the outgrowth of two forces. On the one hand there are those sectors that continue to grow whatever the phase of the cycle, perhaps more rapidly during the boom, but with relatively minor variation in their growth rates. They do so largely because of their ability to obtain funds in any phase of the cycle (although there may be some difficulties in the late stage of the boom); and because of their non-profit community-service orientation. On the other hand, because of the

[28] This is very likely to be the case if the monetary authorities, in attempting to gauge the impact of their policies, are not looking at several 'indicators' of the thrust of their policies.

workings of certain constraints, there will be offsetting movements in expenditures by important sectors of the economy. Some volatile sectors will be pro-cyclical because of their ability to command resources when they are scarce relative to demand, and because of their quick response to profits prospects. In contrast, there are other types of spending that tend to fluctuate rather widely, whose movements tend to be contra-cyclical. These two movements will not be perfectly offsetting however. During the boom some sectors will turn up before others, pulling the economy out of the recession. Typically, these will be the consumer sector, and those groups in the non-profit and business sectors that undertake what we have called family-related expenditures. During the middle stages of the boom, the more dynamic aggressive sectors will also be booming for a time with those that had previously initiated the boom, but the latter are eventually squeezed out as the boom moves into its final stages. On the downswing, there will be a comparable period when most of the volatile sectors will be moving together with the contra-cyclical ones, partially because of the lagged response of the latter. Soon after the downturn, however, the stabilizing sectors will turn up along with the steady growth sectors. But because expenditures by these various sectors are not perfectly offsetting, but tend to overlap and get into phase for a short part of the boom and the recession, mild cycles in final sales are generated around a rising trend. Furthermore, the sooner the stabilizing sectors turn up after the volatile sectors turn down, the less pronounced will be the recession. And, likewise, the less overlap there is during the boom in the growth of these two groups, the less pronounced the boom.

However, it is important to recognize which sectors are squeezed out in the boom, and which are responsible for carrying the boom through to its final stages. What is important is that those squeezed during the boom are the least sensitive to declines in activity, either because of lags, isolation from the general level of activity, or because of needs that have so risen relative to the capacity to satisfy them, that, in spite of the overall state of the economy, expenditures can no longer be postponed. With regard to this last point, anything that operates to postpone these expenditures in the boom will work to stimulate the same expenditures in the recession.

It can be argued that manufacturing investment will give the boom its profile, at least in an economy relieved of defense commitments.[29] This is especially true in an affluent society, where the social overhead capital has been laid and commercial and industrial construction are no longer such an important part of business investment. In addition, one can say that the immediate cause of a recession will be the fall in capacity utilization rates for

[29] Strictly speaking this statement should be qualified further when considering economies where the monetary and fiscal authorities actively pursue stabilization goals. In the limiting case, with a perfect control mechanism, fluctuations would be eliminated. But it must also be qualified to take account of economies lacking an entrepreneurial class keen on expanding capacity during 'boom' times. This, we will argue in Chapter XI, is very much the case in Britain.

manufacturing, leading to a decline in new orders and contracts, and eventually in investment. But the issue can be traced back a step further to find the cause of the fall in capacity utilization rates for manufacturing, and this will tell something about the strength and duration of any boom. For manufacturing, utilization rates will not decline as long as the rate of growth of non-consumption (or overall) demand is as great as the rate of growth of capacity in manufacturing (provided of course that the income elasticity of demand for manufacturing output is one or more). This will depend to a large extent on the diffusion of the boom among the business groups for two reasons. First, the more widely diffused the boom, the stronger will be the rate of growth of demand; and, second, the more backlogs develop in the investment plans of all business sectors, the greater will be the demands on the output of the capital goods industry. This in turn means manufacturing will be less successful and slower in increasing its share of the output of the capital goods industry, and thereby in over-accumulating. While we can expect manufacturers to be on their toes more than consumers and nonprofit institutions, this need not be the case if a comparison is made with firms in, say, the communication or public utility groups.

Thus, the model sketched in these last two chapters is compatible with booms of different duration. And while it is to be expected that investment by consumers and by state and local governments would initiate the boom, its duration and intensity would be dependent upon the degree of diffusion, and the strength behind business investment. Other things being equal, the greater is this diffusion, the sooner and more appreciably will the less aggressive sectors be squeezed, and the larger will be the backlogs of demand by these sectors when the boom tapers off. And, of course, the greater will be inflationary pressures.

What if the degree of diffusion of business investment, as well as the strength of investment demands within this sector, is not great? By our reasoning the booms will be weak. However, it is necessary to be careful at this point. Up until now it has been assumed that the strength of overall demand relative to supply during the boom would inevitably squeeze some sectors, and force them to postpone or stretch out their spending plans. But there may be cases where business demand for capital is weak. Here it is necessary to distinguish two different cases. On the one hand, there may be booms where lack of diffusion of strong business investment demand is due ultimately to technological considerations. Technological change may be capital saving in its simplest sense; i.e. over time the change in capacity generated by a dollar's worth of investment is higher than average, and rising. In this case a given rate of growth of income will induce a relatively small amount of business and manufacturing investment (relative to high employment savings). If this is so, the strength and duration of the boom will be pretty much determined by the strength of investment demand of the consumer sector and other types of family-related investment. If the latter is of no unusual strength, we would expect the boom to be short-lived, although other factors, such as speculation, may prolong it. Consumer investment might grow for a time, causing capacity utilization rates to decline somewhat. But with the assumed lack of strength of business investment demand both by manufacturing and non-manufacturing firms, overall demand could not continue to grow long enough to induce through the multiplier effects even an average sized business investment boom.

On the other hand, it is possible to think of a situation where, given the usual rates of growth of output or final sales during the boom period, a good size investment boom by business would be expected once capacity utilization rates get back up to a more 'normal' rate. However, this never comes about, because the boom in consumer investment and the induced boom in family-related investment outlays never materializes. As a result, capacity utilization rates for manufacturing and other types of business investment that tend to respond to utilizations rates never rise enough to generate a strong boom in business investment, which in turn helps to maintain and even increase utilization rates. The lack of any pronounced boom in consumer investment and related outlays could be traced, in turn, to a premature implementation of a tight monetary policy.[30]

Thus, in both cases there is a lack of any strong investment boom by the business sector. But the causes are different, and so are the consequences. In the first case, family-related expenditures are not cut back because of disintermediation or some other constraint, but are allowed to grow, and when the economy does turn down there is little to cushion the impact. This is not necessarily the case in the second example. In the first case, there is very little left to reverse the decline in activity, save those sectors that tend to grow whatever the phase of the cycle. But even here we may be in difficulty because all sectors can be expected to get into phase if the recession is severe enough. Even though output is declining slowly, without all the usual contra-cyclical forces at work there will come a point when expectations deteriorate for even the most insensitive and isolated groups. At that point a slump equilibrium with negative net investment becomes a distinct possibility.

With this distinction between two types of weak boom and their under-lying causes, it is possible to bring together those factors which will give each boom, and to a large extent each subsequent recession, its strength, form and duration. First, monetary policy, its intensity and timing, will influence the strength of the boom in consumer investment in the early stages of the recovery, and indirectly influence the strength of the house-induced invest-ment. This in turn will influence the strength of the boom in business in-vestment. The stronger the recovery in nonbusiness outlays, the more rapidly will utilization rates rise and the higher will be the proportion of business

---

[30] The boom of 1958–1960 in the United States and that beginning late in 1966 in the United Kingdom are examples of this kind of mini-boom.

firms wishing to step up their investment outlays. Second, if the previous assumption is correct, then the rate of capacity utilization at the beginning of the boom will have an additional influence on the strength of business investment. Third, while the linkage between consumer investment and house-induced investment is strong, there are other factors influencing the strength of, say, public utility and commercial and other investment.[31] These two categories are the most important, after manufacturing investment, in total business investment. Their strength will have an important influence on fluctuations. And, finally, something that has been almost completely disregarded up to this point must be taken into account. This is federal government expenditure, especially that for defense. When this is introduced, the whole nature of the cyclical (and growth) process can be drastically altered.

---

[31] Two investment equations of the Wharton Model are for 'Commercial and Other' (which includes more than the Office of Business Economics definition) and 'Nonfarm Housing'. Both equations assume that expenditures are a moving average of past values of the difference between the long term and short term interest rate. Movements of the latter are used as a measure of the degree of tightness of monetary policy. However, most of the effect of changes in this rate differential are felt quickly in the housing market, but with a longer lag for 'commercial and other' investment.

Chapter VIII **Growth and Cycles in the Postwar United States**

A. Introduction

It is the task of this and the next two chapters to use the theoretical apparatus developed in the earlier chapters, to analyze the development of one particular capitalist system. Our attention will be confined to the period since World War I. The post-World War II period (hereafter referred to as the postwar period) treated in this chapter is viewed as a period when the system was moving along an equilibrium growth path that was stable. In Chapter X the interwar period will be discussed in terms of an economy whose equilibrium path was unstable.

Unfortunately, any attempt to analyze the postwar period in terms of a long-run equilibrium growth path, and deviations around it, runs into three formidable problems. First, because of backlogs created by the war and the depression of the 1930's, much of the period was greatly influenced by the initial conditions. There is a real problem in determining how much of the postwar period can be considered normal (in the sense that the economy was moving along some growth path subject to the kind of deviations described in the last two chapters), and how much of the period was a process of convergence from below (because of large positive discrepancies between desired and actual stocks of capital) toward the neighborhood of the long-run growth path. In an effort to handle this difficulty, the postwar period will be subdivided into the pre and post 1953–1954 recession periods. It is true that even in 1954 it could be said that a housing shortage still existed and that public facilities had not been built up to provide the desired workload. However, the reconversion from World War II and the Korean War had been largely completed by this date, and for this reason we will often find it convenient to divide the period this way, and to concentrate on developments since the 1953–1954 recession.

Second, the Korean War, the cold war and the Viet Nam encounter lead to large variations in defense expenditures. While we would expect growth in non-defense government expenditures at all levels to be natural enough for any developed economy, fluctuations in defense spending had at times a dominating influence, particularly in modifying the nature of the cyclical movements. Both variations in the defense budget and the large backlogs make it difficult to see clearly the workings of the basic growth and cyclical mechanism. Finally, certain other fiscal changes were made during the period that affected the performance of the economy. For the most part, their influence, as well as that of monetary policy, will be treated separately.

B. The Underlying Trends

During the postwar period as a whole, the unemployment rate never exceeded 7 per cent on an annual basis, and averaged 4.7 per cent from 1948 to 1970 and 4.8 per cent from 1954 to 1970. Consumer prices moved upward every year but one, but if the immediate postwar period and the Korean buildup through 1951 are omitted, the average annual increase of prices was 1.4 per cent from 1951 to 1965 and 1.7 per cent from 1951 to 1968. In 1969, 1970 and 1971 prices rose by 6.2, 5.3 and 4.3 per cent respectively. None of this suggests any serious prolonged period of disequilibrium.

As already suggested, the early postwar years were largely dominated by the backlogs of demand built up by the postponements caused by the depression of the 1930's and the war. The situation in 1945 showed a decline since 1929 in the stock of consumer durables, consumer credit outstanding, mortgage and consumer debt, and a huge rise in liquid asset holdings, all measured on a *per capita* basis. Total private debt was lower than in 1929, while state and local government debt was little changed, while the ratio of non-residential fixed capital to GNP had declined over the period by more than 25 per cent. In retrospect, one can see that the stage was set for strong demand pressures for some time to come.

Although the early years are colored by these abnormal backlogs, there are enough observations beyond this period to give some indication of the underlying trends. As is clear from Table 8.1, the postwar period witnessed an upward trend in government expenditures at the expense of consumption, both state and local government expenditures and federal defense expenditures growing at a faster rate than GNP. Fixed non-residential investment as a share of GNP showed little trend during the period, and is little different from the 1929 figure, a boom year for investment. The downward trend since 1929 in non-residential structures as a share of GNP stands out, and

Table 8.1

	G^T/Y	G^F/Y	G^F-G^D/Y	G^{S+L}/Y	C'/Y	C^D/Y	I^H/Y	I^{FNR}/Y	I^{FS}/Y
1929	8·2%	1·2%	N.A.%	7·0%	66·0%	8·9%	3·8%	10·2%	4·8%
1948	12·3	6·5	2·3	5·8	58·6	8·8	5·6	10·4	3·4
1952	21·6	15·0	1·7	6·6	54·2	8·5	5·0	9·1	3·2
1956	18·7	10·8	1·2	7·9	54·3	9·3	5·2	10·4	4·1
1965	20·0	9·8	2·4	16·3	53·6	9·7	4·1	10·2	3·6
1970	22·6	10·2	2·4	12·4	54·0	9·2	3·0	10·5	3·6

Y = Gross National Product; G^T = total government expenditures on goods and services; G^F = federal government expenditures on goods and services; $G^F - G^D$ = federal government expenditures net of defense; G^{S+L} = state and local expenditures on goods and services, C' = consumption expenditures; C^D = expenditures on consumer durables; I^H = residential structures; I^{FNR} = non-residential fixed investment; I^{FS} = non-residential structures. All variables measured in current dollars.

Source: *Survey of Current Business*, various issues.

Table 8.2

	G^T/U	G^F/U	G^F-G^D/U	G^{S+L}/U	U/C'	C^D/U	I^H/U	I^{FNR}/U	I^{FS}/U
1929	24·2%	3·6%	N.A.%	20·6%	50·0%	26·2%	11·2%	30·0%	14·1%
1948	29·5	15·5	5·5	14·0	70·7	21·2	13·5	25·1	8·2
1952	47·2	32·8	3·7	14·4	84·3	18·5	10·8	19·9	7·2
1956	41·0	23·8	2·7	17·2	84·0	20·3	11·2	22·8	9·0
1965	43·1	21·2	5·2	22·0	86·9	20·9	8·8	22·0	7·8
1970	49·1	22·2	5·1	27·0	85·2	20·0	6·6	22·8	7·8

U = gross national product minus consumer expenditures on non-durables and services (C'). All other variables have their previous meanings.

Source: *Survey of Current Business*, various issues.

continues a trend begun early in the 20th century. The downward postwar trend in residential structures is offset by the rise in consumer durable expenditures, so that total consumer investment as a share of GNP is little changed during the postwar period, although typically higher than the 1929 figure. Figures for manufacturing investment as a share of GNP (not shown) show little change during the period, averaging about $3\frac{1}{2}$ per cent.

An alternative way of bringing out some of the structural changes is seen in Table 8.2. The variable, $U = GNP - C'$, measures the sum of all non-consumption expenditures or 'stimulants'. Various components of this sum are then expressed as a percentage of GNP minus consumption. By this measure both consumer and business investment have declined as government outlays have risen. Depending upon whether government expenditures are

Table 8.3

	$\Delta Y/Y$	$\Delta FS/FS$	$\Delta y/y$	$\Delta fs/fs$
1947 (I)–1969 (IV)	3·80%	3·76%	2·30%	2·26%
1954 (II)–1969 (IV)	3·80%	3·72%	2·40%	2·32%

$\Delta Y/Y$, $\Delta FS/FS$, $\Delta y/y$, $\Delta fs/fs$ measure the annual average growth rate of gross national product, final sales, *per capita* gross national product and *per capita* final sales respectively, all in constant dollars.

Source: *Survey of Current Business*, various issues.

more or less stable than consumer or business investment in the face of a decline in overall activity, we can say as a rough first approximation that the economy is more or less prone to serious recessions.

Mention has already been made of the importance of family-related expenditures in total output.[1] Over the postwar period they varied from 10 to 13 per cent of GNP, 1946 excluded. If public utility construction investment is included, the ratio moved between 11 and 14 per cent. A better measure of their importance is in relation to total stimulants, U. This ratio varied from 23 to 30 per cent and from 24 to 33 per cent, depending upon whether public utility construction expenditure is or is not excluded (again omitting the reconversion year 1946). The annual average rate of growth of various measures of economic activity are shown in Table 8.3 for the entire postwar period, including the period from the trough of the first post-Korean recession to the latest peak in overall activity in 1969 (IV). At the same time as population grew 1.5 per cent and 1.4 percent for the longer and shorter periods respectively, the rate of growth of the number of households was even higher for both periods. Diagram 8.1 gives the trends in the distribution of the population for most of the postwar years, together with a projection. As is clear, the rates of growth by age groups was very uneven. In particular, the 25–35 and 35–44 year old group was noticeably below the overall growth of the population. However, the projected growth of these groups in the 1970's and 1980's indicates a sizable potential source of demand for family related expenditures.

C. The Upper Turning Point

To what extent do the cycles of the postwar period resemble the idealized picture of Chapters VI and VII? Monetary policy, the behavior of the economy in the previous cycle, the tie-in between consumer investment and

[1] See pp. 81 and 82.

Diagram 8.1

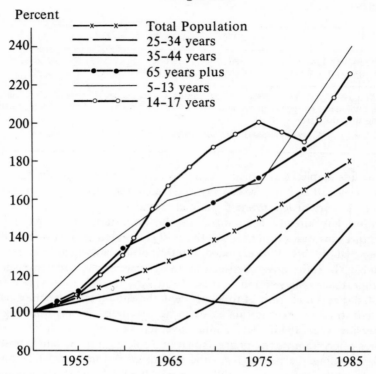

Percent

—x—x—	Total Population
— — —	25–34 years
————	35–44 years
—•—•—	65 years plus
————	5–13 years
—o—o—	14–17 years

Source: 1950 and 1955, U.S. Department of Commerce Bureau of the Census, *Population Estimates*, July 1965. 1960 to 1985, *Population Estimates*, December 1967.

house-induced investment all play a major role during this period. Differences from cycle to cycle can, to a large extent, be traced to differences in the importance of these influences. But, in addition, the federal government played a large role, especially at the beginning and at the end of the postwar period covered.

In Table 8.4, troughs (*T*) and peaks (*P*) are given for GNP in the left hand portion of the table with final sales on the right hand side. Each turning point is shown first in current prices with the same national income measure shown in constant prices immediately below it.[2] The 'basic' causes of

[2] There is no actual downturn in final sales measured in current prices for the boom beginning 1958-(I) and 'ending' in 1960-(III). The dating of the peak for this boom coincides with the period when final sales showed the smallest growth. The same quarter is listed as the beginning of the long boom of the 1960's, during which GNP and final sales in current dollars never declined, even in 1970. Growth during this long boom was somewhat uneven. The economy marked time during a good part of 1966, and in 1964 there was a small one quarter decline in final sales (but not GNP).

Table 8.4

GNP (billions of $)				Final Sales (billions of $)			
T		P		T		P	
—		1948-(IV)	$263·9	—		1948-(IV)	$259·6
—		1948-(IV)	$328·7	—		1949-(II)	$328·8
1949-(II)	$255·2	1953-(II)	$367·5	1949-(I)	$258·5	1953-(IV)	$365·3
1949-(II)	$322·7	1953-(II)	$416·4	1949-(III)	$328·6	1953-(IV)	$413·1
1954-(II)	$360·4	1957-(III)	$446·3	1954-(II)	$363·1	1957-(IV)	$443·8
1954-(II)	$402·1	1957-(III)	$455·2	1954-(II)	$405·7	1957-(III)	$452·2
1958-(I)	$434·7	1960-(II)	$504·7	1958-(I)	$440·1	1960-(III)	$501·0
1958-(I)	$437·5	1960-(I)	$490·2	1958-(I)	$443·1	1960-(II)	$486·0
1960-(IV)	$503·3		—	1960-(III)	$501·0		—
1961-(I)	$482·7	1969-(III)	$730·9	1960-(III)	$484·4	1969-(IV)	$723·0
1970-(IV)	$715·9			1970-(IV)	$712·8		

Source: *Survey of Current Business*, various issues.

differences in the duration and amplitude of booms are somewhat different from the idealized picture painted earlier because Federal government outlays, particularly those connected with defense, are an important part of the postwar picture. Even allowing for offsetting movements in the tax structure, the direct effect of variation in government spending would because of the balanced budget multiplier and the indirect effects of private investment (especially when tied in with defense). allow the central government to have a large and at times dominating effect on the economy. This influence is best discussed systematically later, when the question of the duration of the different booms and recessions is taken up.

We can at this point say something about the immediate cause of the downturn, however. It was argued earlier that the natural course of things in a somewhat simplified world was an overaccumulation of capital by business, especially manufacturing, causing the boom to end. The boom in general activity would eventually lead to a situation where business in general, and manufacturing in particular, would succeed in enlarging their capacity by a larger amount than their sales, partly by obtaining an enlarged portion of the output of the capital goods industry. This would eventually bring about a decline in investment and a recession, other things being equal.[3] Monetary factors might prolong or shorten the boom, but not alter its

[3] The capital goods industry was defined earlier to include that collection of firms producing business equipment, plus all construction firms. Construction firms, especially the larger ones, can produce either for the residential or commercial construction markets.

essential pattern. The business sector's ability to increase its share of the output of the capital goods industry is to a certain extent born out by Diagram 8.2, where the behavior in the postwar period of a measure of family-related construction is shown. The numerator of the ratio of family-related construction to total construction measures as near as possible the construction component of family-related expenditures, as defined in Chapter V, and excludes the volatile types of business investment. Public utility plant investment is excluded, as well as all forms of 'commercial and industrial construction', except the Department of Commerce category 'stores, restaurants and garages'. The major component is naturally residential construction. The shaded areas indicate a recession in final sales. The behavior of the ratio during the middle and late stages of each boom points up the ability of the business sector to increase its share of the output of the construction industry, as family-related construction in percentage terms falls off correspondingly. The even greater propensity for the manufacturing sector to over-accumulate is clear in the postwar period. The middle and late stages of each boom were characterized by substantial increases in manufacturing investment as a share of total business investment (and therefore of total capital outlays), followed by a decline in this ratio in each recession. This, it has been argued, is the result both of a greater sensitivity of manufacturing investment to current profit prospects, and of a greater degree of aggressiveness by manufacturers in obtaining the desired share of the output of the capital goods industry.[4] The net effect is to lead to an even greater likelihood of fluctuations of manufacturing investment. In Chapter IX we will look at this phenomenon from the point of view of the household sector, and the squeezing out of residential construction.

Total non-residential fixed plant and equipment investment leads, or is coincident with, final sales at every peak, whether variables are measured in current or constant dollars (as is the equipment category considered separately).[5] There is somewhat less regularity in timing for these different investment groups and GNP. The peaks in investment tend to coincide with the peaks in GNP, especially after the Korean War period, rather than to

[4] A typical swing for a moderate sized boom and recession; is an increase of manufacturing investment as a percentage of business investment from about 40 per cent at the beginning of 1955, to about 44 per cent during the period mid-1956 to mid-1957, to be follosed by a decline to 35 per cent by the end of 1958.

The failure of the ratio in Diagram 8.2 to rise during the interval from peak to trough in final sales during 1960–1961, is partly accounted for by the heavy business demand for construction throughout 1960; i.e. a construction lag, together with lag in new mortgage acquisitions by thrift institutions.

[5] Unfortunately the fixed non-residential investment series that excludes outlays by agriculture and non-profit institutions, as well as the manufacturing investment series, are in current dollars. This former series is referred to as 'business investment' by the Department of Commerce. It leads or is coincident with final sales at every peak of the latter, except 1969-(IV). We will use the term business investment in this sense to be contrasted with non-residential fixed investment, which includes outlays by agriculture and non-profit institutions.

lead it, because of the lead shown by inventory investment over final sales, i.e., GNP tends to decline before final sales.

More revealing is the behavior of changes in fixed non-residential investment and changes in final sales, beginning with the trough in final sales in 1954-(II). Diagram 8.3 brings out the high correlation between this measure of investment and final sales in the middle and late stages of each boom. If a comparison is made between the changes in final sales and changes in business investment (roughly fixed non-residential investment less investment by agriculture and non-profit institutions), beginning with the point in each boom when business investment has begun to recover until the following trough in final sales, the parallel movements are even more striking. In other words, after that point in each boom when capacity utilization rates have been rising long enough to cause an upturn in the most volatile procyclical types of spending, the movements of final sales for the remainder of the boom, and the subsequent decline in final sales, tend to be highly correlated with movements in these measures of investment outlays. The same relationship holds between changes in final sales and manufacturing investment. Where this relation tends to break down is during periods where defense spending changed fairly rapidly, such as the late 1960's, a matter to be discussed shortly.[6]

The fact that various measures of fixed investment by the business sector tend to coincide or lead movements of GNP and final sales at cyclical peaks, and to be highly correlated with the latter during the middle and later stages of the boom, does not necessarily indicate causation. However, the fact that in general peaks in capacity utilization rates for manufacturing, and new contracts and orders for business, plant and equipment, lead final sales does give more than a hint that there are causal links. The suggestion is that falling capacity utilization rates and falling contracts and orders lead to declines in manufacturing and business investment, and eventually declines in final sales. There are no figures for capacity utilization rates for all business, and while it is true that some categories of business investment have moved counter to manufacturing investment, these movements have never been strong enough to keep total business and manufacturing investment from being practically mirror images of one another. We can only guess, but there

---

[6] This is true for the business investment series (which excludes investment by agriculture and non-profit institutions), manufacturing investment and non-residential fixed investment in current and constant dollars (the latter including outlays by agriculture and non-profit institutions). For example, from 1954-(III) (the point at which fixed non-residential investment picks up), to 1970-(IV), the change in non-residential fixed investment in constant dollars was of the opposite sign as the change in final sales in constant dollars in only eleven of the fifty-eight quarters. Eight of these eleven quarters came during the 1960's, when changes in defense spending loomed so large. The correlation is not as strong earlier because of the influence of the Korean War and the nature of the reconversion period. Fixed non-residential investment is often considered a lagging series. It certainly is not with respect to final sales, as Diagram 8.3 indicates. If the years prior to 1955 were shown in the Diagram, they would reveal a lead of fixed non-residential investment over final sales at the peak and a lag at the trough.

Diagram 8.2

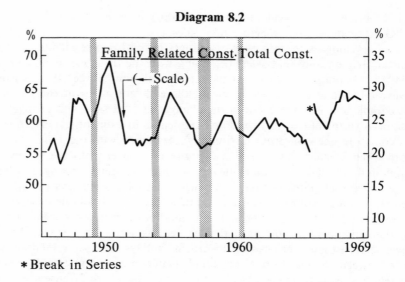

* Break in Series

Source: 1946–1953, U.S. Department of Commerce, Bureau of the Census, *Value of New Construction Put in Place*; 1946–1963 *Revised*; U.S. Department of Commerce, Bureau of the Census, *Construction Review*, various issues.

is no reason to think that business investment in the aggregate does not also turn down, after some analogous measure of capacity utilization rates for all businesses has also begun to fall—partly, to be sure, because of the manner in which manufacturing investment dominates its behavior. The behavior of the 'contract and orders, plant and equipment' series, which includes contracts and orders by other sectors in addition to manufacturing, supports this latter position.[7] We will return to these points later when discussing why the booms differed from one another.

D. The Postwar Recessions

Fortunately, once the recessions set in, final sales declined slowly. In the two most severe recessions, 1953–1954 and 1957–1958, final sales in constant dollars declined in both cases for only two quarters, and at an annual rate of approximately 2 per cent. We would expect this, one reason being the

[7] See *Business Cycle Developments*, U.S. Department of Commerce, September 1968, appendix F. The behavior of both the capacity utilization rates and contract and orders series, preceding cycle peaks in final sales and GNP, is best described in terms of a plateau rather than a peak, suggesting that some sort of moving average of past movement of these series would best explain the timing of the downturn in investment.

Diagram 8.3

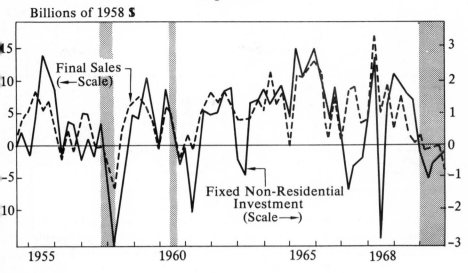

Source: *Survey of Current Business*, various issues.

manner in which producers of capital goods reacted to the booming demand for new capital goods in the preceding boom. There are no figures for unfilled orders and contracts to go with the (new) orders and contracts, plant and equipment series, though unfilled orders of the 'durable goods industries' are available. (Unfortunately this series includes unfilled orders for consumer durables as well as backlogged orders for producers durables.) These orders rose relative to sales for each boom except the immediate postwar expansion, as did a related series, the backlog of capital appropriations for manufacturers. The percentage and absolute increase both in the ratio of unfilled orders to sales and in backlogged capital appropriations was largest in the boom of the 1960's, smallest in the 1958–1959 mini-boom, and somewhere in between in the boom of the mid-1950's, indicating that the longer is the boom the greater will be the accumulated backlogs and average waiting period.

The stabilizing effect of the inelasticity in the supply of capital goods for business can be better seen, perhaps, by comparing, for successive recessions beginning with 1948–49 and ending in 1969–70, (*a*) the percentage decline in contracts and orders by business, *CO*, with the percentage decline in fixed nonresidential investment, I^{FNR}, from the peak in the contract series to the trough in final sales, *FS*; and (*b*) the percentage decline in contracts and orders from its peak to its trough, with the percentage decline in fixed non-residential investment from its peak to its trough, for successive recessions beginning with 1948–49 and ending in 1969–70. This is shown in Table 8.5. The first two columns indicate that once new orders and contracts for capital

Table 8.5

% decline in CO from CO peak to FS trough	% decline in I^{FNR} from CO peak to FS trough	% decline in CO from peak to trough in CO	% decline in I^{FNR} from peak to trough in I^{FNR}
22·0%	7·8%	27·3%	15·6%
29·9	0·2	29·9	6·9
24·4	5·6	24·4	14·2
1·9	1·9	5·2	6·1
7·8	4·8	7·8	1·7

Source: *Business Cycle Developments*, September 1968 and *Survey of Current Business* various issues, all figures based on current dollar magnitudes.

goods by business begin to decline (just before cyclical peaks), the decline in this demand for new capital goods is much greater than the 'supply' of new capital goods from this point until the trough in general economic activity. Had the capital goods industry been able to better match up the supply with the demand for capital goods during the previous boom, the decline in business investment outlays would naturally have been much greater. The final two columns are another indication of the greater instability of the demand for capital goods compared to supply and, therefore, business investment expenditures. It is this response of the capital goods industry to orders that plays such an important role in slowing the rate of decline in expenditures on new capital goods and, thereby, the rate of decline of total output. While not able to stop the decline in overall activity (let alone reverse it), the slowness of the decline (relative to what would occur if the capital goods industry could immediately match supply with demand) acts to keep expectations from becoming perverse, and allows certain groups to remain isolated from the recession for a longer period of time.

The other built-in stabilizers behaved in the expected fashion; transfer payments rose, tax receipts fell and dividend payments hardly changed at all. As a result of these conditions, disposable income in current dollars declined absolutely in only one recession, that of 1948–1949, and then by only 3 per cent. Personal consumption expenditures (defined net of durable outlays) declined by less than 1 per cent, causing a rise in the average propensity to consume from peak to trough from 79 to 81 per cent in this first recession. In every other recession both disposable income and consumption measured in current prices rose absolutely, the latter more than the former, so that each time the average propensity to consume rose approximately 1 per cent. This is what we would expect on the basis of the consumption equation developed in Chapter III. Thus while disposable income and consumption rose during the recession, so did unemployment. Hence the greater

Table 8.6

	ΔFS	ΔI^{FNR}	ΔC^D	ΔI^H	ΔI^C	ΔG^F	ΔG^{S+L}	$\Delta C'$	ΔE
Change	−$0·2	$−1·7	$1·4	$1·5	$2·9	$−0·1	$0·5	−0·8	−1·0
Peak to	−7·4	−1·2	−0·4	1·9	1·5	−13·7	1·1	3·3	1·5
Trough in	−9·1	−4·7	−2·9	−0·1	−3·0	−0·9	1·8	−0·7	−3·5
Final Sales	−1·5	−0·6	−0·6	−1·0	−1·6	0·8	−0·1	−0·7	0·6
	−10·2	−6·6	−8·3	0·8	−7·1	−10·6	2·3	+10·8	1·2
Change	1·2	−0·7	1·1	2·1	3·2	−1·0	0·6	1·9	−2·7
Trough in	4·0	0·4	0·4	1·3	1·7	−2·5	1·0	3·2	0·3
Final Sales	1·4	−2·0	−1·1	−0·1	−1·2	1·2	0·5	2·9	0
To one									
quarter later	2·6	0	−1·5	−0·3	−1·8	0	0·5	1·4	1·7
	14·4	2·2	9·3	1·5	10·8	−1·9	1·1	0·4	1·3

Source: *Survey of Current Business*, various issues. $I^C = C^D + I^H$ and $E =$ net exports of goods and services. All other variables have their previous meanings.

increase of consumption compared to disposable income. Naturally, the built-in stabilizers can at best stop the fall in income, and possibly only slow its rate of decline. But they do play an important role, along with the sectors that pull the economy out of the recession, in keeping excess capacity from rising very rapidly or greatly in the recessions. Together they hasten the turn around both of contracts and orders, and business investment.

In Table 8.6 the change in final sales and its components in successive recessions, beginning with the 1949-(II) trough and ending with that in 1970-(IV), have been calculated for (a) the change in each flow from the peak to trough in final sales and (b) the change in each flow from the trough in final sales to one quarter later, all variables measured in constant dollars. Table 8.6 brings out the mildness of postwar recessions as much as Table 8.4 brought out their brevity. The results are little different if the declines in GNP are considered instead of those in final sales. The amplitude of the declines in the former are a little greater on the average, and the durations of the declines average between one and two quarters longer. The decline in non-residential fixed investment is fairly consistent, as is its lagging the upturn in final sales. A trough in fixed non-residential investment two quarters after the trough in final sales is typical. These investment declines can be described alternatively as being dominated by declines in manufacturing or equipment investment.

On the other hand, the behavior of state and local government expenditures is, with one small exception, stimulating both during the recession and at the lower turning points. Table 8.6 also brings out the stabilizing influence of consumption. When it did decline, the decline was small, and in two recessions it increased substantially. The behavior of federal expenditure (and net exports) is somewhat irregular. For the downturn sometimes the changes are plus, sometimes minus, and this is true for the early period of recovery. In the two early recessions, consumer investment actually increased throughout, undoubtedly because of the strong backlogs of demand for consumer capital goods. This is true even though housing investment was not growing at the beginning of each recession, but only picked up later. In the third and fourth recessions consumer investment didn't turn up until two and three quarters after the trough in final sales, respectively. More will be said about this when discussing the role of monetary policy.

What seems to be happening is that in each recession the behavior of state and local government consistently offsets the negative influence of business investment outlays, with consumption and residential housing playing a helpful role. However, to some extent, the mildness and shortness of the postwar recessions has to be considered the outcome of fortuitous events. The extremely heavy backlog of demand by consumers for capital goods, together with their very favorable net worth position, in the period shortly after the war must have been responsible for the early rise in such expenditures once business demand for funds and resources had declined. While some sort of backlogging of this type of spending is a likely result of any boom, the extraordinary size of the immediate postwar backlog was bound to work itself out sooner or later. Fortunately, federal government expenditures were being cut back during two recessions when we could still count on this large consumer backlog. When these abnormal backlogs cannot be counted on, what seems to be absolutely essential (leaving aside the possibility of federal outlays increasing) is that the decline in business investment be gradual and mild, so that the more or less steady growth of state and local (and other forms of family-related) expenditures and consumption cause final sales to stop declining. When this happens the stage is set for the next boom in consumption and then expenditures on consumer durables will pick up, leading eventually to an increase in all forms of consumer investment.[8]

The insensitivity of state and local expenditures to declines in final sales of the size just described, as well as those of much greater magnitudes, is amply demonstrated by their behavior in the late 1920's and early 1930's. In the interwar period state and local government annual expenditures on construction and current account increased until 1931 and 1932 respectively (this in a day when federal grants-in-aid were almost nonexistent), and in the face of a collapse of financial markets and a more rapid decline in activity.

---

[8] Table 8.6 to some extent does not emphasize enough the stabilizing role of family-related expenditures. Although housing investment does not turn up one quarter after the trough in final sales in the recessions of 1957–1958 and 1960, it does turn up by the second quarter after the trough in both cases. Also most of the decline in expenditures on consumer durables is taken up by declining auto sales. Expenditure on furniture and household equipment hardly declined during the recessions.

We might infer from this that without the stimulating effects of increased federal government outlays in the 1957–1958 and 1960 recessions, the recessions would still be relatively mild, but longer. From all this it is possible to think of two possible cases when recessions will be likely to be severe. In the one case, during a period when there are only the more usual backlogs of deferred demand built up during the boom, federal government expenditures are cut back substantially. On the other hand, in a boom where initially unemployment is relatively high, some constellation of circumstances gives rise only to a very modest boom in business investment. This can lead to a situation where real and financial resources are not drained away from the non-business sector, and backlogs of business demand in the form of unfilled orders are not built up substantially. As a result, when the recession comes, the rate of decline of business investment may be very rapid and the subsequent pick up in consumer investment will fail to materialize. The recession beginning in 1969-(IV) would, but for 'God's grace', have been an example of the first possibility, and is of such interest as to require special treatment at the end of the chapter. The recession beginning in 1929 is an example of the latter.

E. The Booms of the Postwar Period

The theoretical model of Chapter VI and also the actual behavior of the American economy in the postwar period suggested that the immediate cause of the decline in final sales can be attributed to the decline in business and manufacturing investment. At some point in the recovery, business investment would pick up and grow rapidly. Eventually, the capacity effect would catch up with the multiplier effect, so that the growth of investment would decline. Finally, business investment outlays would reach a plateau whereby the stage for overaccumulation was set. This latter event would be preceded by a leveling off or decline of capacity utilization rates, and contracts and orders for plant and equipment. As it turned out, in some instances this leveling off of business investment did not lead to a downturn, say, a quarter or two later. As a result, the booms differed substantially in duration. If we somewhat arbitrarily date the beginning of the first postwar boom as the first quarter of 1946, the duration of the five postwar booms were, in order, 13, 17, 13, 9 and 37 quarters, the peak in each case being measured in terms of final sales in constant dollars. These differences suggest that much remains to be explained. They also suggest that what took place in the long boom of the 1960's was qualitatively different from that in the four earlier ones. We will, therefore, postpone any discussion of this boom until the next section.

Beginning with the trough in final sales in constant dollars, each boom saw capacity utilization rates and contracts and orders for business plant and

Table 8.7

FS-T	CUR-P	CO-P	I^{FNR}-P	FS-P
46(I)	48(I)-48(III)	48(II)	48(I)-48(IV)	49(II)
49(III)	51(I)-53(II)	51(I)-53(II)	50(IV)-53(III)	53(IV)
54(II)	55(II)-56(I)	55(IV)-57(I)	55(IV)-57(III)	57(III)
58(I)	59(II)	59(III)	60(II)	60(II)
60(III)	66(II)-66(IV)	69(I)-70(I)	69(III)-69(IV)	69(IV)

Source: *Survey of Current Business, Economic Report of the President*, various issues, and *Business Cycle Developments*, September 1968, Appendix F, and various issues.

equipment move up with final sales after a short lag that averaged around one quarter. Fixed non-residential investment showed on the average a somewhat longer lag behind troughs in final sales, a lag which tended to increase with each successive boom. Then, with even greater regularity, a peak (or plateau) in capacity utilization rates and contracts and orders was reached five to six quarters after each trough. The one exception was the reconversion period following World War II, where the interval was somewhat longer. In Table 8.7 the troughs and subsequent peaks in final sales are recorded for each boom, together with the 'peaks' in capacity utilization rates (*CUR*), contracts and orders, plant and equipment (*CO*), and fixed nonresidential investment (I^{FNR}).[9] Table 8.7 shows the early peaks of capacity utilization rates and contracts and orders, after the trough in final sales, followed by a leveling off rather than a decline in these series, with, on the average, the plateau in fixed investment outlays reached about a quarter or two later— with the exception of the boom in early 1950's. This lag we would expect as a result of lags involved in the investment process. The slight lead during the early 1950's of outlays over the other two series can be attributed to the unusual chain of events following the Korean War. For any boom, the length of the interval over which fixed investment remained more or less constant, turned out to be correlated with the length of the interval over which contracts and orders and capacity utilization rates remained high. This also is to be expected. What needs explaining is why investment could remain high, but more or less constant for different lengths of time during the first four booms, causing the length of the boom to vary as a result. As stressed earlier, a leveling off of investment outlays would still generate additional capacity, even if it failed to generate additional demand.

As already suggested, the clue to understanding differences in the first

[9] The dating of the various plateaus is somewhat arbitrary. In general a leveling off in any of the series determined the beginning of the interval. The earliest available data for con-contracts and orders and capacity utilization rates is 1948-(I), which makes the dating of this first plateau quite arbitrary.

four postwar booms can be found in the growth of other non-consumption expenditures, expenditures that kept the additions to capacity from having a depressive effect on fixed non-residential investment outlays. This is most easily seen during the Korean War period, when federal government expenditures played such a large role. In constant dollars, these outlays moved from $27 billion in 1950 (IV) to almost $71 billion in 1953-(II). Against this backdrop, a more or less constant level of fixed non-residential investment expenditures for 11 quarters, with high and sustained rates of capacity utilization and contracts and orders, is not hard to understand. It is only when federal government expenditures leveled off in 1953, slowing down the growth of overall demand, that the capacity effect of a high but fixed level of investment caught up, causing a downturn in investment by business. In this sense we can say that while the immediate cause of a decline in final sales can be traced to the overaccumulation of business capital, the basic difference stemmed from a failure of the federal sector to expand expenditures rapidly enough. To be sure, this example oversimplifies matters greatly, but it does illustrate the proper context within which to treat the 'Domar effect', and what might postpone the depressing capacity influence of investment.

F. The Nature of the Booms—Some Further Considerations

A shift in emphasis is necessary in explaining differences between the two other booms of the 1950's (and to a lesser extent that immediately following World War II) and what took place beginning early in the 1960's. It was suggested in the last chapter that three factors, other than the behavior of federal government spending, will account for the differences in the booms:

(1)   The duration and amplitude in the recovery of consumer investment, which in turn is very much determined by the monetary policy employed during the boom.
(2)   The degree of excess capacity at the begining of each boom, especially for the manufacturing sector.
(3)   The investment behavior of the two most important business sectors after manufacturing, 'commercial and other' and 'public utility', whose linkage to consumer investment, as well as their general influence on the growth of demand, is important. Alternatively, the behavior of house-induced investment expenditures other than consumer investment can be considered critical.

Given the lag between the rise in capacity utilization rates for business, as well as in contracts and orders for plant and equipment, and business investment outlays, we would expect that the initial stage of the recovery

Table 8.8

	ΔFS	ΔC^D	ΔI^H	ΔG^{S+L}	ΔG^F	ΔI^{FNR}
Phase I 1954-II to 1955-III	$30·0b	$9·9b	$4·0b	$2·9b	$-5·8b	$5·8b
Phase II 1955-III to 1957-II	15·1	-3·3	-4·9	2·7	0·9	1·9
Phase I 1958-I to 1959-III	31·5	11·8	4·9	2·7	-1·5	1·8
Phase II 1959-III to 1960-II	11·4	0·5	-2·7	1·5	-0·9	2·6
Phase I 1960-III to 1965-I	104·7	19·5	3·3	11·2	4·6	15·5
Phase II 1965-I to 1969-IV	131·4	19·8	-2·3	17·9	17·4	19·3

Source: *Survey of Current Business*, various issues.

(the stage where the decline in capacity utilization rates and contracts and orders are halted and then reversed), would be dominated by non-business types of expenditures. The steady growth of state and local government expenditures was an outstanding feature of the postwar era. It not only stabilized the economy downward but helped push the system on to the next boom. From trough to peak, the rate of growth of state and local government expenditures in constant dollars was 9·7, 4·4 and 5·6 per cent per annum for the booms beginning in 1954, 1958, and 1961 respectively. Its behavior in the early stages of the recovery was no less impressive, as shown in Table 8.8, where, also, the three booms of the post Korean period are divided into two phases: (a) from the trough in final sales to a point where consumer investment in constant dollars reaches its maximum; and (b) from the latter point until the peak in final sales; these are described in the Table as Phase I and Phase II.[10] In addition Table 8.8 indicates the change in expenditures on consumer durables, residential housing, state and local and federal government purchases of goods and services, and fixed non-residential investment—all in constant dollars—during these two intervals. What stands out is the sharp reversal of the relative importance of consumer to business investment, when the economy moves from Phase I to II. This spurt in consumer investment in the early part of a boom was also true for the Korean boom, and for the immediate postwar boom. For the first two booms in

[10] The figures for Phase II of the boom of the 1960's require a somewhat different interpretation from those for Phase II of the other booms. There was actually a spurt in consumer investment after 1966. Hence the less pronounced reversal of the relative importance of consumer to business investment.

Table 8.8 the dividing line between Phase I and II more or less corresponds with the point where capacity utilization rates and contracts and orders first reached the peaks or plateaus indicated in Table 8.7. This is not true for the boom in the 1960's. Then, capacity utilization rates and contracts and orders leveled off six to seven quarters after the trough in final sales, but consumer investment continued to grow until early 1965, and, of course, unlike the two earlier booms, the plateaus in utilization rates, contracts and orders and business investment were not followed soon after by a downturn.

Thus, one outstanding difference between the boom of the 1960's and these two earlier ones is the sustained boom in consumer investment, that continued not only after capacity utilization rates and contracts and orders had leveled off, but also after fixed non-residential (and manufacturing) investment had reached a kind of temporary plateau (mid-1962 until mid-1963). If we now add the 'linkage' effects, whereby the strength of certain types of business investment other than manufacturing (or other forms of family-related outlays discussed in Chapter V) are related to the strength of consumer investment, especially residential housing, then we have the following situation. Leaving aside the behavior of the federal government, the boom of the 1960's was proceeding at such a pace and on such a broad front (after the early stages), that whatever the rate of capacity utilization of manufacturing or business capital at the trough, the early plateau achieved by business investment was not likely to result in an early downturn. The boom in residential housing, together with the growth of state and local government outlays and other types of family-related expenditures, was helping to generate a rate of growth of demand rapid enough to keep the capacity effects of business investment from surpassing the growth of business sales and outlays. Thus, there would be no tendency for the business, especially manufacturing, sector to overaccumulate capital and cut back on investment after only a short boom in final sales, as happened during the 1950's.

This remains true in spite of the fact that at the trough in final sales in 1961, capacity utilization rates for manufacturing stood at 75. This was high by comparison with a similar point in the mini-boom of 1958–1959, when utilization rates were in the low seventies but low compared to the trough in 1954, when such rates were in the low eighties. Even so, when business investment reached a temporary peak in mid-1962, a date comparable to 1955-(IV), this did not result in a recession but in steady growth (with only a one quarter lull in 1964).

The strength and duration of the boom in consumer investment was much less in both booms of the 1950's. As already pointed out, in both cases a peak in consumer investment was reached at more or less the same time as the peak in capacity utilization rates and contracts and orders. Consumer investment then declined fairly steadily. For two reasons, then, we would expect business investment to undergo a mild boom in both cases. On the one hand, the slowing down and decline of consumer investment would mean that the capacity effects of business investment would be more likely to outstrip its multiplier effects, relatively soon after the trough in final sales. And second, the linkage effects would be less strong, which would also mean that business investment in Phase II would undergo a rather weak boom because of a lack of diffusion. For example, the change in 'commercial and other' investment with its high family-related component, increased from $8.15b to $11.0b during Phase I of the 1960's boom, a period that encompassed even the temporary plateau in fixed non-residential and manufacturing investment. And this marked only about one half the boom in the commercial and other investment component. In the booms of the 1950's this type of investment had a much shorter and less pronounced boom. The boom of the 1960's was also the only one of the three where movements of public utility and commercial and other investment were not offsetting one another. By early 1963 both were growing rapidly. Similar examples can be found for other measures of investment complementary to housing investment.

G. Expansion and Federal Outlays in the Post-Korean Period

We have already seen that the behavior of the federal government expenditures worked, after Korea, to shorten the booms of the 1950's compared with the boom that spanned the Korean war. This is even more true when these two short booms of the 1950's are compared with that of the 1960's. In Table 8.9 federal government expenditures in constant dollars, and the federal budget on national income account basis in current dollars, are shown (T^F indicating tax receipts of the federal government) from the beginning of the trough of each boom until nine quarters later, the number of quarters from trough to peak of the 1958–1960 boom. The overall depressive role played by this sector in the first two booms stands out quite clearly.

As between the two booms of the 1950's it would be hard to argue, as some have, that the relative shortness of the boom at the end of the 1950's can be attributed to the behavior of the federal budget. It is true, as Table 8.9 indicates, that the absolute change in the budget from deficit to surplus was greater at the end of the 1950's. However, if there is any truth in the balanced budget multiplier, the less depressing effect of the movements of government expenditures in the second boom should just about balance matters. The fact remains, however, that the post-Korean boom lasted four quarters longer than that of the late 1950's, with a corresponding difference in the two business investment booms. The rate of growth of state and local government spending was higher in the first boom than in the second. But again it is difficult to say whether the influence of all government sectors considered together was greater or more expansive in one boom than the other, because of the difficulty of determining the relative stimulus provided by the federal

Table 8.9

	G^F	ΔG^F	$G^F - T^F$	$\Delta(G^F - T^F)$
1954-(II)	$56·1b		$6·6b	
1956-(III)	48·7	$-8·4b	-4·9b	$-11·5b
1958-(I)	52·2		8·1b	
1960-(II)	51·0	-1·2	-5·6b	-13·7b
1960-(III)	51·8		-1·5b	
1962-(IV)	60·6	8·8	3·2b	4·7b

Source: *Economic Report of the President*, various issues.

government in two booms. However, the other factors singled out as contributing to differences in booms does provide a great deal of insight.

First, excess capacity was substantially higher in the second boom of the 1950's. At the trough, capacity utilization rates for manufacturing were in the low seventies, compared with a figure in the low eighties for the earlier trough. Over the course of the booms this differential was maintained. Whether these figures are representative for business in general or not is difficult to say, but assume that they are. Then if capacity utilization rates are positively correlated with the proportion of firms experiencing shortages of capacity, we would expect the mid-1950's investment boom and the boom in final sales to be longer and more pronounced, other things being equal. This is certainly borne out by the more pronounced investment boom by manufacturing. In addition, there was a stronger boom in the mid-1950's in the non-manufacturing categories of business investment such as public utility, commercial and other and communications investment. Like the behavior of manufacturing investment, this would reflect greater backlog of demand remaining following the Korean war. While it is true, as Table 8.8 indicates, that Phase I lasted one quarter longer in the second boom and consumer investment increased by more, the figures are somewhat misleading. Over the period depicted in Table 8.8 there is some difference between the cumulated outlays for housing: $143.8 billion for the first boom versus $158 billion for the second (as compared to total outlays for housing during Phase I of the boom of the 1960's of $448.0). But housing investment began to turn up two quarters before the trough in the first boom, whereas it was more or less coincident with the upturn in the second boom. If this two-quarter spurt in housing is taken into account, the consumer investment booms of the two recoveries should not be too different in their impact.

The fiscal operations of the federal government had a much more stimulating impact in the 1960's. As Table 8.9 reveals, increased government expenditures played a strong 'pump-priming' role in the early stages of the recovery. By mid-1962 they had leveled off, and actually declined from 1963-(I) until 1965-(I) (although not by enough to reduce them to their pre-1961 levels). Overall the government sectors were not providing much, if any, stimulus during the period 1962-(II)–1964-(I). Yet the economy continued to grow through most of 1964 because of a strong and prolonged consumer investment boom that eventually induced a second and stronger business investment boom that was to last through 1966. There was only one quarter decline in final sales in constant dollars about this time, 1964-(III) to 1964-(IV), but it was miniscule. It coincided with a sharp temporary decline in consumer investment outlays, especially on consumer durables, a slight decline in outlays by federal and state and local government, and a retardation in the growth of fixed non-residential investment. But by 1965-(I) fixed non-residential investment and state and local government expenditures began to boom again. While housing investment declined steadily until 1967-(I), consumer expenditures on durables, although somewhat erratic, had an upward trend.

As we have seen, a large part of this prosperity must be attributed to the behavior of consumers investment outlay. Another part must be attributed to the pickup in outlays interlinked with residential construction, as already mentioned. Commercial and other investment had begun its boom in mid-1961, with public utility investment outlays to follow in early 1963. Both continued to grow through most of the 1960's. Finally, manufacturing investment began its boom in late 1963, so that a strong business investment boom took hold from that period until 1966. Throw in an appreciable cut in income taxes during this period and a reasonable amount of momentum would be built up. Thus, even with federal spending playing if anything a depressive role from mid-1962 until early 1965, the period from the trough in final sales in 1960-(III) until 1965-(I) was longer than the entire length of the Korean boom, the longest postwar boom to date.

Fixed non-residential investment in constant dollars continued to grow through 1965, but leveled off by the end of 1966. The rise in outlays by all levels of governments was not enough to keep the economy from stagnating in 1966, as the decline in housing expenditures accelerated. During 1967 capacity utilization rates in manufacturing fell, as did fixed non-residential investment. Considering the behavior of the private sector alone, one might have expected a recession in 1967. As a matter of fact, Table 8.10 suggests that it might have come earlier, had not the war in Vietnam escalated. Beginning in 1965 defense expenditures increased sharply. In addition, expenditures by state and local governments increased at about the same pace as federal expenditures. This surge in government spending, plus the recovery of housing investment in 1967, kept the economy going until fixed non-residential investment pushed up for the third time during this boom, first moderately in 1968 and then substantially in 1969. What we have beginning in 1965 is something similar to what took place at the beginning of the 1960's: a large increase of government outlays and housing expenditures, followed

Table 8.10

		National defense spending	Other federal expenditures			National defense spending	Other federal expenditures
1965	I	48·2	15·9	1967	I	70·2	16·8
	II	49·2	16·2		II	72·5	17·0
	III	50·3	17·3		III	72·9	18·4
	IV	52·4	17·4		IV	74·6	19·0
1966	I	55·1	17·1	1968	I	76·8	20·3
	II	58·4	16·6		II	79·0	21·0
	III	63·0	16·6		III	79·6	21·5
	IV	65·6	15·9		IV	80·0	21·6

Source: *Economic Report of the President*, various issues. All variables measured in current dollars.

by a business investment boom. There was one major important difference, of course: unemployment stood at 6 per cent late in 1960 but had fallen to $4\frac{1}{2}$ per cent in 1965. The effect on prices, given an unwillingness to raise tax rates, was easily predictable.

What resulted from all this was a period of sustained boom for over nine years. Unlike the 1950's after Korea, the federal government played a large role in the early stages of the boom. This was reinforced by a long housing and housing induced boom, that eventually overlapped with a boom in business investment (and a tax cut). This boom might itself have ended in, say, 1966 or 1967, had it not been for a new upsurge in federal government spending in 1965. Thus, from 1966 to 1968 fixed non-residential investment in constant dollars increased from $74.1 to $75.5 billion. Housing investment increased slightly more during this period, but the overall stimulative effect of fixed non-residential and residential investment together was very slight. In this sense much of the second half of the boom of the 1960's resembles the Korean war boom.

The closing stages of the boom were marked by a sharp cutback in federal outlays, offsetting movements in fixed non-residential and residential invest-ment, and a small rise in consumption outlays. The latter together with a small increase in state and local government spending, was enough to generate a 3 per cent increase in GNP and final sales in 1969. Fixed non-residential investment lagged the downturn in GNP and final sales by one quarter. But like the end of the Korean boom and the subsequent recession, the decline in federal government outlays was sharp and sustained—from $79.4 billion in 1968-(IV) to $65.5 billion in 1970-(IV). Final sales fell from $721 billion in 1969-(III) to $717.2 in 1970-(IV), with GNP declining from $730.9 to $720.3 during this same period.

H. The Effect of Demand on Productivity and Growth

When we look at the post-Korean period of the 1950's as a whole, beginning in 1954-(II) up to the peak of the second boom in 1960-(II), and compare it with the period from 1960-(III) to 1969-(III), some interesting comparative growth statistics emerge. The annual average growth rates of final sales in constant dollars are 3.7 and 5.0 per cent respectively. The differences between decades is quite impressive. Unemployment rates in the trough quarter of 1954-(II) and 1960-(III) stood at 5.8 and 5.5 per cent respectively. However, the figures for the end points were 3.5 per cent in 1969-(III) and 5.2 per cent in 1960-(II). This suggests that some of the difference in growth rates might be considered a short run phenomenon, as the economy had pushed about as close to the full employment ceiling as possible in the 1960's. Even if no attention had to be given to the inflationary problems, a projection of a late growth of 4·5 to 5·0 per cent beyond the late 1960's into the 1970's might seem unreasonable.[11]

However, what stands out more than anything else is the behavior of output per man hour during these periods. From 1954 to 1960 it rose 2·37 per cent per year, compared to an annual average rise of 3·5 per cent from 1961 to 1969. This suggests two things. First, the higher growth rates of the 1960's were to a large extent the result of a more rapid growth of productivity, and cannot be written off as due to a more rapid growth of employment. And second, the difference in growth rates, both of aggregate output and per man hour, might well be attributable to a more rapid and sustained rate of growth of demand, as suggested in Chapter IV. There was barely a setback to the growth of demand through the 1960's, whereas demand was often sluggish in the 1950's.

What the authorities had going in their favor during the 1960's was something that will be the focus of our attention in Chapter XI: namely, 'space', or the ability to sustain demand pressures for a considerable period of time. In particular what we have just described was a situation where the monetary authorities were able to allow market rates of interest to remain relatively low for an extended period of time, beginning in the early 1960's. This permitted a sustained boom in housing and family-related expenditures. As a result Phase I of the boom of the 1960's lasted for $4\frac{1}{2}$ years. This had much to do with the very strong business investment boom which began in 1960-(III). That latter boom showed hardly any interruption of its growth from early in the 1960's until 1969. The pronounced business investment boom in turn had much to do with the high rates of growth of productivity. And, fortunately, productivity grew very rapidly early in the 1960's, keeping

[11] The annual average rate of increase in the consumer price index was 1·60 and 2·2 per cent from 1954 to 1960 and 1961 to 1968 respectively, suggesting that higher growth and employment are bought at the expense of price stability. By 1969 growth had tapered off but inflation had not.

down inflationary pressures. While the former was responsible for the failure of unemployment rates to fall, its effect on stabilizing prices had the effect of creating additional space, as monetary conditions remained relatively easy until late in 1965.

In the second half of the 1960's monetary policy tightened, and the effects on housing were quite dramatic. But as just mentioned, the second half of the 1960's to a large extent duplicated what happened in the first. The major differences were the unemployment rates and rates of inflation.

In the next chapter the role of the monetary authorities throughout the boom of the 1960's, as well as the rest of the period, is discussed along with the discussion of fiscal policy. As we have just said, the monetary authorities as well as the federal government played a central role in generating a boom of the magnitude of that of the 1960's, and can also be held accountable for the sluggishness of demand in the 1950's.

Postscript

The recession beginning in 1969-(IV) was of such an unusual nature as to require special treatment. What we wish to show is that, but for fortuitous circumstances, it might have been by far the most pronounced in the postwar period. A peak in GNP and final sales (FS) was reached in 1969-(III) and 1969-(IV) respectively. Like the 1953–1954 recession (but unlike any other), the decline in overall activity was accompanied by a simultaneous decline in federal government expenditures on goods and services (largely defense expenditures) and non-residential fixed investment. Unlike this one earlier recession, however, there were no large backlogs of demand left over from two decades of abnormal economic conditions. Furthermore, at what turned out to be the trough in final sales in each recession (1954-(II) and 1970-(IV)), capacity utilization rates for manufacturing were very different: 83.7 per cent in the earlier period and 74 per cent in the latter. This latter figure was the lowest rate of utilization on record in the postwar period. Finally, the shift in monetary policy from tightness to ease (mid-1970) lagged the peak in economic activity more than it had in any other recession. One might have expected on the basis of all these circumstances that a severe prolonged recession was in the making.

Relatively speaking, it was a long recession by postwar standards. Measuring from peak to trough in constant dollar GNP and FS, the recession lasted 5 and 4 quarters respectively. This can be compared to earlier postwar recessions, where the average duration of the decline in GNP and FS was 3 and $1\frac{1}{2}$ quarters respectively. From peak to trough the decline in FS was only $10.2 billions or approximately $1\frac{1}{2}$ per cent. What was unusual after taking into account the many forces at work is that the decline in activity was as mild as it was.

Table 8.6 gave a partial picture of what took place during this decline. During this most recent decline, the sum of the three important stimulants, G^F, I^{FNR} and C^D declined by over 10 per cent. Yet, as has just been pointed out, the decline in final sales from peak to trough was only $1\frac{1}{2}$ per cent, and most of that can be accounted for by the decline in 1970-IV in consumer expenditures on automobiles associated with the auto strike. Indeed, if figures for auto sales are averaged over the three quarter period, 1970-(III) to 1971-(I) (when the auto strike had ended), the whole period beginning from 1969-(IV) to 1971-(I) would show the economy merely marking time without any measurable decline in overall activity.

The fact that a simultaneous decline in outlays by the federal government, business and consumers on durable goods did not lead to a serious decline in overall activity can be largely traced to the behavior of consumer expenditures on non durable goods and services, C'. Thus while constant dollar outlays by the federal government, business and consumers on durables together declined $25.5 billion, consumption net of durables rose $10.8 billion from 1969-(IV) to 1970-(IV). At the same time state and local government and residential construction expenditures rose $2.3 and $.8 billion respectively. Without too much exaggeration, it can be argued that consumers acted to keep the recession from becoming severe, and turned the economy around. The question naturally arises as to why consumption outlays net of durables should have risen so during the latest recession, since there was no increase in the propensity to consume. Basically, the answer lies in the fact that the consumption, or better, disposable and ultimately personal income had a large autonomous component. Thus, from 1969-(IV) to 1970-(IV) disposable income in current dollars rose from $650.6 to $701.5 billions. Consumption, in turn, rose by $38 billion, indicating a not unusual marginal propensity to consume (net of durables) of 0.75.

To some extent this rise in disposable income is reflecting the built-in stabilizers of the system. But while personal tax and non tax payments fell by $2.6 billions during this period, personal contributions for social security rose by $1.4 billion. But the explanation of the rise in consumption outlays is best seen as the result of an 'autonomous' growth of personal income during this period. Personal income increased by $46.2 billions in current dollars, or roughly 6 per cent from 1969-(IV) to 1970-(IV). Of this total, approximately one half constituted an increase in wages and salaries. More importantly, employment increased by enough in the trade, services and government sectors of the economy to cause the decline in total non-agricultural employment to be the mildest on record, except for the mini recession of 1960. This and higher wage rates resulted in wage and salary income also growing 6 per cent, while other forms of income grew at approximately 3 per cent. Moreover, transfer payments (which accounted for over one third of the increase in personal and disposable income) grew by approximately 25 per cent. What is interesting here is that of the $15.0 billion increase in transfer payments, only $2.2 billion represented an increase in unemployment benefits. In contrast, in the other recessions increases in unemployment benefits were from about one-third to four-fifths of the increase in transfer payments. The lion's share of the increase in transfer payments during the latest recession came from the welfare programs, e.g., 'Old age, survivors, disability and health insurance benefits, public assistance transfers and veterans benefits'.

In summary, and contrary to popular notions on these matters, consumers acted in such a way as to constrain the downward movements of income.

They were able to do this in spite of the depressing influence of the federal government and business, by the continuous and large rise in personal and disposable income. These flows rose as much as they did because of an expansion of employment in certain sectors, including state and local government, and because of large transfer payments arising from measures adopted on social and welfare grounds. These outlays, together with state and local government and residential construction expenditures, acted to slow the rate of decline of activity, so that by the end of the auto strike the economy turned around. All of this took place in a period of large-scale resentment over expanding welfare payments and government employment.

Chapter IX Monetary Policy in Postwar United States

A. Introduction

Monetary policy has already been assigned a possible role in contributing towards stability. Even though the discussion of the 1920's in Chapter X will show that it is not a sufficient condition for stability, in this chapter we will argue that the direct and indirect influences of monetary policy on spending has allowed it to play a useful role in postwar United States. Mention was made in Chapter VIII of the influence the federal government has had on the duration of booms in the postwar period, but little has been said yet about the stabilizing influence of fiscal policy, especially during recessions. For this reason, it is important to determine to what extent the mildness of recessions in the postwar period can be attributed to deliberate action by federal authorities regulating demand in the interests of stability. This issue must be faced squarely because if it could be shown that the postwar period was one that saw the federal government actively pursue a policy geared to limiting fluctuations in employment to a narrow range and at a high average level, the lack of any collapse during this period might not be too surprising. Explaining the lower turning point is still one of the most important issues of cycle theory. Fortunately, a good deal has already been written on this and the matter can be disposed of in short order.[1]

---

[1] For elaborate and detailed descriptions of policy during much of this period see Hickman, *Growth and Stability . . .* , *op. cit.*, and Lewis, Wilfred, Jr., *Federal Fiscal Policy in the Postwar Recessions*, The Brookings Institution, Washington, 1962.

B. Fiscal Policy in the Early Postwar Period

By common agreement the discretionary fiscal policy had its best showing during the Korean War period. After the outbreak of hostilities in the summer of 1950, there was only a three to four month lag before tax rates were raised to finance the anticipated higher level of government expenditures. However, it is also true that much of the credit for the shortness of the lag in enacting tax legislation after the outbreak must be attributed to the fact that Congress had been working on a tax bill during 1950. Given the separation of power under the American system, this seems to be a necessary condition for speedy enactment of tax legislation.

The record of the immediate, postwar period and the remainder of the 1950's can be described as, at worst, one of timidity and ignorance and, at best, one of being right for the wrong reasons. Immediately following World War II, Congress echoed the sentiments of most professional economists in stressing the desirability of tax cuts. There were, in fact, three tax cuts enacted during this period, The Revenue Acts of 1945, 1947 and 1948. Although the federal budget showed a surplus in 1946 and 1947, this did not prevent prices from rising 11·1 per cent per annum from 1945 to 1947, and at an average annual rate of 9·9 per cent from 1945 to 1948. All in all, it was a period when stabilization policy was nonexistent. On the other hand, under the Truman administration, next to nothing was done once the recession of 1948–1949 set in, primarily because of the common feeling that a little deflation was a good thing, and because of the additional concern over pushing the budget into the red.

Fiscal responsibility, i.e. a balanced budget and a diminished role for the federal government as insurance against inflation, was the cornerstone of the Eisenhower administration. As mentioned in Chapter VIII, the growth of federal government expenditures during the early 1950's accounted for the rather prolonged length of the boom. This growth allowed the economy to absorb the growing capacity generated by a high, but more or less constant, level of business investment. Once government expenditures declined, the downturn was inevitable. Another fortuitous tax cut took place in January 1954, based on an agreement reached between the two branches of the government in May 1953. Even so, the decline in government expenditures during the recession was so great that the budget deficit was actually reduced throughout. This was to account partly for the slower recovery in 1954 compared to 1948–1949. A minor offset in the form of a speeding up of the rate of defense spending was undertaken, but overall a deflationary policy was pursued in the face of a decline in economic activity. Without the large backlogs of demand in the private sector, a fairly serious recession might have resulted.

The paring down of the size of federal expenditures continued during the boom of 1954–1957, as did Congressional pressure for further tax cuts. Talk of the latter died down somewhat even in the face of the recession of 1957–1958, because of the strong possibility of additional government expenditures to meet the Russian challenge posed by Sputnik. Even so, pressure from Congress for lower taxes as well as increased government outlays, continued well into calendar 1958. The 1957–1958 recession was also associated with a decline in government spending in constant dollars. Unlike the previous recession, the (induced) decline in tax revenues was large enough to increase the actual budget deficit, all through the recession and into the early stages of the recovery. Again reliance was placed on speeding up spending for already authorized programs, but a few new elements were introduced. In April 1958 the Highway Act of 1958 was passed, giving the President additional flexibility in administering the rate of the spending on the Interstate Highway Program. Congress also appropriated funds for grants to states for highway construction, provided they could be started and ended within a definite period of time. In addition, there was a speeding up of tax refunds, and a temporary extension of unemployment compensation; but overall, while more potent than the policies of 1953–1954, the anti-recession measures were still modest. Partly this could be ascribed to the administration projection of a $10 billion deficit in fiscal 1959 (made in the first half of calendar 1958); and to the fact that prices continued to rise during 1957. This fear of deficits and inflation carried over to the subsequent boom of 1958–1960, the shortest in the postwar period. There is some room for debate over the blame to be attributed to fiscal versus monetary policy, in the poor showing of the economy in its recovery from the 1957–1958 recession. The budget moved from a deficit of $11 billion in 1958-(II) to a surplus of $6 billion in 1960-(I); but most of this was the natural effect of the built-in stabilizers. It was not until the end of the boom that gasoline tax rates and payroll tax rates were raised.

In summary, then, throughout the period from the end of the war until the final mini-boom of the late 1950's, little credit can be given fiscal policy in reversing the downturn once it began. The moderateness of the recessions during this period must be attributed primarily to the fact that backlogs of demand had been built up during the war, and to the workings of the kinds of constraints, lags and other factors stressed in Chapters VI and VII. Nor can fiscal policy be given particularly high marks for a stimulating role during booms. It is true that, by American standards, inflation became something of a problem after 1956. And concern with inflation throughout most of this period, was partly responsible for a lack of strong stimulation from the federal budget in those stages of the boom when the economy was still below full employment. Thus, whether or not fiscal policy during boom periods was adequate overall is a matter of the relative weights assigned to price stability and low unemployment rates in some kind of social preference function.

C. Fiscal Policy During the 1960's

The poor performance of the late 1950's, together with an election of a president less predisposed to balance the budget, led to some improvement of anti-recession policy in 1961. By the trough of the recession, deliberate contra-cyclical measures (mostly in the form of a speedup in the distribution of a veterans insurance dividend) were beginning to take effect, although the size of the injection was small. Again, a speedup in spending of appropriated funds, especially for defense, together with temporary extension of unemployment benefits, was introduced. But unlike the two previous recoveries, the recovery beginning in 1961 was soon aided by a large increase in federal government outlay.[2] Much of this was earmarked for defense, but the explicit anti-recession measures proposed and carried out during the early period of the Kennedy Administration would lead one to believe that the latter felt that more than one end could be achieved with the same instrument. Two minor tax measures designed to stimulate the economy were passed during this period (1962): one allowing an investment tax credit, and the other liberalizing depreciation guidelines.

As already stated in Chapter VIII, government expenditures leveled off by mid-1962 and remained more or less stationary until early 1964. In the meantime the discussion of the 'full-employment surplus' and the assumed 'fiscal drag' associated with this surplus, gave rise to administration pressure for a tax cut, this in the face of a current budget deficit. Since unemployment rates had failed to fall sufficiently during the boom (they were 5·5, 5·7 and 5·2 per cent in 1962, 1963 and 1964 respectively), much less weight was attached to fiscal orthodoxy. In January 1963 a substantial cut in personal and corporate tax rates was advocated by the Kennedy Administration, but it was not passed until February 1964, after Kennedy's death. The year 1964 also marked the beginning of a sustained decline in the unemployment rate at a time when federal government outlays and housing expenditures in real terms were declining, but in the midst of a substantial business investment boom that was to last through 1966.

Estimates have been made of the stimulating effect of the tax cut. One such estimate of the gain was a growth of GNP of $10 billion per quarter from the beginning of 1964 to mid-1965, compared with a quarterly increase of $6·3 billion without a tax cut.[3] In any case, the escalation in Viet Nam in 1965 was to ensure that the long period of growth was to continue for some time yet, at least through 1968.[4] At the same time the stepped up spending led to a sustained period of inflation. Various minor tax measures were enacted from the mid-1960's on, some expansionary, others inflationary. As already indi-

---

[2] See Table 8.9 in Chapter VIII.
[3] See Okun, Arthur, 'Measuring the Impact of the 1964 Tax Reduction' in *Perspectives on Economic Growth*, Heller, Walter W. (ed.), Vintage Books, New York, 1968.
[4] See Table 8.10 in Chapter VIII.

cated, the 1960's stand out compared to the 1950's as a decade where rising government expenditures accounted for much of the growth of demand. Productivity grew much more rapidly, but there was also more inflation (comparing, say, 1953–1960 with 1961–1969). Government fiscal operations certainly operated (inadequately or not) to prevent even a minor recession up until 1969, but they also led to strong inflationary pressures. Thus, while it is possible to conclude that fiscal operations did little to dampen recessions during the period prior to the 1960's, they did act to prevent all but the most minor downturns at the expense of price stability until the closing years of the 1960's. As indicated in the last chapter, after leveling off in 1968 federal spending on goods and services began a decline that continued into 1971 (largely through cut-backs in defense spending). After leveling off in 1968, federal spending fell from $79.4 billion in 1968-(IV) to $65.5 billion in 1970-(IV). This can be compared to a decline of such spending after the Korean War from a little over $70 billion in 1953 to $50 billion in mid 1955, all figures in 1958 dollars. A rise of consumption outlays (net of durables) of $25 billion, and state and local outlays of $6 billion, prevented economic activity from declining substantially. The net effect was stagnation after 1968.

D. Monetary Policy in the Early Postwar Period

In discussing the role of monetary policy in the postwar period, it is again appropriate to break up the period into two parts, before and after the 1953 recession. The former period was dominated on the one hand by the Korean War, with its exceptional control measures, as well as by the Federal Reserve commitment to support the government bond market. As was argued in Chapter VI, the main impact of monetary policy is felt through the housing market. From 1950 to 1952 Regulation X was in effect, regulating minimum down payments and maximum repayment periods on mortgages. This would have a pronounced effect on the demand for funds even if, for example, the supply of mortgage funds were unaffected by economic conditions.

The pre-1953 period is abnormal in another important respect, namely, the 'pegging' of government bond prices. This resulted in a period of stabilization of long-term interest rates including mortgage rates, up until the Accord of March 1951, when the Federal Reserve abandoned its commitment to stabilize government bond prices. This would explain the extremely liquid position of the commercial banks until the accord (excess reserves exceeded borrowings on average by over one-half billion dollars), because banks found it quite painless to liquidate part of their government securities portfolio whenever there was a rising demand for loan funds. There would seem to be little scope for monetary policy as a contra-cyclical device, as the authorities played largely an accommodating role. In spite of this, residential construction underwent a short cycle that was contra-cyclical. Housing starts, the index of mortgage recordings and residential contract awards all rose early in 1949 and continued to rise until mid-1950. Previous to that, especially in 1948, all these series had declined. Unfortunately, there is no quarterly flow of funds data for this period that would permit any sort of study of possible disintermediation. There is data on down payments on VA home loans as a per cent of value of the home, and also FHA and VA home loans as a per cent of total home loans.[5] The former series fell, beginning in 1949 (the earliest period for which data is available), and only began to rise again in mid-1950. Guaranteed loans as a per cent of total home loans fell during the previous boom, rose early in the recession period, and continued to do so until late in 1950. The decline in down payments reflected undoubtedly a general easing of terms that accompanies easy money periods. The fact that home owners lack saleable assets is less of a concern to lenders when money is easy than when it is tight. This would be true for conventional mortgage lending as well as guaranteed. The increasing importance of guaranteed mortgages also reflects easier money conditions. These loans have traditionally involved a smaller down payment and longer amortization period than conventional mortgages, in addition to having a maximum rate of interest provision. All these qualities lead to a greater supply of funds for guaranteed mortgages only when the supply of funds in general is plentiful. Evidently, both the supply of funds and the demand for funds were affected during this period enough to cause residential construction to respond quickly once the recession set in. Unfortunately, the imposition of Regulation X in 1950 does not allow us to see what effects an ordinary tight money policy might work on the housing market.

E. Thrift Disintermediation in the Post-Korean Period

In discussing in Chapter VI the channels through which monetary policy works, emphasis was on the housing and mortgages markets. In Diagram 9.1, a summary of post-1953 mortgage flows, i.e., the net change or acquisition of mortgages, is shown, beginning with 1953-I and extending through 1971(-II). The total mortgage acquisition by all lenders including government agencies are depicted, along with the same flows at thrift institutions. Also graphed in Diagram 9.1 are residential construction expenditures. The high correlation of these latter expenditures with total mortgage flows is apparent. Peaks (*P*) and

[5] See Guttentag, Jack, 'The Short Cycle in Residential Construction', *The American Economic Review*, June 1961.

Diagram 9.1

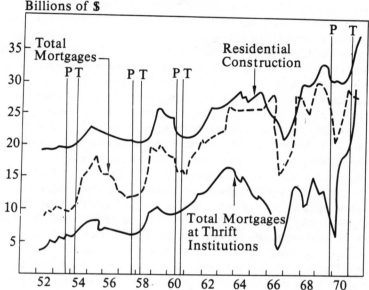

Source: Board of Governors and Federal Reserve System.

troughs (*T*) in GNP are indicated by the vertical lines.[6] The early recovery of the mortgage market and housing during the recessions of the 1950's and early 1960's is very clear, just as it was during the 1948–1949 recession and recovery. This quick recovery is especially true for thrift institutions, where changes in total (and 1–4 family) mortgages tend to increase before the trough in GNP, all through the recessions of the 1950's and the recession beginning in 1960. The squeeze of housing during the boom is also apparent (as changes in both measures of mortgage flows, and housing peak in advance of the peaks in GNP) during the 1950's and in 1960, although somewhat less so for housing in 1969. The decline of these flows in 1966 will receive special comment below.

However, none of this throws any light on the channels through which policy worked during the postwar period. In Chapter VI the importance of such influences on mortgage lending and residential construction as (relative) cost considerations, changes in vacancy rates and the inventory of houses under construction, was deliberately downgraded. The assumption throughout was that the supply of loanable funds and its distribution among lenders

---

[6] The lines designated *P* and *T* represent peaks and troughs in real GNP. When discussing monetary policy, its timing, etc., GNP is a more appropriate measure to work with than final sales. In determining the degree of tightness or looseness of credit conditions, the overall demand and supply of funds will be more closely related to GNP. Also the authorities will be more influenced by the behavior of GNP because of its closer relation with employment.

over the cycle was such an overpowering factor during the postwar period, that a good first approximation of what was happening could still be obtained if other influences were neglected. It did accept the general framework of analysis used in several econometric studies that view the influence of monetary policy on housing as a series of portfolio adjustments by different economic units.[7] This required an analysis of household behavior, a distinction between different types of lenders, their commitment to mortgage lending, and the various factors determining their willingness or unwillingness to supply credit when credit conditions tighten overall. It also required an understanding of the differences in reactions of different types of borrowers to the terms of credit. But by concentrating on the supply of funds, the importance for stability of a monetary constraint was made clear.

We can best begin with the recognition of a fact which became all too apparent during the period of the 'credit crunch' of 1966. Mortgage lending and borrowing is an activity performed through financial intermediaries, not through the capital market. It should therefore be obvious that the change in the flow of loanable funds coming into these different intermediaries would have had a most important bearing on mortgage flows and home building. This would be true even if the terms of lending were unchanged during the course of the cycle. And the more these intermediaries are bypassed the more would housing suffer. Therefore some general measure of that part of the supply of loanable funds passing through financial intermediaries is an appropriate first step in understanding fluctuations during the period in mortgage loans, housing activity and the channels of policy.

In any period of time, the total funds supplied directly to credit markets, i.e., the flow of funds, can be broken down into those funds supplied by:

(a)   the U.S. Government and Federal Reserve System to borrowers;

(b)   commercial banks to borrowers;

(c)   'nonbank finance' to borrowers; i.e., financial intermediaries other than commercial banks, including insurance companies, pension plans, etc., as well as thrift institutions;

(d)   the 'private domestic nonfinancial' sector to borrowers, where this final group is composed of households, business and state and local governments.

---

[7] See, for example, Smith, L. B., 'A Model of the Canadian Housing and Mortgage Markets', *Journal of Political Economy*, September–October 1969; and Sparks, G. R., 'An Econometric Analysis of the Role of Financial Intermediaries in Postwar Residential Building Cycles', in *Determinants of Investment Behavior*, New York, National Bureau of Economic Research, 1967. Unfortunately, Sparks' study uses annual data and omits a treatment of commercial banks. As will be clear from the text, quarterly data are essential in discovering the kind of portfolio responses undertaken by households and financial intermediaries, in response to changing economic conditions. It will be noted that there should be a (negative) correlation between the flow of funds available for mortgage financing on the one hand, and vacancy rates and the profitability of home building on the other. Unfortunately, much of the econometric work, while stressing the channels through which policy affects spending, neglects the importance of the contra-cyclical impact of policy working through these channels.

Disintermediation was earlier defined as the withdrawal of funds from (or the failure to deposit them with) any financial intermediary and their direct placement in the capital market. Intermediation was just the opposite. As a first approximation, the ratio of funds supplied by the private, domestic, non-financial sector to the total flow of funds can be allowed to measure the extent of disintermediation. However, it is possible to think of disintermediation in a narrower sense, the bypassing of thrift institutions or 'thrift disinter-mediation'. This takes place when the (d) sector bypasses an intermediary that is prepared to match deposit liabilities and mortgages, or where the propensity to invest in mortgages out of deposit flows is very high. This type of disintermediation primarily involves the household sector, as households hold approximately 90 per cent of all deposits at thrift institutions. This measure of disintermediation is given by the top panel in Diagram 9.2.

Here total funds supplied directly to the credit markets by households are combined with household savings (or time) deposits at thrift institutions, as well as at commercial banks. The sum of these forms the denominator of a ratio, the numerator of which is simply total funds supplied directly to the credit markets by households, plus change in household time deposits at commercial banks. Fluctuations in this measure of disintermediation are closely correlated with movements of mortgage flows shown in Diagram 9.1. Also shown in Diagram 9.2. is the spread between the Treasury Bill rate and the rate paid on regular savings accounts at a sample of Boston mutual savings banks.[8] The positive correlation between movements of this yield differential and the degree of disintermediation is very strong. In other words, during the booms and recessions (and tight and easy money periods) of the postwar period, the spread between rates paid on marketable securities and fixed-price near-moneys (e.g., savings deposits, savings and loan shares) widened and narrowed. This led households to undertake portfolio adjustments in such a way that a smaller share of the flow of funds was first funneled through thrift institutions during booms as opposed to recessions.[9]

The reason for the widening differential between rates on marketable securities and those on deposits at financial intermediaries, has already been discussed.[10] The induced portfolio adjustments of households were bound to have an effect on mortgage lending, as can be seen by comparing various changes in mortgage flows in Diagram 9.1, with movements in the disinter-mediation indicator and the yield differential in Diagram 9.2.[11] Even a casual comparison points up the importance of fluctuations of the latter two variables

[8] This diagram and part of the analysis of this section is based on a study by Arena, John, 'The Outlook for Financial Disintermediation', *New England Business Review*, December 1967.

[9] See Chapter VI, pp. 116–118.

[10] See Chapter VI, p. 115–116.

[11] Intermediaries could sacrifice profits per dollar loaned out, and even total profits, by raising rates on their total liabilities by more than the increased income coming from higher loan rates on new loans; but the Federal Home Loan Bank Board has taken a dim view of this.

Diagram 9.2

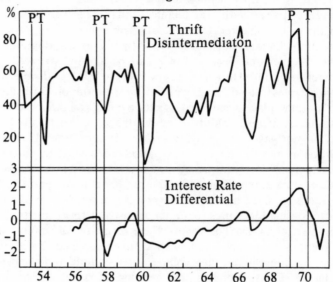

Source: Board of Governors, Federal Reserve System and Boston Federal Reserve Bank.

for mortgage lending and housing. Consider the period up through 1961 first. From peaks to troughs in GNP and then up through the early to mid stages of the recoveries, the disintermediation and rate differential remain relatively low. Due to lags, mortgage flows and housing do not recover immediately after the decline of the disintermediation and the rate differential measure (although the reversal comes very soon for thrift institutions), but all through the period the upturn in mortgage flows came before the trough in GNP. Residential construction was a little slower in recovering, as already implied. In the mid to late stages of the boom, a rise in the rate differential induces a bypassing of financial intermediaries, and disintermediation becomes more pronounced. The result is that with flows into intermediaries cut back, mortgage lending was also cut back.

The period after the early 1960's is different in several important respects. There was no appreciable decline in GNP (although the fourth quarter of 1966 did indicate at least a pause). However, it still remains true that during the early stages of the boom beginning in 1961, the relationship of high mortgage flows and construction to a low value for the disintermediation measure and the rate differential, continued to hold. And as the rate differential slowly rose up to 1966, disintermediation also increased, eventually leading to the crunch of 1966 and the drastic cutback in mortgage lending and residential construction. Furthermore, the decline in the yield spread through mid-1967 and from mid-1970 through much of 1971 had the predictable effect on the disintermediation measure, mortgage lending and construction. The failure of mortgage flows between these two periods to reflect movements of the thrift disintermediation measure can largely be accounted for by the behaviour of governmental agencies.

F. Two Influences on Mortgage Lending

In Chapter VI we argued that one of the most important impacts of monetary policy on mortgage lending is not so much a matter of the private domestic non-financial sector bypassing all financial intermediaries, as it is of their bypassing certain types of financial institutions—hence the stress given to thrift disintermediation. For example, savings and loan associations on the average acquired $.94 in mortgages for every one dollar increase in deposits during the 1960's, with 1–4 family housing accounting for most of this. Mutual savings banks held a wider variety of assets during the postwar period, and showed a greater willingness to substitute different types of assets when yield differentials became large enough. Still mortgages were acquired at the rate of $1.07 for every dollar of deposits, suggesting a matching of assets with liabilities and even a willingness to liquidate other assets in order to expand holdings.

What evidence there is of a matching of mortgages with time deposit flows at commercial banks, indicate that the tie was weak especially during boom (and tight money) periods. That is, during easy money periods flows of time deposits were high, but at a time when customer loan demand was low. Surplus funds were then allocated to the mortgage market, but the acquisition of most mortgages per dollar of new deposits was relatively low. Then when customer loan demand picked up and was growing rapidly compared to flows of time (and total) deposits, mortgage lending tended to be cut back. As a result, flows of time deposits through banks during boom periods, when money was tight enough to impair the banks' liquidity position, had nothing like the effect on mortgage lending of a similar flow of deposits into thrift institutions. A case in point is the boom from 1954 to 1957. Time deposit flows increased substantially at banks during 1956 and 1957 compared to 1955. Yet the increase in mortgage holdings declined from 1955 on, until by 1957 acquisitions of new mortgages had fallen to zero. A similar event took place in 1965–1966. Moreover, a shift of deposits from thrift institutions to banks, even during easy money periods, would also work against mortgage lending. For example, from 1961 through 1965, a period when the net free reserve position of banks did not indicate any strong liquidity problem, banks acquired mortgages at a rate that was less than $.30 for every dollar of additional time deposits received.

Insurance companies have shown a fairly strong inclination to respond to yield differentials in their portfolio management. This is complicated by the extensive use of forward commitments and other factors, but the mortgage loan-corporate bond choice was found to be very much influenced by expected relative yields.[12] An additional influence on mortgage lending by insurance companies, especially in the 1960's, was the ability to obtain an 'equity kicker' in their mortgage loans, enabling them to share in the profits of the enterprise financed by the loan. This applied to 'other mortgages'; i.e. other than 1–4 family mortgage loans as typified by the large apartment house complexes. Thus, again to take two examples, the spread between conventional first mortgages and corporate bonds narrowed from 1·97 per cent early in 1955 to 1·57 per cent by the end of 1957 and from 1·41 per cent beginning in 1963 to virtually nothing early in 1968. In both cases insurance company acquisition of 1–4 family mortgages declined sharply. Other mortgage acquisitions remained more or less unchanged in the earlier period, but rose dramatically during the 1960's when the equity kicker had become more popular. Following the credit crunch, the rate of acquisition of other mortgages fell somewhat, but remained higher compared to the 1950's.

All of these considerations support the need to keep separate two kinds of influences working for and against mortgage lending, especially in trying to derive a useful measure of disintermediation. On the one hand, there is the influence of changes in the flows into and out of intermediaries that have a strong tendency to match mortgages with deposits, if not dollar for dollar, then nearly so. This tendency is strong enough to treat savings and loan associations, (S & L's), and mutual savings banks, (mutuals), as qualitatively different from other intermediaries. On the other hand, there is the fact that mortgages are a less sought after asset for other institutions and become an even less desirable asset to hold for these institutions during tight money periods. This arises because mortgage rates are relatively 'sticky', which leads to cyclical fluctuations in yield spread between mortgage rates and rates on other securities; and because long-run profit considerations dictate a downgrading of the acquisition of such assets in favor of customer loans. These latter considerations will (and did) act as additional factors leading to a monetary ceiling and, in general, causing the supply of funds in the mortgage market to move contra-cyclically. They should be kept separate from the first influence, however, since the flow of funds through intermediaries other than thrift institutions may be large and rising during a boom, though mortgage

---

[12] See Jones, L. D., *Investment Policies of Life Insurance Companies*. Graduate School of Business Administration, Harvard University, Boston, 1968, p. 453. Insurance companies make extensive use of forward commitments whereby lenders agree to make funds available to borrowers at some future date, say six months from the commitment date. The mortgage loan-corporate bond choice was complicated by other factors but yield differentials were very important nonetheless. See especially Chapter IX of Jones' book.

lending is still cut back.[13] The next two sections will discuss at greater length these two influences on mortgage lending. The reader more interested in the actual workings of the monetary ceiling and the related question of the lags in monetary policy can proceed to section I.

G. Portfolio Adjustments by Households

Disintermediation, as we have measured it, will summarize the effects of one type of portfolio adjustment that has an important bearing on mortgage lending and residential construction; the portfolio adjustments undertaken by the household sector in response to changes in different yield differentials. These adjustments will determine the distribution of household liquid assets between deposits at thrift institutions and savings deposits at commercial banks and holdings of primary securities.[14] In addition, there will be the adjustments of thrift institutions in response to variations in deposit (largely household) flows. A study of these two types of portfolio adjustments will allow an isolation of most, if not all, of the disintermediation effect narrowly defined on mortgage lending and housing. And Diagram 9.1 suggests that activities of the thrift institutions (and, therefore, households ultimately) explain a great deal of the variation in total mortgage lending. What is left unexplained can then be studied in terms of the activities of other financial institutions.[15]

[13] Deposit flows at S & L's and mutuals move contra-cyclically, and the spread between mortgage rates and rates on marketable securities widens during recessions and narrows during booms. While this narrowing of the yield differential is not likely to influence S & L's if deposit flows were maintained during a tight money period, it would be likely to influence the acquisition of assets by mutuals. In other words, a decline in deposit flows is not a necessary condition for a cutback in mortgage acquisitions at mutuals (nor at banks or insurance companies), but it is for S & L's, at least in some long run sense. Basically, it is the similarity in the behavior of their liabilities during tight and easy money periods that justifies lumping S & L's and mutuals together.

[14] Hamburger found that time deposits at commercial banks and deposits at thrift institutions were close substitutes. In addition he found that (a) bonds were also a close substitute for all kinds of fixed-price near-moneys (we use short term government securities); and (b) the latter were not good substitutes for equities. See Hamburger, Michael J., 'Household Demand for Financial Assets', *Econometrica*, January 1968, and Tong Hun Lee, 'Substitutability of Non-Bank Intermediary Liabilities for Money: The Empirical Evidence', *The Journal of Finance*, September 1966 for a related study.

[15] The correlation matrix for (1) Total Mortgage Flows; (2) Total 1–4 Family Mortgage Flows; (3) Total Mortgage Flows at Thrift Institutions; and (4) 1–4 Family Mortgage Flows at Thrift Institutions is:

	(1)	(2)	(3)	(4)
(1)	1·000	—	—	—
(2)	0·8969	1·000	—	—
(3)	0·8175	0·8552	1·000	—
(4)	0·7439	0·8550	0·9778	1·000

Thrift disintermediation on the part of households implies a taking advantage of the more favorable terms on variable priced liquid assets, and shifting their assets out of certain fixed-price near-moneys. In the postwar period both household flows of savings accounts at thrift institutions and time deposits at commercial banks have an upward trend, although the latter is more pronounced. Commercial banks during the first decade following the war found themselves losing out to thrift institutions in the competition for deposits. It was during this period that households and others were increasingly accepting nonbank deposits and shares as acceptable forms in which to hold their wealth. When bank holdings of liquid government securities had been worked off sufficiently, banks began to compete more aggressively for time deposits. They were greatly aided in their efforts through a change in the Regulation Q (which determined the maximum rate of interest banks could pay on different types of time deposits) in 1957. Four additional increases in the ceiling rates from 1962 to 1965 permitted a continued rapid growth of time deposits, with households accounting for about one-half of the inflows. The effect of these ceiling rate increases was to cause a narrowing of the spread between rates paid at thrift institutions and commercial banks, as seen in Table 9.1. This narrowing was particularly evident from 1953 to 1957 and

Table 9.1

Annual average yield differentials between deposits at savings and loan associations (i_s), mutual savings banks (i_m) and commercial banks (i_b)

	$i_s - i_b$ (per cent)	$i_m - i_b$ (per cent)		$i_s - i_b$ (per cent)	$i_m - i_b$ (per cent)
1953	1·60	1·20	1961	1·21	0·84
1954	1·60	1·20	1962	0·90	0·67
1955	1·50	1·20	1963	0·86	0·65
1956	1·40	1·20	1964	0·77	0·64
1957	1·20	0·80	1965	0·54	0·42
1958	1·17	0·86	1966	0·41	0·41
1959	1·17	0·83	1967	0·43	0·50
1960	1·30	0·91	1968	0·20	0·28
			1969	−0·09	−0·02

Source: *Savings and Loan Fact Book, 1969* and *Federal Reserve Bulletin*, various issues.

from 1962 through 1968. Looking at the whole period, this downward trend in the yield differential must have worked to keep down mortgage lending and residential construction.

In absolute terms thrift institutions as a group did not experience a noticeable decline in household deposit flows until the mid-1960's, but this was because deposits at S & L's were growing during the period. Mutual savings banks experienced a slight absolute decline in the flow of deposits during the boom of the mid-1950's, and a large decline from 1958-I to 1959-IV (from $2½ billion to $½ billion). Since a high proportion of mutual banks are located in urban centers, an explanation of this difference between thrift institutions has been attributed to the high degree of sensitivity by depositors in cities like New York and Boston, to changes in the yield differential.[16]

The amplitude of the swings in the flows of household savings at thrift institutions increased over time. This would seem to be due for the most part to increased fluctuations of savings accounts held at S & L's, as a kind of learning process seemed to be at work here. In other words, even depositors located some distance from the large city money markets were more frequently taking advantage of changes in yield differentials, and were increasingly prone to shift in and out of savings deposits at thrift institutions. Overall, while it is true to say that a slowdown in the growth of deposits because of thrift disintermediation took place in the 1950's, it is also true to say that disintermediation had its main impact later.

In the late 1950's, rates paid at thrift institutions moved favorably relative to rates on bank time deposits, but unfavorably compared with rates on Treasury bills. Late in the 1960's rates on thrift institutions (and banks deposits) were again low relative to the Treasury bill rate. In both periods thrift institutions suffered largely at the hands of the capital market.[17] During the mid-1950's and the years leading up to the crunch, thrift institutions suffered at the hands of both banks and the capital market (although the impact was much more dramatic during the mid-1960's). As Diagram 9.2 reveals, the rate differential between the Treasury bill rate and the rate paid on deposits at savings banks was greater in 1959 than in either 1957 or 1965, yet thrift disintermediation was greater in the latter two years, especially 1965. Annual figures shown in Table 9.1 partly explain the greater thrift disintermediation in the mid 1960's compared to 1959 (and 1957 as well). With rates on time deposits at banks so favorable (and reasonably so compared to open market rates), households stepped up their acquisitions of bank time deposits at the same time as they cut back their rate of deposit in thrift accounts. But the mid 1960's also saw the introduction by banks of a new type of certificate of deposit geared to households with limited financial resources and paying a relatively high yield. For the first time (since 1953 at any rate) S & L's were finding their deposit flows cut back dramatically in the mid-1960's, while mutuals experienced a decline far in excess of the 1958–1959 experience.

---

[16] See Teck, Alan, *Mutual Savings Banks and Savings and Loan Associations*, Colombia University Press, New York, 1968, Charts 9, 10, and 11; and Anderson, Paul S., 'Mutual Savings Banks and "Tight Money"',' *New England Business Review*, January 1964.

[17] More correctly, they suffered at the hands of the bond market. Unfortunately, the series on short term U.S. government acquisition stops at the end of 1968, but household acquisitions of total U.S. government securities bear out the statement in the text.

Thus, while there is no reason to believe that the response of the household to changes in the spread between rates on bank time deposits and deposits at thrift institutions is not rapid, the postwar period suggests that at least two yield differentials are needed to explain fluctuations in the amount of thrift disintermediation. In addition, announcement effects, the absolute size of a differential and the length of time a differential has persisted, the introduction of new kinds of near-moneys and the influence of stock prices might also be considered. But changes in two yield differentials should account for a large share of variation of the disintermediation measure and deposit flows at thrift institutions.[18]

H. Mortgage Lending at Financial Intermediaries

Fluctuations in the extent of thrift disintermediation and deposit flows at thrift institutions tell a large part of the story behind fluctuations in mortgage lending and residential construction, but not everything. Fluctuations in mortage flows at thrift institutions tend to be of greater amplitude than fluctuations in savings deposits, up until 1966. During recessions deposits tend to run above mortgage flows. At this time liquidity positions are built up or advances (borrowings) from the Federal Home Loan Bank are brought down. During the early and middle stages of the boom, mortgage flows soon surpass deposit flows, as (evidently) lenders become overly optimistic and find themselves overcommitted. Savings and Loans find temporary relief, mainly by borrowing from a Federal Home Loan Bank; the mutuals from sales from their bond portfolio. Eventually, mortgage flows fall below deposits towards the latter stages of the boom as borrowings must be paid off, liquidity positions become impaired or mortgages just become less attractive. The net effect is to generate greater fluctuations in mortgage flows than in deposits (but not by enough to prevent mortgage lending and residential construction from behaving contra-cyclically).

In any case, as Diagram 9.1 indicates, fluctuations in mortgage flows at thrift institutions very strongly influenced changes in total mortgage flows.[19] From mid-1954 to early in 1960, from 1961 through 1963 and from the beginning of 1967 to the end of the period these two series are highly correlated. The same is true for their 1–4 family mortgage counterparts. A period

[18] The correlation between the disintermediation measure and the one interest rate differential shown in Diagram 9.2 shows $R^2 = 0.61$. Household sales of corporate stock rose dramatically towards the end of the 1960's. The fact that the extent of thrift disintermediation was little different in 1969 from 1966, while the interest rate differential had moved appreciably higher in 1969, suggests that some of the funds obtained from sales of stock found their way into thrift institutions.

[19] Recall that the simple correlation between these two flow variables was: $R^2 = 0.67$.

when total mortgage flows and flows at thrift institutions tend to consistently diverge is during the early stages of a recession. Three examples are shown in Diagram 9.1. What distinguished each recession period was the quick turn-around in mortgage flows at the thrift institutions. This was to a large extent due to the quick turnaround in deposit flows at these institutions, near cyclical peaks in GNP. Given the decline in the demand for loanable funds once the recession sets in, together with the easing up in policy, the improvement in the relative yield on deposits at thrift institutions led to thrift intermediation. It also led to large increases in the flow of time deposits at banks. However, given the closer proximity of thrift institutions to the mortgage market, mortgage flows picked up sooner there than with, for example, banks and insurance companies. Thus, in every period of monetary ease, mortgage flows rose first at thrift institutions.

During the mid and late stages of each boom, mortgage lending tended to be cut back sharply at all financial institutions. The explanation for the cutback at thrift and other institutions has already been given. The only period during the middle or late stages of a boom when total and 1–4 family mortgage flows diverged from flows at thrift institutions, was from 1963 to 1965. Mortgage lending at thrift institutions reached a peak by the end of 1963. This was not true for banks until 1965-(III), and not until 1966-(II) for insurance companies (although there was no noticeable increase in mortgage lending at the former after 1963). Increases in both demand and time deposits at commercial banks were large during this period. More than one-half of the growth in the latter could be attributed to the previously discussed behavior of the household sectors who were taking advantage of the relative attractiveness of rates on bank time deposits. This large growth of commercial banks liabilities, to-gether with the monetary authorities' regulation of unborrowed reserves, led to a situation where free reserves remained relatively high until 1966. The result was that banks were willing to increase their rate of acquisition of both 1–4 family and total mortgages up through 1965-(III). Once free reserves moved noticeably negative, banks backed away from the mortgage market. Insurance companies continued to increase their rate of acquisition of 1–4 family mortgages up through 1964-(IV). Even though short term market rates were rising relative to almost all other rates, the spread between mortgage rates and long term bond rates remained high through 1965-(II). But even after that, when mortgages became relatively less attractive as other market rates rose relative to rates on mortgages, insurance companies acquired 'other mortgages'; i.e. other than 1–4 family, at increasing rates up through 1966-(II). To a large extent this reflected a boom in apartment building, together with the ability of insurance companies to obtain an 'equity kicker' in their mortgage loans on apartments, enabling them to share in the profits of the enterprise. But overall mortgage lending, especially on 1–4 family housing, was adversely affected as early as 1963 by thrift disintermediation. While funds supplied to the credit markets by all financial intermediaries rose for some time after 1963, banks and insurance companies were not allocating to the mortgage market anywhere near as large a proportion of their funds, as thrift institutions would have done.

By 1965-(III) total mortgage lending reached a peak. Aside from insurance companies and federal agencies, all lenders were cutting back on their mortgage acquisitions at that point. As Diagram 9.1 and Table 9.2 indicate however, it was the thrift institutions that cut back most dramatically during this period. Like the 1955–1957 period, but to a much greater extent, thrift institutions were losing deposits up through mid-1966 both to the market and to commercial banks. After mid-1966 and until the easing of monetary policy late in 1966, both banks and thrift institutions were unable to raise deposit rates to compete with rates offered on marketable securities. Following that, the turnaround in policy late in 1966 led to a sharp decline in disintermediation as market rates fell sharply relative to rates paid on fixed-price near-moneys. This led to a sharp increase in deposit flows at thrift institutions and banks as well, and a large increase in mortgage lending. The main impact of a subsequent tightening of credit, followed by another short period of ease and a current period of tightness can be seen in Diagram 9.1. Neither total or 1–4 family mortgage lending at thrift institutions ever did quite succeed in recovering their 1963–1964 high until 1970.

Total mortgage acquisitions by insurance companies were only one-half their 1966 level in 1967, and remained so during 1968 and 1969. In all three of these years, this could be attributed to the poor yields on 1–4 family mortgages. With insurance companies actually cutting back on 1–4 family mortgage holdings, and banks more or less acquiring these mortgages at their 1965 rate, total 1–4 family mortgage lending did as well as it did up until 1969 mainly because of net purchases by government agencies.[20] Thus, the disintermediation measure increased substantially from mid-1967 until early 1968, yet total mortgage flows fell little, and 1–4 family mortgage flows did not decline as much as might be expected compared to other comparable periods; and this can largely be traced to purchases by government agencies. The behavior of the disintermediation measure and the interest rate differential in 1970 and 1971 had the predictable effect on mortgage lending.

I. The Monetary Ceiling in the Postwar Period

Except for the period from 1963 to 1965, changes in 1–4 family mortgage lending flows were very much dominated by changes in mortgage lending at the thrift institutions. This was true especially during the mid and late stages

[20] Flow of funds data indicates that net acquisition of 1–4 family mortgages by government agencies amount to approximately one-eighth of total 1–4 family mortgage acquisitions in 1967 and 1968 and rose to one-fifth of the total in 1969.

Table 9.2

Peak in total mortgage flows to peak in GNP	Change in total mort- gage flows	Change in 1–4 family mortgage flows	Change in 1–4 family mortgage flows at thrift in- stitutions	Change in 1–4 family mortgage flows at thrift in- stitutions	Change in mortgage flows at commercial banks	Change in mortgage flows at insurance companies
55-II 57-III	−5·4	−5·2	−4·1	−3·0	−2·0	−1·4
59-II 60-I	−3·7	−3·9	−1·8	−1·4	−1·5	+1·1
66-I 66-IV	−13·0	−10·2	−9·0	−8·2	−2·2	−1·8
68-IV 69-III	−4·9	−2·0	−3·7	−2·6	−4·0	−1·3

Source: Board of Governors of the Federal Reserve System.

of the boom, as seen in Table 9.2. Table 9.2 indicates the changes in total and 1–4 family mortgage acquisitions in billions of current dollars by all lenders, from the peak in total mortgage flows to the peak in GNP.[21] In addition, certain changes in mortgage flows are recorded for the four major inter-mediaries over the same interval.

Two things stand out. First, Table 9.2 indicates clearly that 1–4 family housing has borne the brunt of the cutback of mortgage flows during booms and tight money periods. Second, with one exception all four of the major private lenders in the mortgage market cut back on the supply of mortgage funds during tight money periods. The one exception is insurance companies during the late 1950's and early 1960's. This deviation from the norm can be explained in terms of the early imposition of tight money policy during this boom, together with excessive forward commitments by mortgage depart-ments of insurance companies.[22] However, thrift institutions appear to be the most vulnerable to tight money, hence, the special attention given these institutions (and households). The contra-cyclical behavior of residential construction in the boom, i.e. the imposition of a monetary constraint, can still be seen largely as the result of actions by the household sector: unfavor-able yields of deposits at thrift institutions lead to withdrawal of funds by households, which leads to a cutback in mortgage lending. The effect on residential construction during each of the four intervals listed in Table 9.2 was a decline of −$5.9, −$1.7, −$8.7 and −$2.0 billion, all figures in constant dollars.

The events of the period, especially during the 1960's, should certainly

[21] 1966-(IV) marks not so much a peak in GNP in constant dollars as a sharp shift in monetary policy from tightness to ease. A tight money policy encompasses each of the first three intervals.

[22] See Jones, *op. cit.*, p. 353.

dispel most of the concern about the possible destabilizing role of thrift institutions. Instead, what took place during the mid and late stages of each boom (or more correctly during tight money periods) was a shift upward to the left of the various supply curves of mortgage credit, where the amount supplied can be expressed as a function of the mortgage rate, the value to loan ratio or the amortization period. Given an elastic demand curve, mortgage lending would be cut back at thrift institutions, banks and insurance companies and so would residential construction. Thus, while we come out with the same result as writers like Alberts and Guttentag, the reasons behind the shifts in supply curves of mortgage funds are allowed to differ. It is primarily insurance companies (and to some extent mutuals) that react along the lines suggested by Alberts and Guttentag; i.e., during tight money periods a high cross elasticity of demand for other financial assets leads to a decrease in the available supply of mortgage funds.[23] The shifting supply of funds curves of thrift institutions, especially S & L's, must be traced back primarily to the behavior of deposit flows. The explanation of bank behavior would combine both influences with others.

J. The Lag in Monetary Policy

The monetary authorities as suppliers of funds of the last resort can move their instrument variables in the direction they feel will correctly achieve the ultimate targets of policy. Contrary to much that has been written, credit market conditions will usually reflect and indicate the aims of policy, certainly not on any day-to-day basis, but, say, from one quarter to the next. Movements in such credit market variables as net free (or unborrowed) reserves, the federal funds and the Treasury bill rate from one quarter to the next, have traditionally been the variables used by the authorities as indicators of the thrust of their policy. Of late, changes in certain monetary aggregates such as the money supply have also been given emphasis. Even though all of these variables are influenced by the performances of the economy, the authorities are in a position to offset undesirable movements. These variables are instruments of policy. The peaks (P) and troughs (T) of the Treasury bill rate and net free reserves are shown in Table 9.3, along with the peaks and troughs in the disintermediation measure and interest rate differential variable of Diagram 9.2.

Since the dating of peaks and troughs can sometimes be arbitrary, Table 9.4 shows the correlation matrix for the four variables.

As Tables 9.3 and 9.4 indicate, there is a close relationship between all four variables, especially the two yield variables and net free reserves. This

---

[23] See Guttentag, J. M., 'The Short Cycle in Residential Construction', *op. cit.*, and Alberts, *op. cit.*

Table 9.3

	P	T	P	T	P	T	P	T	P	T	P
(1) i_{TR}	53-II	54-II	57-III	58-II	59-IV	61-II	66-IV	67-II	68-II	68-III	69-IV
(2) $i_{TR} - i_{SD}$	n.a.	n.a.	57-III	58-II	59-IV	61-III	66-III	67-II	68-II	68-III	69-IV
(3) Thrift disinter-mediation	53-II	54-II	57-III	58-II	60-II	61-II	66-III	67-II	68-I	68-III	70-I
	T	P	T	P	T	P	T	P	T	P	T
(4) $(R^E - B)$	53-I	54-III	57-II	58-II	59-III	61-III	66-III	67-III	68-II	68-III	69-II

Source: Figures for net free reserves, $(R^E - B)$, thrift disintermediation and the Treasury bill rate, (i_{TR}), are found in various issues of the Federal Reserve Bulletin and flow of funds data supplied by the Board of Governors of the Federal Reserve System. The interest rate differential variable is denoted by $i_{TR} - i_{SD}$.

suggests that even if the authorities are using the traditional indicators to measure the thrust of policy, i.e. net free reserves and short term interest rates, they will be essentially correct even if the 'true' thrust of policy is measured by the interest rate differential and disintermediation measure. Tables 9.3 and 9.4 point up the lack of any significant lag in the adjustment of household holdings of liquid assets, to changes in yield differentials.

These movements can be compared with the periods of ease and tightness, as defined by the Federal Reserve open market committee, shown in Table 9.5. The beginnings of periods of shifts to ease are closely related to the timing of peaks in the interest rate, yield differential and disintermediation measure, and troughs in free reserves (and the rate of growth of the money supply). If anything, the turning points of the credit market variables lead the announced shift to ease, the average lead being about one quarter.[24] This lead would be a

Table 9.4

	(1)	(2)	(3)	(4)
(1)	1·000	—	—	—
(2)	0·8985	1·000	—	—
(3)	0·5223	0·6126	1·000	—
(4)	−0·7585	−0·8731	−0·6611	1·000

[24] The statements by the open market committee are usually very general, so that too much precision should not be read into the dates. The June 1970 date was arrived at after consultation with Reserve Board staff members.

Table 9.5

Tightness	Ease
March 1952 – June 1953	July 1953 – December 1954
January 1955 – November 1957	December 1957 – July 1958
August 1958 – January 1960	February 1960 – November 1965
December 1965 – October 1966	November 1966 – December 1967
January 1968 – June 1968	July 1968 – December 1968
January 1969 – June 1970	June 1970

Source: Parker Willis, *The Federal Funds Market*, Federal Reserve Bank of Boston, 1964, and statements by the open market committee.

reflection of the workings of the built-in stabilizing properties of the system; for example, free reserves are nothing but the difference between unborrowed reserves and required reserves. The former can be used as a measure of what the system is willing to supply in the way of reserves, while the latter indicates what the commercial banks are demanding. A rise in the free reserve position of banks following cyclical peaks would indicate that, at the margin, demand for reserves is falling relative to supply, even before the central bank deliberately loosens up on credit conditions. This is very likely to happen if the authorities are committed to a policy of 'gradualism' in their tight money policy. In contrast, a period of drastic tightening at and immediately following cyclical peaks, a point at which the demand for loanable funds and reserves begins to decline, would likely lead to a rise in free reserves only after the recession was well under way. This can be seen as follows: since $R^F = R^U - R^R$ where R^F, R^U and R^R are free reserves, unborrowed reserves and required reserves, respectively, a large deliberate cutting back of R^U following a (yet undetermined) cyclical peak would easily swamp the decline in R^R caused by a decline in the demand for reserves by banks, as economic activity declines.

Assume that throughout the 1950's and early 1960's the monetary authorities felt there existed a stable Phillips curve offering the authorities a trade off between wage and price movements on the one hand, and unemployment rates on the other. Assume further that during this period there was no other ultimate target of policy, so that the authorities would not be constrained in their use of general controls to pick some point on the Phillips curve. Then the inside lag in easy money policy can be approximated by comparing the peaks in GNP with the announced shifts in policy. Thus, the respective peaks in GNP were 1953-(II), 1957-(III) and 1960-(II), while the announced shifts in policy were July 1953, December 1957 and February 1960. The shortness of the inside lag so measured is apparent.

In turn, mortgage flows and residential construction increased on the average a little less than $1\frac{1}{2}$ quarters after the announced shift to ease. We might also surmise that because of the built-in stabilizing properties of the system just mentioned, the Treasury bill rate, the interest rate differential and disintermediation measure reached a peak and free reserves a trough before an announced shift. This was especially true during the mini-boom of the late 1950's. This had much to do with the fact that the lag in the upturn of mortgage flows and housing behind announced shifts to monetary ease, was so short. As a result, in the 1953–1954, 1957–1958, and 1960–1961 recessions, mortgage flows reached a trough either before or at the same time as GNP. Residential construction, at most, lagged the upturn in GNP by one quarter, and then only in one recession. In the other two recessions, housing either turned up before or at the same time as GNP. If the outside lag in easy money policy is measured as the inverval from the announced shift to ease and the upturn in housing, it is a little over two quarters during this period.

Sustained declines in GNP were less evident during the remainder of the 1960's and early 1970's. This alone would make it difficult to determine any sort of inside lag, even if only one target were being pursued. But there were other complicating factors during this period as well. Inflation, balance of payments difficulties, the heavy burden being borne by the mortgage and housing sectors, and disorderly security markets were all factors that the authorities recognized as in need of correction during tight money periods of the period. With only one policy instrument at their disposal and several ultimate targets of policy, the correct dial setting of the authorities instruments would have to reflect some sort of compromise.[25] But even if we use the announced shift of policy to ease as the recognition date, there is no way to date the need to shift. We would have to know the exact nature of the preference function supposedly being maximized by the authorities; i.e., the 'trade-offs' between the ultimate targets of policy. Only then could we see the extent of the recognition lag.

We do know that mortgage flows turned up one quarter after the announced shift to ease in 1966, and simultaneously with the announcement in 1970; i.e., 1970-(II). Construction also responded with only a one quarter lag after the announced shift in 1966. However, it did not turn up in the latter period until 1970-(III) if measured in current dollars and not until 1970-(IV) if measured in constant dollars. This could be due to the high proportion of multi-family construction in total construction in 1970.

Interest rates, the yield differential and disintermediation measure reach a trough, and free reserves tend to a peak, somewhat more in advance of the announced shift to a tight money policy—indeed very soon after the troughs in GNP. However, the rate of growth of the money supply peaks *after* the announced shift to a tight money policy. Given the dating of its announced changes in policy from ease to tightness, the authorities evidently do not feel that policy is tight when money market rates rise and free reserves fall, as long as the money supply maintains a fairly high rate of growth. Alternatively, we

[25] Operation 'twist' was an effort to develop a second policy instrument.

can say that the central bank allows the demand for loanable funds to outstrip the supply during a boom, as long as the money supply is growing at a rate above its cyclical average and does not interpret its actions as one of tightening credit.

There is no simple way of measuring the inside or recognition lag for a shift of policy from ease to tightness. Even if there is only one policy target, as was largely the case during the 1950's, there is nothing comparable to the decline in GNP as indication of the need to shift policy. The period immediately following the trough would hardly be the point at which to shift to a tight money policy. Unlike the timing of a shift from tight to easy money, the recognition of a need to shift from easy to tight money must be based on forecasts and estimates of the outside lag in policy.[26]

The outside lag in tight money policy, as measured by the interval from the announcement of a shift to tightness, to the peak in mortgage flows, is seen by comparing Tables 9.2 and 9.5. Announcement dates of a shift to tight money in January 1955, August 1958, and December 1965 can be compared with peaks in mortgage flows in 1955-(II), 1959-(II) and 1966-(II), and the peaks in constant dollar residential construction expenditures in 1955-(II), 1959-(II) and 1964-(I).[27] The lag between peaks and troughs of the four variables in Table 9.3 and peaks and troughs in mortgage flows is naturally longer. But what is important, and this is seen most clearly during the two tight money periods of the 1950's, mortgage flows and construction peaked well in advance of the peaks in GNP.

Those concerned with the possible destabilizing role of discretionary policy might well take heart from the effects of policy on mortgage lending and housing during the postwar period. There is no evidence that shifts from tightness to ease involved such long outside lags, that the stimulus to housing came so late in any boom as to intensify inflationary pressures. As we have seen, the upturn in housing came very soon after the downturn and the switch to ease (which in itself would shorten the recession). And the reversal of this policy led to declines in residential construction well in advance of cyclical peaks, and not after the recessions were under way. The period after 1961 does not give much clear cut evidence that discretionary policy dampens fluctuations. The lack of any pronounced recession, the quick reversals of policy in the late 1960's and the more pronounced intervention in mortgage markets by government agencies, beclouded the issue. But there is nothing to indicate that, during a sustained boom like that of the 1960's, when the supply of loanable funds and resources is limited, a tightening of policy will

---

[26] Theoretically, there is no reason why policy shifts from tightness to ease cannot be based on forecasts and estimates of the outside lag. Indeed the shift to a policy of ease in the second half of 1968 was based on forecasts that later turned out to be most incorrect.

[27] No attempt is made to find even a rough approximation to the outside lag from 1968 on, since policy was reversed so often and rapidly and since government activity in the mortgage market was so pronounced.

not cause a further cutback in housing, and that an easing of policy (such as the second half of 1968) will not lead to an increase in residential construction, with a short lag.

K. An Evaluation of Policy

In focusing our attention the way we did on the supply of loanable funds, it was clear that all the monetary influences mentioned in Chapter VI were at work during the postwar period. In every case, tight money caused the supply of loanable funds to grow less rapidly than the demand, leading to a general overall tightening of credit. It also led to a redistribution of funds away from thrift institutions and other financial intermediaries, to the capital markets. The resulting curtailment of funds led lenders to demand more favorable terms from potential builders and home owners. Given the highly elastic response of these two potential borrowers to the different terms of borrowing, this had to work against mortgage lending and residential construction. In easy money periods the effect was just the opposite.

What was also clear was the quick response of mortgage flows (and housing) to changing credit conditions. The lag of changes in mortgage flows and housing expenditures behind changes in credit policy was short. This was true even though there was strong likelihood that the monetary authorities were not following the 'correct' intermediate indicators in determining the impact of their policies on the economy. The high correlation between movements in what we think of as the more usual indicators—e.g. free reserves, short term market rates of interest, and the rate of growth of the money supply and the 'true' indicators of the thrust of policy, i.e. those depicted in Diagram 9.2—ensured this. Other types of spending may have been directly affected, though the magnitude of such effects are difficult to determine. What stood out, however, was the persistent systematic bias on the part of financial institutions and the public, in their allocation of funds in response to policy changes. This is what disintermediation and intermediation mean.

The effect of the monetary ceiling on housing was reinforced throughout most of the period by the ceiling in the capital goods industry, that led real resources to shift out of residential construction into business-type construction projects. The one possible exception to this was during the short boom at the end of the 1950's. Unemployment rates in the construction industry never fell below 12 per cent in the 1958–59 boom, compared to a low of 9 per cent during the 1955–1957 boom and even lower rates from early 1966 on. The failure of a real ceiling in the capital goods industry to become operative in the 1958–1959 boom, can be traced to the early implementation of tight money soon after the trough in GNP in 1958. As we argued in

Chapter VIII, monetary policy can have both a direct and indirect effect on spending, and if implemented very soon after the trough in activity the direct effect of policy will halt whatever boom in housing investment was just beginning to materialize. This, together with the indirect induced effects on other types of consumer investment spending, will lead to short lived booms in overall activity, such as that which took place late in the 1950's. The more gradual tightening of policy (together with the larger backlogged demands of all types) in the mid-1950's, and then again in the 1960's, allowed for a more sustained boom. The induced indirect effects of policy on spending kept the economy booming long enough to cause a more substantial business investment boom. Only then would the ceiling in the capital goods industry be reached. A tightening up on policy early in the 1960's—say, 1961—might easily have led to another mini-boom like that of the late 1950's. By the same token, if the authorities had not tightened up so early in the boom of 1958–1959, it could have been prolonged.

The authorities can err in their interpretation of the underlying trends in the real sector, and as a result fail to even lean against the wind. This opens up the question of whether policy during the period was optimal in the sense of maximizing, at least implicitly, some objective function that expressed the ultimate aims or targets of policy. In other words, we have argued that the authorities can affect aggregate demand directly and with a short lag. The question is, did they actually contribute to the realization of such goals of high employment, price stability and balance of payments equilibrium? Stated this way it immediately becomes obvious that there is no clear, unequivocal answer to the question. For if general quantitative controls are the only instruments at the disposal of the authorities to achieve a minimum of three ultimate targets, it is extremely unlikely that all three will be realized. The authorities are forced into a compromise, whereby a trade-off between different aims must be made. In the early part of the period up to the late 1950's this was not so much of a problem: there was less concern with the balance of payments position and inflation, and the drastic cut back in housing during a tight money period was yet to come. Thus, policy could concentrate on stimulating spending during recessions and allowing booms to be strong and prolonged, tightening up only after unemployment rates had fallen substantially. The recession of 1957–1958, which witnessed a rise in prices, marks a cutoff point in our ability to evaluate policy more or less in terms of its direct effect on housing and therefore spending. Put another way, after this period it becomes very difficult to evaluate policy in terms of whether or not the 'recognition lag' was short enough to allow the authorities to achieve their goal(s).

Take the case of the boom beginning in 1958. The free reserve position of member banks was not permitted to rise above $0.5 billion at the depth of the recession, and moved from a net free to a net borrowed reserve position while unemployment was $6\frac{1}{2}$ per cent. Unborrowed reserves did not become negative in the earlier boom of the mid-1950's, until unemployment had fallen to $3\frac{1}{2}$ per cent. The result was a lack of any sustained consumer investment boom during the later period, that would push down capacity utilizations rates for business far enough to generate a sustained business investment boom. Unemployment never got below 5 per cent even at the peak of the boom of the late 1950's.

The other periods when policy seemed in error were the quick reversals of policy late in 1966 and again in mid-1968, both at a time when inflationary pressures were strong. The two reversals of policy towards ease in the second half of the 1960's came during a period when unemployment rates were below 4 per cent (closer to 3 per cent in 1968), and had been falling steadily. The consumer price index had increased over 3 per cent from 1965 to 1966 and from 1966 to 1967. It is true that fixed investment in plant and equipment in constant dollars had declined slightly in 1966-(IV), and capacity utilization rates for manufacturing were declining somewhat during 1966. But spending at all levels of government were surging ahead from 1965 until mid-1968. Unfortunately this was to correspond with a large increase in investment by business in mid-1967, helped along no doubt by a $5 billion increase in residential housing outlays (constant dollars) beginning in the second half of 1966 and extending to the beginning of 1968. Business investment outlays declined early in 1968 and federal government expenditures were leveling off in 1968, giving some reason for easing up on the part of the monetary authorities. On the other hand, there was no let-up in the rate of price increase and the large upsurge in business investment by mid-1968 suggests that the authorities might have erred in easing up in mid-1968.

However, except for the last of these three examples, i.e. the final period of ease, it is difficult to say unequivocally that monetary policy was wrong. The difficulties are of several sorts. For example, the Phillips Curve is only a very rough first approximation of the relationship between unemployment and wage and price increases. There are dynamic considerations left out which suggest, quite naturally, that past behavior of wages and prices may be an important influence on current wages and prices, along with the unemployment rate. From this consideration it is possible without too many twists to argue (as some have done) that the sustained boom of the first half of the 1960's, a boom accompanied by a tolerable rate of price increase until 1966, could not have come about unless the inflation psychology developed during the 1950's had been eliminated. Hence the need to kill off the boom of 1958–1960 at an early date in order to stop a possible wage–price spiral. If this had not been done in the late 1950's, so the argument goes, it would have had to be done early in the 1960's. Unfortunately, it would be difficult to prove or disprove this argument.

Evaluating the period of ease beginning late in 1966 presents an entirely different sort of problem. Diagram 9.1 indicates clearly that savings institutions and residential mortgages were bearing a disproportionate share of the burden of tight money. If there is only one policy instrument (general controls) and a minimum of two targets, monetary restraint and some relief for groups connected with housing, the resulting policy will have to be some compromise. Thus, in neither of the two cases just discussed can it be said simply that the authorities erred because they didn't lean against the wind sufficiently.

However, the general easing during the second half of 1968 is different from both these cases. To a large extent the decision to ease was based on an overestimate of the deflationary effects of the surtax enacted by Congress during the period. The estimate was based on a projection of the FRB–MIT model which forecast an 'overkill' if monetary policy wasn't eased. To some extent there were too many targets again and too few instruments. Housing had recovered substantially, although the memory of the events of 1966 was still strong in the minds of the authorities. But in addition, government security dealers' inventories had risen greatly in anticipation of an easing in policy, itself partly based, on the forecast. There was said to be a general fear that if policy was not eased dealers would eventually have to dump large amounts of these securities, thereby creating disorderly securities markets.[28] This may have been a consideration but, on the other hand, the fact remains that much of this would not have happened had it not been for faulty forecasts to begin with.

What comes out of all this is that traditional monetary policy by itself is no longer adequate as an instrument of control. On equity grounds it may seem unfair for housing, especially 1–4 family, and thrift institutions to bear so much of the brunt of policy. This consideration suggests supplementing ordinary tight money policies by such things as mortgage purchases by 'Fannie Mae' or easier long term borrowing facilities at the Federal Home Loan banks.[29] On the other hand, all the evidence cited here points to housing as one sector where monetary policy has a strong effect and with a very short lag. Unless it can be assumed that measures to aid housing will be at the expense of some other type of spending, and that such spending is affected only with a short lag, much if not most of the stabilizing role of traditional monetary policy is lost by efforts to soften the impact of policy on housing.

Traditional monetary policy may also be insufficient to cope with inflation by itself, when the boom gets out of hand as it has in the second half of the 1960's. To be sure it might have been able to cope with inflationary pressures (at the expense of the housing industry) had not the federal government defense expenditures escalated when they did. But whenever there are abnormal spurts in federal expenditures not offset by tax increases, the result can be a situation where most types of non-consumption expenditures get

---

[28] I am indebted to Parker Willis of the Boston Federal Reserve Bank for this suggestion.

[29] During the four intervals depicting a peak in total mortgage flows to a peak in GNP in Table 9.2, the changes in government acquisition of mortgages were $.6 billion, −$1.6 billion, $.2 billion and $4.1 billion.

into phase. And with a commitment to gradualism we can expect the financial community to find means of altering the payments mechanism in such a way as to allow a rising level of expenditures in the face of a declining money stock. Thus, whether the problem is excess or deficient demand, events of the 1960's point up the need for developing additional instruments of policy. This would be true even if there existed no balance of payments problems.

Chapter X What Went Wrong in the Interwar Period

A. Introduction

It was suggested earlier that the interwar period could be viewed as a period when the economy had a long-run growth path, but that this moving equilibrium was an unstable one. By this it was meant that during this period the kind of institutional and technological constraints that normally operate to dampen cyclical fluctuations were absent. Hence, while the 1920's saw reasonably steady growth, forces were building up that could and did lead to one of the worst depressions on record. What stood out is not only the magnitude of the decline in economic activity, but the speed with which the economy moved downward.

In trying to understand what happened during this period, and why it differed so from the post-World War II period, we are handicapped by the paucity of quarterly data and in fact of reliable data of any sort. Furthermore, much of the data that is available is not comparable with the Department of Commerce Data that begins in 1929. Without adequate quarterly data the recursive structure of the system is not at all clear; as annual data seldom picks up the leads and lags at all well. For example, industrial production on an annual basis rose about 5 per cent from 1919 to 1920, and then declined approximately 25 per cent in 1921. However, inspection of monthly data reveals that the decline in industrial production began in March of 1920 and continued more or less uninterrupted until the middle of 1921. If we wish to discover the causes of the recession in production, the monthly data suggests that we look to events earlier than 1920, whereas the annual figures suggest concentration on events later in time. Because of data problems such as this, a great deal of guesswork and speculation will be involved in any attempt to explain the events of this period.

As in the post-World War II period, the interwar period begins with backlogs of demand built up because of postponements during the war. However, the backlogs were nowhere near as large as those stemming from World War II. For example, one estimate shows the backlog of demand for housing to be approximately 122 thousand units in 1918, compared with 2·2 million units in 1945.[1] Barger and Klein's quarterly figures, the National Bureau's reference cycle dates, and monthly figures of industrial production indicate another similarity: the existence of short cycles of two to three year's duration. However, these movements were so damped and of such short duration that they are not even noticeable in the annual data, except for the 1919–1921 short cycle. A comparison of Chawner's quarterly figures on investment by manufacturing with these cyclical patterns lends support to a view stated earlier; namely that in the absence of sharp movements on the defense budget, fluctuations in manufacturing investment will tend to give the boom its shape.[2] These movements are shown in Diagram 10.1. Those cases where GNP did not decline when manufacturing investment declined, can probably be traced to the special nature of the construction boom during the 1920's.

The recession beginning in 1920 was much more severe than either of the other two preceding the depression of 1929. Industrial production fell by about a third from its peak in 1920 to the trough in mid-1921, while the decline from peak to trough in the two subsequent recessions was appreciably less. The data on manufacturing investment shown in Diagram 10.1 also suggest the likelihood of a more severe recession in 1920–1921. Finally, on an annual basis, as already mentioned, GNP and final sales failed to register any decline from 1921 through to 1929. All these considerations suggest that

[1] These figures are found in the following way. From the Department of Commerce, *Historical Statistics, Colonial Times to 1957*, annual figures are available for the number of nonfarm households. Changes in the number of nonfarm households are then compared with estimates of new dwelling units started. Assuming that in 1915 there was no excess of total dwelling units over the total number of nonfarm households, the excess (or deficit) of dwelling units over nonfarm households can be cumulated from one year to the next.

[2] Chawner's quarterly figures on manufacturing investment, Klein and Barger's quarterly figures on current dollar GNP and the values of the monthly index of industrial production, are all found in *Business Cycle Indicators*, Vol. II, G. H. Moore (ed.), National Bureau of Economic Research, New York, 1961. Annual figures in constant dollars for GNP and its components are taken from Kuznets, *op. cit.* Kuznets' breakdown of GNP is not quite comparable with the Department of Commerce estimates. For the purposes at hand, the main difference is his inclusion of government construction figures along with private construction figures in his nonresidential construction outlays. Constant dollar construction figures for public and private construction and various components thereof, are taken from *Construction Volume and Costs, 1915–1954*, U.S. Department of Commerce. In addition, there are annual figures in current dollars for business, consumer and government outlays for new durable goods, as derived by G. Terborgh in the September 1939 issue of the *Federal Reserve Bulletin*. Beginning in 1929, there are annual figures in current and constant dollars for GNP and its components, as derived by the Department of Commerce. See *Survey of Current Business*, August 1965, and various subsequent issues. Unless there is some ambiguity as to the exact source of the data, detailed footnoting of sources will be avoided.

Diagram 10.1

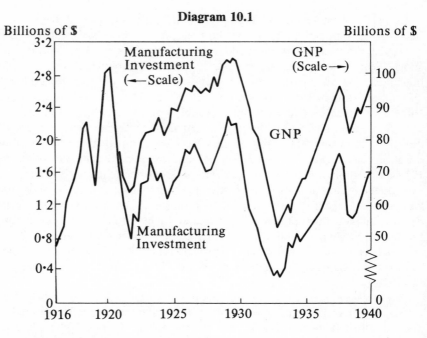

Source: *Business Cycle Indicators*, Vol. II, *op. cit.*

the period immediately following the war, until the first trough in 1921, should probably be treated separately from the period between mid-1921 and 1929. The latter period is best viewed as one long boom with very minor fluctuations superimposed upon it. It is also the period of greatest interest.

B. The First Interwar Cycle

Most writers in discussing the cycle of 1919–1921 stress the speculative nature of the boom, with its rapid rate of inflation ultimately followed by the rapid deflation of wages and prices. Chawner's estimates show manufacturing investment rising in current dollars by the third quarter of 1919, to a peak in the second quarter of 1920, and then declining until the fourth quarter of 1921. Klein and Barger's data only begins in 1921, but the trough in their current dollar GNP figures coincides with Chawner's trough in manufacturing investment (i.e. 1921-(IV)). All things indicate a boom of short duration in comparison with the boom following World War II. The rapid rise of prices and wages following World War I is often cited, together with the speculation in inventories, as a factor that would eventually generate a decline in GNP. Thus, it has been argued that the speculative fever set off soon after the war was bound to generate inelastic price expectations sooner or later, which would in turn lead to a cutback in spending. However, as already mentioned, industrial production had begun to decline very early in 1920. In addition, two outstanding features during the period from 1919 to 1921 which must have had much to do with the eventual downswing, were the large swing in the federal budget from a deficit to a surplus, and the decline in the favorable balance of trade position over the period.

The annual figures reveal a peak in GNP in 1920, and a decline in 1921, followed by a strong recovery in 1922. Final sales, in contrast, were lower in 1920 than in either 1919 or 1921, indicating the large inventory buildup in 1920 (all figures in constant dollars). However, 1921 showed not just a decline in inventory investment. We have already cited the falling off of manufacturing investment. Terborgh's annual estimates confirm the importance of the decline in manufacturing, together with mining and agriculture investment, in accounting for most of the decline in fixed business investment. What stands out during this recession is the strong showing of construction and consumption. Industrial construction declined dramatically from 1920 to 1921, but various estimates both in current and constant dollars show several types of construction, residential and non-residential alike, higher in 1921 than 1920. Thus, in addition to residential construction, public construction increased, and the non-residential construction component included in what was defined as family-related expenditures, was more or less unchanged. Overall family-related construction expenditures, which include residential housing expenditures (but not consumer investment in other forms of durables), increased from $3.0 to $3.2 billion from 1920 to 1921.[3] Meanwhile, Kuznets' estimates show that consumption increased enough from 1920 to 1921 to generate a higher level of final sales in 1921, but not by enough to offset the decline in inventory investment. Hence, overall, GNP declined in 1921.

C. The Boom of the 1920's

The growth performance from 1921 to 1929, using Kuznets' constant dollar figures, was a little over 5.2 per cent. As already mentioned, the growth process was not seriously interrupted. Klein and Barger estimate that the thirty-one quarter period from 1921-(IV) to 1929-(III) contained ten quarters when economic activity declined, but no decline lasted more than two quarters. A more detailed outline of the performance of the economy during the 1920's is shown in Table 10.1, which also reveals first of all that, while growth was so sustained that annual figures do not reveal any recession (other than that

[3] Figures are taken from *Construction Volume and Costs, 1915–1954, op. cit.*

Table 10.1

	GNP	FS	C'	C^D	I^H	$I^{B'}$	I^B
1919	67·8	65·0	42·7	5·0	1·5	10·3	8·3
1920	68·5	64·3	46·4	4·9	1·0	9·7	8·3
1921	65·5	65·5	50·2	4·0	2·1	7·8	6·2
1922	70·4	70·1	51·4	5·1	3·6	9·4	7·7
1923	80·0	77·2	54·6	6·6	4·2	11·3	9·6
1924	81·6	82·5	58·4	6·9	5·0	11·2	9·3
1925	84·3	82·7	56·2	7·8	5·4	12·7	10·6
1926	89·8	88·6	60·3	8·6	5·4	13·9	11·8
1927	90·6	90·2	62·5	8·2	5·1	13·7	11·3
1928	91·9	92·3	64·1	8·4	4·7	14·1	11·6
1929	98·0	96·3	68·1	8·8	3·4	15·3	12·8

$I^{B'}$ is Kuznets' measure of gross fixed capital formation and includes government construction and durable munitions outlays.
I^B excludes government construction.

Sources: S. Kuznets, *Capital in the American Economy*, Princeton University Press, Princeton, N.J., 1961; and *Construction Volume and Costs, 1915–1954*, U.S. Department of Commerce.

from 1920 to 1921), it was uneven. From 1921 to 1923 a strong business and, more especially, consumer investment boom took place leading to an average annual increase of approximately 11 and 9 per cent respectively for GNP and final sales during this two-year period. From 1923 until 1928 both consumer and business investment grew, but at a much diminished rate, and from 1928 to 1929 they hardly moved at all. This was reflected in a much slower rate of growth of GNP and final sales from 1923 on: 3.5 per cent for GNP if 1929 is included, 2.8 per cent if it is not. The comparable figures for final sales are 3.8 and 3.7 per cent respectively. From 1923 through 1929, changes in economic activity were very much related to increases in consumption (net of durables).[4]

When non-consumption spending is broken down, the annual figures show that residential construction did not move in a contra-cyclical fashion as in the post-World War II period, and that total business investment failed to grow appreciably after 1923. Consider the behavior of housing first. Constant dollar annual figures on residential construction indicate an absolute increase in such outlays, beginning in 1920 and extending through 1925, and probably

---

[4] It is true that nonfarm unemployment rates fell from 19·5 per cent in 1921 to 4·1 per cent in 1923, which might account for some of the slowdown, but these same rates had risen to 8·3 and 5·4 per cent in 1924 and 1925, respectively. Furthermore, as argued in Chapters III and IV, a more sustained business investment boom in the 1920's could easily have set in motion forces creating an adjustment on the supply side, allowing growth to proceed more rapidly. Unemployment figures are taken from Lebergott, *op. cit.*, Table A-3.

Diagram 10.2

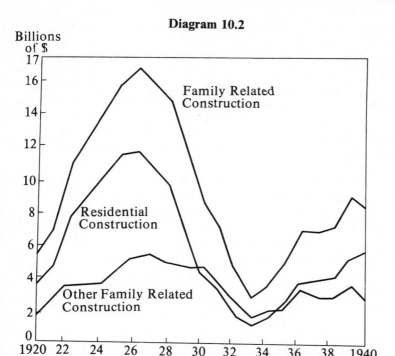

Source: U.S. Department of Commerce, *Construction, Volume and Costs, 1915–54.*

into 1926.[5] This can be compared with the two longest booms in residential construction in the post-World War II period (again using annual data), from 1952 to 1955, and 1961 to 1963. The fact that much of the stimulus in the boom of the 1920's was due to construction outlays is not unusual from a long historical point of view. But unlike most other construction booms, this one was dominated by residential construction. For example, in the construction booms of 1871 to 1893, and 1898 to 1911, 62 and 82 per cent respectively of the increase in construction outlays was accounted for by non-residential construction. In contrast, during the boom in construction from 1920 to 1926, non-residential construction accounted for only 39 per cent of the increase in total construction outlays.[6] This is true whether annual figures or moving averages are used. Furthermore, the first half of the 1920's saw a boom in other types of construction that constituted a large share of

[5] These figures by Kuznets are confirmed by Terborgh's current dollar estimates, as well as by those of the Department of Commerce. The figures for business investment in constant 1929 dollars are obtained by subtracting from Kuznets' fixed nonresidential expenditures, government construction outlays in current dollars. Construction costs were fairly constant during the 1920's, in 1929 hardly differing from the index of costs in 1921.
[6] The figures are from Kuznets, *op. cit.*, pp. 576–579.

what was earlier termed family-related expenditures: e.g., stores, hospitals, educational facilities, etc. Using Department of Commerce data, these outlays, together with those for housing, are shown in Diagram 10.2. Beginning with 1921, these related construction outlays rose from 2.6 billion to a peak in 1927 of 5.2 billion, followed by a decline of about $13\frac{1}{2}$ per cent by the end of 1929.[7] The peak year for residential construction, plus these other family-related types of construction, was 1926, the earlier downturn for the total being attributed to the fact that housing reached a peak in 1925 or 1926 (all figures in constant dollars). At that time they amounted to 50 per cent of total construction outlays.

We would expect family-related construction outlays to be curtailed in the event of competition with the business sector for resources and funds. The fact that they actually expanded would seem to confirm the earlier observation that there existed a lack of strong demand by the business sector, even during the short period from 1921 to 1923, but especially from 1923 up to 1928.[8] Chawner's annual figures for manufacturing investment in constant dollars lends further support. The boom in manufacturing investment after World War I seemed to be confined to the years 1918, 1920 and 1929. From 1923 to 1928 Chawner's constant dollar figures for manufacturing investment show a rise from $2.1 billion to $2.3 billion. This is confirmed by Terborgh's current dollar estimates for manufacturing and mining investment, as well as by his current dollar estimate of $7.9 billion in 1923 and $8.8 billion in 1928 for total business investment. And most of the increase in the latter can be attributed to 'commercial and miscellaneous' investment. It is true that Kuznets' constant dollar figures for total business investment show a rise from $9.7 billion in 1923 to $11.6 billion in 1928, depicting a somewhat stronger business investment boom. But even if these figures are closer to the mark, this increase of 20 per cent over a five-year period has only to be contrasted with a 72 per cent increase in fixed plant and equipment investment from 1961 to 1966—a period with comparable unemployment rates—to see the relative weakness of business investment. It would seem that the real business investment took place before 1923, possibly before 1921. Taking the period 1921–1929 as a whole, over one half the growth in business investment in this eight year interval was achieved in the two-year interval from 1921 to 1923.

Since housing and other forms of family-related construction also showed pronounced growth from 1921 to 1923, the strongest spurt in business investment and family-related construction outlays coincided. Not only that, but as Table 10.1 indicates, of the $8.2 billion increase in consumer and business fixed investment outlays combined from 1921 to 1923, $4.7 billion was due to the increase in consumer investment outlays, with higher housing expendi-

---

[7] All figures from *Construction Volume and Costs, 1915–1954, op. cit.*
[8] See Diagram 8.2 in Chapter VIII for the post World War II picture.

tures alone accounting for $2.1 billion of the increase. Following the slowing down in the growth of business investment in 1923, the non-business groups sustained the boom through 1926. By 1926 residential construction outlays had begun to decline, and other forms of family-related construction expenditures were to shortly follow. From 1926 through to 1928, the sum of all non-consumption expenditures were declining according to both Terborgh's and Kuznets' estimates. Only rising consumption expenditures allowed GNP and final sales to rise at all. Thus, from 1926 to 1928 consumption, excluding durables, rose by $3.8 billion and final sales rose $3.7 billion, while the increase in consumption so measured was identical with the increase in final sales from 1928 to 1929.[9]

D. The Decline in Residential Construction and its Causes

As just mentioned, the peak in residential construction in constant dollars came in 1925 or 1926. The peak in non-residential family-related construction expenditures came in 1927. These facts in themselves would be no cause for alarm, since the decline in family-related construction could merely have been reflecting a ceiling effect. And if this were the case, it would be all to the good from the point of view of stability, since this would have allowed for backlogs to have been built up that could be worked off when other types of business investment turned down. Unfortunately, this would not be an accurate interpretation of what was taking place at the time, and of what would be the likely reaction of family-related construction expenditures to a decline in business investment. It has already been pointed out that business construction expenditures did not dominate the growth of construction up to 1926. Furthermore, Kuznets' figures on total non-residential construction by business in constant dollars show, if anything, a decline from 1926 through 1928. This weakness in business construction outlays during a period when residential and other forms of family-related construction outlays were turning down, is confirmed by Chawner's constant dollar estimates for manufacturing expenditures for plant, and by Terborgh's current dollar figures for total business plant investment. If the demand were there, especially for residential building, there should have been more than enough excess capacity in the construction industry to supply these demands. Instead, estimates point to an overbuilding of houses during the period up to 1926. Table 10.2 shows the number of new households formed (ΔF), the annual number of dwelling units started (DU), and the cumulated excess of dwelling units over non-farm households, $\sum(DU\text{-}\Delta F)$, during the 1920's. From 1923 on, new dwelling units started exceeded the change in the number of families in every remaining

[9] See Table 10.1.

Table 10.2

Year	DU	ΔF (thousands of units)	Σ(DU − ΔF)
1920	217	361	−120
1921	449	587	−258
1922	716	525	−67
1923	871	712	92
1924	893	690	295
1925	937	563	669
1926	849	580	938
1927	810	616	1132
1928	753	475	1410
1929	509	435	1484
1930	330	417	1397
1931	254	208	1443
1932	134	65	1512
1933	93	112	1493
1934	126	465	1154
1935	216	547	823
1936	304	588	539
1937	332	664	207
1938	399	601	5
1939	459	731	−267
1940	530	752	−489

The symbols DU, ΔF and $\Sigma(DU - \Delta F)$ indicate the number of non-farm dwelling units started, the change in the number of non-farm households and the cumulative surplus (+) or deficit (−) of dwelling units in existence over the number of non farm families, respectively. It is assumed that in 1915 $\Sigma(DU - \Delta F) = 0$.

Sources: Grebler, L., Blank, D., and Winnick, L., *Capital Formation in Residential Real Estate, Trends and Prospects*, Princeton, Princeton University Press, 1956; and *Historical Statistics*, Bureau of the Census.

year of the decade. Even the cutback in housing starts beginning in 1926 failed to cut into the surplus, so that by the beginning of the depression the cumulative supplies were the highest to date. And when the downturn came, there would be no deferred housing demands to slow down and eventually stabilize the economy, nor would there be much help from other related types of investment spending.

E. The Investment Spurt of 1929

There remains the perplexing problem of explaining the spurt in investment and aggregate activity in 1929. According to Kuznets, from 1928 to 1929

GNP rose $6.1 billion, final sales $4 billion, consumer outlays excluding durables $4 billion and fixed investment $1.2 billion, the latter largely due to a $1 billion increase in producers durables. Since government construction outlays were unchanged in constant dollars from 1928 to 1929, Kuznets' estimates indicate that the increase in fixed investment was for all practical purposes an increase in business fixed investment, and of the order of magnitude of 10 per cent. Now the period from 1923 to 1928, as we have already seen, was not one of spectacular growth, at least compared to the period between the end of the war and 1923: except for the change from 1925 to 1926 there was no dramatic increase in activity. The only thing that seemed to be sustaining the economy from 1926 through 1928 was the growth of consumption, and to a lesser extent government outlays. With the economy virtually stagnating from 1926 on, while business investment, though not growing, was certainly large enough to be adding to productive capacity, one would have expected capacity utilization rates to be falling during the final stages of the boom. Yet there occurred an inexplicable increase in business investment.

Terborgh's data indicates that railroads, public utilities and communication, which in 1928 accounted for about 20 per cent of business investment outlays, accounted for about 40 per cent of the increase in business investment from 1928 to 1929. Investment by the 'commercial and miscellaneous' sector, which includes trade, service, finance and construction, on the other hand, accounted for 30 per cent of total business outlays in 1928, but only for 14 per cent of the increase. Part of the spurt in public utility investment has been attributed to the need to expand distribution and transmission facilities.[10] The bad showing of commercial and miscellaneous investment, which includes stores and other trade facilities, could be expected on the basis of the previously discussed overbuilding, and eventual decline in residential construction. With the former kind of construction probably geared to the latter, the need for house-induced types of construction would have been more than satisfied by 1929. Manufacturing investment just about held its own, in the sense that it accounted for 35 per cent of business investment in 1928 and 39 per cent of the increase in the latter from 1928 to 1929. But Chawner's quarterly data for manufacturing investment shown in Diagram 10.1 shows that the final boom in manufacturing investment was the weakest on record during the 1920's.[11] In addition, quarterly data show that while on an annual basis manufacturing investment was higher in 1929 than in 1928, this was due largely to the fact that upon reaching a peak in 1929-(II) it had not fallen far enough by 1929-(IV) to pull the annual flow for 1929 below the annual

---

[10] The 1920's was a period when electricity and electrical appliances came into their own.
[11] The boom in manufacturing investment beginning in 1921 lasted no longer than this final boom, but its amplitude was much greater. And while the amplitude of the boom in manufacturing investment was not much greater from 1924-(III) to 1926-(IV), it lasted nine quarters compared with six quarters for the boom beginning in 1927-(IV).

Table 10.3

Physical volume of new orders for durable goods
(seasonally adjusted)
1923–1925 = 100

	J	F	M	A	M	J	J	A	S	O	N	D
1928	100	101	96	98	103	99	98	97	91	90	106	85
1929	95	102	107	97	102	91	90	89	84	93	72	77
1930	71	72	64	60	60	56	58	50	53	47	45	49

Source: *Business Cycle Indicators*, Vol. II, pp. 157.

figure for 1928. There are no figures for contracts and new orders received by producers of capital goods *per se* (which we have argued earlier is a good leading indicator of future investment outlays). But there are figures for new orders received by manufacturers of durable goods, a large part of which are new orders for capital equipment. Table 10.3 shows seasonally adjusted monthly figures for such new orders from 1928 through 1930. By September of 1929 new orders had fallen 16 per cent from the beginning of the year. There is a one-month recovery in October 1929, but the steady decline in new orders throughout the year suggests that a decline in investment outlays by business (and other purchasers of durable goods) towards the end of 1929 would be most likely without a market crash.

Two final bits of information on the likely future course of events are the figures for the diffusion index of new orders for investment goods, and the index of industrial production. Taking the percentage of the total number of sectors (70 in all) expanding their orders for capital goods, as a measure of strength of demand for new investment goods, a peak was reached in October of 1928, when 56 per cent of the sectors were expanding. The value of the index then declined steadily, so that by September 1929 only about 28 per cent of the sectors were increasing their orders for investment goods.[12] Finally, industrial production had stopped growing by June 1929 and began its decline in August 1929.

Thus, a sizeable increase in business investment outlays in 1929 following a two-year period of near stagnation, is not so difficult to understand; nor, incidentally, need we look upon 1929 as the beginning of a boom that was nipped in the bud by the stock market crash in the fall of 1929. A good deal of the increase in business investment can be accounted for by increased outlays by manufacturing. Evidently manufacturing investment, with its relatively short cyclical period, was merely undergoing a short boom

---

[12] The diffusion index for new orders of investment goods is found in *Business Cycle Indicators*, op. cit., p. 158.

generated by the fact that utilization rates had risen as a result of a decline in investment outlays from 1926-(IV) to 1927-(IV), coupled with a modest but still positive increase in economic activity. The boom was weak, however, because total non consumption expenditures from 1928 to 1929 grew very little. This can be traced to the decline in residential housing expenditures and various other non consumption outlays related to housing. Much of the remaining increase in business investment can be attributed to sectors such as public utilities, that would be least affected by the stagnating conditions of the immediately preceding years.

With fixed non consumption outlays increasing little if at all from 1928 to 1929, it could not be expected that consumption expenditures could grow much longer, to sustain this mini-boom. Residential housing, manufacturing and commercial and miscellaneous investment constituted 30 per cent of fixed non consumption expenditures in 1929. A simultaneous decline in these spending categories, when housing and related expenditures (some included in the commercial and miscellaneous category) are declining because of excess capacity rather than because of any squeeze, would certainly forbode for 1930 a marked deterioration in economic conditions. This would be true whatever the state of the stock market.

F. The Relation between the Recession of 1930 and the Previous Boom

We commented in Chapter VIII on the behavior of residential housing and other types of family-related expenditures during the post-World War II period. This spending, as a per cent of total construction, declined in each boom, and rose in each recession as already mentioned. Family-related construction in particular, and what we have defined as family-related expenditures in general, acted not just as a cushion dampening the extent and rate of decline of activity, but behaved in such a way as to reverse the downswing and lead the economy in its recovery. This was very much due to two factors: that this type of capital formation was cut back during each boom so that backlogs of unsatisfied demands were built up; and that spending of this sort is the least likely to get into phase in the recession. Now one of the reasons why backlogs of these demands were built up during the post-World-War II booms, was the strong demand by the business sector for the resources of the capital goods industry. And these demands were so strong that not only the non-business sector but also the business sector built up backlogs, as evidenced by such things as accumulated but unspent appropriations by manufacturers, and unfilled new orders and contracts by business, for capital goods. This was true in spite of a belief that the business sector would be more successful than the non-business sector in garnering resources, if they had to compete. In contrast, the 1920's has just been shown as a period when business investment demands were very weak; so weak that two related sources of instability were present by 1929 that were not evident at the peak of any boom in the post-World War II period. First, the demands for family-related construction were more than satisfied—there were far too many vacancies in residential housing during the height of the boom to lead to anything but an eventual collapse of residential construction. The decline in outlays for other forms of family-related construction must also have been the result of an over-accumulation of this kind of capital. Thus, in the event of a decline in general activity, these types of expenditures could not be expected to turn up. Second, with a weak business investment boom, unfilled orders relative to shipments of capital goods to business would have been relatively low (or non existent), and could thus be worked off quickly, so that expenditures on business plant and equipment would turn down relatively soon, and very rapidly after new orders and contracts fell off. This would in itself tend to speed up the rate of decline in activity compared to the postwar period. Not only was there no ceiling in the capital goods industry to cause postponement of residential housing outlays (and evidently none to cause a large backlog of new orders and contracts for business), there is little evidence that any sort of monetary ceiling was in effect either. In Table 10.4 non-farm mortgage holdings for selected financial institutions are shown. The net acquisitions are large for all institutions until 1929. And even part of this decline in growth can be attributed to a falling off in the demand for funds by mortgage holders, since some of the latter were refinancing their homes during the period, to invest in the stock market. Behind this steady flow of funds into mortgages lie certain other characteristics of the period.

Table 10.4

Non-farm mortgage holdings by institution (in billions of $)

	Total outstanding	Commercial banks	Mutual savings banks	S & L's	Insurance companies
1920	$13·5	$1·9	$2·4	$1·9	$1·1
1921	14·7	2·0	2·6	2·2	1·4
1922	16·2	2·5	2·9	2·5	1·5
1923	18·8	3·1	3·2	2·9	1·8
1924	21·3	3·8	3·7	3·5	2·2
1925	24·5	4·4	4·0	4·2	2·7
1926	27·6	4·8	4·4	4·8	3·4
1927	30·8	5·1	4·9	5·5	4·0
1928	34·1	5·3	5·3	6·1	4·6
1929	35·8	5·3	5·4	6·5	5·2

Source: Goldsmith, R., *A Study of Savings in the United States*, Vol. I, Princeton, 1955, pp. 723 and 729.

Table 10.5

Year	Deposits at mutuals ($ bil.)	Savings shares at S & L's ($ bil.)	r_{SB} (per cent)	r_C (percent)	r_M (per cent)	r_A (per cent)
1920	5·4	1·7	3·69	7·50	5·1	6·1
1921	5·6	2·0	3·86	6·62	5·5	6·0
1922	6·0	2·3	3·83	4·52	5·4	5·1
1923	6·4	2·6	3·92	5·07	4·3	5·1
1924	6·8	3·2	3·93	3·98	4·7	5·0
1925	7·2	3·7	3·98	4·02	5·2	4·9
1926	7·7	4·3	4·06	4·34	5·0	4·7
1927	8·3	5·0	4·06	4·11	4·9	4·6
1928	8·8	5·6	4·18	4·85	4·2	4·6
1929	8·8	6·2	4·46	5·85	4·9	4·7

Sources: Goldsmith, R., *op. cit.*, Vol. I, pp. 425 and 413; *Historical Statistics of the United States*, Bureau of the Census, p. 654; *Banking and Monetary Statistics*, Federal Reserve Board, p. 460; and J. Lintner, *Mutual Savings Banks in the Savings and Mortgage Markets*, Harvard University, 1948, p. 504.

In Table 10.5 deposits at thrift institutions are shown together with the average rate paid on mutual savings bank deposits, (r_{SB}), the prime commercial paper rates, (r_C), the average of mortgage rates charged at mutual savings banks, (r_M), and Moody's AAA corporate bond rate, (r_A). Consider the deposit flows at thrift institutions first. Savings shares at S & L's grew steadily throughout the 1920's, so that from 1920 to 1929 they had increased by $4.5 billion. Mortgage loans outstanding increased by $4.6 billion over the same period. Deposits increased by over $3.4 billion at mutual savings banks, while mortgage loans increased by a little over $3 billion. The ratio of mortgage loans to deposits rose as a result, from 44 per cent to 62 per cent at mutual savings banks. While it cannot be concluded from these flows alone that disintermediation was not a problem in the 1920's, Table 10.5 contains additional information that is helpful. From 1920 until 1928 the spread between the prime commercial rate and the rate on deposits at mutual savings banks, i.e., $r_C - r_{SB}$, had a definite downward trend. Only in 1928 and 1929 did this movement reverse itself in any noticeable way. Of course, by then a cut back in housing starts had been underway for two years for other reasons, and the disintermediation that did occur was not likely to have much of an effect on housing. Even so, flows into thrift institutions were maintained through 1928. If anything, yield spreads were moving in such a way during most of the 1920's as to lead one to believe that the actual flows through thrift institutions were reflecting a process of intermediation rather than disintermediation. Table 10.4 also indicates that mortgage acquisition at other financial institutions also grew substantially. For life insurance companies, and to a lesser extent for mutual savings banks, this can be partially explained in terms of the behavior of yield differentials between mortgages and other securities. If it can be assumed that Moody's AAA corporate bond rate is the relevant yield to compare with mortgage rates (or else can be taken as representative of the general trend in rates on marketable securities), then again we see that movements of rates up until the end of the period were certainly such as to make mortgages attractive acquisitions. The explanation behind the flow of mortgages into commercial bank portfolios can only be inferred, but clearly a lack of strong demand for funds by the bank's traditional customers is consistent with their failure to cut back during the period. Total loans and investments at all commercial banks increased from $37.7 billion in 1923 to $49.7 billion in 1929. Of this $12 billion increase, $8.6 billion was an increase in loans, but only $2.9 billion was an increase in 'other loans'; i.e. loans other than real estate and collateral loans. This can be compared with an increase in corporate bond holdings of $2.4 billion and an increase in all investments of $3.4 billion.[13]

G. Spending During the Downswing

Current dollars figures are available for total receipts and expenditures of the federal government, state and local, and total government on national income and product account basis, and are shown in Table 10.6. Up through calendar 1931 all levels of government were increasingly stimulating. The increase in federal government expenditures in 1931 was for the most part accounted for by a large but temporary increase in transfer payments to individuals. These payments declined more or less steadily until 1936, when they again increased dramatically. By 1933 total government expenditures were only slightly above their 1929 level, although the overall government budget had turned from surplus to deficit. What is interesting is the stabilizing effect of state and local governments, who increased their outlays and the size of their deficit up through 1931. If construction outlays are excluded, state and local expenditures remained fairly stable through 1932.[14] In any case, during the

---

[13] Unfortunately before 1929 loans were only broken down into three broad categories. Loans on collateral include any collateral loan, provided the collateral is not real estate, and include, for example, loans secured by merchandise. Figures in the text are taken from *All-Bank Statistics, United States, 1896–1955*, Board of Governors, Federal Reserve System.

[14] See Maxwell, *op. cit.*, p. 21. The large decline in construction outlays in 1932 has been attributed to the inability of state and local governments to market their securities. This inability to obtain finance may have been true for city governments as early as 1931, although long-term borrowing by state governments increased through 1931. See Gayer, A. D., *Public Works in Prosperity and Depression*, National Bureau of Economic Research, New York, 1935, pp. 127 and 168. In any case, the fact should not be lost sight of that total outlays by state and city governments increased through 1931.

Table 10.6

Receipts and expenditures on national income and
product account basis, 1929–1940 (billions of dollars)

Calendar year	T^T	G^T	T^F	G^F	T^{S+L}	G^{S+L}
1929	$11·3	$10·3	$3·8	$2·6	$7·6	$7·8
1930	10·8	11·1	3·0	2·8	7·8	8·4
1931	9·5	12·4	2·0	4·2	7·7	8·5
1932	8·9	10·6	1·7	3·2	7·3	7·6
1933	9·3	10·7	2·7	4·0	7·2	7·2
1934	10·5	12·9	3·5	6·4	8·6	8·1
1935	11·4	13·4	4·0	6·5	9·1	8·6
1936	12·9	16·1	5·0	8·7	8·6	8·1
1937	15·4	15·0	7·0	7·4	9·1	8·4
1938	15·0	16·8	6·5	8·6	9·3	9·0
1939	15·4	17·6	6·7	8·9	9·6	9·6
1940	17·7	18·4	8·6	10·0	10·0	9·3

In the table T and G refer to tax receipts and expenditures, respectively. The superscripts T, F and $S + L$ refer respectively to total, federal and state and local expenditures or receipts as the case may be. All variables are in current dollars. Total figures are less than the sum for the two government levels because of some double counting involved. The difference between G^T and G^F and G^{S+L} is equal to grants in aid.

Source: *Economic Report of the President*, 1968

early stages of the downswing, all levels of government were acting so as to dampen the decline, and during the critical year, 1930, state and local governments actually increased expenditures 7 per cent compared to 1929. But with the exception of outlays by government (and those by public utilities), all types of business and consumer investment outlays were declining. Viewed another way, while total government expenditures rose by 8 per cent and 12 per cent, consumer investment fell 28 and 15 per cent, and non-residential fixed investment fell 18 and 35 per cent from 1929 to 1930 and from 1930 to 1931 respectively, all in constant dollars. Thus, the fiscal performance of all levels of government was helpful. But when activity was falling so rapidly, and family-related expenditures not rising on a front broad enough to stabilize this rapid decline in output, capacity utilization rates of businesses, especially manufacturing, could only continue to fall during 1930. By the beginning of 1931 we could expect a retrenchment of almost all types of private expenditures.

To illustrate the importance of contracyclical movements of family-related expenditures, we can assume that the peak in final sales coincided with that of manufacturing investment; i.e. 1929-(II). A reasonable calculation of the contribution of residential housing alone, had it behaved countercyclically, can be obtained as follows. Final sales in constant dollars fell on an annual basis from $200.1 billion to $184 billion from 1929 to 1930. The decline in residential housing during this period was $4.1 billion. Now in the post Korean recessions, if we pick a point in time six quarters after the peak in final sales, and compare residential housing expenditures with their value at the previous peak, such investment had increased on the average by 17 per cent. Assume that the level of residential investment for 1929-(II) (on an annual basis) was the same as the annual figure for 1929, namely $10.4 billion.[15] If this figure is increased by 17 per cent, we obtain a figure of roughly $12 billion which can be used as the hypothetical figure for 1930. In other words, if conditions in the 1920's had been anything like those that prevailed in the post World War II period, housing investment (if independent of the stock market crash) would have increased by $1½ billion; whereas in fact it had declined about $4 billion. If we assign a multiplier value of two to changes in non consumption expenditures, we obtain a decline in final sales of between $4 and $5 billion or a little over 2 per cent, rather than the $16 billion decline that actually took place.

If anything, this estimate exaggerates what would have to be done, since the same forces that cause backlogs of family-related demands also cause unfilled or backlogged orders for business. In other words, when the ceiling or constraint in the capital goods industry is operative it causes a relatively large amount of postponement or backlogging of housing; but it also lengthens the waiting time for business investment projects. Thus, the same factors that would have caused backlogs in housing would have caused the same in business investment demands, making the decline in final sales from 1929 to 1930 less rapid. Given some average lag before housing picks up when it has been backlogged, this means a smaller decline in overall activity to be offset by housing and other types of spending linked to housing. The fact of the matter is that it doesn't take much to reverse a downward trend, if at the outset of a downturn there are backlogs of demand by spenders who are not especially sensitive to current conditions, and if the decline in activity is slow. This would have been the case had there been a strong business investment boom in the 1920's; but, in fact, once the economy started to decline, there was nothing much other than the government sector to act out of phase with the rest of the economy.

The severity of the depression has been well documented: GNP and final sales in constant dollars fell from $203.6 and $200.1 billion in 1929, to $141.5 and $145.7 billion respectively by 1933; unemployment rose from 3.2 per cent

---

[15] In fact, annual figures for residential housing during the post-World War II period were less than the quarterly figure for housing in the quarter when final sales and GNP peaked, because of the lag in the pick up of housing after the downswing. But the annual figure for housing in that year following the peak in overall activity was also lower than the quarterly figure for housing six quarters after the downturn.

Table 10.7

	GNP	*FS*	*C*	I^C	I^H	I^{PD}	I^{FS}
1929	203·6	200·1	123·3	26·7	10·4	12·6	13·9
1930	183·5	184·1	116·4	19·2	6·3	9·9	11·8
1931	169·3	171·7	115·0	16·3	5·1	6·6	7·5
1932	144·2	150·4	106·3	11·1	2·7	3·8	4·4
1933	141·5	145·7	104·6	10·4	2·1	4·3	3·3
1934	154·3	157·0	108·6	12·3	2·9	5·6	3·6

All figures are in constant 1958 dollars. I^{PD} = producers' durables investment. I^C is the sum of consumer durable expenditures plus residential housing, I^H. All other variables have their previous meanings.

Source: *Survey of Current Business*, August 1965.

of the labor force in 1929 to 25·2 per cent in 1933.[16] Table 10.7 describes quite well what happened. It was argued earlier that the severity of a depression can largely be explained in terms of what happened (or failed to happen) during the previous boom. In our discussion of the lower turning point in Chapters VIII and IX, much stress was placed on the behavior of the non business sectors. State and local governments, non profit organizations, and consumers increased their outlays in the face of a decline in general activity in the post-World War II period, by enough to offset the downward movements of business expenditures. Once a 'floor' had been reached the stage was set for a full fledged boom in consumer investment. Table 10.7 illustrates the enormity of the job that these stabilizing sectors would have had to do in the interwar period, to reverse the trend before a serious depression had set in. But as we have already stressed, the large size of this stabilizing operation, and the remoteness of the possibility that residential housing and similar outlays would turn up, were very much related. Fixed non residential investment, $(I^{PD} + I^{FS})$, fell as rapidly as it did in the early 1930's, for the same reason that residential housing failed to turn up: demand pressures on the capital goods industry, most clearly on construction firms, had been relatively slight compared to capacity during the 1920's: as a result consumer and other non-profit investment demands for housing, as well as business demands, were satisfied during the period. This lack of unfilled orders and demands contributed greatly to the rapidity of the decline in all forms of construction and producer's durables. Although the behavior of the government sector was stabilizing, its effect was nowhere near enough to cause an early turn-around. Quarterly and monthly data indicate that the trough was

[16] Figures are taken from the *Survey of Current Business*, August 1965, and Lebergott, *op. cit.*, p. 512.

reached early in 1933, with industrial production and manufacturing investment picking up a little earlier.

The end of the downswing finally came in 1933, which is fairly explicable: consumption net of durables as a share of GNP rose from 70 per cent in 1929 to 80 per cent in 1933. If total government expenditures on goods and services is added to consumption, the resulting figures—again as a per cent of GNP—rose from 80 per cent in 1929 to 90 per cent in 1933. The American economy had practically achieved a circular flow situation where further declines were very unlikely.[17] By the same token fixed non-residential investment at $7.6 billion would hardly be considered adequate to match depreciation of business capital.

H. The 'Free Cycle' of the 1930's

Unlike the booms of the post World War II period, the early stage of the recovery was not dominated by a boom in consumer investment. It grew after 1933, but so did business investment and government outlays. The initial stimulus for recovery is probably best attributed to the government sector, especially at the federal level, since grants-in-aid by the federal government provided a source of funds allowing expansion of state and local expenditures as well. Government expenditures on goods and services in constant 1958 dollars increased from $23.3 to $26.6 billion from 1933 to 1934, after having fallen continuously since 1931. The period from 1933 to 1934 also marks the reversal of the increasingly depressing influence exerted by all levels of government, measured in terms of changes in the deficit in the national income and product accounts, as seen in Table 10.6. The economy picked up at the same time as the government sector became expansionary and continued to boom for another three years. The boom from early 1933 to 1937 differed from any other discussed in this and the previous two chapters, to a large extent because there was so much surplus labor and capacity throughout the economy. This difference can be seen with the aid of Table 10.8. By 1937, neither consumer investment, nor business plant, and equipment investment, nor

---

[17] The Hoover Administration consistently argued in favor of a balanced budget as the surest way to recovery, but in spite of the Revenue Act of 1932, which increased both personal and corporate tax rates, continuous deficits were run. There was the decline in transfer payments in 1932 already referred to, but by 1933 federal government purchases of goods and services and grants-in-aid to state and local governments had increased by enough almost to offset this. With the advent of the Roosevelt Administration expenditures shot up, this in spite of the campaign rhetoric of 1932 and the Economy Act of March 1933.

Despite the manner of conflicting views and policies it is difficult to imagine government expenditures, particularly at the federal level, declining from their 1933 levels. Hence their inclusion with consumption as part of a circular flow. For a discussion of the period see: Kimmel, L. H., *Federal Budget and Fiscal Policy 1789–1958*, The Brookings Institution, Washington, D.C., 1959, Chapters IV and V.

Table 10.8

	GNP	*FS*	*C′*	I^C	I^{PD}	I^{FS}	I^H	G^T
1933	141·5	145·8	104·6	10·4	4·3	3·3	2·1	23·3
1934	154·3	157·0	108·1	12·3	5·6	3·6	2·9	26·6
1935	169·5	167·1	113·8	15·7	7·5	4·0	4·0	27·0
1936	193·0	189·9	123·9	20·0	10·3	5·4	5·1	31·8
1937	203·2	197·7	128·0	20·7	11·8	7·1	5·6	30·8
1938	192·9	194·3	128·0	19·9	8·1	5·6	5·7	33·9
1939	209·4	207·2	133·7	22·7	9·4	5·9	8·2	35·2
1940	227·4	22·3	139·0	25·9	12·1	6·8	9·2	36·4

All figures in constant 1958 dollars. G^T = total government expenditures on goods and services. All other variables have their previous meanings.

Source: *Survey of Current Business*, August 1965.

residential housing outlays had reached their 1929 levels. Especially noticeable is the poor showing of either type of construction. In 1937 residential housing (I^H) and business plant investment (I^{FS}) were each just over 50 per cent of their 1929 levels. To a large extent the failure of business plant expenditures to grow reflects the poor showing of public utility investment, with its large plant component—if this category is broadened to include railroad and telephone investment. For example, if agricultural investment is ignored, Terborgh's investment categories can be combined into three different groups: public utility (in the broad sense of the word), manufacturing and mining, and commercial and miscellaneous. In 1929, investment outlays in current dollars by these groups stood at $2.74, $2.84 and $3.60 billion respectively. The same groups in 1937 were investing at the rate of $1.54, $2.00 and $3.12 billion per year or 60, 70 and 87 per cent of their respective 1929 highs. As a result, the investment boom of this period is best seen as a boom in business and consumer equipment outlays; i.e. producers' durables, cars, household furnishings etc.[18]

Table 10.8 contains some additional important information. GNP and final sales increased by 43.6 and 35.6 per cent between 1933 and 1937 respectively. During that same period fixed non consumption expenditures, ($G^T + I^C + I^{PD} + I^{FS}$), increased from $41.3 billion to $70.4 billion, or by about 70 per cent. Table 10.8 reveals that while part of this latter increase can be attributed to a growth of total government expenditures and consumer investment outlays, this growth was small compared with the growth of fixed non-residential investment. The growth of the latter was of the order

[18] The boom of the 1960's saw all three investment categories expanding substantially, whereas during the 1950's there were offsetting movements in public utility and commercial and other (or miscellaneous) investment. See Chapter VIII.

of magnitude of 150 per cent. Fixed non-residential investment as a per cent of GNP rose, as a result, from 5 to 9 per cent from 1933 to 1937.

In other words, in spite of the fact that by 1937 fixed non-residential investment had nowhere near recovered its 1929 level, the increase in these outlays, especially for equipment, was a very important factor in the recovery. Chawner's constant dollar estimate of manufacturing investment shows a similar growth. In no other boom since 1919 has the rate of growth of business investment so exceeded the growth of GNP. There are no records of capacity utilization rates for manufacturing (or business) during this period, but it is difficult to escape the conclusion that business and manufacturing investment could not have continued to grow at this rate much longer, in the light of the comparatively slow growth of GNP and final sales. This modified Domar effect is seen most dramatically at the end of the 1933–1937 boom. The increase in fixed non-residential investment was approximately 20 per cent from 1936 to 1937, and was accompanied by an increase in GNP and final sales of only a little over 5 per cent. Total non-consumption expenditures were just not growing rapidly enough to generate an increase in consumption and overall activity large enough to absorb the additional capacity that business, especially manufacturing, was generating throughout its rapid growth of investment.

There were, of course, no labor shortages. GNP rose from $141.5 billion in 1933 to $203.2 billion in 1937 in constant dollars. This can be compared with a GNP in 1929 of $203.6 billion. In the meantime, labor force and productivity growth had been going on so that unemployment in 1937 was over 14 per cent, compared to 3.2 per cent in 1929.[19] The boom of 1933–1937 was part of a 'free cycle', a cycle unconstrained by the workings of any kind of resource ceiling. It could have been prolonged only if total non-consumption expenditures could somehow have been induced to grow rapidly enough, both before and after what turned out to be the downturn to absorb the growing capacity of the economy. Following so shortly after a depression as serious as that of 1929–1933, even a decline in the rate of growth of activity would be likely to have a pronounced depressing influence on investment by business.

As it was, consumer investment outlays tapered off in 1937, and government outlays on goods and services actually declined. And, as Table 10.6 shows, for the first time since 1929 total government expenditures fell short of receipts. From 1936 to 1937, the budget for the government sector swung from a deficit of $3.2 billion to a surplus of $.4 billion. This depressive influence is also shown in an estimate of the full employment budget deficit, approximately the difference between actual government expenditures and

---

[19] Because of the growth in maximum output between 1929 and 1937, we would expect (on the basis of the consumption function developed in Chapter IV) that consumption out of disposable income would be higher in 1937 than 1929. The figures are 88 per cent versus 82 per cent respectively.

tax receipts at full employment. This deficit declined substantially from 1936 to 1937.[20] The leveling off of consumer investment outlays in 1937 can be explained with the help of monthly and quarterly data. By July 1937—the unemployment rate had reached its lowest point since late 1930—11 per cent. Yet by December of 1937 it had increased to almost 16 per cent. The data for new orders for manufacturers' durable goods and corporate profits after taxes showed a peak in 1937-(I). Industrial production reached a peak in July 1937, and GNP and investment by manufacturing peaked in 1937-(III).[21] Given the fact that the recession was under way well before the end of 1937, it is little wonder that consumer investment outlays, especially on durable goods, should have leveled off over the year in 1937. The quick turn around of the budget for all governments in calendar 1937 can largely be explained in terms of a decline in payments to veterans, together with a large increase of receipts over benefits under the social security program. Behind it all lay a desire to return to fiscal orthodoxy, as the federal government (incorrectly) assumed that inflation was the real danger. It seems clear that to have kept the boom of the 1930's going, a sizeable increase in government expenditures, accompanied by continued deficits, was necessary beyond 1937. Sooner or later, the continued growth of economic activity would have led to increased outlays by most sectors, as capacity utilization rates would eventually have risen enough to cause the most reluctant groups to expand capacity, even when this meant sizeable outlays for plant. Only at that point could the 'pump priming' cease or, at least, taper off.

The slowdown in government expenditures that occurred in 1937 was quickly reversed in 1938. The decline in GNP of approximately $10 billion in constant 1958 dollars from 1937 to 1938 was not mirrored in final sales, as inventory investment fell almost $8 billion. Consumption net of durables was unchanged. Industrial production and manufacturing investment fell for three to four quarters, and then turned around in mid 1938. The turnaround in GNP in 1939, like the decline in GNP in 1938, appears to be partially a delayed reaction to government outlays; but there were other factors as well. Thus, whereas from 1929 to 1930 housing expenditures and total family-related construction expenditures declined by more than 40 and 25 per cent respectively, Diagram 10.2 depicts an increase from 1937 to 1938 of approximately $2\frac{1}{2}$ and 3 per cent for those two types of expenditures.[22]

This difference can in turn be related to housing starts relative to household formation during the 1920's and 1930's. For example, Table 10.2 shows that by the end of 1929 the cumulative excess of non farm dwelling units

---

[20] See Brown, Cary, E., 'Fiscal Policy in the Thirties: A Reappraisal', *American Economic Review*, December 1956, Figure 4.

[21] See Moore, *op. cit.*, pp. 129 and 147.

[22] The figures for residential construction for 1929 and 1930 were $7.2 billion and $4.3 billion and those for total family-related construction expenditures, $11.7 billion and $8.8 billion respectively, all figures in constant dollars.

built over non farm households formed, was almost one and one-half million. This can be compared with a total of 22.9 million non farm households in 1929. Throughout the 1930's new households were formed and new dwelling units started, but at a greatly diminished rate compared with the 1920's. However, for most years the rate of household formation greatly exceeded the rate of construction of new dwelling units, so that by 1937 the cumulated excess was practically non existent. It is true that during this period many existing units were being reconverted into multi-dwelling units, because of the adverse economic conditions. But this trend must be set along side the fact that some households were migrating within the country, so that additional housing would be needed even if there were no change in the number of households during the 1930's. The net result was that when the downturn came sometime in 1937, there were groups who were in need of housing and related capital facilities, and were determined to purchase it. As a result, housing and related expenditures increased from 1937 to 1938. It should be emphasized that in 1938 family-related construction expenditures other than housing accounted for 23 per cent of total construction. If residential construction is included, the percentage rises to 53 per cent. Thus, while total government expenditures increased both from 1929 to 1930 and 1937 to 1938 (it was largely state and local government that stepped up expenditures in 1930, while the federal government played the stimulating role in 1938), a large part of the reason for the shortness and mildness of the recession of 1937–1938 must be attributed to the same factors that stabilized the economy in the more recent period.

I. Could Monetary Policy Have Saved the Day?

A great deal has been made of the failure of monetary policy to act more vigorously in combating the recession in the early 1930's. Various writers have singled out the desire to offset gold inflows, a change in leadership at the Federal Reserve, and a failure to choose the correct indicators of policy, as causes of the failure of the central bank to act aggressively in combating the recession. Whatever the cause or causes, the critics are agreed that the monetary authorities did not expand federal reserve credit outstanding, reserves and the money supply by anything near the amount that the economic situation required. It has been argued that, had monetary policy been more forceful and in the right direction, the recession would not have developed into a depression, and the downswing could have reversed much earlier than 1933. It is important to keep separate the different points raised here. It is one thing to argue that monetary policy was bad in the early 1930's (which it was), and another thing to assert that had it operated correctly we would have experienced nothing more than a recession of the post World War II variety.

Here it is useful to divide the period between the decline in economic activity and the eventual trough in 1933 into subperiods, separated from one another by successive financial difficulties. In particular, it is helpful to follow the scheme of Friedman and Schwartz and use the dates of successive banking crises.[23] Each of these dates was soon followed by a large scale internal drain from the banking system, as depositors rushed to convert deposits to currency. In turn, the fact that banks during these periods did not restrict the ability of depositors to convert deposits into cash, led to serious liquidity problems for the banking system. In the banks' panic to convert income earning assets into liquid form, bank failures became widespread and the money supply declined sharply. The question is whether a 'correct' monetary policy, one that resulted in substantial increases of reserve bank credit outstanding and member bank reserves in periods prior to the various crises, would have been either a necessary or sufficient condition for reversing the downswing before early 1933.

Although the peak in stock prices was reached in September 1929, the slight dip was followed by a recovery, so that by 10 October 1929, the average of stock prices was only $2\frac{1}{2}$ per cent below its September peak. In the meantime, industrial production and personal income had been falling since August 1929. From the latter date until one month before the 'first banking crisis' of October 1930, the index of industrial production fell from 60 to 45 (1947–1949 = 100). From 1929-(III) to 1930-(III) GNP fell 12 per cent, manufacturing investment declined over 60 per cent, while corporate profits after taxes were down from $6.8 billion at annual rates to $1.4 billion, all figures in current dollars. During this same period, federal reserve credit outstanding declined by about $\frac{1}{2}$ billion, as bank borrowings declined by substantially more than the amount by which Federal Reserve securities and bill purchases increased. At the same time excess reserves remained small and little changed, so that net free reserves rose due to the decline in borrowings of between $600 and $700 million seasonally adjusted. Member bank reserves were up slightly (from $2.33 to $2.41 billion), but demand deposits fell from $22.56 billion to $21.41 billion, a little more than one and one-half times the decline in borrowings. It is worthy of note that currency held by the public declined by a little less than 10 per cent, evidence that the decline in the stock of money took place within a framework free of any important banking and financial difficulties.[24]

We have argued earlier that customer loan demands are one of the highest on the list of priorities in the allocation of bank funds. Had these been high and rising, borrowings by commercial banks would surely also have risen during this period. For if, to take a hypothetical example, purchases of government securities by the Federal Reserve had not been greatly affected by a large (hypothetical) increase in loans demanded and granted, borrowings

[23] See Friedman, M., and Schwartz, Anna J., *The Great Contraction 1929–1933*, Princeton University Press, Princeton, 1965, pp. 66–111.
[24] This is the conclusion that Friedman and Schwartz draw; *op. cit.*, p. 12.

would surely have risen, causing member bank reserves to rise, thereby permitting and, in this case, generating an increase rather than a decrease in demand deposits.[25] In other words, although the decline in the money stock was fairly large (but less than that in 1920–1921, 1937–1938), its actual decline can be attributed just as much to a decline in the demand for loanable funds, as to the low level of government security purchases. And the failure of loan demand actually to increase is understandable, when the figures cited above outlining the behavior of the real sector are recalled. Comparatively speaking, with such a substantial decline in activity and no help to be expected by family-related construction, it could not be expected that loan demand would increase to finance business or any other kind of outlays. Thus, up to the first banking crisis of October 1930 it can be argued that a 'correct' monetary policy was not even a necessary condition for recovery during this period. What was necessary was an increase in loan demand. Increased government securities purchases on a large scale might have led only to increased excess and free reserves. Even if they had not, and the initial increase in reserves had been 'put to work', it would most likely have led only to an exchange of securities for demand deposits by the public, with little or no effect on spending for goods and services.

Once financial crises are brought into the picture the question that must be posed is different.[26] In the rush to convert deposits to cash, the commercial banks in October 1930 were forced into the first of several liquidity crises. This first crisis was to last until the beginning of 1931. It was to be followed by further banking difficulties (each of which resulted in declines of the money stock) in March 1931, September 1931 and early 1933. As in the other banking crises, large-scale dumping of securities by banks and widespread bank failures were the vehicles whereby the money supply declined, set off, of course, by an internal cash drain.

Clearly, widespread large-scale open market purchases by the system would have prevented many, perhaps most, of the bank failures during this whole period. They would not necessarily have led to an increase in the money supply, but for the sake of argument let us assume that they would

[25] Brunner and Meltzer argue that the Federal Reserve was using short-term interest rates as the sole indicator of the strength and thrust of policy. If so, an actual increase in loan demand would have caused interest rates to rise more than they did, given the government security purchases that took place during the period. An increase in loan demand would be likely, then, to have led to greater purchases of securities by the system in an effort to keep rates low. See Brunner, K., and Meltzer, A. H., 'What Did We Learn from the Monetary Experience of the United States in the Great Depression?', *Canadian Journal of Economics*, May 1968.

[26] 'The bank failures were important not primarily in their own right, but because of their indirect effect. If they had occurred to precisely the same extent without producing a drastic decline in the stock of money, they would have been notable but not crucial. If they had not occurred, but a correspondingly sharp decline had been produced in the stock of money by some other means, the contraction would have been at least equally severe and probably even more so.' Friedman and Schwartz, *op. cit.*, p. 56.

have done. We can go even further and assume that such monetary policies from October 1930 on were always a necessary condition for recovery. This can be interpreted to mean either that public confidence in the banking system is required, or that banking crises by their very nature create a situation whereby both the capital and money markets cannot function properly, and the supply of loanable funds dries up. The question is whether correct monetary policy prior to any crisis would have been sufficient to reverse the downward trend of the real sector before early 1933.

Take the period immediately following the first banking crisis. After a decline in 1930, the excess of cumulated dwelling units over cumulated households again rose, and was above 1.4 million units by the end of 1931. With the implied high level of vacancy rates for housing, it would be very hard to argue that, had monetary policy become very easy, housing and related expenditures would have been stimulated.[27] From 1930-(III) to 1931-(I) corporate profits after taxes fell from $1,428 millions to $336 million, with manufacturing investment falling an additional 25 per cent over its 1929-(III) to 1930-(III) decline. In contrast, industrial production was little changed from the first to the second banking crisis—an increase in the index from 42 to 43 during the first three months of 1931 is not much in the way of an upsurge.[28] It is possible to argue that some of the decline in the real sector between the first two banking crises was due to the shock provided the system by the initial financial difficulty in October 1930. But, as just suggested, this in itself would hardly account for the decline in housing and related outlays. Furthermore, the decline in manufacturing (and other) investment between 1930-(III) and 1931-(I) would largely reflect a decline in new orders before the first crisis. These fell from 69 in 1930-(I) to 54 in 1930-(II) (1935–1939 = 100).[29] A better case can be made for the adverse influence of improper monetary policy on state and local government construction outlays, which fell slightly from 1930 to 1931. However, even here those who have considered the adverse effect of economic events on state and local bond flotations were thinking in terms of 1932.[30] One is left with the feeling that events in the real sector up until the second banking crisis of 1931-(I) would have been very little different, even had policy been different in October 1930.

After the crisis in March 1931 it becomes almost impossible to disentangle events. Financial crises were bound to curtail lending and borrowing operations. However, it is difficult to imagine that either business or consumer

---

[27] Total deposits at thrift organizations increased from 1930 to 1931 from $15.9 to $16.4 billion while mortgage loans fell from $12.1 to $11.8 billion.

[28] In addition Friedman and Schwartz cite a slowdown in the rate of decline of factory employment and an increase in personal income during this period, largely due to increased veterans benefits. The slowdown in the decline of employment is hardly a clause for optimism. See Friedman and Schwartz, *op. cit.*, p. 17.

[29] See Moore, *op. cit.*, p. 81. As before, this figure is for new orders received by durable goods manufacturers.

[30] See reference cited in footnote 14.

borrowings would have been large in any case. The cumulative excess of dwelling units over new households formed actually rose in 1932 and remained high in 1933. It is true that gross fixed non residential investment had declined greatly by the end of 1931, but at an annual rate of $14.1 billion (compared to $26.5 billion in 1929) it could still be argued that net investment even in 1931 was positive. If so, this meant that capacity was still growing in the face of a large decline in overall activity. Only by 1932, when gross fixed non residential investment had declined to $8.2 billion, was it likely that a process of using up the capital stock of business had begun.

Let us assume that, had monetary policy been correct throughout the whole period, all of the decline in state and local government outlays from 1931 to 1932 could have been averted, and perhaps even some increase achieved. Thus, instead of a decline in total outlays from $21.1 to $19.6 billion, assume an increase of 10 per cent. Even so, this must be set against a decline in non residential fixed investment of $5.9 billion, and a decline in consumer investment outlays of $5.2 billion from 1931 to 1932.

J. Conclusion

The very best that can be concluded is that, had monetary policy not been perverse, the decline in overall activity would have been marginally less rapid, and marginally less pronounced. There were simply too many sectors in phase, once the decline set in, and too few sectors prepared to increase their outlays despite the decline in activity, to prevent a serious depression. These facts could, in turn, be traced to the nature of the boom of the 1920's. It is at this point that we see the relevance of the secular stagnation thesis. If at some point in history full employment savings tend to exceed full employment investment (for whatever reason), for extended but nevertheless limited periods of time, the possibility and likelihood of a boom being followed by a serious decline in activity looms very large. This happens because of a failure of certain constraints to operate, so that backlogs are built up during the boom that can be satisfied only during the subsequent recession. We have argued that these constraints were effective in the post World War II period, but not in the interwar period.[31] The secular stagnation thesis merely carries the argument one step further, and tries to explain why investment opportunities might be so depressed as to put little pressure on the capital goods industry

[31] One author has argued that long swings in economic activity can develop out of the kind of constraints cited in the text. See Easterlin, R., 'Economic-Demographic Interactions and Long Savings in Economic Growth', *American Economic Review*, December 1966.

and financial markets during a boom.[32] But whatever the reason, conventional monetary policy can in such circumstances be of little help. Even though the channels through which policy might work are no different in deep depressions or mild recessions, the demand for funds will not be strong once policy is eased. Given the additional induced effects of declines in housing outlays, serious problems for stability can follow. Thus we find a recession complement to a difficulty that monetary policy might face during a boom. It was argued in Chapters VIII and IX that should a very strong, widely diffused boom get underway, aggravated in the case of the mid-1960's by increased government outlays without a corresponding increase in taxes, policy may be too gradual and ineffective in stopping the boom before serious inflationary trends develop. Here we see that policy may be ineffective (or at very best slow) during a downswing when the latter is widely diffused.

---

[32] For a detailed discussion of the capital saving nature of innovations during this period in selective industries, see Lorant, J. H., *The Role of Capital-Improving Innovations in American Manufacturing During the 1920's*, unpublished Ph.D. dissertation, Columbia University, 1966.

Chapter XI Growth and Stability in the British Economy

Part 1 Some General Considerations

A. Introduction

The discussion of growth and stability up to this point has been centered on an economy where: (1) the long run growth rate has been largely determined by the workings of market forces and: (2) the critical stability problem was seen as that of dampening fluctuations in unemployment rates. In the United States, no deliberate sustained effort has been made by the central government to try and alter the long run growth rate of the economy (other than creating a 'favorable climate for business'). Periodic attempts have been made to 'get the economy going again' but these attempts should be viewed as temporary efforts to push down unemployment rates. In terms of Diagram 4.1 in Chapter IV, this amounts to stating that in postwar America the position picked on the BC segment cannot be attributed to any well defined policy strategies by government. As Chapter VIII argued, forces were such in the 1960's as to lead to a rate of growth of demand, and therefore output, further to the right on the BC segment than in the 1950's. But the more sustained stimulating monetary policy of the first half of the 1960's and the expansionary fiscal policy in the second half must be primarily attributed to a desire to reduce unemployment and to pursue military ends respectively. At the same time, our discussion of the postwar period in the United States revealed that attempts to dampen fluctuation in aggregate demand, output and employment have been very crude. So much so that what success there has been in preventing serious unemployment (and inflationary) problems must largely be attributed to certain institutional and technological factors that acted as built-in stabilizers.

In contrasting the economic goals and activities of the authorities in post-war United States and Britain, two things stand out. First, there has been a greater reluctance to accept inflation in the former and a much greater commitment to high level of employment in the latter. Second, the British authorities have been more willing (and able) to use a much wider range of policy instruments to regulate demand in order to achieve an employment target. They have undertaken policy measures that influenced demand and other key variables in an effort to deliberately affect long term growth rates.

What we hope to make clear in this chapter is that, in spite of these and other basic differences, much of what has been said in earlier chapters will be very helpful in our understanding of what has taken place in Britain. Thus, while the analysis of Chapters III and IV had little to say on the effect of policy on growth, it will soon become clear that the basic source of disagreement among British economists in the postwar period has been the influence of demand pressures on long term growth. To rely on Diagram 4.1 once again, the argument has concerned itself with both the existence of a BC segment and with whether policy measures can move the British economy up along its BC line should it exist. The discussion has been made more complicated by the need to consider the affects of demand on the balance of payments. But the question of the importance of (policy induced) demand pressures on growth has been paramount.

Chapters VI and VII outlined an interaction between an income generating mechanism and certain constraints that led to mild fluctuations in output and employment. In the British case, where lower levels of unemployment were bought at the expense of greater inflation, much the same sort of inter-action has been at work. However, because of this greater relative commit-ment to 'full employment', the British economy underwent cycles in growth rates rather than cycles in levels of aggregate activity as in the United States. Rather than business (or manufacturing) investment giving the cycle its profile, it tended to give the 'growth cycle' its shape. Nonetheless, an inter-action of the kind outlined in Chapters VI and VII was evident in both economies. We wish further to show that only by having a clear picture of the workings of this constrained cyclical mechanism is it possible to see the short comings of growth policy in postwar Britain.

For reasons made clear in Chapter VIII in our discussion of the stability of the American economy, emphasis has been on the problem of dampening fluctuations in aggregate demand and output in the interest of keeping reces-sions from getting out of hand. Dampened fluctuations certainly work to dampen inflationary pressures, but that has not been our main concern. For the most part this emphasis has resulted from a desire (and need) to under-stand this problem, which is still very real in the United States, much better. In our study of the British economy, the problem of price instability must play a central role. This arises from the importance of price movements on the balance of payments and therefore, as we shall see, the long term growth rate of the British economy. Thus, with the strong commitment to keeping unemployment at a minimum, and the resulting lack of any significant decline in the level of output, the question of such matters as explaining the lower turning point need not detain us. Instead, our attention in this chapter will be centered on the problem of growth and the influence of price instability on growth in the British economy. In particular, our concern will be with the interaction of various policy inducements to growth with the other factors singled out in Chapters III and IV as important for influencing long term growth rates. Thus, while the basic structural and institutional differences between two mature economies do not necessarily require a different theoretical apparatus in order to understand the basic forces at work, these differences do affect the kinds of issues that need to be discussed.

B. Growth and the Payments Ceiling

In Chapter IV we discussed at some length under what conditions an increase in the rate of growth of demand would result in a higher rate of growth of maximum output. Diagram 4.1 depicted these possibilities. It is reproduced here with some modifications as Diagram 11.1. The length of the BC segment was earlier considered to be a function of such things as the quality of entrepreneurship and, the structure and development of factor markets along with other institutional arrangements that influenced the speed at which resources could be moved within the economy. It is clear that the length of the BC segment will vary from country to country depending upon these and other factors, and that this will be true even when allowances are made for differences in the rate of growth of the labor force. It will also be recalled that the analysis of Chapter IV neglected the impact of price changes and repercussions in the foreign sector.

What must be noted is that not all points along a given BC segment facing any economy are 'feasible' points in the sense that such growth rates can be freely chosen without causing serious political and economic disruptions. Foreign trade considerations especially cannot be neglected when considering Britain, and this will require certain refinements of the analysis of Chapter IV. For example, as the rate of growth of demand is permanently increased above that level corresponding to point B (but less than that corresponding to C), an equal increase of supply will be forthcoming. But serious inflationary pressures may also develop and these will increase with the rate of growth of demand. Among other things, the more rapidly resources are already shifting, the more difficult it becomes to speed up the rate of transfer of resources without increasing the 'price' inducements. Since the rate of growth of imports will

Diagram 11.1

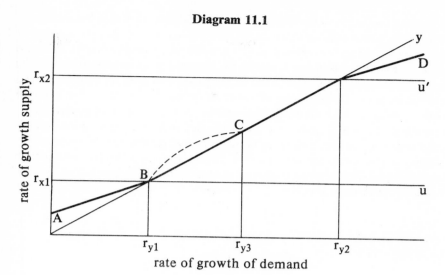

rate of growth of demand

also vary positively with the rate of growth of demand, increased imports and the higher rate of inflation associated with a movement from point B towards point C will mean that balance of payments difficulties are likely to be intensified as demand increases beyond r_{y1}. When considering the British economy, it will simplify matters without materially affecting the outcome if we hereafter speak of a balance of payments constraint limiting a country to some subsegment of the BC segment. For countries not heavily dependent upon foreign trade or who, like Sweden, seem to have been relatively free of payments difficulties, an inflation constraint is more binding. In the British case, the payments constraint is more inclusive.[1]

What we wish to argue here is that the length of both the BC segment and that appropriate subsegment that can be freely chosen by any country because of a payments constraint are largely dependent on the same group of more fundamental influences stressed in Chapter IV, e.g. the quality of entrepreneurship, the adaptability of the capital goods industry and the organization of

---

[1] Balance of payments difficulties can arise for reasons other than the inflation of export prices as we will see. It should be added that since the pound acts as a key currency, Britain is further constrained in the amount of demand pressure that can be sustained.

labor and capital markets. But when considering the United Kingdom economy it must be recognized that another important factor may be at work. A considerable effort has been made in the postwar period through different policy measures to lengthen both the BC segment and the subsegment that is feasible. In spite of this, we wish to argue that, relative to many other developed capitalist economies, the BC segment for the United Kingdom is rather narrow, as is the even narrower subsegment of feasible points. In particular, it is the inability and desire and lack of policy inducements to transfer sufficient resources quickly into those lines of production that are, or soon will be, profitable that accounts for much of Britain's comparatively poor growth performance. One of the symptoms of this failure is Britain's low ratio of business investment to output.

C. A Deflationist View

Having related the balance of payments ceiling to the rate of growth of domestic demand, it is clear from the outset that we are treating exports as well as imports as endogenous variables. This approach is quite in keeping not only with the views to be advanced here but also with those economists who deny that one can permanently increase the rate of growth of output and productivity by increasing the rate of growth of demand. Instead, this latter group of economists, who for simplicity we will call the 'deflationists', argue that Britain's ills—slow growth, too rapid inflation and balance of payments difficulties—have been due to too much demand pressure.

There are several gaps in the argument advanced by the deflationists, but a summary of their views would run something like this: Britain's balance of payments difficulties as well as its poor growth performance are caused by excessive demand pressure. Expansionist, high pressure policies, resulting in the so-called 'go' policies, must always be reversed eventually to ease balance of payments pressures. And the result of alternating between stop and go policies only leads to a lower rate of growth of productivity than a policy which stabilizes demand at a permanently higher level of unused resources over the cycle. In the long run, a full employment-high capacity utilization rate policy target must be lowered relative to foreign competitors and to the 'payments ceiling', i.e. the rate of unemployment at which payments difficulties first arise.[2] This will lead to more competitive pricing in international markets, keep production from being diverted to the home market, shorten the tea break, shake out marginal firms, and decrease the turnover of labor.

[2] For example, if the authorities feel that in the interests of 'social justice' a 2 per cent rate of unemployment should be aimed at, other things being equal, and if during a boom balance of payments difficulties·arise as soon as unemployment falls below the 4 per cent mark, we may say that a payments ceiling is reached before the 'full employment' ceiling.

In terms of our diagram, this position states that for all practical purposes there is no *BC* segment, only a line such as *u* indicating that the rate of growth of supply does not respond to demand pressures. However, if some slack is maintained in the economy, productivity will grow more rapidly, leading to an upward shift of the horizontal line over time to something like *u'*. In the long run, growth will be higher but so will unemployment and unused capacity. Unemployment and capacity utilization rates should be kept high, as productivity is a negative function of the level of demand relative to supply (and not a positive function of the rate of growth of demand).[3]

D. An Expansionist Policy for Getting onto the Virtuous Circle

In contrast there are the 'expansionists' who believe not only that a permanent increase in the rate of growth of demand can lead to a permanent increase in supply but also to a situation where balance of payments difficulties may be lessened. This group does not deny that a payments problem can be solved if the employment target is scaled down. What they deny is that this attack can lead to a higher growth rate in the long run. Like the deflationists, they advocate a policy which they feel will simultaneously increase the growth rate and resolve balance of payments difficulties. But unlike the deflationists, this group believes that the solution to Britain's slow growth and payments difficulties is not to scale down the employment target, but to pursue a policy that raises the employment target toward a full employment ceiling and in so doing raises the payments ceiling.

This view of the response of exports and productivity is seen clearly in the notion of a virtuous circle, which provides a useful way of formulating the issues. The virtuous circle describes a situation where a country finds itself in a position of high rates of growth of demand, output, productivity, and supply at the same time that balance of payments difficulties are minimized. The writers who have developed this notion are economists who stress the

---

[3] Two notable proponents of this position are Paish, F. W. *Studies in an Inflationary Economy: The United Kingdom, 1948–1961*, (Macmillan, London 1962) and Dow, J. C. R. *The Management of the British Economy, 1945–60*, (Cambridge University Press, Cambridge 1964). Dow argues that policy should 'aim to keep demand at a point which left a rather greater margin of spare capacity than on average in the past'. At times he seems to be arguing that more rapid growth could have been achieved by merely dampening the fluctuations of demand around some trend. At other times he seems to be saying that this must be accompanied by policies that 'influence the rate of growth of supply directly', e.g. greater planning if growth is to be speeded up. It is hard to dispute this latter position. See especially pp. 361, 397 and 404.

It must be stressed that what is not at issue here is (1) whether or not 'stop-go' policies have intensified fluctuations in overall activity and the balance of payments, and (2) whether or not deflationary policies will solve payments difficulties. The issue is whether or not a certain type of policy will increase the long term growth rate.

importance of high and sustained rates of growth of demand for getting onto the virtuous circle. For example, if the fiscal and monetary authorities will follow stronger expansionist policies, this will reduce macro risks in such a way as to increase not only the investment ratio but the proportion of investment that we earlier termed 'enterprise' investment.[4] This in turn will so stimulate the rate of growth of productivity that labor costs will rise less rapidly than in the case of: (1) a competitor who pursues a less ambitious employment policy; and (2) the country in question had it chosen to pursue a less ambitious employment policy. With export prices set on a mark-up basis, the expansionist policy will then lead to prices rising less rapidly than under case (1) or (2).

If we let p represent domestic prices and p_f export prices of competitors who behave more like those described under (1) above, then running 'flat out'—i.e. increasing the rate of growth of demand r_y—will have the following results. It will first increase the investment ratio I/Y, which will cause a more rapid growth in labor productivity ρ. This then leads to a decline in p/p_f which in turn leads to an increase in the rate of growth of exports r_{ex}, which feeds back on the rate of growth of demand r_y, etc. This is shown schematically in Diagram 11.2.

Diagram 11.2

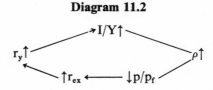

The point to be emphasized here is that if initially a country is not on the virtuous circle experiencing rapid growth, the solution is not to lower the employment and capacity utilization target from the full employment-utilization ceiling. Rather the strategy is to let demand increase, leading to lower rates of unemployment over the cycle, which then speeds up the growth rate of output and productivity and in the process raises the payments ceiling. Exports, it is argued, will be so increased in the process that even though imports may grow more rapidly, they need not exceed the higher growing exports until unemployment has been pushed to very low levels.

---

[4] See, for example, Maddison, A. *Economic Growth in the West: Comparative Experience of Europe and North America*, (Twentieth Century Fund, New York 1964); Lamfalussy, A. *The United Kingdom and the Six: An Essay on Economic Growth in Western Europe*, (Richard Irwin, Homewood Ill. 1963) and, Beckerman, W. 'The Determinants of Economic Growth', in *Economic Growth in Britain*, Henderson, P. D. (ed.) (Weidenfeld and Nicolson, London 1966). See page 72 for a brief discussion of enterprise investment, a concept originally formulated by Lamfalussy, *ibid.*

E. A Critique of the Expansionist View

The expansionist view correctly stresses the need for higher rates of growth of demand to somehow favorably affect investment and productivity. Internal demand management by itself is not sufficient, and there is evidence to support the view that higher demand pressures, by reducing capacity utilization rates, favorably affect the propensity to investment.[5] But, as has been pointed out, this added inducement to invest may be quickly extinguished through the imposition of a stop policy prompted by balance of payments difficulties soon after the pick up in demand.[6] The difficulty that has faced Britain in an effort to get onto the virtuous circle has been a lack of 'space' for developing an expansionist program. For one thing with a slump equilibrium that is never far from a full employment-full capacity utilization level of output, expansionist policies can be expected to generate strong inflationary pressures and a strong upturn in imports in response to rising incomes soon after the implementation of the policy. In addition there is evidence that British firms tend to shift output to the home market when domestic demand increases.[7] If no additional policy instruments are employed to combat these tendencies, a balance of payments ceiling will soon be encountered and the policy must be quickly reversed.

The need for space, or an ability to sustain demand pressures if an expansionist policy is to work, can be seen in another way. As just mentioned, expansionists are given to (correctly) stressing the favorable effect of sustained demand pressures on the desire to invest. But what must also be stressed is the need for space if the supply of new capital goods is to grow rapidly. Thus, higher demand pressures, even if they generate an increase in demand for capital goods by local producers, will not generate an increase in investment unless the capacity of the capital goods industry is expanded to meet this demand. Viewed this way, the importance of demand pressures being sustained at a high level is seen very clearly. Thus, in Chapter VI the

[5] See, for example, the remarks by Kaldor, N. 'Conflicts in National Economic Objectives' in *Conflicts in Policy Objectives*, Kaldor, N. (ed.), (Augustus M. Kelly, New York 1971) on the matter of internal management of demand. See Junankar, P. N. 'The Relationship between Investment and Spare Capacity in the United Kingdom, 1957–66', *Economica*, August 1970, and Beckerman W. and Associates, *The British Economy in 1975*, (Cambridge University Press, Cambridge 1965) for comments on the response of investment to demand. It should be recalled that in Chapter IV we argued that along the BC segment, changes in the ratio of investment to output have a long run influence on the rate of growth of output.
[6] Eltis, W. A. 'The Achievement of Stable Growth at the Natural Rate', in Eltis, W. A. Scott, M. F. G. and Wolfe, J. N. (eds.), *Induction, Growth and Trade: Essays in Honor of Sir Roy Harrod*, (Oxford University Press, London 1970).
[7] Two of the more recent studies emphasizing the unfavorable effects on British exports of a rise in the level of domestic demand are Henry, G. B. 'Domestic Demand Pressure and Short-Run Export Fluctuations', *Yale Economic Essays*, Spring 1970, and Artus, J. R. 'The Short-Run Effects of Domestic Demand Pressure on British Export Performance', *International Monetary Fund Staff Papers*, July 1970.

discussion centered upon the response of producers of capital goods to excess demand situations. Typically excess demand situations lead to longer waiting times and some response to shortages of capacity through the entrance of second and third line producers along with expansion of capital and labor employed by first line firms. But available evidence indicates that large expansionary programs by producers of capital equipment do not take place unless the demand for capital goods has a prolonged trend that reduces the importance of any cyclical component in demand.[8] Thus growing and sustained demand is necessary if the capacity of the capital goods industry is to be enlarged.

We can, therefore, single out three conditions that must be satisfied if an expanionist policy is to have any chance of success in permanently raising the long run growth rate. First, the increased demand pressures must not be accompanied by a diversion of current production to the home market in the short run. Exports must continue to grow even though productive capacity is more or less fixed, so that whatever small amount of space an expansionist policy has to work with will not be squandered. Without this space the induced expansion of investment and productivity growth will not be forthcoming for reasons just outlined. This requires a high degree of export consciousness in the short run on the part of business.

Second, under a system of relatively fixed exchange rates, it is not simply the response of productivity to demand pressures that is critical for creating space, but the productivity response relative to the response of money wages in those industries engaged in foreign trade. This determines the effect of demand on labor costs (and export prices) which must then be compared with one's competitors. Therefore, an expansionist policy must somehow lead to a more favorable response of productivity compared to money wages in this sense. Proponents of the demand pressure school, while aware of the distinction, give little explanation of why the relative response should always be so favorable. Third, firms producing goods with both a potential or actual foreign and domestic demand must be strongly export oriented in their investment programs. As we shall see, conditions two and three are interrelated in the sense that if one is satisfied it is likely that the other will be also. We have already pointed out that satisfaction of the first condition is necessary if the second is to be fulfilled. While these points may seem obvious, failure to make them explicit has in the past led to incorrect formulation of policy. In particular, a lack of explicitness has led to a failure to specify an appropriate set of additional instruments required to get onto the virtuous circle.

---

[8] The strong trend in demand for 'business office equipment' in America has been matched by an equal increase in capacity. No such expansion in the capacity of the American machine tool industry has taken place, an industry with a highly unstable demand.

F. Export Led Growth

At the very least growth must be export led in the sense that production is not diverted from the foreign to the home market when labor markets become tight and capacity strained. One might argue that it is possible to think of export led growth in a more basic sense, namely when exports boom very soon after policy has become expansionist. But this is only likely to happen after a country has gained the virtuous circle and when expansionist policies are being pursued simultaneously by a country's chief foreign customers. In this situation, an expansionist policy coincides with a boom in world trade (or at least a boom in the demand for imports by a country's customers). Something like this seems to have taken place in Sweden in the post-war period.[9] But such an export led boom is certainly conditional upon a country having allocated its resources into the production of goods with high international income elasticities of demand, and with exports almost certainly growing more rapidly than total activity as well as imports. Therefore, let us retain a definition of export led growth that has less demanding implications.

It is possible to think of cases where firms price competitively and output is diverted to the home market simply because domestic demand curves shift to the right more rapidly than the demand curves of foreigners for domestic goods. In this case exports are priced out of the market at least in the short run.[10] To sharpen the issue, this kind of diversion will be ignored at this point.

Instead, consider the case where British goods remain competitive in terms of price because firms do not behave according to the competitive model, but exports suffer because production is diverted to the home market by producers for other reasons. In other words, prices may be held constant in the short run as a general lengthening of the time foreign buyers of British goods must wait is allowed to develop when capacity becomes strained. Alternatively, British firms may cut back sharply on their outlays on marketing or selling services in foreign markets during boom periods. This is bound to have detrimental long run as well as short run effects on exports, as will any deterioration in the non-price terms of international competition. Indeed the lengthening of the waiting period for exports is very easily tied in with the importance of servicing both consumer and business durable goods. It has been argued, for example, that the success of certain German and Japanese exports can be partially explained by firms in these countries establishing an efficient servicing system in the foreign markets they serve. The ready availability of spare parts is an integral part of such an efficient servicing system. Although the evidence is far from overwhelming, there are enough studies indicating that this diversion to home markets during booms exists to cause concern among British officials.[11]

[9] See Lundberg, E. *Instability and Economic Growth*, (Yale University Press, New Haven 1968) pp. 202–212.
[10] See Henry, *op. cit.*, pp. 48–50.
[11] See Henry and Artus, *op. cit.*

G. The Impact of Demand on Labor Costs

Even if there is not a diversion of production to the home market during periods of domestic boom (for whatever reasons), the space required for an expansionist policy may still fail to develop. Under a system of relatively fixed exchange rates, a country can remain competitive only if its labor costs (and, therefore, export prices) in terms of foreign currencies do not rise in relation to labor costs in other countries. An expansionist policy must result in a more rapid growth of productivity relative to the rate of growth of money wages at home as compared with foreign competitors if the policy is to succeed.

Utilizing Diagram 11.1 once again, it is fairly clear that as one moves to the right of r_{y1}, pressure on money wages will increase steadily, other things being equal. If the rate of growth of the labor force, r_n, is held constant, the straight line BC segment in Diagram 11.1 assumes that the rate of growth of labor productivity, ρ, increases at the same rate as the rate of growth of demand (and supply) since $r_y = r_x = \rho + r_n$. What may be critical then is whether or not at growth rate r_{y1} productivity is growing at a rapid enough rate compared to money wages for inflationary pressures not to be too strong at least initially. If this is true at the outset, then it increases the possibility that the authorities can increase the rate of growth of demand beyond r_{y1} without intensifying inflationary pressures.

However, this kind of supply response between r_y and r_{y3} was only assumed for convenience in Chapter IV. The BC segment could be drawn with, say, a bulge beginning at point B indicating that, as demand increased beyond r_{y1}, the rate of growth of supply initially increases by more than that of demand because of a very rapid induced rise in the rate of growth of productivity. If then the authorities attempted to maintain demand somewhere between r_{y1} and r_{y3} because of a fear that higher demand pressures would result in too rapid a rise in wages and prices, this situation could soon correct itself. For with demand growing less rapidly than supply between r_{y1} and r_{y3} (when the bulge of Diagram 11.1 is substituted for a continuous straight line), the unemployment rate would rise lessening the pressure on wages. Sooner or later the authorities could increase demand to a rate corresponding to r_{y3} or even beyond. Thus, the existence of the kind of bulge in the supply response shown in Diagram 11.1 gives the authorities a little more leeway when contemplating a sustained go policy.

This problem of initial conditions suggests that in order to get onto the virtuous circle, you may need a running start from a position of relative price stability. Let us assume that somehow the problem of the initial conditions has been taken care of in the sense that there is not so much inflation taking place when a go policy is initiated that it is doomed to failure from the beginning. If then the rate of growth of demand is increased beyond r_{y1}, the critical issue is still the relative growth of productivity and wages. While we are dealing here with matters that are not well understood, we can perhaps outline what would be essential for the success of such a program.

Recall from Chapter IV that the overall growth in productivity could be broken down between that due to productivity growth within any sector (or firm) and that due to shifts in resources between sectors. It will help matters if the discussion is carried out simply in terms of the influence of demand pressures on productivity growth within a sector. In the first instance, we can say that higher rates of growth of demand must lead to enterprise investment by firms in those industries that are involved in foreign trade, if high rates of growth of productivity are to result from this policy.[12] By this we mean that firms must opt for the 'best practice' or 'optimal' techniques that aim to expand capacity in growing markets instead of merely permitting marginal improvements in production.

The expansionists argue that this kind of response will be forthcoming since the justification for implementing these advanced techniques, techniques that are likely to lead to economies of scale but which are also likely to be very capital intensive, will be the high current and prospective rates of growth of demand for output induced by an expansionist policy. However, if the capacity of the optimal technique and its subsequent expansion through a learning process, capital replacements, etc., is much larger than anything which can be utilized by domestic demand and its policy-induced growth, a strong expansionist policy may never succeed in generating enterprise investment. This possibility is minimized if firms producing goods with a potential or actual foreign and domestic demand are export oriented.

This brings us to our third condition, the importance of firms gearing their investment programs to foreign markets. Producers must not only attempt to meet foreign demand in the short run, but must strive to meet it in the long run through their investment policies. If they do, the likelihood that an expansionist policy will succeed should be greatly enhanced. This not only maximizes the likelihood that labor costs will fall in relation to those of a country's competitors; many other favorable responses are also likely to be forthcoming. For firms that expand capacity in anticipation of satisfying a growing foreign as well as domestic demand will tend to be promoting export sales through strong marketing and servicing programs. They will also be tailoring their pricing policies to promote exports and they are likely to be channeling resources into the growth industries of the future. All of this will ensure that exports continue to grow rapidly beyond the early stages of the expansionist policy so that expansion can now be sustained. And it cannot be emphasized enough that this long run export orientation with its implied

[12] We ignore for the moment whether such investment is channeled into the right lines, i.e. those with high international income elasticities.

sustained demand for capital goods is exactly what is required to induce a rapid expansion of the capital goods industry.[13]

H. Entrepreneurship Once More

By now what should be emerging all too clearly is the importance of the quality of entrepreneurship in getting onto the virtuous circle. Not only must business be expansion minded, it must be expansion minded in a particular way. It must be willing and eager to expand capacity so that foreign and domestic demands can be satisfied simultaneously allowing exports to grow when domestic demand pressures are intense. This is equally true for the demanders and suppliers of capital goods. With an entrepreneurial class so inclined, investment programs will be such that the possibility of a diversion of output, both in the long and the short run, will be minimized, as will the likelihood of labor costs rising more rapidly than a country's competitors.

Success involves not only being able to meet existing demands for particular goods but also anticipating those goods which, while perhaps luxury goods now at home and abroad, are about to become 'necessities' as growth of incomes internationally lead to consumers everywhere moving up the hierarchy of goods described in Chapter III. In that chapter, great stress was laid on the importance of channeling resources into new lines of production. Historically, this has contributed to the overall increase in productivity of different economies. The importance of resource movements has a doubly important function for a country so heavily dependent upon international trade. By more rapidly moving capital and labor into those industries just beginning to produce the mass consumption of goods of the immediate future (or about to produce the intermediate products and capital goods needed for such production), not only may the overall rate of growth of output and productivity be increased, but new profitable export markets may also be found, thus allowing growth to be sustained.[14] Success or failure here is but another manifestation of the quality of the business class. It might be mentioned in passing that this emphasis on entrepreneurship as the factor of greatest importance is consistent with the deflationist view as well. Creating a margin of

---

[13] There is popular argument to the effect that an expansionist policy will lead to an increase in exports because the expanding home market will lead firms to seek sales abroad. We have argued that an expansionist policy cannot be sustained and cannot even lead to a rapidly expanding home market unless firms follow a particular type of investment policy that seeks to expand exports and satisfy domestic demands simultaneously.

[14] Mr. Kaldor is undoubtedly right in stressing the need for manufacturing output to expand. This is true both because productivity grows more rapidly in this sector, and because by expanding capacity foreign demands can be better satisfied during periods of domestic prosperity. But without an entrepreneurial class prepared to expand production and orientate it in a particular way, the Selective Employment Tax or any other such device is not likely to be successful.

unused resources and thereby cutting down inflationary pressures will only succeed in increasing the growth rate if it leads to a situation of export orientation of production and investment policies. The issue between the expansionists and deflationists comes down to which policy is most liable to make business the more export oriented in their production, marketing and investment policies in the long run. We have sided with the expansionists.

I. The Need For a Consistent Set of Policy Instruments

Most of the conclusions that have been reached would be accepted by deflationists and expansionists alike. Indeed we seem to be belaboring the obvious when checking off our list of conditions required for more rapid growth: an unwillingness to divert production to the home market when capacity is strained; a growth of labor costs at a rate less than one's competitors; export oriented investment programs, and ultimately an entrepreneurial class with the scope and imagination to carry through these measures. But the point is that there is no simple and cheap way to get onto the virtuous circle and our laying down in an explicit fashion what may be required at least points up what policy measures might be helpful.

This approach has the additional benefit of indicating some of the inadequacies of postwar policies. To begin with, a certain amount of scepticism is in order regarding the ability of an incomes policy to contain wages and prices. In the past, such a policy has had only a limited amount of success;[15] the same can be said for the various manpower programs.[16] This, is not to argue, however, that these latter programs are incorrect. Locating industry in regions of high unemployment, retraining programs and various other manpower schemes, especially those designed to increase the mobility of labor, have been extensively tried in Britain (and the Scandinavian countries). These programs seem absolutely essential for countries heavily engaged in foreign trade who at the same time pursue high employment policies. If nothing else, they tend to reduce the amount of frictional unemployment associated with any rate of unemployment (and, therefore, any unemployment target), and this must work to reduce inflationary pressures. But singly or in combination these policies have not been sufficient to get the British economy into orbit.

[15] See Smith, D. C. 'Incomes Policy', in Caves, R. E. *Britain's Economic Prospects,* (The Brookings Institution, Washington 1968).

[16] An alternative 'policy' suggested by Kindleberger's analysis is to liberalize immigration laws since, according to Kindleberger, a rapidly growing labor force tends to keep down money wages. It is not at all clear, however, how this can be achieved in the long run without actually exploiting the immigrants. See Kindleberger, C. P. *Europe's Postwar Growth,* (Harvard University Press, Cambridge 1967). For a critique of this position see the author's 'Postwar Growth in Western Europe; a Reevaluation,' *The Review of Economics and Statistics,* August 1968.

The main difficulty with postwar policies in Britain is that they have tended to squander what little space there has been available for an expansionist policy. As will become all too clear in Part II of this chapter, expansionist policies in Britain in the postwar period have been consistently led by consumer investment booms, i.e. residential construction and outlays for consumer durables. The pattern is very similar to that described earlier for the United States.[17] It was argued above that it would be too much to expect that, if an expansionist policy were used in an attempt to get onto the virtuous circle, such a policy induced boom would be led by exports. But it certainly should not be beyond the means of the British authorities to devise instruments to promote booms which are led by business investment. The current policy instruments act to squander what little space there is for a policy to operate by allowing consumer investment demands to absorb part of the excess labor (and capacity) available at the beginning of the boom. This leads to a situation where inflationary pressures can and do become acute before a business investment boom even gets under way.

Thus it is one thing to view consumer led booms as a blessing for an economy like the United States where the fiscal and monetary authorities show a general unwillingness to devise additional and more sophisticated instruments that reflate the economy. It is quite another matter in a country where the leaders are willing to find and use additional instruments that both increase aggregate demand and stimulate business investments. To this end such instruments as 'initial allowances' (accelerated depreciation), 'investment allowances' (an allowance against tax of more than the cost of investment, or a permanent tax break for investors), and 'investment grants' (the payment by the government of part of the cost of investment) have been tried in the past. Their lack of success in appreciably stimulating investment in general and in preventing consumer led booms in particular has been traced to a faulty implementation of these instruments.[18] The Swedish success suggests something can be done along these lines.[19]

More recently economists of the expansionist school have turned to a different policy instrument as a means of generating the space needed if an expansionist policy is to succeed. As we have stressed here, an important element in getting onto the virtuous circle is to keep labor costs in terms of foreign currencies from rising too rapidly. Attempts in the past have been directed to altering this relationship by changing labor costs in sterling while keeping exchange rates between the pound and other currencies constant. But

---

[17] See Chapter VIII. There is one difference between the two countries, however. In Britain, extensive use has been made of variations in the terms of borrowing to finance the purchase of consumer durables, i.e. hire purchase terms. This policy instrument has been used very rarely in the United States.

[18] See Musgrave, R. 'Fiscal Policy' in Caves, R. E. *op. cit.*

[19] See Lundberg, *op., cit.* pp. 220–232.

alterations of the exchange rate itself will directly and immediately affect labor costs and export prices in terms of foreign currencies. Thus, it is argued that a managed rate that allows for frequent (but perhaps small) changes in the exchange rate, especially when an expansionist policy has been undertaken, will generate that space needed to sustain the expansionist policy.[20] Not only can the payments ceiling be pushed to the full employment-utilization ceiling (if it were ever below it), but the economy can be allowed to remain at this latter ceiling in spite of inflationary pressures.

There is much to be said for this policy. However, if the main aim of policy is stepping up the growth rate, there is certainly a limit to how far the terms of trade can be allowed to turn against Britain as a result of constant devaluation. If so, what this means is that a more flexible foreign exchange rate can create some additional space for an expansionist policy but it cannot do the whole job. It is again necessary that the more pronounced boom should induce the kind of investment demand and supply response in the capital goods industry that has been stressed above.

Not only must the set of policy instruments induce a business investment boom, but it must also be a business investment boom that is export oriented. From time to time government authorities have 'encouraged' private lenders to favor the financing of exports and investment projects in export industries. But this policy instrument has been hardly sufficient to keep production from being diverted to the home market in the short run and to make British business more export oriented in their investment policies, and a solution to the latter problem would most likely take care of the former (expanding capacity to handle foreign and domestic demand should decrease the probability that capacity is inadequate to handle both in the short run). Certainly, flexible exchange rates together with the use of policy instruments that enable booms to be led by business investment should help to generate some additional enthusiasm by British firms for expanding foreign sales in the long run, but what is really needed here is a whole host of measures that discriminate very strongly in favor of firms that are export oriented in their production and investment programs.[21]

It has become popular in recent times to blame a large part of the slow growth in the postwar period of the British economy on the quality of

---

[20] See Kaldor 'Conflicts in National . . .' *op. cit.*

[21] If nothing else, a large scale effort on the part of British authorities to provide information to firms with an interest in foreign sales would be most helpful. The studies by Japanese officials of international income elasticities and their subsequent use by Japanese business is often cited as an example of this kind of information. Some perception of the kind and degree of market penetration that will be tolerated by the vested interests in different countries would also be helpful. Other examples can easily be found. The point is that much of the uncertainty connected with exporting can be eliminated if the authorities will only get involved in the business of exporting. And if this uncertainty can be reduced, creating the capacity for expanding export sales should follow.

business leadership.[22] On the other hand, it has been argued that because of the high degree of unionization of British labor, because of the predominant craft structure of British trade unions (and their apprenticeship system), because of 'bloodymindedness' left over from the interwar period, etc., even the finest business class among developed economies could not succeed in getting Britain onto the virtuous circle.[23] From our reading of the British situation, there is a third culprit: public officials, who up to this point have been unable to formulate a consistent set of policy instruments that will get the economy onto the virtuous circle.

Part II The British Experience

A. Growth in Historical Perspective

The growth record of the British economy in the postwar period can be considered good or poor depending upon the basis of comparison. Compared to the performance of the British economy during the interwar period, the postwar period was one of relatively rapid growth. This we would have expected: economic and technological trends during this period worked to prevent the revival of Britain's chief export industries and the required adaption to new world economic trends was not forthcoming; maintaining the pound at pre-1914 parity intensified the difficulties facing British exporters; furthermore, there was no boom in consumer investment during the 1920's as we would have expected on the basis of the high interest rates prevailing throughout the period. These high interest rates were the result of a deflationary policy followed by the authorities in their efforts to maintain the pound at the pre-1914 rate and they adversely affected housing and related expenditures.

What we have in the 1920's is a general breakdown of the mechanism that hitherto had brought demand and supply into life at low levels of unemployment. It differed very markedly from the American collapse of 1929. As we argued in Chapter X, in America the depression was the natural outgrowth of

---

[22] As an example of the inability of British business to compute *vis-à-vis* Germany in terms of exporting to rapidly growing customers see Willey, H. D., 'Growth Patterns and Export Performance: Britain and Germany', in Kenen, P. and Lawrence R. (eds.), *The Open Economy* (Columbia University Press, New York 1968). But overall, British entrepreneurship can be found lacking in this respect. One study found the income elasticity of demand for British exports to be only half that for British imports; Japan's export elasticity was found to be three times its import elasticity. This comparison may seem unfair, but Sweden had an export elasticity almost 25 per cent greater than its import elasticity. See Houthakker, H. S. and Magee, S. P. 'Income and Price Elasticities in World Trade', *The Review of Economics and Statistics*, May 1969.

[23] See Ulman, L. 'Collective Bargaining and Industrial Efficiency' in Caves, R. E. *op. cit.*

events that took place in the previous decade. In Britain events in the 1920's were the result of policies of the period plus a drastic change in Britain's external trade position. Although both consumer and business investment declined sharply in Britain in the 1920's and in America in the 1930's, the differences in the underlying causes should not be lost sight of.

The breakdown in Britain was to continue as long as officials persisted in their efforts to maintain the pound at pre-1914 parity.[24] Following the abandonment of the gold standard and the depreciation of the pound in 1931, monetary policy shifted decidedly to one of ease. This, together with the underinvestment in housing during the 1920's, led to a building boom in residential housing that helped reduce unemployment by almost 50 percent between 1932 and 1937. It is not clear if this consumer-led boom could by itself have pushed the British economy through to a situation of low unemployment by pre-World War I standards. In any case, the rearmament of the late 1930's assured Britain that there would be no fall back to the condition of the early 1930's.

But the growth record of the British economy in the period following the Second World War compares favorably with almost any other period in modern times going back as far as the beginning of the last quarter of the 19th century[25] It is only when Britain's growth record is compared with other mature capitalistic economies in the postwar period that the growth record looks poor. It is this 'cross-section' comparison with Britain's contemporaries that has generated so much concern. Table 11.1 brings together some of the relevant data.

Even after adjustments for population growth, the British growth performance is relatively poor. This can be seen by comparing the figures in parenthesis which give *per capita* growth rates in GNP. Various explanations can be offered for the 'super growth' of countries that lost the war. What has been disturbing, however, is the unfavorable record of postwar British growth compared to a country like Sweden. This difference is harder to explain.

B. Stability of the British Economy

However, by almost any measure of fluctuations in aggregate output, Britain has been a very stable economy.[26] For example, quarterly data in constant prices is available since 1956-(I). During the fifteen year period from 1956–

---

[24] See Arndt, *op. cit.*

[25] See Deane and Cole, Table 74, pp. 284, and Fernstein, C. *National Income Expenditure and Output of the United Kingdom, 1855–1965*, (Cambridge University Press, Cambridge 1972).

[26] We will work with final sales throughout most of the chapter, but the text statement applies to the other common measures of aggregate activity.

Table 11.1

Annual Average rate of growth of
Gross National Product in constant prices

	United Kingdom	Japan	Sweden	West Germany	United States
1950–62	2·7 (1·7)	9·9 (8·8)	3·7 (3·1)	7·8 (6·7)	3·9 (2·1)
1963–69	2·7 (2·1)	11·2 (10·1)	4·5 (3·7)	5·0 (4·0)	4·7 (3·5)

Source: Erik Lundberg, *Instability and Economic Growth*, Yale University Press, New Haven 1968, Appendix, and *National Institute Economic Review*, November 1971, pp. 19 and 21 and *United Nations Demographic Yearbook* 1957, 1968 and 1969.

1971, no 'recessions' in final sales lasted more than two quarters.[27] This lack of fluctuations in levels of economic activity was very much tied up with Britain's commitment to high employment (although constrained by a need to maintain an external balance). The price of this commitment was a rather severe rate of inflation by American standards.[28]

Overall the postwar profile of the British economy shows fluctuations in rates of growth rather than in levels of aggregate activity. Schematically the period breaks down in subperiods of moderate growth, slow growth and stagnation. If we disregard the period from 1956-(I)-1957-(I), a period of three quarters of stagnation followed by a one quarter spurt in final sales, we obtain the sub periods shown in Table 11.2. Average annual growth rates for each sub period are shown in brackets to the right.[29]

The last quarter of each of the first two periods of stagnation mark the peak in unemployment rates, 2.5 and 3.3 per cent respectively. However, severe weather conditions dominated events during the winter of 1962–1963. As a rough guess the unemployment figure of 2.3 or 2.4 per cent in 1962-(IV) and 1963-(II) respectively could be considered a more appropriate measure of the 'space' available for the period of moderate growth that was to follow.

---

[27] Unless otherwise stated, all quarterly data are taken from the *National Institute Economic Review*. Whenever possible data was converted to 1963 prices. As with the American economy, we will work with final sales which are found by subtracting from 'final expenditures at market prices' the figure for 'imports of goods and services' and 'value of physical stock change'.

[28] For example the average annual rate of inflation from 1953 to 1970 was 3.3 and 2.2 per cent in the United Kingdom and the United States respectively. From 1960 to 1970 the rates were 3.8 and 2.7 per cent.

[29] The designation of the final five year period as one of stagnation would be questioned by some who would cite 1968 as a boom year. However, what actually took place in 1968 was essentially a 'one shot' increase in final sales from 1967-(IV) to 1968-(I) generated by a short boom in consumption and exports following devaluation in November, 1967. From 1966-(I) to 1967-(IV), final sales hardly grew at all, and from 1968-(I) to 1971-(I) they grew at an annual rate of 0.8 per cent.

Table 11.2

Stagnation		Moderate Growth		Slow Growth	
1957(I)-1958(IV)	[1·0%]	1958(IV)-1960(I)	[7·9%]	1960(I)-1961(III)	[3·9%]
1961(III)-1963(I)	[0·3%]	1963(I)-1965(I)	[6·0%]	1965(I)-1966(I)	[1·8%]
1966(I)-1971(I)	[1·4%]				

For similar reasons the dating of the end of this stagnation period could be adjusted one quarter in either direction. With the data available at this time of writing (the spring of 1972) it is too early to say whether unemployment has reached a peak at 3.73 per cent in 1971-(IV).[30] On the other hand, troughs in the unemployment rates correspond very closely to the end of the two periods of slow growth, 1.4 per cent in 1961-(III) and 1.2 per cent in 1966-(I).

Throughout this whole period, Britain underwent a series of 'policy cycles' generated by periodic balance of payments difficulties.[31] This involved the use of a 'package' of policy measures, restrictive when international reserves had been run down too far in the eyes of the authorities and expansionist when reserves had been built up enough. For example, policy shifted to ease 6, 4 and 4 quarters respectively after the beginning of each designated period of stagnation. These periods of shift in policy reflected various degrees of optimism about the improvement in the reserve position which could, in turn, be related to the previous restrictive policy. It is worth noting that before each of the three shifts in policy from restrictiveness to ease, market rates of interest declined just as they did in the United States. For example dates for shifts of policy to ease can be fixed at 1958-(III), 1962-(III) and 1967-(II).[32] Meanwhile, the 2½ per cent consol rate peaked in 1957-(IV), 1961-(IV), and 1966-(IV). We return to this built-in stabilizer later.[33] Generally speaking the shift to a tight or restrictive policy coincided with the end of a period of moderate growth. This we might expect for an economy not on the virtuous circle, since the rate of growth of imports both absolutely and relative to the growth of exports would be highest during these growth periods. For example, the period from 1958-(III) to 1960-(II) was a period of monetary and fiscal ease and relatively rapid growth of final sales. During that period imports grew at an annual average rate of 10.1 per cent while exports grew at 8.6 per

[30] A consumption boom beginning in 1971-(II) led to a spurt in overall activity indicating that a new period of moderate growth was underway just as the coal strike interfered.

[31] For a discussion see Lundberg, *op. cit*, Chapter 4, and Kareken, J. H. in *Britain's Economic Prospects, op. cit.*, pp. 69–89.

[32] See Kareken *op. cit.*, p. 72.

[33] See the earlier discussion in section J of Chapter IX for a comparison with the United States.

cent.[34] The exception to this timing of a shift to restrictive policy was the abrupt reversal of policy towards the end of 1967.

C. Stability of the Components of Final Sales

The high degree of stability of overall activity is mirrored in the relatively stable trend behavior of almost all the components of final sales. Total government outlays, which include current fixed investment in industries, services and public housing, showed a strong upward trend with only minor short run declines until 1968. In contrast, there were two substantial cutbacks in total government expenditures on goods and services in the United States, one following Korea when these expenditures declined by 17 per cent, and one during the recent period when they declined by 8 per cent. Taking fixed investment for all 'industries and services', (the British counterpart to fixed non-residential investment in the United States), both quarterly and annual data reveal fewer and less intense declines than in the United States, partly due to the strong upward trend in public investment that lasted until 1968. For example, the most severe decline in fixed investment by all industries and services was from 1968-(IV) to 1969-(I) and amounted to 9 per cent, all figures in constant 1963 prices. The next most serious investment decline was during 1967 and this amounted to a less than 3 per cent decline. In contrast fixed non-residential investment in the United States declined by 15 per cent in the 1957–1958 recession and by 7 per cent in the 1970–1971 recession. It is true that in the winter of 1962–1963 investment in Britain fell 10 per cent, but much of this must be attributed to the severity of the winter.

Diagram 11.3 gives annual figures in constant prices for fixed non-residential investment in the two countries. The greater stability of these outlays in Britain is apparent. What was missing from the British experience (and was very much a part of what happened in America) were pronounced 'business' investment booms followed by relatively sharp declines. The periods of expansion in fixed investment, industries and services, tended to be followed by periods of stagnation of this category of fixed investment rather than declines. Unlike the United States, changes in total investment by industries and services did not reflect changes in manufacturing investment primarily because of offsetting movements in fixed non-residential investment by the public sector.

The lack of any noticeable decline in overall activity cannot be attributed solely to the behavior of fixed investment, industries and services, however.

---

[34] The discrepancy was not as large from 1962-(III) to 1965-(III), but nevertheless there were two periods of 'Sterling Crisis' during this period.

Diagram 11.3

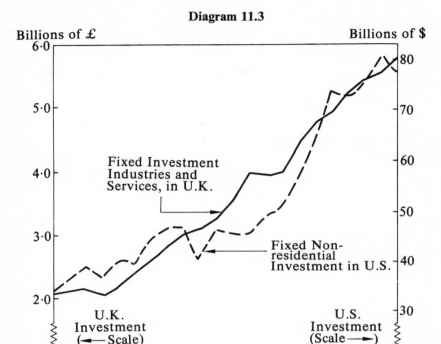

Billions of £

6·0

5·0

4·0

Fixed Investment
Industries and
Services, in U.K.

3·0

Fixed Non-
residential
Investment in U.S.

2·0

U.K.
Investment
(◄— Scale)

U.S.
Investment
(Scale —►)

Billions of $

80

70

60

50

40

30

1950   1955   1960   1965   1969

Source: *National Income and Expenditures* and *Survey of Current Business,* various issues˙

We have already commented on the stabilizing behavior of the government sector (at least up until 1968). Diagram 11.4 makes abundantly clear that expenditures on housing in constant prices had a very pronounced upward trend until 1968. The contrast with housing expenditures in the United States as shown in the Diagram is very marked. Diagram 11.5 below makes very clear that this is due to the behavior of public housing outlays not to those by the private sector, a matter to which we will return shortly. If one recalls the tie-in of other forms of non-consumption outlays with housing that was stressed in earlier chapters, the effect of housing investment on the overall trend in output throughout most of the period is clear. As we will see in the next section, booms (or more correctly the initial phases of periods of moderate growth) were dominated by household investment outlays followed by an upsurge of fixed investment by industries and services. In this sense there was a Phase I and a Phase II during expansion periods in Britain, but it was less pronounced than in the American economy.

Overall, if fixed investment, industries and services were added to housing expenditures (public and private) and 'public authorities current spending'

Diagram 11.4

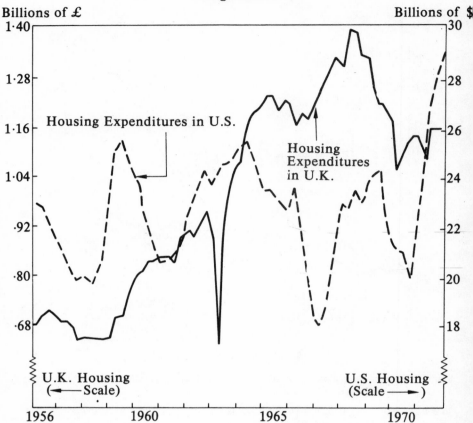

Billions of £   Billions of $

Housing Expenditures in U.S.

Housing
Expenditures
in U.K.

U.K. Housing
(◄——Scale)

U.S. Housing
(Scale ——►)

1956   1960   1965   1970

Source: *National Institute Economic Review* and *Survey of Current Business*, various issues.

(which has a steady upward trend), the resulting sum of these 'offsets' tended to determine movements in final sales. Fixed investment, industries and services, either grew (when there was a spurt in investment by the private subsector) or stagnated as public investment, industries and services, tended to pick up any slack when private investment fell off.[35] Public investment in housing was such a strong trend during most of the period that it dominated movements in total housing outlay. As a result, final sales either grew or stagnated, they did not decline for all practical purposes. The behavior of outlays for consumer durables and net exports only slightly modifies this picture.

[35] For example, 1956-IV to 1958-(IV), 1961-(III) to 1962-(IV) and 1966-(IV) to 1968-(I) were periods when public investment acted to stablize total investment.

D. Some Important Similarities

There are some important similarities in the British and American experiences. Manufacturing investment did show one cyclical swing that resembled the American experience, that from 1959-(I) to 1963-(I). But if one ignores 1962-(IV) and 1963-(I), when total investment was so dominated by the severe weather conditions, this swing in manufacturing investment was not enough to keep total investment by industries and services from more than stagnating. 'Net new orders for machine tools' and 'total engineering net orders' tended to lead fixed investment outlays, especially those for manufacturing. And during the boom of the late 1950's-early 1960's and that ending in mid-1960 (to be discussed presently), engineering orders on hand (the closest counterpart for the American series on unfilled orders) both for export and the home market were built up, introducing the same kind of a stabilizing element into the system that similar backlogs created in the American economy.[36]

While housing expenditures had a stronger, less interrupted upward trend in the British economy as compared to the American, there is substantial evidence that disintermediation was having an important effect on private residential construction.[37] The pattern was similar to the American one. For example, falling interest rates from late 1957 to late in 1959, from late 1961 to late 1963 and again from 1966-(IV) to 1967-(II), led to an increase in inflows into building societies (the British counterpart to thrift institutions in the United States) which, after a short lag, was followed by an increase in mortgage advances and then private housing starts. Conversely, rising interest rates from late 1959 to late in 1961, from late 1963 until 1966-(IV) and from 1967-(II) until 1969-(II), led to disintermediation and a leveling off of private residential construction in the early 1960's and declines from early 1965 to 1966-(IV) and 1968-(II) to 1970-(I). Thus both a ceiling in the capital goods industry and a monetary ceiling were in effect in both economies during the postwar period, creating backlogs of demand.

Finally, because of the implementation of easier monetary conditions during stagnation periods (and after balance of payments problems had been lessened), booms tended to be led by consumer investment much as they were in the United States. This was both because easier money led to a fall in market interest rates (absolutely and by inference relative to rates paid on deposits at building societies), and because of the easier terms on borrowing to finance purchases of certain consumer durables. Furthermore, the relative strength of the recovery from the three periods of stagnation since early 1956 was very much related to the strength and duration of the boom in consumer

---

[36] See Chapter VI.
[37] See Vipond, M. J. 'Fluctuations in Private Housebuilding in Great Britain, 1950–1966', *Scottish Journal of Political Economy*, June 1969.

Diagram 11.5

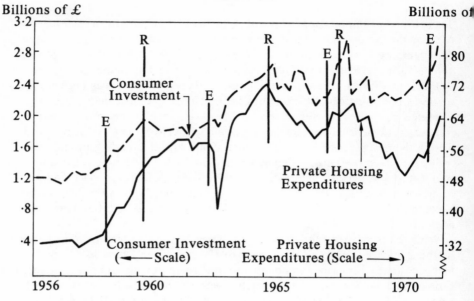

Source: *National Institute Economic Review*, various issues.

investment, i.e. private residential construction and outlays on consumer durables.[38] And as we shall see, the strength of the booms in consumer investment were, in turn, very much related to the period over which policy was expansionist—as was the case in the United States.

Diagram 11.5 brings out these points. Consumer investment (outlays for consumer durables plus private housing expenditure) in constant prices are shown along with expenditures on private housing alone. The initiation of a period of ease or restriction in policy is indicated by E and R respectively. The rise of both series just before a shift to a period of ease and their decline or leveling off during periods of restriction are quite pronounced. A comparison of Diagram 11.5 with Table 11.2 also points up the importance of consumer investment for leading the economy out of a period of stagnation. The declines in consumer investment coincided with the declines in the growth rate from 'moderate' to 'slow'. In between these periods of early growth and eventual decline of consumer investment, fixed investment, industries and services grew rapidly. The result of this overlap of consumer and industrial investment growth was a period of moderate growth in final sales.

[38] There is no reason to believe that matters were any different in the earlier years of the 1950's.

E. Consumer Investment in the Postwar Period

The fact that the first two stagnation periods were relatively short in comparison to the last can be largely traced to similar causes. In the first two periods of stagnation, expansionist policies were instituted in 1958-(III) and 1962-(III). These measures included tax cuts, favorable 'initial allowances' and 'investment allowances', increased public investment, less restrictive terms on hire purchases of consumer durables and the easing of monetary restrictions of the kind that have been employed in America.[39] Interest rates had begun to fall somewhat earlier in both periods (early in 1958 and towards the end of 1961), no doubt due to the built in stabilizing properties of the system.[40] The easing of interest rates, and by implication their decline relative to rates paid on deposits at building societies, led to an increase in flows to building societies in 1958-(I) and in 1962-(II) that was to remain high throughout 1959 and into 1960 during the first period of ease and well into 1964 during the second.[41] The results were two sustained booms in private residential construction of approximately three years in each case.[42] This was also reflected in the behavior of total residential expenditures.

The easing of hire purchase regulations in the second half of 1958, in January 1961 and again in the second half of 1962 led to strong upsurges of expenditure on consumer durable outlays from 1957-(III) until early 1960 and from 1961-(IV) until the end of 1964. Together, the increase in consumer durable and private residential construction outlays led to consumer investment booms from 1957-(III) to 1960-(I) and from 1962-(I) to 1964-(IV) as Diagram 11.5 clearly shows.

Starting from a trough in 1959-(I) and 1963-(I), industrial investment continued to grow until 1961-(III) and 1965-(I) in the two periods of moderate growth. Taking into account the periods of consumer investment booms this meant that (1) consumer investment outlays rose for 6 quarter before the upturn in industrial investment in the first boom and for 5 quarters in the second, and (2) the booms in consumer and industrial investment overlapped for 4 quarters during the first boom and 6 quarters during the second. As in the American case, booms in Britain have been led by consumer investment and this in spite of the fact that the package of expansionist proposals have aimed at stimulating both consumer and business investment outlays.

But of greater importance is the effect this sequence of events had on the

---

[39] For details see Dow, *op. cit.*, chapters VII–IX.

[40] Recall from Chapter VII that even if the monetary authorities are pursuing a tight money policy, their commitment to 'gradualism' leads to situations at the end of the booms where a decline in the demand for funds can more than offset the restrictiveness of policy and market rates will, therefore, decline.

[41] See Vipond, *op. cit.*, Appendix, Table II.

[42] The dating of the second housing boom treats the events of the winter of 1962–1963 as a temporary interruption or shock. Certainly, the behavior of inflows at building societies bears out the assumption.

space available for an expansionist policy. After making allowances for the effect of the severe winter on unemployment rates, we concluded earlier that both periods of moderate growth began with comparable rates of unemployment, roughly 2.4 to 2.5 per cent. By the time that restrictive policy measures (and whatever else was involved) had succeeded in bringing the boom in consumer investment to an end (1960-I and 1964-IV), unemployment rates had fallen to 1.8 and 1.4 per cent respectively.[43] At their lowest during these periods, unemployment rates were 1.4 per cent in 1961-(II) and 1.2 per cent in 1966-(II). In this sense, much of the space for an expansionist policy was eaten up by the boom in consumer investment.

F. The Stagnation of the Late Sixties

It is, however, in comparing the period beginning in 1966-(I) with the previous ten years that the contrast stands out. Deflationary policies were implemented late in 1964 (with interest market rates already beginning to rise (1964-(I)) and policy remained deflationary until April 1967. There was a short period of ease from April 1967 to November 1967. This had the effect of generating a boom in consumer investment up through 1968-(I). The easing of market rates of interest beginning in the fall of 1966, together with the discretionary monetary measures taken in the spring of 1967 led to an increase of flows to building societies beginning in 1966-(III) and lasting until 1967-(III). However, early reversal of policy (including tougher borrowing terms to finance consumer durable purchases) coinciding with devaluation in November, 1967 resulted in a consumer investment boom of only five quarters duration compared to booms of 10 and 11 quarters in the previous two periods of consumer investment booms. Thus the expansionist policy following the period of stagnation beginning in 1966-(I) was short lived. The acute payments difficulties developing in 1967 led to very restrictive monetary and fiscal policies that were to persist until 1971.

There was a slight industrial investment surge beginning late in 1967 and running through 1968 due primarily to an increase in manufacturing investment. Some of this was due to a bunching of investments in the last two quarters of 1968 in order to take advantage of special investment grants. However, the simultaneous decline in residential construction (both public and private) and industrial investment by the public sector, and the lack of any upward movement in outlays on consumer durables ensured that overall the economy could only stagnate for some time.

Unemployment increased fairly steadily from 1966-(I) until 1971-(II). The

---

[43] The end of both booms in consumer investment marked the end of periods of moderate growth.

annual average rate of growth in final sales during this period was less than $1\frac{1}{2}$ per cent and most of this 'growth' was due to a one quarter spurt. Industrial and manufacturing investment did a little better than this, but with the general stagnation of the economy it could not be expected to grow rapidly without some exceptional policy inducements.

During 1970 inflows at building societies increased rapidly and private and public residential construction picked up as well. This was accompanied by a boom in consumer durable outlays. Both forms of consumer investment grew rapidly during 1971, as did net exports. However, this consumer investment boom was accompanied by a decline in industrial investment, especially in private industries, so that while final sales grew during 1971 growth was not rapid enough to keep unemployment from rising to 3.73 per cent by 1971-(IV).

G. A Summing Up

This description of the postwar behavior of the British economy ends with the coal miners' strike of January 1972 and on the eve of Britain's entry into the Common Market. It would seem that several lessons can be drawn from the postwar experience that have a bearing on what was said earlier in the chapter. Much has been made of the possibility that policy measures have intensified fluctuations in postwar Britain.[44] For reasons similar to those given in Chapter IX, we would have to argue that the case is anything but proven. With too many policy targets for the policy instruments to handle, it is next to impossible to evaluate the success of policy by merely looking at the data or performing simple tests. Our criticism of official policy is based on different grounds.[45]

With British governments committed to maintaining high levels of employment, reflationary measures have been implemented when unemployment rates were still relatively low; 2.3, 2.1, 2.0 and 3.2 per cent in mid-1958, mid-1962, 1967-(I) and 1971-(II) respectively. This lack of space was discussed earlier and was seen as one of the reasons that authorities have been unable to sustain a expansionary policy for any length of time. But what should also be clear from the description of the postwar period is that policy measures have succeeded in compounding the difficulties created by this lack of space. For when expansionist policies have been introduced, their immediate impact has been to create a boom in consumer investment outlays and only later does a business investment boom get going. Now it may be true that some

[44] See Dow, *op. cit.*, p. 384.
[45] See Chapter IX, pp. 197–201. A more general critique of the position that policy has been destabilizing is found in Worswick, G. N. D. 'Fiscal Policy and Stabilization in Britain' *Money, Credit and Banking*, August 1969.

resources required to produce consumer capital items are specialized and so would not be drawn into industries specializing in industrial capital. As a result this sequence of events may not greatly curb output of firms producing industrial capital in the short run. However, in the long run, this type of boom is bound to have a sizeable effect on the capacity of the capital goods industry since the sequence of events we are describing will prevent the authorities from sustaining a reflationary policy, and this will operate to keep producers of industrial capital from expanding their capacity in the long run. It is difficult in these circumstances to see the incentive for producers of such capital goods to appreciably expand capacity during the boom.[46] To a certain extent, a policy of flexible exchange rates will work to offset the unfortunate choice of policy instruments, but, as suggested in Part I, more is certainly needed for getting onto the virtuous circle. Some extra space may now be available for an expansionist policy because of the higher unemployment rates prevailing in the early 1970's. But without some additional instrument, it is likely that the balance of payments ceiling will be encountered before an investment boom has left the ground.

[46] An alternative way of putting the problem is to argue that if a boom is led by industrial investment, at least the spending category that sets in motion the multiplier is one that adds the most to the growth of productivity per time period. The longer the period of business investment led booms, the less will be the pressure on prices. The business investment 'boom' beginning late in 1967 took on something of this character, but it was not self-sustaining. The slow growth of final sales, itself partly related to policy measures, and the termination of investment grants were bound to eventually lead to a situation where the capacity effects of investment outstripped the multiplier effects.

Chapter XII A Summing Up

A. The Importance of the Unemployment Rate Along the Equilibrium Path

The earlier chapters outlined a model with an equilibrium growth path on which demand and supply grew at the same rate. Chapters VI and VII attempted to set out in as concrete a fashion as possible the conditions that must prevail if this growth path is to be stable in a world where only a minimum effort is made by the authorities to stabilize demand. Two types of ceilings or constraints were particularly singled out as important stabilizing influences: i.e. the ceiling in the capital goods industry, especially construction; and a monetary ceiling. The lack of sensitivity by certain sectors to declines in output was also emphasized, as this kind of 'inertia' was important for explaining the lower turning point. This lack of sensitivity could be attributed to several factors, but one very important prerequisite was a forced or voluntary postponement of spending plans during the previous boom. Chapters VIII–XI described the cyclical and growth record of two advanced capitalist systems over a half century of their history. The American experience illustrated the importance of strong booms led by the business sector, even when these interfere with price stability. For unless profit considerations and technological requirements together are such as to lead to business demanding (and obtaining) an increased share of financial and real resources, backlogs of demand by consumers and other units of the non-profit sector will not be created during the boom. This will lead to the subsequent downturn, turning into a serious depression that is widely diffused over the whole economy.

All of this suggests that if growth is to proceed in a relatively steady fashion, uninterrupted by serious depressions of the 1930's variety, it is important not only that demand and supply grow at the same rate but also that the average rate of unemployment along this growth path be relatively low. Expressed in terms of the model of Chapter IV, what matters is that the ratio of the long run equilibrium level of income, Y_t^E, to full employment or maximum output, X_t, be close to one.

The British economy in the postwar period illustrated quite well how an economy can succeed in eliminating the kind of instability that may still be troublesome in the United States. The British authorities have shown a strong predisposition to utilize a variety of policy instruments in an effort to regulate aggregate demand, and they have shown a willingness to implement policies with such speed and courage as to astonish economists of other countries. But while actions of the British authorities in the postwar period give every indication that large scale unemployment in Britain is a thing of the past, they have not been able to make more than a beginning in developing policy instruments that can succeed in increasing their growth rate and at the same time eliminate chronic balance of payments difficulties.[1]

The problems facing the United States in the last quarter of the 20th century are somewhat different. It is true that both Britain and America at this juncture have not found the means to handle inflation (save by creating a level of unemployment that would be intolerable). But America, unlike Britain, has not even made a beginning in establishing an adequate set of stabilization instruments to handle problems either of serious inflation or unemployment. Ignoring the 'freeze' and 'Phase II', measures that have been considered only temporary, general quantitative monetary controls have been the chief instrument of stabilization. This instrument has been helpful in the postwar period but, as we have argued, it is not adequate to handle serious recessions (or inflations). Yet there is no certainty that a capitalist system will always be operating in an employment and capacity utilization region that brings the various stabilizing constraints into play during a boom. This does not mean that if conditions like those that prevailed in the interwar period should come into play a depression like that of the 1930's would develop. Sooner or later, as a recession intensifies, the fiscal and monetary authorities would devise new instruments to stimulate demand. But given the division of power under the American political system (and the quasi independence of its Central Bank), there exist serious lags in implementing policies that do not exist under a parliamentary system. This difficulty is naturally compounded by the fact that there is no package of instruments already developed and tried, from which the American authorities could choose. So there could still develop a recession serious by postwar standards.

It might be useful then in drawing this study to a close to concentrate on certain trends in the development of the most mature capitalist system, with particular emphasis on the shifting composition of output.[2] This might give some insight into whether the offsets to full employment savings—i.e. business and consumer investment, net exports and government outlays—will be

---

[1] This statement is made in spite of the fact that unemployment exceeded 3 per cent in Britain in 1971, a very high level by British standards.
[2] Most mature in the sense of having developed a distribution of output that other economies will achieve only after *per capita* incomes have risen further.

sufficient to continue to generate a moving equilibrium at high levels of employment. If they will not, fairly substantial changes will have to be made in the number and kinds of instruments utilized in the interests of stability.

B. The Classification of the Offsets to Savings

Let U again represent all desired or *ex ante* spending other than consumption (net of durables), and let U' represent the amount of such spending at full employment; i.e. the amount of offsets to savings forthcoming at full employment output. If S represents all private savings and T total tax collections, then S' and T' represent the savings and tax yields that will be forthcoming at full employment, given the consumer spending propensities and the tax structure. The condition for full employment is naturally $S' + T' = U'$. The fact that unemployment in the United States typically has varied from 3 to 6 per cent means that the discrepancy over the cycle between $S' + T'$ and U' is either zero or relatively small, depending on how we choose to define full employment. Since the offsets determine income through the multiplier, and savings and tax yields depend on income, the problem is how to divide up U the better to understand why it is that offsets and leakages *ex ante* have tended toward equality at tolerable levels of unemployment in the past, and whether they are likely to do so in the future.[3]

For example, the early secular stagnation theory of Hansen suggested a division between family- or population-related spending, and other types of business investment.[4] This division was suggested because the early stagnationists believe that the relation between full employment output, X, and the equilibrium level of output, Y^E, very much depended on demographic growth, the opening of new frontiers and extent of capital saving innovations in the business sector. The stimulating effect attributed to population growth and investment due to the opening of new frontiers can be traced largely to the effect these two influences had on housing and other forms of family-related expenditures, which in turn led to an increase in the ratio of non-consumption spending to output. There is an implicit assumption in the Hansen argument that higher rates of growth of the demographic variables lead not only to

[3] One could just as well speak of dividing up full employment output and the equilibrium level of income, Y^E, and ask under what conditions will the leakages plus consumption at full employment, be equal to the offsets plus consumption at full employment. But since consumption can be dropped from both sides, the usual way of handling the problem is in terms of leakages and offsets. It should be emphasized that the form of the consumption function does not in any way determine how the offsets and leakages must be classified.

[4] Alvin Hansen, 'Economic Progress and Declining Population Growth', *American Economic Review*, March 1939.

higher levels of non-consumption expenditures but to higher levels per family; otherwise the deflationary gap will not be closed.[5]

We have had several occasions to assert that, other things being equal, the share of non-consumption expenditures in output rises with the rate of growth of the population.[6] Thus, other things being equal, a more rapid rate of growth of the population by pushing up the ratio of non-consumption expenditures to output will cause the long run equilibrium level of output, Y^E, to rise, generating a lower level of unemployment along the long run path. This of course intensifies inflationary pressures; but it also means that on the average recessions will start from a lower level of unemployment than otherwise. This, in turn, increases the likelihood that any boom will encounter the kinds of restraints described earlier, and that backlogs of deferred demand will develop in certain sectors to dampen the subsequent downswing. On the other hand, a declining rate of demographic growth will result in a lower U/Y^E and Y^E/X, other things being equal, increasing the likelihood that recessions will be more severe for reasons already outlined. Thus, there is a limited sense in which the analysis here is in sympathy with one of the tenets of the stagnationist doctrine.[7]

The stagnation argument fell into disrepute in the early postwar period—partly because of the (unpredicted) strong boom following the war, partly because of the different interpretations of the doctrine itself (even though in the second half of the 1950's a kind of neostagnationist position developed).[8] However, it is necessary to be quite clear about what is meant by the stagnationist position before rejecting it, and the usefulness of dividing the offsets along the lines suggested. If one interprets it simply as meaning that a capitalist system is bound to generate an ever increasing level of unemployment, weak booms and prolonged recessions no matter what, then clearly the doctrine is wrong. The postwar record in the United States and the record of other capitalistic systems in the postwar period clearly disprove a 'vulgar stagnationist doctrine'. A more convincing way to express the theory is to state that in the absence either of new frontiers, reasonably high rates of demographic growth, an active fiscal policy or an exogenously given export boom, a capitalistic system will be subject to weak booms leading to recessions

[5] Assume for convenience that family incomes are identical, labor productivity the same for each worker, and that the number of families and workers are always the same. Then if an increase in the number of families (workers) leads to a marginal increase in non-consumption demand, no greater than the average amount of such demand per family in the absence of demographic growth, demand per family will be unchanged. Since the labor force has increased by the same percent as aggregate demand, the unemployment rate will not fall.

[6] See, for example, Chapter V, pp. 93–94.

[7] Needless to say, there are other ways to ensure stability.

[8] For a lively discussion see the views of the Council of Economic Advisors and Arthur Burns in *The Morgan Guaranty Survey*, Morgan Guaranty Trust Company of New York, May and August 1961.

of the 1929 variety followed by weak recoveries etc., so that in the long run unemployment rates will be high. The neostagnationist doctrine can be interpreted to mean that a capitalistic system like the American one will tend toward high and rising levels of unemployment unless the government sector actively pursues a full employment policy through fiscal means. In particular, this position can be defined as the belief that, given the present level of government expenditures, present tax rates and propensities to spend, the full employment offsets to full employment savings and taxes are inadequate (or soon will be), and that there is a chronic tendency for this to be the case. It is but a short step from this to the idea of the fiscal drag: the notion that the current budgetary system acts to thwart the achievement of full employment, because the budgetary surplus is too large or the budgetary deficit too small. If private spending propensities at full employment were otherwise, it would be appropriate to refer to the current fiscal structure as a fiscal stabilizer. Since estimates of the full employment receipts and expenditures in the early 1960's (when this theory was popular) denoted a surplus, the expression fiscal drag and full employment surplus went hand in hand.

Write $S'/X = I^{C'}/X + I^{FNR'}/X + (G' - T')/X$, where G' and T' represent government expenditures and tax receipts at full employment. $I^{C'}$ and $I^{FNR'}$ represent consumer and business investment outlays (or, more correctly, business plus investment by agriculture and non-profit institutions) at full employment. X is full employment output and income and the foreign sector is again ignored as are any distinctions between levels of government. The argument popular before the 1964 tax cut can now be seen as the assertion that given $(I^{C'} + I^{FNR'})/X$, i.e. our estimate of what they would be *ex ante*, $(G' - T')/X$ is not sufficiently positive to satisfy this full employment equilibrium condition. Of course, one of the reasons why full employment equilibrium may not have been possible is that the fiscal structure was such as to generate too great a surplus. It is primarily the development of this notion of inter-dependence of the offsets that distinguishes the more recent stagnation from the old. Fiscal policy is elevated to the role that Hansen assigned to population growth and new frontiers, since not only does the budget determine the size of $(G' - T')/X$, but it also affects the size of $(I^{C'} + I^{FNR'})/X$. To put matters differently, emphasis and concern has shifted from finding ways of inducing the private sector to save less, to getting the public sector to do so. Thus, if the tax structure is progressive and government spending rising more slowly than full employment tax receipts, periodic reductions in tax rates may be necessary if full employment is to be maintained. Alternatively, a more rapid rate of growth of the public sector is called for. The actual behavior of this 'required' budget over time will depend upon the propensities of the consumer and business sectors to invest. The matter is discussed in greater detail in the Appendix.

C. Trends in Business Investment

It is not possible to dismiss the neostagnationist doctrine out of hand. And its suggested breakdown of the offsets to savings is consistent with the method utilized in this book, in that it separates expenditures related to family formation from other non-consumption outlays. Throughout the earlier chapters these family-related expenditures have been singled out as an important stabilizing force in non-consumption expenditure. Their behavior in the past and future is certainly an important determinant of the stability properties of an economy. Unfortunately, a continuous series spanning the interwar and postwar period is unavailable for this spending category. As an alternative, non-consumption expenditures will be divided into investment outlays by the consumer, and business sectors and all government outlays. A large share of consumer investment outlays is related to family formation and business, and government outlays can always be further subdivided to isolate that part which is also tied in with demographic movements.

Write $I^{FNR'}/X = (I^{FNR'}/\Delta X)(\Delta X/X)$, where business investment as a share of full employment output is shown to be equal to the marginal business capital–output ratio, and the rate of growth of maximum output. Assume that business investment tends to be capital saving, as Hansen earlier argued. If, then, full employment growth of output is given (or falling) and if full employment savings as a per cent of full employment output is constant, either the consumer or government sector or both must offset this decline in $I^{FNR'}/X$ caused by an alleged decline in $I^{FNR'}/\Delta X$, if full employment is to be maintained. And if there is a limit to the increase of I^C/Y, either because of the size of the income elasticity of demand for consumer capital, or because a constant per cent of the purchase price is financed by borrowing and there is a limit to the debt–income ratio, then the government sector must play an increasingly larger share in generating offsets to full employment. This is equivalent to saying that government saving must decline and dissaving eventually increase.

Several studies undertaken in the postwar period, including the studies of capital formation under the direction of Kuznets, show an eventual secular decline in the average capital–output ratio in mining, manufacturing and public utilities, and in most subsectors of these sectors.[9] The historical pattern is typically an inverted U with the peak varying in time from one sector to the next. One exception is the public utility sector, where the ratio falls steadily from the beginning of the period covered. Obviously, if the capital–output ratio is falling, the marginal capital–output ratio must be falling,

[9] See Kuznets, *op. cit.*, pp. 78–90; Israel Borenstein, *Capital and Output Trends in Mining Industries, 1870–1948*, Occasional Paper 41, National Bureau of Economic Research, New York 1954; and Ulmer, Melville, *Capital in Transportation, Communications, and Public Utilities: Its Formation and Financing*, National Bureau of Economic Research, New York 1960.

which is just the issue under discussion.[10] Various arguments have been advanced to explain these alleged trends. It is a well known fact that the share of plant in business fixed investment has declined historically, and continues to do so in the postwar period. One reason cited for this is the switch by manufacturing firms from producing their own power to purchasing electrical power, which means that output can be produced with less capital, since the optimum size plant for any level of output will be smaller.[11] Creamer suggests that during the 19th and early part of the 20th century, manufacturing investment was strongly affected by an increase in the number of new firms which accompanied territorial dispersion—an argument similar to Hansen's new frontiers.[12] Couple this with sizeable indivisibilities and limited facilities for distribution, and a high ratio of plant to equipment investment will result. Once the frontier closes this ratio will then drift downward. With regard to public utilities, the point has been made that railroad building involved working with plant indivisibilities large enough to have created excess capacity for several decades. As demand grew historically, further increases in capacity could be handled by equipment investment such that the marginal capital–output ratios were small enough markedly to pull down the average.[13]

The falling capital–output ratio for public utilities has not aroused much dissension. However, it has been suggested that the alleged decline in manufacturing is due to measurement errors. Anderson contends that the initial increase of the capital–output ratio may be due to increased reporting of capital assets from 1879 to 1919, while the decline resulted from more complete adjustments for depreciation after the income tax became important.[14] Furthermore, Goldsmith has argued that historical capital–output ratios in manufacturing fail to take account of the changing structure of

---

[10] Unfortunately for this view, one estimate shows that the incremental capital–output ratio began to rise in manufacturing, at least between 1948 and 1955. See Creamer, Daniel, 'Postwar Trends in the Relation of Capital to Output in Manufactures', *American Economic Review, Papers and Proceedings*, May 1958. This could easily be a temporary phenomenon associated with backlogs built up during the 1930's and 1940's.

[11] See Kuznets, *op. cit.*, Chapter 4, and Wooden, Donald, and Wasson, Robert, 'Manufacturing Investment Since 1929', *Survey of Current Business*, November 1956, pp. 8–20, for a discussion of the substitution of equipment for plant.

[12] Creamer, *Postwar Trends . . ., op. cit.*

[13] Ulmer, *op. cit.*

[14] Anderson, Paul, 'The Apparent Decline in Capital-Output Ratios', *Quarterly Journal of Economics*, November 1961. Anderson further argues that because the gross savings ratio has been fairly constant historically, while the rate of growth of output has fallen, the marginal capital–output ratio should rise historically and, presumably, pull the capital–output ratio up. This conclusion is unwarranted. Write: $S/Y \div \Delta Y/Y = S/\Delta Y$. Anderson states that since *ex post* savings and investment are equal, the marginal capital–output ratio has risen. However, S in the above formula is not the same thing as gross fixed non-residential investment, I^{FNR}, in the Department of Commerce sense, Rather, $S = I^C + I^{FNR} + G - T$ (ignoring the foreign sector). Dividing both sides by ΔY gives $S/\Delta Y = I^C/\Delta Y + I^{FNR}/\Delta Y + (G - T)/\Delta Y$. A rising $S/\Delta Y$ is clearly compatible with a falling $I^{FNR}/\Delta Y$.

Table 12.1

	Gross investment as a per cent of GNP (current dollars)	Gross investment as a per cent of GNP (constant dollars)
1899–1908	14·6%	15·3%
1909–1918	12·4	13·7
1919–1928	13·4	13·8
1946–1955	13·4	11·1
1956–1962	13·6	10·5
1946–1962	13·5	10·8

Source: F. Thomas Juster; *Household Capital Formation: Growth Cyclical Behavior, and Financing, 1897–1962*, Tables A-1 and A-2.

assets and allow purely financial assets to distort the picture.[15] Finally, these estimates fail to adjust for the degree of utilization of capital, and Goldsmith shows that a reasonable adjustment for changes in utilization will eliminate any change in the coefficient.

In any case, Kuznets' study reveals a decline in gross investment (which includes residential housing and some government outlays but excludes consumer durables), as a per cent of GNP in constant dollars, beginning with the decade 1889–1898.[16] Due to the more rapid rise of prices of capital goods, the trend is missing for the same ratio measured in current prices. But since Kuznets includes government investment in the numerator, and excludes certain types of government expenditures from the denominator, both of which have been growing more rapidly over time than business investment or GNP, even in current dollars the share of business investment plus residential housing in GNP should be falling. Goldsmith's findings updated by Juster are in substantial agreement with those of Kuznets.[17] In Table 12.1 gross investment (defined as business plant and equipment investment plus residential housing but excluding any government outlays) is shown as a per cent of GNP (Department of Commerce definition). The depression years are omitted for obvious reasons.

However, the figures in Table 12.1 include residential housing, which may have had a downward trend historically, and this may be dominating the figures. In addition, when housing is included along with business plant and

[15] See the discussion of Creamer's paper, *Postwar Trends . . ., op. cit.*
[16] Kuznets. *op. cit.*, Table 8. Strictly speaking these ratios and others discussed in the text use actual GNP, while the concern is with the trend in certain offsets relative to X. Since there does not seem to be any noticeable trend in unemployment rates during the period, the trends in both ratios should be little different.
[17] See Goldsmith, Raymond, *A Study of Savings*, Princeton University Press, Princeton 1955; and Juster, F. Thomas, *op. cit.*

Table 12.2

	Plant, equipment and rental housing investment as a per cent of GNP (current dollars)	Plant, equipment and rental housing investment as a per cent of GNP (constant dollars)
1899–1908	12·4%	13·0%
1909–1918	10·6	11·9
1919–1928	9·6	9·9
1947–1962	9·7	8·0

Source: Same as Table 12.1.

equipment investment, outlays by the business and consumer sectors are confused. Eliminating all residential housing outlays from the figures is one way of getting closer to the heart of the matter. An alternative method, and one better for our purposes, is to divide residential housing into single family and all other, and to assume that single family housing is synonymous with owner-occupied housing. New outlays for single family homes then become investment expenditures by the household sector, while all other housing expenditures are assumed to be made by the business sector.[18] Adding housing expenditures by the business sector so defined to plant and equipment expenditures, and dividing by GNP, gives the figures in Table 12.2. The downward trend in investment outlays by the business sector shown in Table 12.2 is quite clear. Department of Commerce figures, while not strictly comparable to those of Table 12.2, indicate some reversal through the 1960's of the downward trend in plant and equipment expenditures as a per cent of GNP.[19] But the downward trend still stands out. In addition, Census figures confirm a further continuation of the trend toward owner-occupied housing. All in all, the evidence indicates that, as a potential offset to full employment savings, outlays by the business sector have since the turn of the century played a lesser and lesser role. There seems little to indicate that its role might increase in the near future, without a major technological revolution.

D. Trends in Consumer Investment Outlays

The downward trend in business outlays as a share of GNP does not however signal the advent of an era of secular stagnation, unless there is also no

[18] Juster, *op. cit.*, Tables A-1 and A-2.
[19] Fixed non-residential investment as a share of GNP rose from 9·6 per cent during the 1946–1962 period, to 10·2 per cent during the strong investment boom of the 1963–1969 interval.

offsetting trend in any of the other offsets (or there is a decline in the private savings ratio). At a popular level, discussion of a coming of age of mass acquisition of consumer durables, an era beyond affluence, points up the possibility of consumer investment rising in importance at some stage of development. Thus, substitutions of private transportation for public, and of services provided in the home for those provided by business, such as are made possible by the acquisition of consumer durables, are cited as examples of rising consumer investment at the expense of public and business outlays. At a more technical level, this possibility has been seen by Oshima as a means of counteracting any deflationary tendencies generated by a decline in the business investment ratio.[20] Thus, the business sector may be an increasingly unreliable source of offsets to full employment savings, as an economy becomes increasingly affluent.

As *per capita* incomes rise and as most sectors of business become rationalized and achieve high levels of productivity, they are alleged to generate surplus savings. Savings that at an earlier date would be plowed back into the sector are superfluous, and must be borrowed by other sectors to maintain aggregate demand. But the reason that these savings are superfluous is that businesses producing non-durable goods and services are either experiencing a slow rate of growth of demand because of a low income elasticity of demand, or are producing under conditions of low capital intensity (i.e. high capital

Table 12.3

| | All durables as a share of GNP | | Major durables as a share of GNP | |
	(*current* $)	(*constant* $)	(*current* $)	(*constant* $)
1879–1888	6·6	7·3	—	—
1889–1898	6·6	7·7	—	—
1899–1908	6·4	7·2	2·2	2·8
1909–1918	6·8	7·3	3·4	3·2
1919–1928	8·4	8·4	5·5	5·4
1946–1953	9·4	9·5	—	—
1946–1962	—	—	6·0	7·2

Sources: Kuznets, *Capital in the American Economy*, and Juster, *Household Capital Formation, op. cit.*

[20] See Oshima, Harry, 'Consumer Asset Formation and the Future of Prosperity,' *Economic Journal*, March 1961. What is new in this model of development is the lack of stagnationist overtones, since Oshima assumes that the consumer sector would offset the decline of investment by the business sector, and would borrow the surplus funds of the latter. Presumably, the capital–output ratio (somehow measured) of the consumer sector would rise over time.

productivity), or both.[21] Under such conditions what saves the economy from collapse is a rise in consumer capital formation as a per cent of GNP. This model of development assumes that the consumer sector will grow in importance as an offset, as consumer capital formation (never well defined) increases as a per cent of GNP. Sometimes it is total expenditure on residential construction that is included in the numerator; sometimes it is expenditure on owner-occupied residential construction. Kuznet's figures for total consumer durables as a per cent of GNP show an increase over time, whether measured in current or constant dollars. Juster's figures for major durables as a per cent of GNP show a more pronounced trend when measured in constant dollars, with the share in current prices changing somewhat less. Table 12.3 summarizes the findings for decade averages.[22]

The behavior of non-farm residential housing tends to show a less clearcut pattern. Beginning in the last quarter of the 19th century, non-farm residential housing as a per cent of GNP measured in current dollars, tends to move between 3 and 4 per cent, with two large deviations above the average, one in the late 1890's and 1900's and the other in the 1920's.[23] If all housing outlays are combined either with outlays on all consumer durables, or just with major consumer durables, the trend for the 20th century is upward when measured in both current and constant dollars. But it would be more in keeping with our distinction between the consumer and business sector to assume that single family homes are owner-occupied while all other dwelling units are rental units. As before, all new single family homes are then considered to be investments undertaken by the consumer sector, the value of all other residential construction being assigned to the business sector. Both in current and constant dollars, the trend in investment in housing and major durables by the housing sector is quite striking. From just before the turn of the century until 1946–1962, investment by the

[21] Thus, let $\Delta Y_i/Y_i$ represent the rate of growth of demand for the output of the ith industry determined by: $\Delta Y_i/Y_i = (ie)r_y + r_f$, where (ie) is the income elasticity of demand (on a per family basis), r_y is the rate of growth of family income, and r_f the rate of growth of the number of families. Since, $I_i/Y_i = I_i/\Delta Y_i \times \Delta Y_i/Y_i$ the higher the capital intensity of production, $I_i/\Delta Y_i$, *ceteris paribus*, the larger will be I_i/Y_i.

[22] Juster, *op. cit.*, Tables A-1 and A-2. Major durables include expenditures on furniture, household appliances, the entertainment complex, passenger cars and dealer gross margins on used passenger cars. Vatter and Thompson in their critique of Oshima's theory had the two postwar periods in mind, when arguing that cross section comparisons (say Japan and the United States at one point in time) do not carry over to a single country's experience over time. Had they extended their own analysis back further in time, they might have modified their position. See Vatter, H., and Thompson, R., 'Consumer Asset Formation and Economic Growth—The United States Case'. *The Economic Journal*, June 1966. It is in this context that Oshima's use of consumer asset formation in two different senses is confusing. If he had referred to owner-occupied housing and its behavior over time, he would have had a better case, as the text makes clear. Oshima also failed to consider the capital intensity of production in those industries producing consumer capital, which are supposed to be high growth industries. They might be heavy demanders of savings.

[23] *Historical Statistics of the United States*, Series F1. F104, F114, N115, and current issues of *Statistical Abstract*.

consumer sector so defined grew from around $4\frac{1}{2}$ per cent to 10 per cent of GNP in current prices, and from 5 to 10 per cent in constant prices. Table 12.4 reflects the underlying trends that were earlier depicted by Table 12.1.[24]

To a large extent, these trends can be attributed to the fact that families are substituting owner occupied housing for rental; but data in Table 12.3 indicate also that part of the increased importance of consumer capital formation is probably at the expense of business fixed investment. Families as investors in consumer capital must be assigned an ever increasing role in generating high levels of employment during the past sixty years. The Department of Commerce data in the remaining years of the 1960's (though the figures are not strictly comparable) reveal a slight reversal of this trend, largely accounted for by the decline in residential housing as a share of output from 1963 on. But the reversal is so slight that it cannot be interpreted as a reversal of the underlying patterns shown by Tables 12.3 and 12.4.[25]

Table 12.4

	Consumer investment a share of GNP	
	Current prices	Constant prices
1899–1908	4·4%	5·1%
1909–1918	5·2	5·4
1919–1928	9·3	9·3
1946–1955	9·7	9·4
1956–1962	10·1	10·8
1946–1962	9·8	10·0

Source: Juster, *op. cit.*, Tables A-1 and A-2.

Whether or not this shift in the composition of the offsets is stabilizing or not depends largely on whether or not such shifts affect the ability of constraints to come into play in any boom. But this is a matter of whether the relationship between the long run equilibrium level of income and full employment income has changed, in such a way as either to raise or lower Y_t^E/X_t. For even if one wished to argue that consumer investment is less sensitive to movements in GNP or final sales than business investment, this is only likely to be true within the kind of situation sketched earlier. In other words, one reason consumer investment (or, to change the classification system, family related) outlays tend to be less sensitive in the downswing, is

[24] See Chapter II, p. 25. No attempt has been made to update Juster's findings.

[25] As already mentioned, fixed non residential investment as a share of GNP rose slightly from the period 1946-1962 to 1963-1969. During these two periods, the figures for residential housing as a share of GNP moved from 5 to 3·7 per cent, while major durables as a share changed from 7·8 to 8·1 per cent. See *Survey of Current Business*, various issues, and *Business Statistics*, 1969, U.S. Department of Commerce.

that they were postponed during the previous boom. If fluctuations are not around a trend with such a low level of unemployment over the cycle that the constraints come into effect in a boom, the substitution of consumer for business investment will not increase the stability of the system. We would then be back to the situation prevailing during the interwar period. The basic issue is still that mentioned at the outset: whether trends in the 20th century have led to a rise or fall in Y_t^E/Y_t.

E. The Public Sector

What is missing in this discussion so far is a consideration of the development of the public sector in an age of affluence. And the one obvious dramatic change in the composition of output has been the increase, at the expense of consumption, of government expenditures at all levels as a per cent of GNP. If government purchases of goods and services are taken as the measure of government activity, the data reveals a rise of total government expenditures from a little over 8 per cent in 1929 to 22·4 per cent of GNP in 1970, and a decline of consumption from 66 per cent to 52·1 per cent of GNP. With respect to the composition of government outlays, state and local government expenditures on goods and services have expanded since the Korean War at a more rapid rate than GNP (and federal expenditures), so that by 1970 state and local governments expenditures surpassed federal government purchases —12·4 versus 10·2 per cent of GNP.

The other side of the coin to a substitution of government outlays for consumption, is a rise in tax receipts as a share of GNP. Because of the alleged differences in the tax and government spending multipliers (giving rise to the balanced budget multiplier), this substitution has two stability aspects. Thus, on the one hand, we might ask (as we could with the substitution of consumer investment outlays for business investment) whether or not the substitution of government expenditures for consumption is substitution of a more stable type of spending for one less so. On the other hand, the possibility of a balanced budget multiplier allows for the possibility that the mere increase of the size of the public sector has raised the equilibrium level of output relative to full employment output.[26] If this is true, the increased importance of the public sector has increased the stability properties of an advanced capitalist system on this ground alone. For the moment we can ignore the possible balanced budget multiplier effect, and concentrate on the first issue: whether government expenditures are more stable than consumption outlays.

There are two possible ways to interpret the expression 'more stable' in

[26] See the appendix.

this context. First, it can refer to the possibility that one type of spending is more likely than another to change substantially, in a way quite independent of the general performance of the economy (e.g. large changes in government expenditures on defense, or 'autonomous' shifts in the consumption function). Second, stability can refer to the relative response of consumption and government expenditures to changes in income, induced by a change in some other type of spending.

In neither sense of the term is the issue clear cut. On the one hand, the large variations in federal government defense outlays from the end of World War II up through the 1950's had an important impact on the economy even when matched by changes in tax receipts. Fortunately, the cutbacks following World War II and the Korean War came at a time when there were still substantial backlogs of demand for goods, especially those related to family formation. But the overall effect tended to be depressive. The same is true of the cutbacks beginning in the late 1960's.

In the opposite direction, the post-1965 build up in Viet Nam was not accompanied by any substantial offset in spending by the private sector (except in housing), so serious price instability followed. The only comparable example in the consumer sector was the scare buying at the outbreak of the Korean War (itself induced by expected increases in federal government outlays). This suggests that large changes in government outlays, even when balanced by changes in tax receipts, can play an even more destabilizing role in the future, if little regard is paid to their effect on the economy. For example, without backlogs of demand, large downward shifts in the budget could easily lead, if poorly timed, to serious recessions.[27] To be set against this is the fact that expenditures by state and local governments have increased with virtually no interruption, in an effort to catch up with postponed expenditures, and eventually to maintain the workloads for a growing population.

The relative response of consumption and government expenditures to changes in income, poses the question of whether, because of some sort of budget constraint, a given decline (increase) in income or receipts causes one type of expenditure to decline (increase) more than another. Our discussion in earlier chapters indicated that in situations other than that prevailing in the early 1930's, changes in GNP and tax receipts not only did not induce changes in government outlays at any level of government in the same direction, but if anything induced movements that are contra-cyclical.[28] The federal government did not show a great deal of imagination in its use of fiscal instruments to counteract changes in demand by the private sector. But state and local governments tended to vary their expenditures in a contra-cyclical manner, especially during recessions, as state and local outlays increased throughout

[27] See the postscript to Chapter VIII.
[28] The Viet Nam buildup is not an exception, as this increase in government outlays was not induced by growing receipts related to the booming economy.

every postwar recession. Only when a decline in activity is as severe, rapid and pronounced as it was in the 1930's, can we expect state and local government outlays to respond in a pro-cyclical way. Set against this is the (slight) decline in aggregate consumption in constant dollars in three out of four recessions, and the even larger implicit decline in per family consumption.

All things considered, it is difficult to take any very strong position on whether the higher government expenditures are more or less stable, than the consumption expenditures they replaced in the United States. There is another aspect to the stability question, however, that has to do with a possible change in the equilibrium growth path of the system relative to full employment, which would result from a more or less proportionate increase in government expenditures and taxes. By our reading, if the balanced budget multiplier applies in a dynamic setting, the chief stabilizing effect of an increased government sector is best seen in this context. By raising the ratio of Y_t^E/X_t, the public sector has (inadvertently) acted throughout the 20th century, other things being equal, in such a way as to push the equilibrium path closer to the full employment growth path. Evidently the increase in the size of public sector outlays (and receipts) from approximately 8 per cent at the turn of the century to 12 per cent in the 1920's, was not sufficient to offset the other influences pulling down the business investment ratio. In the 1950's and 1960's the growth of the public sector (together with other factors) was sufficient to keep the economy, again by inference, moving close to full employment output.[29]

F. Trends in the Near Future

Unfortunately it is difficult to disentangle the importance of the growth of the public sector from other influences in the postwar period. The backlogs of demand left over from the war and the 1930's were important during the 1950's, but not much after that. Of greater importance was (and is) the stimulating influence derived from the willingness of individuals to go into debt at an earlier age, or stage of their life cycle, to finance consumer investment outlays. For example, *per capita* short- and intermediate-term consumer credit outstanding rose about tenfold from 1929 to the 1960's, while *per capita* mortgage debt on 1-to-4 family houses rose almost as rapidly. This surely must have had much to do with the increase in consumer investment as a

---

[29] From 1929 to 1966 total government expenditures on goods and services and total government receipts net of transfer, interest and subsidies increased by roughly the same amounts, $146 billion and $148 billion respectively. Over the same period, GNP increased $640 billion. Applying a balanced budget multiplier of one would suggest that roughly one-fourth of the increase in GNP can be accounted for by a larger public sector. This is all very crude, and some additional complications are introduced in the appendix.

proportion of output. More importantly, both types of debt have risen much more rapidly than *per capita* income. Given some limit of the debt to income ratio that a family can maintain, a slowdown in the spending associated with these types of indebtedness must be expected.[30]

One measure of the net impact of all these factors is the behavior of the public sector's budget during years when the economy more or less experienced full employment. Thus, since $G - T = S - (I^C + I^{FNR})$, if in the neighborhood of 3 or 4 per cent unemployment an actual budget deficit is run, this would indicate that investment fell short of savings at full employment by an equal amount. If one retains these same assumptions and includes net exports, (E), i.e., $G - T = S - (I^C + I^{FNR} + E)$, the interpretation changes only slightly: investment plus net exports of goods and services at full employment were inadequate to offset full employment savings. Without a tax and expenditure relationship that generated this deficit, the economy would have achieved an equilibrium at something less than full employment. This possibility was earlier described as a sophisticated version of the stagnationist doctrine.

In the period from 1966 through 1971, unemployment rates were below 4 per cent for four of the six years, with an average rate of unemployment over the whole period of 4·3 per cent. The annual average deficit from calendar 1966 through calendar 1971 for all governments (National Income Accounts basis) was $7.5 billion.[31] Since net exports were positive in all these years, the budgetary deficit required for (or consistent with) full employment was reduced. However, the steady decline in net exports during this period (due to a more rapid rise in imports than in exports) gives no cause for comfort in the future.

Nevertheless, one is reluctant to assume that the underlying savings–investment relationship of the second half of the 1960's, that required *ex post* a deficit in order to reduce unemployment to around the 4 per cent level, will necessarily continue into the future. There seems no reason to assume that major technological changes are under way, such as would cause business investment as a share of output to reverse its historical downward trend. But at least for the immediate future, there appear to be factors at work that could cause consumer investment as a share of output to rise. Thus Diagram 8.1 in Chapter VIII indicates that there will be a large increase in the 25–34 year age group from 1970 to 1980 or 1985, and a similar spurt in the 35–44 year age group after 1975. At the same time the 14–17 and 18–24 year age groups (the latter group not shown) will be growing relatively slowly. Since at least one of

[30] The fact that over time different people are getting into and out of debt is really not relevant here. An increase in the *per capita* debt to income ratio will mean that, on the average, families at any stage of the life cycle have increasingly larger debt burdens to finance relative to their incomes.

[31] The average deficit for the federal government was much larger than this. Adjustments have been made in the text calculation to avoid duplications associated with grants-in-aid.

the age groups with which we associate high rates of family-related spending is expected to grow rapidly all through the 1970's and the other such group is expected to grow rapidly after the mid-1970's, there should be substantial pressure put on resources to satisfy the demands of these two groups. Other things being equal, this should lead to strong demand pressure for ten or fifteen years at least, to push the economy towards the full employment level.

G. A Need for Additional Instruments

But either as an intermediate or long run solution to the stability problem, rapid demographic growth in certain age groups is unsatisfactory. Even if it could be assumed that such demographic trends will persist, high demographic growth has become increasingly identified with a more rapid deterioration of the environment, and while this deterioration can be traced both to rising per family incomes and population growth (and their possible interaction), the latter must share the blame. Let us assume that the bulge in the high spending age groups is only temporary, so that eventually other sources of high demand pressures must be found. The Keynesian revolution taught us that only the 'vulgar stagnationist' doctrine was incorrect. Rapid population growth, new frontiers, or capital using innovations are neither necessary nor sufficient conditions for preventing periodic breakdowns such as in the 1930's. Over the long run, trends in government spending and taxation can easily fill any demand deficiency caused by a slowdown in demographic growth, capital saving innovations or any other influence. This may necessitate a growth in the national debt as years of excess *ex ante* savings at full employment will outnumber those of excess *ex ante* investment. It might even be necessary for continuous deficits to be run, the size of which will fluctuate in a contra-cyclical fashion. In other words, the relationship between actual government, expenditures and the average tax yield over the cycle may have to be altered, in such a way as to generate an annual deficit that displaces the equilibrium path of the economy, to a position where unemployment over the cycle will average some smaller amount, say, 5 per cent. This basically requires a willingness to accept more or less steady growth of the national debt. It also requires a much greater willingness and readiness to intervene when recessions do set in.

Second, what is also required is the development of additional and more sophisticated monetary and fiscal instruments in the interests of equity. Merely to raise the equilibrium level of income by increasing the offsets to 'full' employment relative to the leakages, will not solve certain discriminatory effects of conventional monetary policy, the chief instrument used for stability in the postwar period. This is true even if the long run policy is thought to be one of decreasing the present stimulating role of the public sector rather than increasing it.[32]

What seems to be called for is a consensus on how much of the burden of monetary and fiscal policy should be borne by the household sector relative to business and others; and then a decision as to what forms of household, business and other spending should be influenced by policy. In the interests purely of overall stability it would appear that the more the non-business groups are affected during the boom, the less serious will be the recession, other things being equal. But this may be because we are accustomed to thinking in terms of general monetary controls as stabilizing instruments. The Swedish example of investment controls in the postwar period suggests that fiscal measures can be used to cause business outlays to behave in a less procyclical manner.

But the behavior of prices in the second half of the 1960's and early 1970's indicate that additional instruments may be necessary at times, merely to promote overall stability of another sort. Heretofore, it has usually been implicitly assumed that there existed a relatively stable Phillips curve with a selection of unemployment-rate of inflation choices that are politically acceptable. However, one lesson to be learnt from the escalation in Viet Nam in the mid-1960's is that once prices and wages start to rise and continue for several years, there may no longer exist any unemployment-rate of inflation combination that is politically acceptable. In other words, only during a period of price stability is it possible, through regulating aggregate demand, to get unemployment rates down to a tolerable level and still maintain relatively stable prices. Once prices become unstable upward, more than one instrument is necessary to dampen fluctuations in employment rates at high levels, and to achieve relatively stable prices. When one considers the types of additional instruments suggested for solving this problem—e.g. an incomes policy, wage and price controls—it is clear that even greater structural changes are required than would be called for to distribute more equitably the burdens of monetary policy.

Finally, it should be noted that, in this discussion of the need for additional instruments, nothing has been said about the need to develop additional

---

[32] And by our reasoning many of the current proposals for eliminating the discriminating effects of monetary policy will do so only at a heavy cost. For example, increased intervention of government agencies in the mortgage market, through increased purchases of existing mortgages, will most likely allow lending institutions to expand mortgage holdings during boom periods. But if business borrowers, together with the financial community, are able to find alternative methods of financing their desired spending, the supply of loanable funds will increase. This will result in greater demand, and therefore greater inflationary pressures, during the boom. And if the greater availability of funds for home builders, together with an unchanged supply of loanable funds to business, also succeeds in generating a response on the supply side, the backlogs of demand necessary for cushioning the recession may be less. To a large extent the same criticism applies to the suggested introduction of variable mortgage rates and greater portfolio diversification for thrift institutions.

instruments for affecting the rate of growth of output. This was deliberate. It will be recalled that in Chapter IV the process of growth was described as one of a changing composition of demand and output. A higher rate of growth of output was synonymous with a more rapid rate of transformation and a more rapid reallocation of factors of production. It has become increasingly clear that the rise in *per capita* and family incomes that has accompanied growth, has had much to do with the increased pollution of the environment. The argument is usually framed in such terms as the increased use of automobiles, and a general problem of disposal of waste that affluence causes. But the adverse effect of growth on the environment can just as well be expressed in terms of the contamination that comes from an uncritical and unplanned reallocation of resources. More particularly, stepping up the growth rate may require fewer restrictions on the control and care of the environment, in the interests of speeding up the mobility of resources. This may be a price that many are unwilling to pay. Hence, the lack of concern with finding instruments for stimulating growth in the United States.

But it would be hard to find a consensus any more that high levels of unemployment might be desirable. The unwillingness of modern societies to tolerate long run unemployment at high levels requires us to develop adequate instruments to deal with this problem. In a country like Britain this may mean developing instruments that lead to more rapid growth. Thus, in Chapter XI it was argued that raising the balance of payments ceiling to the full employment ceiling may be conditional upon developing a policy that increased the rate of growth of output. But for those economies who have solved their payments problems, in the sense that they can maintain unemployment at a reasonably low rate without creating a payments crisis, the growth problem may well take care of itself. As long as net investment is positive, some growth will occur. And it is difficult to believe that, by settling for a normal rather than a super rate of growth, we cannot also find additional instruments that will allow qualitative improvement as we move beyond affluence.

Appendix

A reinterpretation of the secular stagnationist doctrine suggests the possibility that government must offset the *ex ante* shortfall of investment relative to private savings at full employment, by running a deficit. To see this more formally, the target-instrument approach to policy can be used. Write:

$$C_t = m(1 - \lambda)Y_t + n(1 - \lambda)X_t, \tag{1}$$

$$I_t = b(1 - \lambda)Y_{t-1} - cK_{t-1}, \tag{2}$$

$$Y_t = C_t + I_t + G_t, \tag{3}$$

$$K_t = K_{t-1} + I_t, \tag{4}$$

$$X_t = X_0 (1 + r_x)^t, \tag{5}$$

and

$$X_t = Y_t. \tag{6}$$

Equation (5) expresses the target of policy: full employment output. The instrument in this model is government expenditures, G_t, with the tax rate, λ, assumed given. Unlike most models which are solved for income, this model is solved for G_t, as income is to be made equal to full employment income. Thus, equations (1)–(5) can be solved down to;

$$G_t = (1 - c)G_{t-1} + \left\{ \frac{(c + r_x)\,[1 - (m + n)\,(1 + \lambda)] - b(1 - \lambda)}{(1 + r_x)} + \frac{b(1 - \lambda)}{(1 + r_x)^2} \right\}. \tag{7}$$

This has as its solution:

$$G_t = J_1(x_1)^t + G_t^E = J_1(x_1)^t + G_0 X_0 (1 + r_x)^t, \tag{8}$$

where x_1 is the root obtained from the homogeneous part of the model, and is real and less than one if $0 < c < 1$. The equilibrium path for government expenditures is determined by the growth of maximum output, X_t. Since $|x_1| < 1$, the long run behavior of G_t is dominated by X_t. This means that the

278

long run relation between government expenditures and maximum output is:

$$\lim_{t \to \infty} \frac{G_t}{X_t} = \frac{G_t^E}{X_t} = G_0 = \left[1 - (m+n)(1-\lambda)\right] - \left[\frac{b(1-\lambda)r_x}{(c+r_x)(1+r_x)}\right]. \quad (9)$$

Assume that the tax structure, λ, is given. Then, since equation (2) can be written $I_t = c(b/c)(1-\lambda)Y_{t-1} - K_{t-1}$, the expression $b/c(1-\lambda)Y_{t-1}$ is seen as some kind of measure of the desired stock of capital, and $b/c(1-\lambda)$ as the value of the desired capital–output ratio. Ignore $(1-\lambda)$ and write $b = (b/c)\cdot c$. A decline in the desired capital–output ratio, because of a capital-saving innovation, is now seen as a decline in b/c. Assume this to take place with c unchanged. Then equation (8) clearly indicates that $\{(G_t)/(X_t)\} = (G_t)/(Y_t)$ must rise in the long run. If initially $G_t/Y_t = \lambda$ then over the long run deficits must now be run more, causing a growth in the national debt. The sophisticated version of the secular stagnation doctrine posits just this. A model using taxes as the instrument variable to achieve $Y_t = X_t$ is also easily formulated again, to show the importance of the spending propensities on the long-run budget.

The static textbook formulation of the balanced budget multiplier is easily reformulated in dynamic terms. Write as a modified version of the final model developed in Chapter III:

$$C_t = m(Y-T)_t + n(X-T)_t, \quad (1)$$

$$I_t = b(Y-T)_{t-1} - c\,K_{t-1} \quad (2)$$

$$Y_t = C_t + I_t + G_t, \quad (3)$$

$$K_t = K_{t-1} + I_t, \quad (4)$$

$$X_t = X_0(1+r_x)^t. \quad (5)$$

G and T are government expenditures on goods and services and tax receipts, respectively, and all other variables have their previous meanings. Assume that government expenditures and tax receipts are given. Then, the solution of this model is:

$$Y_t = Y_t^{E1} + Y^{E2} + Y^{E3} + H_1(x_1)^t + H_2(x_2)^t$$

where x_1 and x_2 are the roots of the endogenous part of the model and

$$Y^{E2} = \frac{\mu''C}{1 - \mu''(1-c)(1-m)}G$$

and

$$Y^{E3} = -\frac{\mu''c(m+n)}{1 - \mu''(1-c)(1-m)}T,$$

where

$$\mu'' = \frac{1}{1-m} \cdot Y_t^{E1}$$

is the particular solution resulting from the inclusion of X_t in the model, and can be ignored. The net effect of a once over increase in G and T by the same amount is to raise the level of income if $\Delta Y^{E2} > \Delta Y^{E3}$. This will be true if

$$\frac{\mu''c}{1 - \mu''(1-c)(1-m)} > \frac{\mu''c(m+n)}{1 - \mu''(1-c)(1-m)}$$

or $1 > m + n$. Since $(m + n)$ represent the full employment marginal and average propensity to consume, this inequality should be satisfied. If, instead of equation (1) $C_t = a(Y - T)_t$ had been used, the resulting inequality would have been $1 > a$.

Next allow a fixed rate of growth for both expenditures and tax receipts so that $G_t = G_0 (1 + r)^t$ and $T_t = T_0 (1 + r)^t$. The model now has as its solution:

$$Y_t = Y_t^{E1} + Y_t^{E2} + Y_t^{E3} + H_1 (X_1)^t + H_2(X_2)^t.$$

Ignoring Y_t^{E2} as before, it is found that

$$Y_t^{E2} = A_0 G_t = \frac{\mu''(1+r)(c+r)}{(1+r)^2 - \mu''[(1-c)(1-m)+b](1+r) + \mu''b} G_t$$

and

$$Y_t^{E3} = B_0 T_t = -\frac{\mu''\{(m+n)(1+r)^2 - [(m+n)(1-c)-b](1+r)-b\}}{(1+r)^2 - \mu''[(1-c)(1-m)+b] + \mu''b} T_t.$$

A once over displacement of government expenditures and tax receipts to a higher growth path will raise the level of income if

$$1 > m + n + \frac{br}{(r+c)(1+r)}.$$

The average and marginal propensity to consume full employment output must now be somewhat smaller if income is to be raised through a simultaneous increase in G_t and T_t. Alternatively, we can say that $(m + n)$ must be smaller than in the example where G and T were constant, if the government expenditure multiplier is to exceed the tax multiplier.

Author Index

Subject Index